BALANCE-OF-PAYMENTS THEORY
AND THE UNITED KINGDOM EXPERIENCE

Balance-of-Payments Theory and the United Kingdom Experience

FOURTH EDITION

A. P. Thirlwall

Professor of Applied Economics
University of Kent at Canterbury

and

Heather D. Gibson

Lecturer in Economics
University of Kent at Canterbury

First edition 1980
Second edition 1982
Third edition 1986
Reprinted 1988
Fourth edition 1992

Published by
MACMILLAN ACADEMIC AND PROFESSIONAL LTD
Houndmills, Basingstoke, Hampshire RG21 2XS
and London
Companies and representatives
throughout the world

ISBN 0–333–54311–4 hardcover
ISBN 0–333–56648–3 paperback

A catalogue record for this book
is available from the British Library.

Printed and bound in Great Britain by
Billing and Sons Ltd, Worcester

Contents

Preface to the Fourth Edition

This book has three main purposes: first, to provide an elementary exposition of the balance of payments and of balance-of-payments adjustment theory; secondly, to describe the historical evolution and contemporary position of the United Kingdom's balance of payments, and thirdly, to critically appraise conventional balance-of-payments adjustment mechanisms, particularly in the light of the poor record of changes in nominal (and real) rates of exchange in rectifying balance-of-payments disequilibria in the world economy in the last decades. We emphasise the importance of non-price factors as determinants of export and import performance, which are reflected in the income elasticities of demand for exports and imports.

As far as the United Kingdom is concerned, it is argued strongly in the book, particularly in Chapters 12, 13 and 14, that the balance of payments should be viewed in a growth context, and that at the heart of the UK's poor post-war growth performance relative to other industrialised countries is its relative neglect of the tradeable goods sector which is reflected in a low propensity of other countries to buy UK exports and a high propensity in the UK to import foreign goods (particularly manufactures). This problem cannot be tackled by exchange rate depreciation or monetary manipulation. It requires real economic policies of a structural nature related to the wider characteristics of goods, such as their quality, design, reliability, marketing and delivery. Exchange rate depreciation simply ossifies the industrial structure and makes producers temporarily more competitive in the export of goods with given characteristics which were the source of payments weakness in the first place. In our view, the UK's inferior economic record in relation to other countries is largely a function of its balance-of-payments strait jacket caused by the slow growth of exports and high propensity to import, and until this underlying weakness is rectified, the UK will be condemned to a low growth rate (and the spectre of rising unemployment) whatever other domestic policies are pursued.

The idea that countries may be constrained in their growth performance by balance-of-payments weakness leads to the concept of balance-of-payments constrained growth. We formally derive a formula for a country's growth rate consistent with balance-of-payments equilibrium which turns out to be a remarkable predictor of growth rate differences between advanced industrial countries since the Second World War.

Since the book was first published in 1980, it has been widely used as a preliminary text on balance-of-payments theory, and as a source of reference on the performance of the UK balance of payments. This fourth edition provides the opportunity to bring up to date all the tables relating to the balance of payments, imports and exports, the commodity and geographic composition of trade, the exchange rate, and so on, and also the text relating to the history of the UK balance of payments. The tables and text now extend to 1989/90.

In addition, the analysis and exposition has been extended in several places. The most significant change, which has led to co-authorship of the book, has been the addition of two new chapters on the capital account of the balance of payments and on the determination of exchange rates. A detailed analysis of these two topics was a major omission from previous editions.

Other changes include the following: the book continues to argue strongly that the focus of balance-of-payments policy ought to be on the current account, but in Chapter 1 there is a fuller account of why the current account of the balance of payments matters for the functioning of the real economy. It has become fashionable in some quarters to argue that current account deficits do not matter if they are not government induced and can be voluntarily financed. We argue that they do matter. Chapter 4 on the balance of payments and the national economy retains one of its distinctive features of presenting the foreign trade multiplier relating imports to expenditure rather than to income, which is obviously more realistic if the import coefficients of various components of domestic expenditure differ. In this chapter, the worsening trade-off between the balance of payments on current account and the level of unemployment in the UK is also highlighted. Chapter 9 extends the history of the UK balance of payments to 1990 with particular emphasis on exchange rate policy and the worsening current account deficit in the latter years of the 1980s. Chapters 10 and 11 contain up to date information on import penetration and export performance in the UK. Chapter 12 on the balance-of-payments equilibrium growth rate reports recent work by other researchers of applying the model of balance-of-payments constrained growth to a range of countries for the most recent years. We also show how the model can be used for simulation and forecasting purposes. Chapter 14 on the balance of payments as a structural problem has an extended discussion of non-price factors as determinants of trade performance, and gives the results of some tests of the theories of non-price competition. The link between balance-of-payments weakness and deindustrialisation in the UK is further developed in a new Chapter 15.

In the original writing of the book a debt was incurred to a number of organisations and individuals. The Economic and Social Research Council (formerly the Social Science Research Council) financed the initial research on the structural aspects of the UK balance of payments. The Treasury and Department of Trade and Industry provided statistics. Mr John Goy and Mrs Julia Stevens of the University of Kent Library obtained and checked references. The editors of *Banca Nazionale del Lavoro Quarterly Review*, *Applied Economics*, the *Oxford Bulletin of Economics and Statistics*, the *Journal of Common Market Studies* and the *National Westminster Bank Quarterly Review* gave permission to reproduce certain material which first appeared in their journals. Finally, colleagues – Richard Disney, John Craven, Charles Kennedy, Bob Dixon and Thea Sinclair – read the first edition and helped to improve the book with their constructive comments on various chapters. For this new edition we must also thank Euclid Tsakalotos for constructive criticism; Keith Povey and Steven Gerrard for editorial assistance, and Celine Noronha for typing various drafts of the manuscript.

A. P. THIRLWALL
HEATHER D. GIBSON

Acknowledgements

The authors and publishers wish to thank the following who have kindly given permission for the use of copyright material:

Cambridge University Press, for tables from *Abstracts of British Historical Statistics*, by B. R. Mitchell and P. Deane; The Controller of Her Majesty's Stationery Office, for tables from U.K. *Balance of Payments*, *Key Statistics*, and *Economic Progress Reports*; Lloyds Bank Ltd, for a table from *Lloyds Bank Review* (January 1975), by M. Panić; Institute for International Economics, for a table from *The Exchange Rate System*, by J. Williamson; National Westminster Bank Ltd, for a table based on figures from *National Westminster Bank Quarterly Review* (May 1975); Organization for Economic Co-operation *and* Development, for a table derived from *OECD Manpower* and *Labour Force Statistics*; Martin Robertson & Company, for an extract from *Modern Capitalism: Its Growth and Transformation*, by J. Cornwall (1977); *Financial Times* for a diagram by T. O' Shaughnessy in an article published 1 February 1989; Heinemann Publishers for the use of text from *Deindustrialisation*, by S. Bazen and A. P. Thirlwall.

Every effort has been made to contact all the copyright-holders, but if any have been inadvertently omitted the publishers will be pleased to make the necessary arrangement at the earliest opportunity.

1
Balance-of-Payments Accounting and the Foreign-Exchange Market

CONCEPTS OF THE BALANCE OF PAYMENTS

There are two distinct concepts of the balance of payments which must not be confused: the market balance of payments, and the accounting balance of payments. The market balance of payments refers to the balance of supply and demand for a country's currency in the foreign-exchange market at a given rate of exchange. If the exchange rate is fixed, the market balance of payments would be in balance only by chance. If it is not in balance and the exchange rate must be maintained, the monetary authorities would have to intervene to achieve balance by buying their own currency with foreign exchange if the home currency were in excess supply or by selling their own currency for foreign exchange if the home currency were in excess demand. If the exchange rate is allowed to float freely, however, the market balance of payments must always balance because the exchange rate is the price which equates the supply and demand for a currency in the foreign-exchange market.

The accounting balance of payments is a record of all the financial transactions in goods, services and capital assets which have taken place between a country's residents and the residents of other countries within an arbitrary accounting period, normally one year. Like most accounting records, this concept of the balance of payments is an *ex post* concept, the record of accounts being compiled by double-entry book-keeping. For there to be a deficit or surplus on the balance of payments, using this concept of the balance of payments, certain sections of the account must be taken. Which sections should be looked at is considered later when we examine the question of what is meant by balance-of-payments equilibrium, and how equilibrium should be defined for the sensible conduct of economic policy.

Given these two distinct concepts of the balance of payments, the meaning of a balance-of-payments deficit or surplus will be different in each case, and movements in the different balances might be quite unrelated. In particular it must be stressed, and this will be a constant theme throughout the book, that a market balance of payments does not guarantee a balance-of-payments equilibrium in any objective sense. It depends how equilibrium is defined within the framework of the accounting balance of payments. As we shall see later, only if there is no concern about the balance between the exchange of real goods and services and complete indifference to the value of the exchange rate can the market balance of payments be said to give balance-of-payments equilibrium within the accounting framework. This feature of the book distinguishes it from many others in which the belief is expressed that if exchange rates are left to find their own level, giving a market balance of payments, there will be a balance-of-payments equilibrium obviating the need for corrective action. This view is not only naive in principle, because there are many different definitions of equilibrium, but is contradicted by the facts – no more so than by the continual corrective discretionary actions of governments since exchange rates were floated in the early 1970s.

THE ACCOUNTING BALANCE OF PAYMENTS

The accounting balance of payments is a record of a country's financial transactions with the rest of the world in an accounting period, normally one year. It is constructed on the principle of double-entry book-keeping, and as such always balances. For every credit there is a debit, and for every debit there is a credit. The financial transactions recorded include payments and receipts for physical goods (imports and exports), which are called visible items; payments and receipts for services, which are called invisible imports and exports, and capital transactions. Any receipt from the rest of the world which increases the net claim on foreigners is recorded as a credit in a country's balance of payments, but the net claim on foreigners itself is recorded as a debit. Similarly, any payment to the rest of the world which increases a country's net liabilities to foreigners is recorded as a debit in a country's balance of payments, but the increase in liabilities to foreigners itself is recorded as a credit. To see how the principle of double-entry book-keeping works, making the accounting balance of payments always balance, let u , give some examples. First, the accounting balance-of-payments state ment must be divided to distinguish between transactions on current account 'above the line', and transactions on capital account 'below the line'. Items above the line in the current account affect a country's current level of national income. Items in the capital account below the line affect a country's debtor – creditor status, or its wealth position. Exports of goods and services (both visible and invisible) will appear as a credit item in the current account above the line because the demand for a country's goods abroad affects current national income. By the principle of double-entry book-keeping, however, the increase in the net claim on foreigners that the exports represent will be recorded as a debit in the capital account. For example, if payment for £100-worth of exports from the United Kingdom to the United States is made by the US importer making a dollar deposit in New York in favour of a British bank, the £100 of exports would be recorded as a credit above the line but as a capital outflow below the line. Similarly, imports of goods and services will appear as a debit item in the current account of the balance of payments above the line because the demand for another country's goods also affects a country's current national income. The increase in the net liabilities to foreigners that imports represent will be recorded as a credit in the capital account. For example, if payment for £100-worth of imports from the United States is made using sterling cheques drawn on London banks, the £100-worth of imports would be recorded as a debit above the line but as a capital inflow below the line.

Unilateral transfers between one country and another, such as government transfers and private remittances, will also be recorded twice even though no real goods are exchanged. For example, if a gift is sent by an individual to a resident in another country, the gift would be recorded as a debit in the country of origin and as a credit in the recipient country, and then would be 'accounted for' on the credit side of the account in the country of origin and on the debit side of the account in the country of destination.

Capital movements involving financial transactions are also re-corded on both sides of the account below the line. The export of capital (investment abroad) is treated as a debit, while the payment itself is recorded as a credit representing an increase in the net liabilities to foreigners. Conversely, imports of capital are recorded as a credit and the receipt itself is recorded as a debit involving an increase in the net claim on foreigners.

The sale of gold and foreign currencies by the monetary authorities is recorded as a credit, with the corresponding receipt recorded as a debit.

With each transaction recorded twice, the sum total of debits and credits should be equal. In other words the current and capital accounts of the balance of payments should sum to zero. In equation form:

$$\text{current account} + \text{capital account} = 0$$

or

$$(X - M) + (LTC + STC + G) = 0 \tag{1.1}$$

where X is exports of goods and services (visible and invisible), M is imports of goods and services, LTC is net long-term capital flows, STC is net short-term capital flows, and G is the net increase in gold and foreign currency reserves (a net loss is recorded as credit and a net gain is recorded as a debit). It can now be clearly seen that if the current account is in surplus, this represents a net claim on foreigners, and this shows up in the capital account as a debit equivalent to the export of capital or the accumulation of reserves. Similarly, if the current account is in deficit, with a country importing more than it exports, the country must either be borrowing abroad or losing reserves, which show up as a credit on the capital account. A real change on current account must always be matched by a corresponding financial transfer on the capital account.

In practice, because of errors, omissions and so-called 'leads' and 'lags', the current and capital accounts never sum exactly to zero, and it is this which gives rise to the *balancing item* in the balance of payments. The balancing item is the difference between the total value of transactions recorded and the amounts of the supply of and demand for foreign exchange recorded (in the United Kingdom, by the Bank of England). Errors may arise if the real and monetary sections of the balance-of-payments accounts are compiled independently, as happens to a large extent in the United Kingdom. Trade and long-term investment flows are calculated mainly from customs records, while monetary movements are largely derived from reports by the banking system. Omissions may arise through the sheer difficulty of recording all transactions, particularly short-term capital movements. Leads and lags refer to the difference in timing between the recording of transactions in goods and the recording of transactions in currencies. Traders in goods and services, for example, may delay or hasten payment depending on expectations about the future value of the exchange rate. Within an accounting period this may cause a discrepancy between the value of goods recorded and the value of currency transactions.

BALANCE-OF-PAYMENTS EQUILIBRIUM

While in a book-keeping sense the balance of payments must balance, in an economic sense the accounts may be in severe imbalance because individual components of the accounts may be in surplus or deficit. This leads to the notion of balance-of-payments equilibrium/disequilibrium, which is defined in terms of a selected group of items within the accounting balance. The question is, which group of items? To answer this it is helpful to ask the prior question, why does a country bother to construct a balance-of-payments account in the first place if it always balances? One answer is that a country wishes to know its changing economic strength relative to other countries for the sensible conduct of economic policies, and one measure of this is what is happening to its balance of payments. Looked at in this way, what is happening to exports and imports on the current account of the balance of payments is of crucial importance because changes in exports and imports affect a country's national income. Exports rising relative to imports will be expansionary, while imports rising relative to exports will be contractionary. What is happening to the balance of overseas investment is also important because this affects employment and the level of future income. If deficits arise on the current account of the balance of payments, they have to be financed, and the balance-of-payments account will show this. The accounts are useful for this purpose, too. In fact, while there are a number of ways of defining balance-of-payments equilibrium within the accounting balance, there would seem to be two criteria, alluded to above, which are important in deciding on which items to focus within the accounts. First, what is the best measure of equilibrium for the conduct of economic policy which is designed to maximise the long-run welfare of society? Second, which measure shows up those items which are contributing to a balance-of-payments surplus or deficit on the one hand and financing the surplus or deficit on the other? Let us look at possible definitions of balance-of-payments equilibrium in terms of these two criteria.

The Balance of Trade

The balance of trade measures the difference between earnings from visible exports and visible imports. While it is interesting to see what this balance is, and to note that for the United Kingdom it has been in deficit for most of the nineteenth and twentieth centuries, focus on the balance of trade as a measure of equilibrium would be rather narrow, especially in a country like the United Kingdom which over the years has developed a comparative advantage in the provision of financial services and other 'invisible' exports.

The Balance on Current Account

The current-account balance is the difference between total exports and total imports ('visibles' and 'invisibles'). During the mercantilist period in Europe, equilibrium was conceived of in terms of the current-account balance. Taking the components of equation (1.1), balance-of-payments equilibrium would be represented as

$$X - M = 0 \tag{1.2}$$

Using this concept of equilibrium no account is taken of the balance of capital movements or changes in gold and foreign currency reserves. In mercantilist times the objective of economic policy was to maximise the current-account surplus in order to accumulate gold. This, it was argued, was the means to prosperity. While we now know better, focus on the current account as a measure of equilibrium has much to recommend it, particularly in considering the functioning of the real economy and the conduct of economic policy.

There are two major reasons why the current account matters from the point of view of the performance of the real economy. First, current account deficits must be financed. If this requires higher interest rates than otherwise would be the case, this will impair the long-run performance of the economy by discouraging investment in productive assets at home. Secondly, in the long run, no country can grow faster than that rate consistent with balance-of-payments equilibrium on current account unless it can finance *ever-growing* deficits. There is a limit to every country's credit worthiness and ability to borrow which imposes the ultimate constraint on growth. Countries with a weak balance of payments will find their external constraint on growth much tighter than countries with a strong balance of payments: witness the contrast between the UK and Japan or Germany. We shall have much more to say on this topic in Chapter 12 where we formally define a country's balance-of-payments equilibrium growth rate.

If the current account of the balance of payments is integrated into the national accounts, it can be seen that the emergence of a deficit implies that a country's expenditure exceeds its income, and this cannot go on for ever unless financed by a continual inflow of long-term capital investment. As debts grew, it would be increasingly difficult to finance a current-account deficit by the issue of monetary assets.

National income is defined as

$$Y = C + I + (X - M) \tag{1.3}$$

where Y is income, C is total consumption, I is investment and $(X - M)$ is the current-account balance of payments. In a closed economy total expenditure $(C + I)$ could not exceed income (Y). In an open economy expenditure can exceed income if there is an import surplus $(M > X)$. An import surplus (a current-account deficit) implies that a country is 'living beyond its means'. Rearranging equation (1.3), another way of saying the same thing would be

$$S - I = X - M \tag{1.4}$$

where $S (= Y - C)$ is saving. In a closed economy saving must equal investment (in an accounting sense). In an open economy, however, saving and investment may diverge depending on the foreign balance. An import surplus $(M > X)$ implies investment in excess of saving (financed by foreign borrowing), but this also cannot go on indefinitely unless there is a continual inflow of direct long-term capital investment.

The danger of a country not worrying about the state of the current-account balance, and being willing to finance a deficit on current account by any form of capital inflow, is that if the capital inflows are highly liquid, the country is put at the mercy of international speculators, and this may then reduce the freedom of government action in other important fields of economic and social policy. Likewise, if there is recourse to international financial institutions such as the International Monetary Fund (I M F) to support a deficit on current account, freedom of economic action by government may also be reduced, as it has been in the United Kingdom in the past and is the case in many developing countries.

The Basic Balance

The fact that a current-account deficit may be financed on a continuing basis by the inflow of direct long-term capital investment from abroad gives rise to the concept of the basic balance, which is another possible measure of balance-of-payments equilibrium. This concept of equilibrium was used by the United States until 1955 and by the UK authorities up to September 1970. Like the current balance, the basic balance measures underlying trends in the balance of payments in relation to the performance of the real economy, abstracting from volatile short-term capital movements. Using the concept of the basic balance, equilibrium would be defined as

$$X - M + LTC = 0 \qquad (1.5)$$

As long as LTC is not volatile, and domestic economic policy is not constrained by it, there is little to choose between defining equilibrium either in terms of the current balance or in terms of the basic balance from the point of view of the conduct of economic policy.

From the basic balance to the final balance of zero there has been a long-standing discussion and controversy as to which liquid assets and liabilities should be considered as contributing to the surplus or deficit on the balance of payments and which should be regarded as financing it. In the United Kingdom prior to 1970 all monetary movements, including private short-term capital movements, were regarded as accommodating or financing the deficit or surplus (including the balancing item) because balance-of-payments equilibrium was defined in terms of the basic balance. It then became the practice in the United Kingdom and elsewhere to consider private short-term capital movements (and the balancing item, in the United Kingdom) as contributing to the deficit or surplus, with only official monetary transactions accommodating the resulting deficit or surplus. To reflect this change of view, the measure of equilibrium in use in the

United Kingdom up to 1981 was the *balance for official financing* (or total currency flow) and the concept of *total official financing*, both of which are akin to the concept formerly in use in the United States called the balance of official reserve transactions.[1]

Total Currency Flow[2]

Extending equation (1.5), the total currency flow measure of equilibrium is defined as

$$X - M + LTC + STC_p = 0 \qquad (1.6)$$

where short-term capital flows are now divided into private flows (p) and official or compensating flows. Thus private short-term capital movements become part of the balance-of-payments deficit or surplus 'above the line' to be financed 'below the line' by official accommodating transfers. This concept of equilibrium gives a measure of the financial pressure on the monetary authorities from the point of view of maintaining the external value of the currency. Under floating exchange rates the measure takes on less relevance because some of the pressure on the exchange rate may be released by allowing the exchange rate to fall, and the amount of official financing will be correspondingly smaller. Indeed, if the exchange rate were completely free to float, the balance of payments would always be in equilibrium in the total currency flow sense and there would be no need for official financing and the holding of gold and foreign currency reserves. There would be a coincidence between the market balance of payments and the accounting balance of payments. However, to claim an equilibrium in the total currency flow sense when the exchange rate is free to find its own level, the authorities would have to be completely indifferent to the value of the exchange rate and the balance on current account. The authorities rarely are indifferent, and currencies in practice are not allowed to float freely. A disequilibrium balance of payments in the total currency flow sense can then be observed. But the disequilibrium may be very much smaller than disequilibrium in the basic balance or current balance if a basic or current-account deficit is being matched by a surplus of private short-term capital inflows.

The International Monetary Fund expressed the view as early as 1948 that it was of great importance to know the financial pressures on the monetary authorities resulting from international transactions, and how they are met. In fact, the distinction between autonomous and compensating (or accommodating) transactions was largely developed by the IMF. The distinction was supposed to provide a measure of payments problems more relevant to the activities of the IMF than the state of the current balance of payments alone. From the individual country's point of view, however, the danger of focusing on *all* autonomous (private) transactions, as distinct from those on the current account alone, is that the real economic problems of the country might be disguised by large private short-term capital inflows. Alternatively, the real economic problems may be made to appear worse than they actually are by speculative capital outflows which bear no relation to any adverse movements in the real economy. Thus a measure of equilibrium which indicates the pressure on the monetary authorities in the foreign-exchange market is not necessarily the best measure of equilibrium for focusing on problems in the real sector of the economy. Coppock and Metcalfe (1974) argued with respect to the changed presentation of the UK balance-of-payments accounts that 'problems might arise if a basic deficit were obscured for a number of years by forces leading to a relatively persistent short-term capital inflow which was then reversed, leaving the official reserves and borrowing facilities vulnerable to a speculative crisis'. This is the danger of the total currency flow measure of balance-of-payments equilibrium.

The official reasons given by the Central Statistical Office in favour of the changed presentation from the concept of basic balance to the total currency flow were fourfold; first, the volatility of certain capital flows previously regarded as being long-term ones, making the distinction between long-term and short-term capital movements arbitrary and misleading; second, the growing importance of directly related short- and long-term flows, for example United Kingdom direct investment overseas financed by short-term borrowing in foreign currencies which might be regarded as joint autonomous transactions yet were shown under the old presentation in separate accounts; third, the growing tendency for export and import trade credit to reflect long-term elements even though these transactions were by convention regarded as short-term accommodating movements; and fourth, it was thought that the balancing item was difficult to fit into the old classification and could prove awkward if the size of the balancing item was large.

Net Transactions in UK Assets and Liabilities

In 1985 a further change was introduced into the presentation of the
UK balance of payments accounts. The 1986 *Balance of Payments
Pink Book* describes the change as follows:

> official financing . . . brought together under one heading all
> transactions undertaken by or on behalf of the UK monetary
> authorities for the purpose of reserve management . . . . Over
> recent years, however, the monetary authorities' use of the re-
> serves for balance-of-payments related purposes has been much
> reduced and the official financing category has consequently lost
> much of its significance. It has, therefore, been decided to drop the
> category from the accounts and to associate the transactions pre-
> viously included under the heading with similar transactions re-
> corded elsewhere in the accounts.

In other words, both public and private transactions in capital assets
are now lumped together in the accounts. Transactions previously
included under official financing (e.g. changes in the level of reserves)
generally remain identifiable in the accounts, but the change in
presentation effectively does away with an official concept of what
constitutes balance-of-payments disequilibrium.

Table 1.1 summarises a comparison of the earlier presentation of
the accounts with the new, and Table 1.2 gives an historical summary
of the UK balance of payments up to the present time based on the
latest presentation of the accounts. Tables 1.3 and 1.4 show the
composition of the current and capital accounts. Table 1.2 is useful
for seeing movements in the visible and invisible account and the
extent to which net transactions in capital assets mirror the current
account deficit – the difference being the balancing item (apart from
gold subscriptions to the IMF and the allocation of SDRs). The
balancing item, reflecting unrecorded (or under-recorded) transactions, most probably on the capital and invisible accounts, has become worryingly large in recent years. Table 1.3 is useful for giving a
detailed breakdown of the composition of the current account, and
Table 1.4 shows the magnitude of both short and long-term, public
and private transactions, including government borrowing and
changes in reserves. It will be noticed that despite the abandonment
of the concept of official financing, the late 1980s saw massive
changes in official reserve holdings resulting from the attempt to

TABLE 1.1

Summary of old and new presentations of the balance-of-payments accounts

Pre-1970	1970–80	1980–84	Post-1985
Visible balance	Visible balance	Visible balance	Visible balance
+ Invisible balance	+ Invisible balance	+ Invisible balance	+ Invisible balance
= Current balance	= Current balance	= Current balance	= Current balance
+ Balance of long-term capital	+ Balance of private and other autonomous capital flows	+ Total investment and other capital transactions	+ Net transactions in U.K. assets and liabilities
= *Basic balance*	+ Balancing item	+ Balancing item	+ Allocation of special drawing rights
+ Balancing item	= *Total currency flow*	+ Allocation of special drawing rights	− Gold subscription to IMF
+ Balance of monetary movements	+ Allocation of special drawing rights	− Gold subscription to IMF	+ Balancing item
= 0	− Gold subscription to IMF	= *Total official financing*	
	+ Total official financing	+ Methods of financing	
	= 0	= 0	= 0

stabilise the exchange rate. The balance-of-payments experience of the United Kingdom historically, and up to the present, is discussed in Chapter 9.

MORE ON THE CONCEPT OF EQUILIBRIUM

The arbitrariness over the choice of components within the accounting balance of payments for the measurement of balance-of-payments equilibrium has led to such statements by economists as 'the balance of payments deficit cannot be measured, it can only be analysed'. While there may be agreement with this sentiment, and agreement that more than one number should be given, none the less some definition of equilibrium is required for the conduct of economic policy. Otherwise, how is balance-of-payments adjustment policy to be gauged? But having chosen the most appropriate measure of equilibrium for the purpose at hand, is equilibrium or disequilibrium then diagnosed regardless of the economic policies in effect at the time and independently of the achievement of other domestic objectives? Kindleberger (1969) comes out boldly with his definition of equilibrium as 'that state of the balance of payments of a country . . . for a given set of parameters which can be sustained without intervention'. This gets close to the balance for official financing definition of equilibrium, holding domestic policy constant: but should there be no constraints on the parameters and other domestic goals, e.g. on the level of interest rates, tariffs, employment, and so on? Suppose equilibrium on this definition is achieved because very high interest rates are leading to a large inflow of private short-term capital, and at the same time high interest rates are choking off domestic investment. Is that equilibrium? Or suppose that equilibrium is achieved solely as a result of a very high tariff on imports, or at the expense of high unemployment depressing the demand for imports. Is that equilibrium?

The question being raised here is, should equilibrium on the balance of payments be defined regardless of the level of restrictions and the achievement of other domestic goals? Economists seem to be divided on this matter. Some say no, but some say yes because specifying levels of restrictions and other goals infuses value judgements into the concept of equilibrium. Machlup (1950) calls such a practice 'disguised politics'. He argues that 'by infusing a value judgement, a political philosophy or programme, or a rejection of a

TABLE 1.2
Summary balance of payments

£ million

	1968	1969	1970	1971	1972	1973	1974	1975	1976	1977
Current account										
Visible balance	−712	−209	−14	210	−742	−2 568	−5 233	−3 257	−3 961	−2 322
Invisibles										
Services balance	312	366	421	547	623	686	961	1 315	2 415	3 238
Interest, profits and dividends balance	359	531	596	553	594	1 327	1 508	891	1 560	265
Transfers balance	−223	−206	−182	−196	−272	−443	−422	−475	−786	−1 128
Invisibles balance	448	691	835	904	945	1 570	2 047	1 731	3 189	2 375
Current balance	−264	482	821	1 114	203	−998	−3 184	−1 524	−772	53
Capital transfers	—	—	—	—	—	−59	−75	—	—	—
Transactions in UK assets and liabilities										
UK external assets	−1 120	−1 336	−1 438	−3 823	−883	−3 012	−2 833	−1 607	−3 961	−13 844
UK external liabilities	1 773	476	550	2 319	1 331	3 936	5 952	3 135	4 317	9 952
Net transactions	653	−860	−888	−1 504	448	924	3 119	1 528	356	−3 892
EEA loss on forward commitments	−251	—	—	—	—	—	—	—	—	—
Allocation of special drawing rights	—	—	171	125	124	—	—	—	—	—
Gold subscription to IMF	—	—	−38	—	—	—	—	—	—	—
Balancing item	−138	378	−66	265	−775	133	140	−4	416	3 839

Source: Central Statistical Office, *The Pink Book 1990: United Kingdom Balance of Payments* (London: HMSO, 1990).

programme or policy, into the concept of equilibrium designed for economic analysis, the analyst commits the fallacy of implicit evaluation or disguised politics'. While it may be conceded that attaching to equilibrium some level of restriction or some other defined goal is to make a value judgement, and that equilibrium, conceived analytically, is compatible with any level of restriction, it cannot make sense

											£ million
1978	1979	1980	1981	1982	1983	1984	1985	1986	1987	1988	1989

1978	1979	1980	1981	1982	1983	1984	1985	1986	1987	1988	1989
–1 592	–3 342	1 357	3 251	1 911	–1 537	–5 336	–3 345	–9 485	–11 223	–21 078	–23 840
3 700	3 895	3 653	3 792	3 022	4 064	4 519	6 687	6 692	6 624	4 502	4 709
806	1 205	–182	1 251	1 460	2 854	4 379	2 519	4 927	3 820	4 971	4 582
–1 791	–2 210	–1 984	–1 547	–1 741	–1 593	–1 730	–3 111	–2 157	–3 402	–3 546	–4 577
2 715	2 890	1 487	3 496	2 741	5 325	7 168	6 095	9 462	7 042	5 927	4 714
1 123	–453	2 843	6 748	4 649	3 787	1 832	2 750	–24	–4 182	–15 151	–19 126
—	—	—	—	—	—	—	—	—	—	—	—
–4 377	–40 189	–43 439	–50 769	–31 407	–30 172	–32 041	–52 919	–92 888	–83 633	–56 244	–86 253
1 506	39 447	39 499	43 334	28 820	25 622	24 119	45 677	84 375	84 103	63 258	90 255
–2 871	–742	–3 940	–7 436	–2 589	–4 551	–7 923	–7 241	–8 512	469	7 015	4 002
—	—	—	—	—	—	—	—	—	—	—	—
—	195	180	158	—	—	—	—	—	—	—	—
—	—	—	—	—	—	—	—	—	—	—	—
1 748	1 000	917	530	–2 060	764	6 091	4 491	8 536	3 713	8 136	15 124

for the purpose of the conduct of economic policy to measure the balance of payments without regard to the level of restrictions and the achievement of other goals. It is the easiest thing in the world to achieve balance-of-payments equilibrium on any definition by becoming a siege economy or running the economy at less than full employment, but at what price? One can sympathise with both sides

TABLE 1.3
Composition of the current account (£m)

	1979	1980	1981	1982	1983	1984	1985	1986	1987	1988	1989
Credits											
Exports (f.o.b.)	40 471	47 149	50 668	55 331	60 700	70 265	77 991	72 656	79 446	80 776	92 792
Services											
General government	265	315	401	404	470	474	483	511	521	551	449
Private sector and public corporations											
Sea transport	3 807	3 789	3 731	3 215	3 043	3 244	3 211	3 216	3 282	3 526	3 870
Civil aviation	1 755	2 210	2 359	2 741	2 665	2 931	3 078	2 786	3 159	3 192	3 758
Travel	2 797	2 961	2 970	3 188	4 003	4 614	5 442	5 553	6 260	6 184	6 877
Financial and other services	5 803	6 373	7 487	8 283	9 389	10 575	12 285	13 839	14 893	14 358	15 150
Interest, profits and dividends											
General government	816	946	971	979	765	818	735	764	931	1 456	1 948
Private sector and public corporations	16 689	22 735	36 559	43 419	41 706	50 818	51 387	46 709	46 856	55 078	72 652
Transfers											
General government	550	958	1 675	2 154	2 235	2 392	1 760	2 138	2 282	2 115	2 143
Private sector	850	935	1 117	1 248	1 528	1 652	1 775	1 732	1 670	1 707	1 750
Total invisibles	33 333	41 222	57 269	65 360	65 803	77 516	80 157	77 248	79 855	88 168	109 098
Total credits	73 804	88 371	107 937	120 691	126 503	147 781	158 148	149 904	159 301	168 944	201 890
Debits											
Imports (f.o.b.)	43 814	45 792	47 416	53 421	62 237	75 601	81 336	82 141	90 669	101 854	116 632
Services											
General government	1 073	1 165	1 264	1 754	1 522	1 655	1 781	1 920	2 141	2 351	2 698
Private sector and public corporations											
Sea transport	3 625	3 739	3 818	3 589	3 665	3 600	3 508	3 312	3 317	3 754	3 840
Civil aviation	1 498	1 863	2 005	2 184	2 363	2 676	2 877	3 194	3 775	4 097	4 261

Interest, profits and dividends											
General government	683	895	940	1 090	1 188	1 329	1 479	1 668	2 024	2 307	2 435
Private sector and public corporations	15 618	22 970	35 338	41 847	38 429	45 927	48 126	40 879	41 944	49 257	67 583
Transfers											
General government	2 566	2 738	3 282	3 493	4 165	4 491	5 187	4 371	5 559	5 363	6 420
Private sector	1 044	1 139	1 057	1 200	1 191	1 283	1 459	1 656	1 795	2 005	2 050
Total invisibles	30 443	39 736	53 773	62 621	60 479	70 348	74 062	67 787	72 814	82 241	104 384
Total debits	74 257	85 528	101 189	116 042	122 716	145 949	155 398	149 928	163 483	184 095	221 016
Balances											
Visible balance	-3 342	1 357	3 251	1 911	-1 537	-5 336	-3 345	-9 485	-11 223	-21 078	-23 840
Services											
General government	-808	-850	-863	-1 350	-1 052	-1 181	-1 298	-1 409	-1 620	-1 800	-2 249
Private sector and public corporations											
Sea transport	182	50	-87	-374	-622	-356	-297	-96	-35	-48	30
Civil aviation	257	347	354	287	302	255	201	-408	-616	-905	-503
Travel	688	223	-302	-452	-87	-49	571	-530	-1 020	-2 032	-2 413
Financial and other services	3 576	3 883	4 690	4 911	5 523	5 850	7 510	9 135	9 915	9 287	9 344
Interest, profits and dividends											
General government	134	52	30	-112	-424	-511	-744	-903	-1 092	-851	-487
Private sector and public corporations	1 071	-235	1 221	1 571	3 278	4 891	3 261	5 830	4 912	5 820	5 069
Transfers											
General government	-2 016	-1 780	-1 607	-1 789	-1 930	-2 099	-3 427	-2 233	-3 277	-3 248	-4 277
Private sector	-194	-204	60	48	337	369	316	76	-125	-298	-300
Invisibles balance	2 890	1 487	3 496	2 741	5 325	7 168	6 095	9 462	7 042	5 927	4 714
Of which: Private sector and public corporations: Services and IPD	5 774	4 268	5 876	5 943	8 394	10 591	11 246	13 931	13 156	12 122	12 027
Current balance	-453	2 843	6 748	4 649	3 787	1 832	2 750	-24	-4 182	-15 151	-19 126

Source: Central Statistical Office, *The Pink Book 1990: United Kingdom Balance of Payments* (London: HMSO, 1990).

TABLE 1.4

Analysis of capital transactions (UK financial account and capital transfers)

	1979	1980	1981	1982	1983	1984	1985	1986	1987	1988	1989
Capital transfers	—	—	—	—	—	—	—	—	—	—	—
Transactions in external assets and liabilities*											
Investment overseas by UK residents											
Direct	-5 889	-4 867	-6 005	-4 091	-5 417	-6 033	-8 456	-11 780	-19 198	-20 685	-19 365
Portfolio	-887	-3 310	-4 467	-7 565	-7 193	-9 869	-19 426	-23 072	3 323	-9 870	-36 781
Total UK investment overseas	-6 776	-8 175	-10 474	-11 656	-12 611	-15 902	-27 882	-34 853	-15 875	-30 555	-56 146
Investment in the United Kingdom by overseas residents											
Direct	3 030	4 355	2 932	3 027	3 386	-181	3 865	4 987	8 681	9 218	18 344
Portfolio	1 549	1 431	257	-11	1 701	1 288	8 913	10 911	17 710	13 220	10 860
Total overseas investment in the UK	4 579	5 786	3 189	3 016	5 087	1 107	12 778	15 898	26 391	22 438	29 204
Foreign currency lending abroad by UK banks	-30 104	-29 836	-36 900	-16 521	-16 162	-9 439	-20 200	-47 885	-45 684	-14 698	-24 378
Foreign currency borrowing abroad by UK banks	30 752	30 505	36 763	19 904	17 192	18 648	25 306	58 361	44 277	20 301	32 841
Net foreign currency transactions of UK banks	648	669	-137	3 383	1 030	9 209	5 106	10 476	-1 407	5 603	8 463
Sterling lending abroad by UK banks	210	-2 778	-3 019	-4 019	-2 232	-4 933	-1 635	-5 955	-4 638	-4 570	-2 887
Sterling borrowing and deposit liabilities abroad of UK banks	2 788	3 044	2 497	4 421	3 945	6 149	4 155	5 605	8 537	13 544	10 280
Net sterling transactions of UK banks	2 998	266	-522	402	1 713	1 216	2 520	-350	3 899	8 974	7 393
Deposits with and lending to banks abroad by the UK non-bank private sector	-1 138	-2 502	-1 864	-598	863	-3 213	-1 240	-2 724	-5 177	-3 644	-9 375

Borrowing from banks abroad by											
UK non-bank private sector	693	471	1 042	985	73	-2 215	2 618	3 817	2 109	4 137	7 495
Public corporations	246	-15	-178	-36	-35	-47	64	-31	-166	-253	-1 132
General government	46	-40	-192	58	78	49	87	100	104	-10	-65
Official reserves (additions to −, drawings on +)	-1 059	-291	2 419	1 421	607	908	-1 758	-2 891	-12 012	-2 761	5 439
Other external assets of											
UK non-bank private sector and Public corporations	-1 184	-209	-1 026	126	-161	1 281	528	1 930	550	875	2 036
General government	-137	351	93	-161	-478	-743	-730	-509	-796	-891	-942
Other external liabilities of											
UK non-bank private sector and Public corporations	605	301	224	119	-55	517	731	547	1 381	2 187	10 145
General government	-263	-553	-14	351	-661	-89	-64	78	1 468	914	1 487
Net transactions in assets and liabilities	-742	-3 940	-7 436	-2 589	-4 551	-7 923	-7 241	-8 512	469	7 015	4 002
EEA loss on forward commitments	—	—	—	—	—	—	—	—	—	—	—
Allocation of special drawing rights	195	180	158	—	—	—	—	—	—	—	—
Gold subscription to IMF	—	—	—	—	—	—	—	—	—	—	—

* Assets: increase−/decrease+. Liabilities: increase+/decrease−.

Source: Central Statistical Office, *The Pink Book 1990: United Kingdom Balance of Payments* (London: HMSO, 1990).

of the argument, but ultimately a reconciliation is called for. One such reconciliation is to use the actual balance of payments in comparison with an estimate of the full-employment, restriction-free balance of payments, and this would highlight more clearly the policies that need to be pursued for the reconciliation of objectives. This is the approach preferred by Meade (1951), who draws the distinction between the 'true' and 'potential' balance of payments, the latter being the full-employment, restriction-free balance and the 'true' balance being the balance of autonomous trade and transfers which must be matched by accommodating transfers. Meade says 'it is, of course, this potential deficit (or surplus) which is the proper measure of balance of payments disequilibrium'. Adopting this reconciliation, there will be a different equilibrium for each level of restriction and for each level of employment.

The same questions that have been raised about the meaning of balance-of-payments equilibrium in the presence of restrictions, and when economies have other goals, can also be asked about the meaning of exchange-rate equilibrium: that is, about the market balance of payments. Under fixed exchange rates, if the monetary authorities are intervening in the market to maintain the fixed parity, the exchange rate cannot be an equilibrium rate in the sense that there is no tendency for it to change. But similarly, even if the exchange rate is free to find its own level, it is hardly proper to call the prevailing rate in the free market an equilibrium rate if at the same time trade is highly restricted and there is depression and unemployment at home. Like the balls in Marshall's bowl, everything in the economic system is determined simultaneously and nothing is determined unless everything else is given. Thus there will be a different equilibrium exchange rate for each given set of the other variables and parameters in the economic system. If other factors are taken into consideration, there can be no such thing as *the* equilibrium exchange rate, just as there can be no unique measure of balance-of-payments equilibrium.

Finally, we return to the question of whether equilibrium in the foreign-exchange market gives balance-of-payments equilibrium. The first point to make is that there is not a complete coincidence of the items covered by the market balance of payments and the items covered by the accounting balance of payments because the latter includes some transactions which never pass through the foreign-exchange market, for example unilateral transfers in kind, barter deals and direct investments of plant and machinery. Ignoring this factor, however, it is sometimes argued that the market balance of payments gives an accurate indication of balance-of-payments equilibrium or disequilibrium in the accounting sense, with the implication that if only the exchange rate were left to find its own level, giving a market equilibrium, this would automatically achieve balance-of-payments equilibrium within the accounting balance. The argument is that when the supply and demand for foreign exchange balances at the current exchange rate, this must mean that autonomous transactions requiring foreign currency payments are equal to autonomous transactions involving foreign receipts. In the new presentation of the UK balance-of-payments accounts this is tantamount to saying that when the foreign-exchange market is in equilibrium (net transactions in capital are zero), there will be balance-of-payments equilibrium. As was argued earlier, however, this balance-of-payments equilibrium may be the result of net inflows of private short-term capital, perhaps of a speculative nature, which have little, if anything, to do with the state of the real economy. An equilibrium exchange rate in a free market may coincide with balance-of-payments equilibrium in one sense but not in another. Changes in the balance of payments which affect people's real living standards are changes in the current balance and this may move into disequilibrium as the exchange market moves towards equilibrium. When balance-of-payments adjustment policy is considered in detail later, particularly in Chapter 5, we will discuss many ways in which movements in the exchange rate towards a market-clearing equilibrium may be disequilibrating for the current balance of payments and, indeed, for the economy as a whole.

If movements in the exchange rate do cause disequilibrium between other items in the accounting balance of payments, this in turn will have repercussions on the exchange rate, and there is really no way of knowing what the long-run equilibrium exchange rate is. A cumulative appreciation or depreciation of the exchange rate may be set in motion, with the rate moving from one temporary equilibrium to another in an upward or downward spiral. Inflation may produce a spiral of depreciation; so may speculation against a currency. Most balance-of-payments adjustment theory is about the movement from one temporary equilibrium to another, with very little discussion about the path of the exchange rate or the behaviour of the domestic economy between the temporary equilibria. The assumption seems to be that the path of the exchange rate to long-run equilibrium is smooth, but from the experience of the world economy in the 1970s and 1980s this assumption must surely be challenged. The very idea that there is a long-run equilibrium to which exchange rates will move may itself be a chimera. The subject of exchange rate determination is dealt with in Chapter 3.

THE FOREIGN-EXCHANGE MARKET

Behaviour in the foreign-exchange market depends on the supply of and demand for currencies. Under a system of fixed exchange rates or managed floating in which the monetary authorities wish to preserve the exchange rate at a particular level, a positive total currency flow will increase the level of foreign-currency reserves because the supply of foreign currency to a country will exceed the demand. Conversely a negative total currency flow will lead to a decrease in foreign-currency reserves because the demand for foreign currency exceeds the supply. Under a system of freely floating exchange rates a positive total currency flow will lead to an appreciation of a country's exchange rate (i.e. a fall in the home price per unit of foreign currency), and a negative total currency flow will lead to a depreciation of a country's exchange rate (i.e. a rise in the home price per unit of foreign currency[3]). A good deal of balance-of-payments theory, and particularly the theory of balance-of-payments adjustment policy, under both fixed and flexible exchange rates, is concerned with the influence of different policies on the level of foreign-currency reserves and whether a policy will rectify a loss of reserves in the case of a balance-of-payments deficit or whether the policy will be destabilising. Here, therefore, we focus on the foreign-exchange market, outlining the determinants of the supply of and demand for foreign exchange, and the conditions for the market to be stable in response to a change in the home price of foreign exchange.

The shape and position of the supply and demand curves for foreign currency are determined by the nature and magnitude of the underlying transactions. Taking the current account of the balance of payments we can show how the curves can be derived from the supply and demand curves for imports and exports. For illustrative purposes we take the dollar ($) as the foreign currency and consider the supply and demand for dollars in relation to the sterling (£) price of dollars. In working out what happens when a change in the exchange rate takes place it matters whether the analysis is carried out measuring the effects in the home currency (sterling) or in the foreign currency.

Since the normal balance-of-payments problem is one of rectifying a foreign-exchange shortage, the analysis here will be undertaken measuring changes in terms of dollars. If interest were in the domestic repercussions of exchange-rate changes, however, it would be more appropriate to measure the effect of exchange-rate changes in terms of the home currency, as Joan Robinson (1937) did in her early classic paper on the foreign exchanges. At that time, however, the economic problem was recession rather than balance-of-payments difficulties. We concentrate first on the demand for and supply of foreign currency for trading purposes.

THE DEMAND FOR DOLLARS

The quantity demanded of dollars in relation to the sterling price of dollars can be derived from the UK demand for imports from the United States and the US supply curve of imports. If it is assumed for simplicity that the supply curve of US goods is infinitely elastic (so that the dollar price of imports does not rise as the demand for imports from the United States increases), the elasticity of demand for dollars with respect to a change in the sterling price of dollars will equal the UK elasticity of demand for US goods.

Imports may be either competitive or non-competitive with domestic goods. Competitive imports fill the gap between the domestic demand for a commodity and its domestic supply. For most of these goods the demand for imports will be more elastic than the demand for the goods that the imports compete with (importables) because as the domestic price of the goods falls not only does domestic demand increase but also supply contracts. Exceptions to this would be if domestic supply is completely inelastic or if domestic supply becomes non-existent because the price is too low. Figure 1.1 illustrates these propositions.

Take the importable commodity, steel. Figure 1.1(a) shows the domestic demand for steel and the domestic supply in relation to price. Figure 1.1(b) shows the demand for imported steel. At price P_1 the total domestic demand for steel is met by domestic supply. At prices lower than P_1 the demand for steel exceeds the domestic supply, and the demand for steel imports to make up the difference is greater than the increase in demand for steel itself because domestic supply contracts. At price P_2 no domestic supplier is willing to supply steel, and the demand for imported steel then has the same elasticity

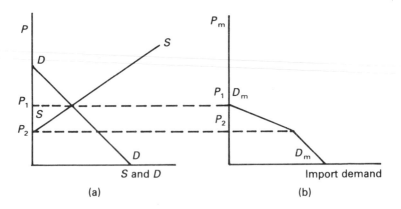

FIGURE 1.1

as the demand for the importable, as shown by the same slope of the two demand curves below P_2. Above P_2, however, the demand curve for imported steel is more elastic than the total demand for steel. It is easily shown that the elasticity of demand for competitive imports is a weighted sum of the domestic demand and supply elasticities. Let $M = D - S$ and

$$E_m = \frac{\mathrm{d}M}{\mathrm{d}P_m} \times \frac{P_m}{M} = \frac{P_m}{M}\left(\frac{\mathrm{d}D}{\mathrm{d}P_m} - \frac{\mathrm{d}S}{\mathrm{d}P_m}\right)$$

where E_m is the elasticity of demand for imports and P_m is the domestic price of imports. Therefore

$$E_m = \left(\frac{D}{M} \times d_m\right) + \left(\frac{S}{M} \times s_m\right)$$

where d_m is the domestic demand elasticity, and s_m is the domestic supply elasticity. The smaller the amount imported relative to total domestic demand, the higher E_m will be relative to d_m. Only if there is no domestic supply will the elasticity of demand for imports equal the domestic demand elasticity for the commodity. For non-competitive imports the demand curve will depend on the good's own characteristics and the structural relationships that exist between domestic output and necessary inputs that must be imported.

Aggregating the demands for all imports and converting into foreign currency ($) gives the demand for foreign exchange at a given

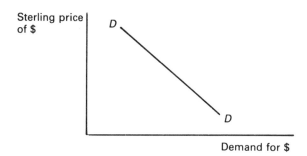

FIGURE 1.2

rate of exchange. As the home price of foreign exchange falls, the demand for foreign exchange may be expected to rise, the elasticity of demand depending on the elasticity of demand for imports. The demand for dollars in relation to the sterling price of dollars is shown in Figure 1.2. In interpreting the curve it is helpful to remember that a fall in the sterling price of the dollar implies an appreciation of sterling and a depreciation of the dollar, which means that the sterling price of dollar goods will fall in the home market and more imports and dollars will be demanded. Conversely, a rise in the sterling price of dollars means a depreciation of sterling and an appreciation of the dollar, which will raise the sterling price of dollar goods and reduce the demand for imports and dollars.

THE SUPPLY OF DOLLARS

On to Figure 1.2 can be superimposed the supply curve of dollars to give an equilibrium sterling price of dollars at which the supply of and demand for dollars is equal in the foreign-exchange market. The supply of dollars depends on the US demand for UK exports or, in other words, on the US demand to import goods from the United Kingdom. If the demand for UK goods in the US market is of unitary elasticity (if demand changes in the same proportion as the dollar price of UK goods does), the supply of dollars will remain unchanged with respect to a change in the sterling price of dollars. The supply curve of dollars will be vertical (S_1S_1 in Figure 1.3). If the elasticity of demand for UK goods is greater than unity (i.e. if the demand changes more than in proportion to price), the supply curve of dollars

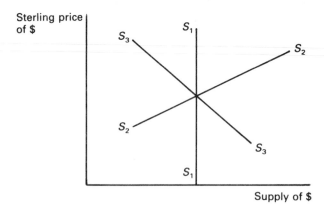

FIGURE 1.3

will be positively sloped in relation to the sterling price of dollars
(S_2S_2). If the elasticity of demand for UK goods is less than unity (i.e.
if the demand changes less than in proportion to price), the supply
curve of dollars will be negatively sloped in relation to the sterling
price of dollars (S_3S_3).

In interpreting the supply curves it is again helpful to remember
what a change in the sterling price of the dollar means. If the sterling
price of the dollar rises, this implies a depreciation of sterling and an
appreciation of the dollar. The dollar price of UK goods in the US
market will fall if the sterling price of goods remains unchanged. If
the demand for UK goods then rises in proportion to the fall in the
dollar price, the supply of dollars will remain unchanged (supply
curve S_1S_1). If the demand for UK goods rises more than in proportion, the supply of dollars increases (S_2S_2); and if the demand for
UK goods rises less than in proportion, the supply of dollars decreases (S_3S_3). The argument is reversed for a fall in the sterling price
of dollars, or an appreciation of sterling.

Combining Figures 1.2 and 1.3 the equilibrium sterling price of
dollars is obtained at P_1 in Figure 1.4. In Figure 1.4 two negatively
sloped supply curves of dollars are drawn, one steeper ($S_{3a}S_{3a}$) than
the demand curve for dollars and the other flatter ($S_{3b}S_{3b}$). The
importance of this difference will become apparent when we consider
the conditions for the foreign-exchange market to be stable.

From Figure 1.4 it is clear that if the sterling price of the dollar is
free to vary, as under a system of freely floating exchange rates, the
foreign-exchange market will be cleared. The market balance of
payments will be in equilibrium and the total currency flow will be

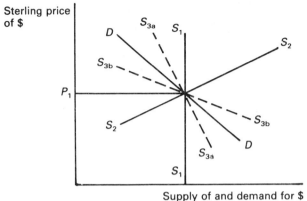

FIGURE 1.4

zero. The theory of how exchange-rate changes are supposed to preserve balance-of-payments equilibrium in an accounting sense is then as follows. Starting from the equilibrium rate of exchange P_1 an increase in import demand in the United Kingdom will increase the demand for dollars and cause the UK balance of payments to go into deficit. In 'normal' circumstances this causes the sterling price of the dollar to rise, which will make the sterling price of imports from the United States dearer and the dollar price of UK exports to the United States cheaper, which should tend to rectify the imbalance. Conversely, an increase in the demand for UK exports will increase the supply of dollars and cause the balance of payments to go into surplus, reducing the sterling price of dollars. This will make imports cheaper and exports dearer, which again should tend to rectify the imbalance.

It is clear from Figure 1.4, however, that a change in the exchange rate will not rectify imbalance in all circumstances; it depends on the relative slopes of the demand and supply curves of foreign exchange. Starting from a position of imbalance where the demand for dollars exceeds the supply, a rise in the sterling price of dollars will restore balance as long as the demand for dollars is reduced by more than the supply. This will be so as long as the supply curve of dollars is either positively sloped or not more negatively sloped than the demand curve. Likewise, starting from a position of imbalance where the supply of dollars exceeds the demand, a fall in the sterling price of dollars will restore balance as long as the demand for dollars is increased by more than the supply. This condition will also be met as long as the supply curve of dollars is either positively sloped or not flatter than the demand curve if it is negatively sloped. Stability of the exchange rate when there is disequilibrium in the market thus depends on the relative slopes of the supply and demand curves for foreign exchange. In Figure 1.4, if the supply curve of dollars is $S_{3b}S_{3b}$ a rise in the sterling price of dollars, when there is an excess demand for dollars, would create even greater excess demand, and a fall in the sterling price of dollars when there is an excess supply of dollars would create an even greater excess supply. In these circumstances variations in the exchange rate will not produce equilibrium and the market will be unstable. Note that for stability it does not matter that the demand for UK exports is inelastic, provided that the inelasticity does not give a supply curve of dollars with a flatter negative slope than the demand curve for dollars. We shall derive more precisely in Chapter 5 the precise elasticity conditions with respect to the demand for exports and imports for a depreciation of the exchange rate to improve the balance of payments starting from equilibrium (the so-called Marshall-Lerner condition).

It is possible, of course, for the elasticity of demand for UK exports to the United States to be elastic over one range of prices and inelastic over another range of prices, so that the foreign-exchange market is stable at one rate of exchange but unstable at another rate of exchange. Suppose, for example, that the demand for UK exports is elastic at a low sterling price of dollars (i.e. at a high dollar price for UK goods) but inelastic at a high sterling price of dollars (i.e. at a low dollar price for UK goods). The supply curve of dollars would then look like that drawn in Figure 1.5, bending back on itself at the point of unitary elasticity of demand for exports (point L). P_1 is a stable equilibrium exchange rate, but any depreciation of the currency beyond point L will either reduce a surplus (from L to P_2), or increase a deficit (beyond P_2). A freely floating rate will tend to move away in either direction from A (to P_1 in the downward direction).

The discussion so far has been about 'static' stability and instability. The foreign-exchange market may also be subject to 'dynamic' instability caused by the supply and demand curves themselves shifting in a destabilising way as the exchange rate changes. Indeed, this type of instability may be more common in practice. Speculation, and domestic inflation sparked off by the rapid depreciation of a currency, may be sources of dynamic instability. Consider Figure 1.6, which shows the supply and demand for dollars in relation to the sterling price of dollars.

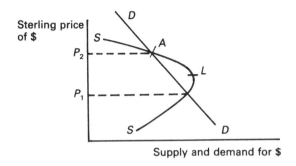

FIGURE 1.5

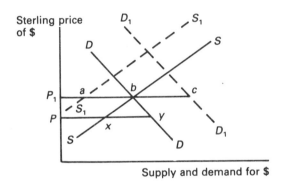

FIGURE 1.6

Suppose that at exchange rate P there is an excess demand for dollars equal to xy. To rectify this disequilibrium sterling is either devalued or allowed to depreciate to P_1. If the demand and supply curves (DD and SS) do not shift, equilibrium will be achieved. However, suppose that depreciation of the currency generates so much domestic inflation that the supply curve of dollars from the sale of exports shifts from SS to S_1S_1. At the exchange rate P_1 there is now a greater excess demand for dollars, ab, than there was at P. Alternatively, suppose currency depreciation generates so much pessimism among currency traders that instead of demanding more pounds and less dollars, they demand more dollars, shifting the demand curve for dollars from DD to D_1D_1. At the exchange rate P_1, with the old supply curve SS, there is now a greater excess demand for dollars, bc, than there was at *P*. If both the supply and demand curves shift, the excess demand for dollars at the lower sterling exchange rate would be *ac*, greater than before the depreciation. It should also be mentioned, of course, that income expansion in the 'depreciating' country will also increase the demand for dollars, offsetting some of the gain from depreciation.

CAPITAL MOVEMENTS AND SPECULATION

So far we have been concerned with the supply of and demand for foreign exchange arising from the international exchange of goods and services. Transactions in capital and currency speculation also give rise to the supply of and demand for foreign exchange and affect the current (spot) rate of exchange. The wish of residents of a country to export capital and acquire foreign assets such as bonds, equities, property, and so on, leads to a demand for foreign exchange, while the desire of foreigners to acquire capital assets in the home country adds to the supply of foreign exchange. The effect of a net inflow of capital on the exchange rate will be to cause the exchange rate to appreciate in the same way as a trade surplus; and a net outflow of capital will cause the exchange rate to depreciate in the same way as a trade deficit. The foreign exchange market in most advanced industrialised countries is now dominated by the demand for and supply of currency for transactions in capital.

If the exchange rate is adjustable, or free to vary of its own accord, the buying and selling of currencies for profit will cause variations in the demand for and supply of foreign currency. The essence of speculative activity, as it is called, is that traders will buy a currency when its price is 'low' if they expect the price to rise, and sell a currency when its price is 'high' if they expect the price to fall. If speculators forecast correctly, they make a profit and, so it is argued, stabilise the exchange rate at the same time by adding to demand when price is low relative to its equilibrium value and adding to supply when price is 'high'. The rate of return from speculative activity can be very high. An example will illustrate. Suppose the current price of a dollar is 50 pence and the speculator expects the price to rise to 52 pence, so he buys. If he held the dollars for a week, before selling, and assuming no costs, he would make a return of 4 per cent on the week, or approximately 200 per cent per annum.

The notion that speculation will on balance be stabilising rests on the assumption that speculators are profit-maximisers who must buy cheaper than they sell, and if they do the current exchange rate will be brought closer to its long-run average. For speculation to be destabilising, it is argued, speculators would have to lose money and would eventually go out of business. In his classic paper on the case for flexible exchange rates Friedman (1953) says: 'people who argue that speculation is generally destabilising seldom realise that this is largely equivalent to saying that speculators lose money, since speculation can be destabilising in general only if speculators on the average sell when the currency is low in price and buy when it is high'. Friedman also admits, however, that 'it does not, of course, follow, that speculation is not destabilising; professional speculators might, on the average, make money while a changing body of amateurs regularly lose large sums'. He also adds that his remarks that speculation must be stabilising if it is to be profitable are

a simplified generalisation of a complex problem . . . A full analysis encounters difficulties in separating 'speculative' from other transactions, defining precisely and satisfactorily 'destabilising speculation' and taking account of the effects of the mere existence of a system of flexible rates as contrasted with the effects of actual speculative transactions under such a system.

It can in fact be shown that profitability is neither a necessary nor a sufficient condition for speculation to be stabilising. It is not necessary because perfectly competitive speculation under perfect foresight would lead to perfect stability of the exchange rate but zero profits. It is not sufficient, either, if the exchange market exhibits multiple equilibria in the absence of speculation with unstable regions in between (like Figure 1.5 above if the supply curve were to bend back on itself again and cut the demand curve from below). In this case profitable speculation could cause fluctuations that would not have occurred in its absence. Thus profitable speculation need not always be stabilising, and destabilising speculation can be profitable.

Ultimately the question of whether speculation is stabilising or not is an empirical one: the matter cannot be decided by theoretical reasoning alone. The empirical evidence, however, may be very difficult to interpret. The major difficulty is knowing what a freely fluctuating exchange rate would have been in the absence of speculation. How do we know, for example, whether speculation has been stabilising or destabilising since the general abandonment of fixed exchange rates in the world economy in 1973? The fact that exchange rates have shown instability since 1973 may be the result of de-stabilising speculation, or may reflect the fact that the 'non-speculative' rate is subject to variation which was not allowed to express itself under the former fixed exchange-rate system. The instability could also have been part of a process of adjustment towards a more stable long-run equilibrium after a period of exchange-rate rigidity.

Whether or not speculative activity is stabilising in the long run, there is no doubt that speculative activity can be destabilising and very harmful to economies in the short run, especially when the speculative activity starts a spiral of depreciation necessitating dom-estic economic policy inappropriate to the functioning of the real economy. If speculative capital movements could be controlled, the harm done to the domestic economy would constitute a powerful argument for doing so. It is, of course, absolutely vital to be able to control capital movements in a fixed exchange-rate system (see Chapter 3) unless the foreign-currency reserves can take the strain of a speculative outflow. One of the reasons the par value system of exchange rates established at Bretton Woods broke down from 1971 onwards was the inability of countries to defend the par values of their currencies in the face of movements of short-term capital, the volume of which grew so rapidly in the 1960s (Lamfalussy, 1976). But those who argued that under a system of flexible exchange rates movements around the trend would be limited (because speculation would be stabilising?) seem to have been confounded by the experi-ence of the 1970s and 1980s.

Government transactions also affect the supply of and demand for foreign currency. Governments provide foreign currency to other countries, thus depreciating their own currency, and themselves receive foreign loans, which appreciate their currency. The central banks of countries also intervene on behalf of governments to stabilise exchange rates – buying foreign currencies to stop their own currency from appreciating and selling foreign currencies to prevent their own currency from depreciating.

THE FORWARD RATE OF EXCHANGE

The rate of exchange that we have been considering so far is the so-called 'spot' rate of exchange, which is determined in the free market by the immediate supply of and demand for currencies. Many international transactions, however, do not require immediate settlement but instead involve contracts to pay in the future. To facilitate the implementation of contractual arrangements involving future obligations there exists in addition a forward exchange market at which traders can buy and sell currencies 'forward' at an agreed rate. Thus whereas in the spot market the buyers and sellers of foreign currency accept the ruling market price, in the forward market the buyers and sellers agree to a price in advance, sometimes more than a year into the future but usually less. The two markets, and the two rates of exchange, are linked by three main factors: interest-rate differences between countries; speculation; and 'hedging' and 'covering'.

If there were no cost or risk in the transfer of funds from one country to another, and interest rates were the same at home and abroad, there would be no difference between the spot and forward rates of exchange within and between countries. For example, if the forward rate was higher than the spot rate, it would pay to purchase currency spot and sell it simultaneously at the higher forward rate, investing the funds in a foreign bank (paying the same interest rate as domestic banks) until the forward contract expired. By a process of arbitrage, i.e. the switching of funds between the two markets, the two rates would be equalised.

If the rate of interest on monetary deposits differs between two countries, however, the forward rate will tend to diverge from the spot rate, being higher (at a premium) in the country with the lower interest rate, and lower (at a discount) in the country with the higher interest rate. As a first-order approximation, ignoring transfer charges, risks and other factors affecting the forward rate, the currency will sell forward at a premium or discount equal to the interest-rate differential.

Suppose that the spot rate between the dollar and the pound is $2 to £1, and that the interest rate is higher in the United Kingdom than in the United States. It would then pay investors to switch funds from the United States to the United Kingdom provided that the interest gain is not offset by a lower rate of conversion of sterling to dollars when the investment matures than when the original investment in sterling assets was made. To ensure against this contingency investors will sell pounds (and buy dollars) forward at an agreed rate. The forward rate of exchange will fall below the spot rate of $2 to £1, and funds will tend to move from the United States to the United

Kingdom until the differential yield on investment in the United Kingdom is just offset by the forward exchange conversion loss in the United Kingdom. The equilibrium forward rate of exchange giving 'interest-rate parity' between the two currencies is given by the formula

$$R_F = \frac{(1 + i_{US})}{(1 + i_{UK})} R_s \qquad (1.7)$$

where R_F is the forward rate of exchange in the United Kingdom, R_s is the spot rate, i_{US} is the interest rate in the United States, and i_{UK} is the interest rate in the United Kingdom. For example, supposing $i_{US} = 0.05$; $i_{UK} = 0.1$ and $R_s = \$2:\£1$, then

$$R_F = \frac{(1 + 0.05)}{(1 + 0.1)} \times \frac{\$2}{\£1} = \frac{\$2.1}{\£1.1} \approx \$1.9:\£1$$

As a rate of discount against spot sterling this is $(2 - 1.9)/2 \approx 0.05$, or 5 per cent. If the discount were less, it would continue to pay US investors to switch their funds to the United Kingdom. In practice funds move when the difference between the forward discount or premium and the interest differential is minutely small, perhaps as narrow as 1/100 of 1 per cent.

If the interest-rate differential between the two countries were the only factor affecting the relationship between the forward and spot rates of exchange, the discount (or premium) on sterling should equal the interest-rate difference. In practice other factors also influence the forward rate of exchange and its relation to the spot rate.

Risk and liquidity considerations will affect the forward rate of exchange and its relationship to the spot rate. Importers who have to pay in foreign currency in the future, and exporters who expect to be paid in foreign currency in the future, may wish to 'cover' against the risk of exchange-rate changes. For example, a UK exporter may expect to be paid $100 in three months' time but be worried that in the meantime the dollar will depreciate and sterling appreciate so that he would get less pounds for his $100. He may therefore decide to sell forward his $100 at an agreed rate knowing exactly how much sterling he will then receive in three months' time when he delivers the $100. Selling dollars forward in anticipation of a depreciation of the dollar will influence the forward rate of exchange. Likewise, a

UK importer may have to pay a supplier in dollars in three months' time and be worried that the dollar will appreciate and sterling depreciate in the meantime, involving him in a higher sterling payment for a given amount of dollars. He may therefore decide to buy dollars forward knowing exactly how much sterling he must pay in three months' time when he collects the dollars. The importer may, of course, decide to pay immediately or expect sterling to appreciate, in which case it would be the supplier who would presumably attempt to cover. Expectations that traders hold about future exchange-rate movements are a major contributor to leads and lags and to the *balancing item* in the balance-of-payments accounts that we discussed earlier.

Forward cover is also sought by business firms holding foreign assets who are obliged for accounting reasons to convert the value of their foreign assets and liabilities at the current spot of exchange. To avoid exchange risks firms may continually cover. This practice is called 'hedging', and tends to be insensitive to expected exchange-rate changes.

Speculation is another factor that affects the relation between the spot and forward rates of exchange. If a speculator believes that the future spot rate will be higher than the current forward rate, the 'bull' speculator will buy forward in order to sell spot at the higher rate than he bought forward. For example, if the current forward rate is $1.9 to £1 and the expected spot rate is $2 to £1, a profit will be made by speculators who agree to buy sterling forward at $1.9 per £, and who then sell the sterling for $2 per £. The forward rate will tend to move up towards the expected spot rate, and if this encourages buying in the spot market, expectations about the future spot rate will become self-fulfilling. Conversely, a speculator who expects the spot rate in the future to be below the current forward rate will sell sterling forward in order to buy spot at a lower rate than he sold forward. Suppose the current forward rate is $1.9 to £1 and the expected spot rate is $1.8 to £1. A profit will be made by speculators who agree to sell sterling forward at $1.9 per £, and who then buy sterling back again at $1.8 per £. In this case the forward rate will tend to move down towards the expected spot rate, and if this encourages selling in the spot market, expectations about the future spot rate will again be self-fulfilling.

If the spot rate of exchange is fixed within limits but the forward rate is free to vary without limit (as was the case under the Articles of Agreement of the IMF), a situation may arise where the covering operations of commercial traders in forward markets depreciates the forward rate of exchange in excess of the interest-rate differential. It then becomes profitable to buy *foreign* currency spot and sell it forward, exerting considerable pressure on the rate of exchange of the home country, which under a system of fixed exchange rates must be preserved by the monetary authorities using its reserves and selling foreign currency.

Alternatively, the monetary authorities may intervene to support the forward rate of exchange by forward sales of foreign exchange to reduce the forward discount for domestic currency. The authorities would, of course, have to deliver the foreign exchange at a later date but in the process some foreign-exchange loss that would otherwise have occurred might be prevented. If, however, the intervention is unsuccessful, and the currency has to be devalued (or depreciates further under a system of flexible exchange rates), the monetary authorities stand to lose heavily. The UK Exchange Equalisation Account lost nearly £400 million in its attempt to prop up the forward value of sterling before the devaluation of sterling in November 1967. Some would argue that many of the UK foreign-exchange crises have not been predominantly of a purely speculative nature but the result of interest arbitrage arising from the spread between the spot and forward rates of exchange. In theory stabilisation of the spot rate should give stability to the forward rate if arbitrage funds are perfectly elastic with respect to the (covered) interest differential. In practice, however, they are not; and there may be controls. In these circumstances it may be preferable for the authorities to stabilise the forward rate in order to keep the spot rate stable.

2
The Capital Account of the Balance of Payments

The capital account of the balance of payments is a record of all transactions which alter the external assets and/or liabilities of a country. Let us take it from the point of view of the UK. The external assets (or wealth) of the UK include shares, property, companies, and bank accounts held abroad by UK residents. Analogously, the external liabilities of a country include borrowing by residents of that country from overseas, non-resident holdings of shares, property, companies etc. and bank accounts held by non-residents in UK banks. Changes in these external assets or liabilities can result either from transactions which result from the buying or selling of goods and services (i.e. current account transactions) or from exports and imports of capital (i.e. pure financial transactions).

With respect to current account transactions, the purchase of an import, for example, will appear as a credit in the capital account because the importer reduces his/her holdings of foreign assets to pay for the import. Such a reduction in external assets held by UK residents is equivalent to a capital inflow and thus appears as a credit in the capital account. On the other hand, an increase in resident holdings of overseas assets, associated, for example, with an export, is equivalent to an outflow of capital and thus appears as a debit in the capital account.

We can also illustrate the second case of a pure financial transaction. Let us examine what happens when a UK resident buys a share on the Japanese stock exchange, for example. The purchase of the share results in a capital outflow which increases the stock of overseas assets held by UK residents. The transaction thus appears as a debit on the capital account. However, there is an equivalent credit which also appears on the capital account. If the share is purchased by drawing on a foreign bank account, by borrowing from abroad or by drawing a cheque on a UK bank account, all these will be recorded as a debit on the capital account either because external assets have fallen or because external liabilities have risen.

The purpose of this chapter is to outline and explain the various components of the capital account and their determinants. In addition, we discuss the conceptual role which the capital account plays in any analysis of the balance of payments.

THE COMPONENTS OF THE CAPITAL ACCOUNT

Table 2.1 lists the items found in the UK capital account. In the detailed balance-of-payments accounts of the United Kingdom (see, for example, Balance of Payments Pink Book), transactions are divided into those affecting external assets and those affecting external liabilities.

Items in the capital account are divided either according to the type of investment being undertaken (e.g. portfolio or direct) or according to the sector of the economy to which the transactor belongs (e.g. government or non-bank).

Direct investment (Table 2.1, A.1(a) and B.1(a)) is defined as transactions which involve the purchase or sale of an interest in a firm in which the owner has 'an effective voice in the management of the enterprise' (Balance of Payments Pink Book, 1989, p. 41). For example, if a British multinational company sets up a components factory abroad, the value of the investment would be itemised under direct investment overseas by UK residents. Direct investment is influenced, *inter alia*, by unit labour costs, geographical factors (which influence transport costs), taxes, subsidies and tariffs. The recent growth in direct investment in the UK is often attributed to the desire of non-EC companies to gain access to the EC market, especially in preparation for the single market in 1992. Direct investment is usually thought to be long-term in nature. The costs involved in setting up a subsidiary or affiliate overseas are usually quite large, making this type of capital transaction unsuitable for short-term speculative purposes.

Portfolio investment (Table 2.1, A.1(b) and B.1(b)) includes the sale and purchase of company, government and local authority securities. Outward portfolio investment involves transactions in securities undertaken by UK banks, financial institutions and UK

TABLE 2.1
The capital account of the balance of payments

A. *Transactions in external assets*
1. Investment overseas by UK residents
   (a) direct
   (b) portfolio
2. Lending abroad by UK banks (in sterling and foreign currency)
3. Deposits with and lending to banks abroad by the UK non-bank private sector
4. Other external assets of
   (a) UK non-bank private sector
   (b) Public corporations
   (c) General government

B. *Transactions in external liabilities*
1. Investment in the UK by overseas residents
   (a) direct
   (b) portfolio
2. Borrowing abroad by UK banks (in sterling and foreign currency)
3. Borrowing from banks abroad by
   (a) UK non-bank private sector
   (b) Public corporations
   (c) General government
4. Other external liabilities
   (a) UK non-bank private sector
   (b) Public corporations
   (c) General government

C. *Official reserves*

D. *Allocation of special drawing rights*

E. *EEA loss on forward commitments*

F. *Gold subscriptions to IMF*

G. *Balancing item*

---

residents. Inward investment involves foreign banks, financial institutions and non-residents. Portfolio investment is influenced by factors such as the expected relative returns and the desire of individuals or institutions to diversify portfolios. As a result portfolio investment is normally categorised as long-term – by the International Monetary Fund, for example. However, this distinction is not so clear-cut in practice, and portfolio investment could also be influenced by speculative factors such as the expected depreciation (appreciation) of the home (foreign) currency. The fact that well-developed secondary markets for securities exist in many countries implies that securities are fairly liquid and might be considered as an appropriate vehicle for speculation.

Transactions of UK banks (excluding portfolio and direct investment) include both foreign and domestic currency lending and borrowing abroad (Table 2.1, A.2 and B.2). The largest component results from London's role as a major eurocurrency (especially eurodollar) centre. A eurocurrency is a currency which is lent or borrowed outside its country of origin. Thus, for example, a eurodollar loan is a dollar loan which is made by a bank based outside the US: a eurodollar deposit is a deposit account held with a bank outside the US. Foreign currency lending by UK banks represents an increase in UK external assets and thus is categorised as a capital outflow on the balance of payments. On the other hand, an increase in deposits held by UK banks for non-residents represents an increase in UK external liabilities and is a capital inflow. A second important component of bank transactions in external assets and liabilities arises from their role in the provision of trade credit. UK banks provide trade credit not only for UK trade but also for trade between other countries. Banks provide facilities for trade credit in either sterling or foreign currencies.

Transactions by UK residents other than banks and general government (excluding direct and portfolio investment) include transactions undertaken by public corporations and non-bank private residents (Table 2.1, A.3, A.4(a)(b), B.3(a)(b) and B.4(a)(b)). These transactions are mainly conducted with banks abroad. In Table 2.1 we distinguish between external assets held by public corporations and the non-bank private sector with banks abroad (A.3) and other assets (A.4(a)(b)). A similar breakdown exists for external liabilities: borrowing from banks abroad (A.3(a)(b)) and other liabilities (B.4(a)(b)). Bank assets and liabilities include items such as bank deposits held by private individuals or UK companies, borrowing from banks abroad by UK companies, trade credit arranged by overseas banks etc. Other assets and liabilities include, for example, trade credit, transactions in commercial bills and overseas residents' deposits with UK building societies.

Transactions by general government include transactions under-taken by both central government and Local Authorities (Table 2.1, A.4(c), B.3(c) and B.4(c)). If the central government or a Local Authority borrows from either a bank or non-bank abroad this represents an increase in the external liabilities of general government. Alternatively, if central government lends, perhaps on a con-cessional basis, to a developing country government, this is included as an increase in the external assets of general government. Subscrip-tions to international organisations such as the IMF are also included in general government transactions (although gold subscriptions to the IMF are itemised separately (Table 2.1, E)[1]).

The Exchange Equalisation Account (EEA) is the record of transactions carried out in the foreign exchange markets to influence the value to sterling. It is essentially the government's account held at the Bank of England for the purpose of foreign exchange market intervention (see UK Balance of Payments, 1989). Line E in Table 2.1 records any losses following forward exchange market intervention.

Of the final three items in Table 2.1, official reserves and allo-cations of special drawing rights by the IMF are normally included under transactions of general government. The balancing item, on the other hand, does not usually appear in the capital account but rather in the consolidated balance of payments accounts. These three items deserve some special attention.

Official Reserves

Official reserves comprise holdings of convertible currencies and gold by the monetary authorities of a country (in the case of the UK this is the Bank of England).[2] The balance of payments records changes in these reserves which take place in a given time period. Additions to reserves appear as a minus entry: a decline in reserves appears as a plus. This counter-intuitive method of recording changes in reserves results from the double-entry bookkeeping nature of the balance-of-payments accounts. Official reserves are assets: an increase in re-serves thus represents an increase in the external assets of the UK and as such are a debit item in the balance of payments in much the same way as an increase in UK holdings of overseas securities. By contrast, a decrease in reserves represents a decrease in the external assets of the UK and hence appears as a credit item in the balance of payments.

Changes in official reserves indicate the degree to which the monetary authorities have intervened in the foreign exchange market. As such, we expect the magnitude of this variable to vary according to the exchange rate regime in operation. If exchange rates are floating cleanly, we would not expect any official intervention by the monetary authorities in the foreign exchange market – changes in reserves would be zero. In practice the case of cleanly floating exchange rates is not to be found. Countries are rarely indifferent about the level of their exchange rate, so that even if exchange rates are floating there is some intervention by the monetary authorities. Changes in reserves are rarely zero.[3]

On the other hand, if the government is committed to maintaining the level of the exchange rate at some agreed level, as under the Bretton Woods system and now under the exchange rate mechanism of the European Monetary System, then we would expect changes in reserves to be non-zero. Assume, for example, that the government has committed itself to maintain the exchange rate at e_1 (Figure 2.1). In this case, there is an excess supply of dollars. In the absence of intervention by the monetary authorities, the sterling price of dollars would be expected to fall towards e^*, the equilibrium rate (i.e. sterling would appreciate). In order to maintain the exchange rate at e_1, the monetary authorities would have to intervene and buy up the excess supply of dollars, thus experiencing an increase in their official foreign exchange reserves. On the other hand, were the monetary authorities trying to peg the sterling price of dollars at too low a level, for example, e_2, there would be an excess demand for dollars leading to pressure for depreciation of sterling. The monetary authorities in this case would have to intervene to supply the dollars demanded in the foreign exchange market: their foreign exchange reserves would be decreasing.

What factors are likely to influence the volume of reserves which a country would wish to hold? Reserves can be viewed as a buffer-stock (Triffin, 1947) which allow countries to finance a balance-of-payments deficit whilst maintaining their exchange rate or at least allowing it to depreciate slowly.[4] They allow a country time to correct the deficit, in the hope that this breathing space reduces the costs of adjustment in terms of slower growth of national income and unemployment. The higher the costs associated with speedy adjustment,

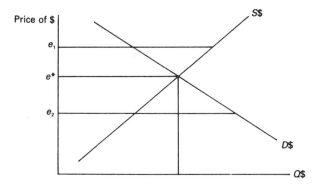

FIGURE 2.1   *Government intervention under fixed exchange rates*

the larger will be the demand for international reserves.

However, there are costs associated with holding reserves. If the foreign exchange was not being held as international reserves, then it could be earning a return from investment either in the country itself or abroad. The costs of holding reserves therefore have to be weighed against the benefits which they provide.

Our analysis of Figure 2.1 above suggests that the demand for reserves might also depend on the exchange rate regime. If a country is pegging its currency to another, then one might expect its demand for reserves to be higher than if it were allowing the exchange rate to float. However, Black (1985) has shown that increased uncertainty associated with the move towards flexible exchange rates (resulting from their volatility) could have tended to increase the demand for reserves. The evidence on whether the move towards floating exchange rates in 1973 has reduced the demand for reserves is mixed.[5]

Table 2.2 shows the growth of international reserves from 1950 and gives us some information about their composition. The main problem associated with the valuation of reserves is the question of whether or not gold should be included. Table 2.2 includes the total value of reserves with gold valued at market prices, with gold valued at $35 per ounce (the official price of gold during the Bretton Woods system) and without gold. The wide divergence between these three measures indicates the importance of the decision about the inclusion or exclusion of gold. The market price of gold during the 1950s and 1960s was kept very close to the official price of $35 per ounce. Thus if one includes gold in foreign exchange reserves, its valuation only becomes an issue in the 1970s. Although the official price of gold was

TABLE 2.2

International reserves – all countries (billions of SDRs)

	1950	1955	1960	1965	1970	1975	1980	1985
Total reserves								
– gold at market prices	48.2	53.7	60.7	71.3	95.6	282.2	762.0	687.8
– gold at $35 per oz	48.4	53.8	60.0	71.2	93.2	195.8	355.0	438.5
IMF related reserves								
(as percentage of total reserves excluding gold)	11.3	10.2	16.3	18.4	19.2	12.7	8.9	14.0
(as percentage of total reserves with gold at $35 per oz)	3.5	3.5	5.9	7.6	11.6	10.9	8.0	13.0
– reserve positions	1.7	1.9	3.6	5.4	7.7	12.6	16.8	38.7
(percentage of total reserves)	3.5	3.5	5.9	7.6	8.1	4.5	2.2	5.6
– SDRs					3.1	8.8	11.8	18.2
(percentage of total reserves)					3.2	3.1	1.5	2.6
Foreign exchange	13.3	16.7	18.5	24.0	45.3	138.8	292.9	348.3
(percentage of total reserves)	27.6	31.1	30.5	33.7	47.4	49.2	38.4	50.6
Total reserves excl. gold	15.0	18.6	22.1	29.5	56.2	160.2	321.6	405.2
Gold								
– at market prices	33.2	35.1	38.6	41.9	39.5	122.0	440.5	282.6
(percentage of total reserves)	68.9	65.4	63.6	58.8	41.3	43.2	57.8	41.1
– at $35 per oz	33.4	35.2	37.9	41.8	37.0	35.7	33.3	33.2
(percentage of total reserves*)	69.0	65.4	63.2	58.7	39.7	18.2	9.4	7.6

* Total reserves valued with gold at $35 per oz.
All other percentages are with respect to total reserves with gold valued at market prices.
Source: Calculated from IMF International Financial Statistics.

not abandoned until 1976,[6] the price of gold began to rise on the London market in the early 1970s.

If we include gold in our measure of total reserves, then we can see that its importance as a reserve asset has declined since 1950 even if we value it at market prices. The decline is of course much more marked if gold is still valued at $35 per ounce: in 1950 it accounted for 69 per cent of total reserves whereas in 1985 it accounted for only 7.6 per cent. Accompanying this decline in the importance of gold, there has been an increase in the importance of foreign exchange reserves. The importance of the IMF as a provider of reserves has been variable: IMF reserves generally increased in importance up to 1970 and declined thereafter.

Table 2.3 illustrates the composition of UK international reserves. The patterns displayed are very similar to the pattern for all countries. It

TABLE 2.3

International reserves – United Kingdom (millions of SDRs)

	1950	1955	1960	1965	1970	1975	1980	1985
Total reserves								
– gold at market prices	3 418.9	2 626.1	4 255.1	3 011.3	2 906.5	6 446.4	24 898.8	17 373.2
– gold at $35 per oz	3 442.6	2 627.8	4 207.1	3 003.5	2 827.2	4 663.1	16 850.4	12 374.1
IMF related reserves								
– reserve positions	0.0	236.0	488.0	0.0	0.0	304.0	1 045.0	1 810.0
(percentage of total reserves)		9.0	11.5		0.0	4.7	4.2	10.4
– SDRs					266.0	696.0	447.0	1 030.0
(percentage of total reserves)					9.2	10.8	1.8	5.9
Foreign exchange	581.0	380.0	918.0	739.0	1 213.0	2 927.0	14 699.0	8 868.0
(percentage of total reserves)	17.0	14.5	21.6	24.5	41.7	45.4	59.0	51.0
Total reserves excluding gold	581.0	616.0	1 406.0	739.0	1 479.0	3 927.0	16 192.0	11 707.0
Gold								
– at market prices	2 837.9	2 010.1	2 849.1	2 272.3	1 427.5	2 519.4	8 707.8	5 665.2
(percentage of total reserves)	83.0	76.5	67.0	75.5	49.1	39.1	35.0	32.6
– at $35 per oz	2 861.6	2 011.8	2 801.1	2 264.5	1 348.2	736.1	659.4	666.1
(percentage of total reserves*)	83.1	76.6	66.6	75.4	47.7	15.8	3.9	5.4

* Total reserves valued with gold at $35 per oz.

All other percentages are with respect to total reserves with gold valued at market price.

Source: Calculated from IMF International Financial Statistics.

TABLE 2.4
Composition of foreign exchange reserves of industrial countries (%)

	1979	1980	1981	1982	1983	1984	1985	1986	1987
Dollar	83.5	77.6	78.7	77.1	77.4	73.6	65.4	68.4	70.6
Sterling	0.7	0.7	0.7	0.8	0.8	1.6	2.1	1.6	1.5
Deutschmark	9.4	14.3	12.8	12.2	12.8	14.8	19.4	17.5	16.5
French Franc	0.6	0.5	0.4	0.3	0.3	0.4	0.5	0.6	0.8
Swiss Franc	1.4	1.7	1.7	1.7	1.4	1.4	1.8	1.4	1.1
Guilder	0.6	0.7	0.8	0.7	0.5	0.6	1	1.1	1.1
Yen	2.6	3.3	3.7	4.4	5.1	6.3	8.8	8.2	6.6
Other	1.2	1.2	1.2	2.8	1.7	1.2	1	1.2	1.8

Source: *IMF Annual Report, 1988.*

can be noted, however, that while gold in 1950 was more important to the UK as a reserve asset, its importance in 1985 had declined to below that of the average for all countries.

Table 2.4 shows the composition of foreign exchange reserves. This highlights the continued domination of the dollar as the principal reserve currency. However, we can note that its attractiveness has been much reduced over the 1980s. This trend has been noticeable since the move towards floating exchange rates. Monetary authorities have been keen to diversify their reserve holdings and the Deutschemark and the Yen have proved to be the most attractive currencies for this purpose.

Special Drawing Rights (SDRs)

SDRs are a reserve asset created by the IMF in 1969 in response to the perceived shortage of liquidity in the international system. During the Bretton Woods system, gold and the dollar were the main reserve assets. Since the volume of gold in the world economy grew only slowly, dependent as it was on gold production, it was the dollar which provided the increased liquidity required to finance international trade. To allow the dollar to assume this role, the United States had to run a balance-of-payments deficit, thus increasing the supply of dollars to the rest of the world. A balance-of-payments deficit implies that the US is exporting less than it is importing. Thus it pays out more dollars (on imports) than it receives (from exports). The supply of dollars in non-US ownership thus increases. Triffin

(1960) pointed out the dilemma inherent in this strategy. As holdings of dollars outside the US grew relative to the stock of US gold, confidence in the convertibility of the dollar into gold at the official price of $35 per ounce would come into question. In short, the longer the US ran a balance-of-payments deficit, the lower confidence in the dollar would become. On the other hand, if the US adjusted their balance-of-payments to a surplus, confidence in the dollar would be restored at the cost of an increasing shortage of dollars to finance international trade. This became widely known as the Triffin dilemma.

The SDR was envisaged as a means to get around this dilemma.[7] During the 1950s and early 1960s, there was indeed a shortage of international liquidity since the US balance of payments was in surplus. By the mid-1960s, it had moved into deficit. It was envisaged that as the supply of dollars dried up when the US deficit fell, so SDRs would replace them as the main reserve asset. Moreover, even if the US deficit continued and international liquidity remained in good supply, it was envisaged that SDRs would remain popular as a reserve asset. If the US deficit continued, then European central banks would continue to accumulate dollars as they intervened in the foreign exchange market by buying dollars to prevent it from depreciating. At some point, eventually European central banks may become unwilling to accumulate further dollar balances, as the probability of dollar devaluation grew. Thus it was expected that this potential lack of confidence in the dollar may lead to increased demand for SDRs.

SDRs are created simply by the IMF taking a decision to do so. For a decision to be taken at least 85 per cent of the quota-determined votes must favour an allocation. An SDR is not backed by any commodity, gold or otherwise. In other words, it cannot be converted into anything other than world currencies. In that sense, it is exactly like a national currency, which circulates because it is widely accepted as a means of payment. Indeed, IMF members are required to accept SDRs for financing international transactions up to three times their original allocations.

The first allocation of SDRs took place over the three years 1970–72. SDR 3 billion was distributed at the beginning of each year to IMF members according to each country's quota.[8] The UK received SDR 410 million, SDR 300 million and SDR 297 million in each of these years. It was originally envisaged that allocations of SDRs in the initial period and subsequent years would form the major component of increases in international reserve assets. In the event, however, the anticipated shortage of reserves, which the creation of the SDR was supposed to ease, did not materialise. Instead, the US balance-of-payments deficit averaged some SDR 17 billion per annum between 1970 and 1972 rather than the SDR 1–1.5 billion which the IMF had predicted (Von Furstenberg, 1983, p. 494). Excessive reserve creation rather than a lack of reserves became the major problem and it was decided not to allocate any more SDRs between 1973 and 1977.

The second allocation of SDRs took place over the years 1979–81. By 1978, when the decision to further allocate SDRs was taken, it was clear that the SDR was unlikely to become the major international reserve asset. Rather, the allocations were seen as a means to help reduce the amounts that developing countries were having to borrow from the international capital markets. Since SDRs can be used as an international means of payment, LDCs can use them instead of, say, dollars, to purchase goods and services from developed countries. Accordingly SDR 4 billions were allocated in each year over the period 1979–81. Allocations were still made according to quotas. Thus developed countries with larger quotas receive more SDRs than LDCs with relatively small quotas. The UK, for example, received SDR 304 million in the first two years and SDR 298 million in the last allocation. Thus while LDCs were helped to some extent by the allocations, they would have been better off if all the SDRs created had been allocated to them, with none allocated to the developed countries who had little need for them. Since 1981 there have been no further allocations of SDRs.

The value of the SDR was originally linked to the dollar price of a fixed amount of gold. Initially therefore one SDR was equal to one dollar and the exchange rate of other currencies *vis-à-vis* the SDR was the same as their dollar exchange rate. After August 1971, when the dollar convertibility into gold was suspended, the link between the SDR and gold became tenuous. Before the dollar devaluation, one dollar was equal to 0.888671 grams of gold. Following its devaluation, the dollar was worth less than this. However, the SDR maintained its value relative to gold *at its official price*. Its value relative to the dollar therefore rose. Its link to gold, however, became more tenuous as the *free market price* of gold rose. The SDR could still buy 0.88671 grams of gold at its official price, but on the free gold market it was worth much less. Thus its purchasing power relative to gold depended on whether gold was valued at its official or free market price.

On 1 July 1974 it was decided to link the value of the SDR to a basket of 16 currencies (the currencies of the top 16 trading nations). This move to opt for a basket valuation system was an attempt to make the SDR more attractive, allowing it to compete more effectively with other currencies for a role as an international reserve asset. The advantage of such a valuation method is that the value of a basket of currencies is more stable than the value of individual currencies. It provides holders with ready-made portfolio diversification. The basket was subsequently reduced to five currencies on 1 January 1981 to allow for easier calculation of its value: the currencies included were the US dollar, the Deutschemark, the Yen, the Pound sterling and the French franc. It was also hoped that the private sector would begin to denominate loans and deposits in SDRs and that the new basket would make this easier since the five currencies all have well-developed spot and forward markets.

As we can see from Table 2.2 the importance of SDRs as a reserve asset has remained very low, in spite of numerous attempts to make them more attractive.[9]

The Balancing Item

The balancing item in the balance-of-payments accounts is always of equal magnitude but of opposite sign to the sum of the current account, capital account and official financing components of the balance of payments (see Chapter 1). It is the item which ensures that the balance of payments as a whole sums to zero. In theory every transaction in the balance of payments is recorded twice, once as a credit and once as a debit, because of the double-entry bookkeeping nature of the balance of payments. However, in practice, the entries are often derived from separate sources so errors can easily arise. Moreover, amounts denominated in foreign currencies may be converted to sterling at different times and hence at different rates of exchange, again leading to an anomaly between the two entries for one transaction. It is generally recognised (see UK Balance of Payments, 1989) that errors are more likely to be associated with a misrecording of capital account items rather than current items. The balancing item in the UK has been rather large in recent years: since 1984 it has varied between £5 and £12 billion. The UK Balance of Payments (1989) attributes these errors in the main, first, to the large increase in the number of financial instruments available particularly as a result of deregulation in the city of London. Secondly, the

abolition of capital controls in October 1979 destroyed the reporting
system which the Central Statistical Office had used for collating
information on capital movements. New reporting systems appear to
have taken some time to implement and moreover their coverage is
less than 100 per cent.

In countries where capital controls still exist, the balancing item is
often thought to represent illegal and therefore unreported capital
account transactions.[10]

THE CAPITAL ACCOUNT AND THE NET EXTERNAL WEALTH OF
THE UK

The capital account of the balance of payments records capital flows
over a given period. The flows affect the stock of external assets and
liabilities of the UK. For example, a capital outflow may result in the
purchase of a share overseas, thus increasing the stock of external
UK assets. Alternatively, a capital inflow, associated for example
with a UK company borrowing from abroad, will increase the stock
of external UK liabilities. The stock of external assets and liabilities
in turn affect the current account. An increase in the stock of assets
held by UK residents abroad might be expected to lead to an increase
in interest, profits and dividends in future periods. The return on
assets held abroad is recorded in the current account. Thus an
increase in the stock of external UK assets would be expected to
improve the current account in the near future. Alternatively, an
increase in external UK liabilities would be expected to cause the
current account to deteriorate as interest, profits and dividends which
the UK pays to the rest of the world increase. High interest rates to
cut import demand never improve the balance of payments to the
extent of the fall in import demand, because interest payments on the
current account increase.

The capital account records transactions which result in increases
or decreases in the stock of external assets and liabilities. However
the stock of external assets and liabilities can change as a result of
changes in the value of assets or liabilities already held. These
valuation changes can come about either through a change in the
price of marketable assets/liabilities or through changes in exchange
rates.

Table 2.5 shows the volume of UK external assets and liabilities
from 1962 to 1987. Table 2.6 focuses specifically on portfolio invest-

ment. These two tables will help us to illustrate the four main factors which have influenced the value of external assets/liabilities of the UK.

The first factor which has on two significant occasions strongly influenced the value of external assets/liabilities of the UK is changes in share prices. The value of external portfolio assets and liabilities of the private sector fell sharply over the period 1972 to 1974, with the fall being more marked in 1974. Table 2.6 breaks the changes in market value into changes due to transactions and those due to changes in valuation. The latter were largely responsible for the decline in the value of both assets and liabilities. It should, however, be noted that falling share prices in 1974 caused a large repatriation of funds, with net transactions reducing the value of UK portfolio investment overseas by £675 million. The second instance where share prices have been a major influence on the value of overseas assets/liabilities was the stock market boom during the mid-1980s which was followed by the crash of October 1987. Overseas portfolio assets had risen by £23 billion due to valuation changes during 1986. However, during 1987 their value fell by £22 billion (Table 2.6): three-quarters of the fall was due to the fall in share prices; only one-quarter was the result of repatriation of wealth. By contrast, overseas portfolio liabilities grew by £6 billion in 1987 due to a large inflow of funds into the London market. This can probably be explained by the desire of wealth holders to move their wealth to markets with more depth and resilience.

The second major factor affecting the value of external assets/ liabilities of the UK is changes in the value of sterling. When sterling depreciates, the sterling value of external assets which are largely denominated in foreign currencies increases. The value of UK external liabilities also increases but since a smaller proportion of UK liabilities is denominated in foreign currencies, the increase is smaller than the increase in the value of assets. Overall, therefore, *net* external assets tend to rise when the pound depreciates. The 1976–7 period is highly illustrative of the impact which exchange rate changes can have on the value of external assets/liabilities. In 1976 sterling depreciated substantially (from $2.02 at the end of 1975 to $1.47 at the end of 1976). This increased the value of UK overseas investment by £1.5 billion. Overall, in 1976, the value of UK overseas assets increased by some £1.35 billion since some funds were repatriated (see Table 2.6). By contrast, during 1977, when sterling appreciated, the value of portfolio investment overseas fell by £1.35 billion.

TABLE 2.5

UK external assets and liabilities, 1962–87 (£ million)

UK external assets	1962	1964	1966	1967	1968	1969	1970	1971	1972	1973	1974	1975
Private sector												
– Direct (incl. bank)	4 870	5 585	6 285	7 280	7 750	8 440	8 930	9 290	10 790	11 590	13 085	15 040
– Portfolio (incl. bank)	3 200	3 900	3 650	4 850	6 150	5 650	5 600	5 900	9 490	7 600	5 400	6 850
Banking/commercial	2 205	3 170	4 830	6 330	9 425	15 000	18 200	20 550	28 640	41 685	50 680	66 270
Public sector	2 250	2 110	2 270	2 195	2 140	2 290	2 520	4 885	4 020	4 565	4 910	4 875
– Official reserves	1 540	1 270	1 285	1 125	1 010	1 055	1 180	3 390	2 405	2 795	2 956	2 700
Total	12 525	14 765	17 035	20 655	25 465	31 380	35 250	40 625	52 940	65 440	74 075	93 035
UK External liabilities												
Private sector												
– Direct	2 135	2 590	3 230	3 575	4 050	4 520	5 210	5 980	6 540	8 600	10 920	12 940
– Portfolio	1 030	1 135	1 150	1 635	2 455	2 290	2 075	3 000	3 370	2 640	1 625	3 000
Banking/commercial	2 875	3 870	5 275	6 595	9 275	14 550	18 355	21 950	29 905	43 445	52 295	68 220
Public sector	4 995	5 375	5 895	6 675	7 860	7 335	5 890	5 600	5 795	6 610	9 000	10 630
Total	11 035	12 970	15 550	18 480	23 640	28 695	31 530	36 530	45 610	61 295	73 840	94 780
Net external assets	1 490	1 795	1 485	2 175	1 825	2 685	3 720	4 095	7 330	4 145	235	-1 745

UK external assets	1976	1977	1978	1979	1980	1981	1982	1983	1984	1985	1986	1987
Private sector												
– Direct (incl. bank)	19 613	22 265	25 460	31 570	33 849	44 649	51 808	57 649	78 898	74 233	87 850	91 366
– Portfolio (incl. bank)	8 550	7 800	9 000	12 000	18 100	25 400	40 292	50 324	83 479	101 383	145 493	117 834
Banking/commercial	91 125	95 045	113 315	134 096	157 667	238 051	303 280	348 621	440 962	401 361	471 540	457 821
Public sector	4 835	13 575	13 355	18 464	18 699	17 512	20 082	20 501	22 501	22 457	27 292	36 397
– Official reserves	2 485	10 975	10 380	13 170	13 275	11 960	12 939	12 805	13 219	13 201	17 424	27 008
Total	124 125	139 395	161 565	196 130	228 315	325 612	415 462	486 390	625 840	599 434	732 175	703 418
UK external liabilities												
Private sector												
– Direct	15 233	16 000	17 120	21 880	26 422	30 012	32 301	37 232	40 092	43 521	48 177	53 444
– Portfolio	3 390	4 700	4 580	4 530	5 100	5 800	7 246	9 728	13 359	18 973	27 707	33 368
Banking/commercial	91 590	95 320	111 655	140 838	164 934	247 258	317 503	367 946	473 720	436 428	519 216	500 338
Public sector	14 625	18 160	15 460	15 852	14 838	13 467	16 377	17 147	18 417	20 197	23 825	26 776
Total	124 840	137 170	152 985	183 100	211 294	296 537	373 427	432 053	545 588	519 119	618 925	613 926
Net external assets	–715	2 225	8 580	13 030	17 021	29 075	42 035	54 337	80 252	80 315	113 250	89 492

Source: *Bank of England Quarterly Bulletin*, various issues.

TABLE 2.6
Portfolio investment (£ million)

	1970	1971	1972	1973	1974	1975	1976	1977	1978	1979	1980	1981	1982	1983	1984	1985	1986	1987
UK investment overseas																		
Change in market value	-200	-50	2 300	-1 300	-2 650	1 155	1 350	-1 350	1 050	1 450	4 800	5 500	13 300	19 500	22 600	10 300	38 700	-22 100
– transactions	80	55	685	0	-765	-20	-155	-105	910	873	2 925	4 060	5 900	6 200	8 800	8 000	15 300	-6 200
– valuation*	-280	-105	1 615	-1 300	-1 885	1 175	1 505	-1 245	140	577	1 875	1 440	7 400	13 400	13 800	2 300	23 400	-15 900
Overseas investment in UK																		
Change in market value	-300	650	150	-750	-1 145	1 355	310	1 340	-60	-50	570	700	900	2 800	3 700	4 300	6 700	6 100
– transactions	-10	100	10	100	140	30	220	440	65	350	230	315	100	900	800	2 300	4 900	7 200
– valuation*	-290	550	140	-850	-1 285	1 325	90	900	-125	-400	340	385	800	1 900	2 900	2 000	1 800	-1 200

* Valuation changes include currency adjustment.
Source: *Bank of England Quarterly Bulletin*, various issues.

The third factor which influences UK external assets/liabilities is the importance of London as an offshore banking centre. Most of the external assets and liabilities of the banking sector are associated with their eurocurrency business. Thus factors influencing the growth of the euromarkets play a large role in determining the value of external assets/liabilities of UK banks. Table 2.5 shows the large growth in external assets and liabilities of the banking and commercial sector. For example, the large increase in external assets in 1969 reflected the large demand for eurodollars from US banks who were facing a shortage of funds in the domestic US market as a result of tight monetary conditions there[11] (*Bank of England Quarterly Bulletin*, 1970). On the other hand the slowdown in the growth of bank external assets and liabilities during 1974 can be attributed to difficulties in the euromarkets following large foreign exchange losses by a number of banks (*Bank of England Quarterly Bulletin*, 1975). These losses had led to the failure of Bankhaus I D Herstatt (a Cologne bank) in June 1974. Confidence in the euromarkets fell and their growth slowed.

The fourth and most important factor influencing the volume of external assets and liabilities of the UK is exchange controls (see Bank of England Quarterly Bulletin, 1981b, 1985). Exchange controls or capital controls seek to limit either capital outflows or inflows or both, by closely regulating access to foreign exchange. They were first introduced in the UK during the First World War. In the post Second World War era, exchange controls were operated according to the Exchange Control Act of 1947. Exchange controls were essentially aimed at preventing capital outflows.[12] Banks were allowed to deal in foreign currencies only within the limits laid down by the Bank of England. UK residents were unable to transfer either cash or securities abroad without the permission of the Bank, and the availability of forward cover was limited to prevent its use for speculative purposes. UK residents were able to purchase foreign securities and other assets such as property, but at a premium. These transactions, however, had to be conducted through a special foreign exchange market, known as the investment currency market. The price of foreign exchange in this market was usually higher than in the official market. The extent of the premium depended on the demand and supply of currency in the market. Let us assume a UK resident wished to purchase some foreign asset. The foreign exchange would be bought in the investment currency market at a price higher than the official one. If the UK resident wished to sell the

TABLE 2.7

Distribution of UK external assets and liabilities (percentages of total assets or liabilities)

Assets	End-1979	End-1984
Non-bank private sector	68.9	75.5
– direct	41.2	37.4
– portfolio	14.9	29.8
– other	12.8	8.4
UK banks	7.2	14.9
General Government	23.9	9.6
Liabilities		
Non-bank private sector	59.4	51.5
– direct	34.3	29.4
– portfolio	7.7	10.8
– other	17.4	11.3
UK banks	18.9	32.5
General Government	21.1	16.0

Source: *Bank of England Quarterly Bulletin*, 1985.

foreign asset and repatriate the money from the sale, then until the beginning of 1978, only 75 per cent of the foreign exchange could be sold in the investment currency market. This allowed the potential to recoup the premium that had originally been paid. However, 25 per cent of the foreign exchange had to be sold in the official market, offering no possibility of recouping the premium. When the 25 per cent surrender rule, as it was known, was abolished at the beginning of 1978, portfolio investment abroad rose quite substantially owing to increased transactions (Table 2.6).

Exchange controls were finally removed completely on 23 October 1979. This had a major impact on capital flows. Table 2.5 shows the rapid growth in external assets and liabilities since 1979, especially portfolio and banking/commercial investment. This has led to a large change in the composition of UK external assets and liabilities. Table 2.7 compares the composition of assets and liabilities at end 1979 with that at end 1984. The major changes are the increased importance of overseas portfolio assets and bank assets and liabilities. These changes are confirmed in Table 2.8 which shows transactions in UK external assets and liabilities over the periods 1975–9 and 1980–84. Increased capital outflows can be attributed to UK banks and non-

TABLE 2.8

Transactions in UK external assets and liabilities (billions, annual averages). Note: an increase in assets is recorded as a minus: an increase in liabilities as a plus

	1975–9 current prices	1980 prices	1980–84 current prices	1980 prices
Outward investment				
Non-bank private sector				
– direct	–3.1	–4.3	–5.2	–4.5
– portfolio	–0.3	–0.3	–3.1	–2.7
– other*	–0.8	–1.1	–1.2	–1.1
UK banks	–0.5	–0.8	–4.1	–3.5
General Government	–1.8	–2.6	0.8	0.7
Inward investment				
Non-bank private sector				
– direct	2.1	3.1	3.2	2.8
– portfolio	0.2	0.3	0.5	0.4
– other*	1.1	1.6	0.5	0.4
UK banks	1.1	1.4	5.0	4.3
General Government	1.1	1.8	0.2	0.1

* Includes mainly trade credit and lending/borrowing to/from banks abroad.

Source: *Bank of England Quarterly Bulletin*, 1985.

bank portfolio investment. Increased inflows have resulted from increased bank activity.

These tables broadly indicate two major effects of the removal of exchange controls. The first effect has been on portfolio investment by the non-bank private sector. Between 1979 and 1987, the market value of UK investment overseas has increased by £78.3 billion. Around 50 per cent of the increase can be attributed to an increase in the value of existing assets, and around 50 per cent to increased transactions. Most of this investment overseas has been undertaken by non-bank financial institutions such as pension funds, insurance companies, investment trusts and unit trusts.

The second effect has been on the banking sector. There has been a large growth in private sector foreign currency deposits and sterling lending and borrowing by UK banks. When exchange controls were in operation, UK banks were unable to offer non-residents sterling deposits or loans unless they were trade-related. The abolition of controls has seen an increased integration between the domestic inter-bank market and the offshore eurosterling market.

3
Exchange Rate Determination

In this chapter, we examine the question of exchange rate determination. In the first section we present some theoretical models of exchange rate determination. Many early models of exchange rate determination focused mainly on the current account of the balance of payments. The exchange rate was seen as the price which would alter if the current account was in disequilibrium. The main current account models are purchasing power parity, the elasticities approach and the absorption approach. We consider the purchasing power parity theory in this chapter. The other two are dealt with later in the book. Indeed, they are not usually seen as models of exchange rate determination, but rather current account determination. Looking at them from the point of view of exchange rate determination, they argue that the exchange rate can be seen as being influenced by the export of goods and services relative to the import of goods and services.

More recently, since the 1970s, the importance of the capital account has been recognised. As we argued in Chapter 1, capital flows create a demand for and supply of foreign exchange, thus affecting the exchange rate. Moreover, capital flows have grown in importance and are now thought probably to have more influence on exchange rate determination than the current account. There are a number of models which examine the current and capital accounts together – the Mundell–Fleming model, the Dornbusch overshooting model and portfolio models. Indeed, the portfolio models look at the interaction between current and capital accounts. A current account deficit implies that a country's net holdings of foreign assets are declining and vice versa for a surplus. In this way, the portfolio models have sought to break down the dichotomy which was developing between the two accounts and their role in the determination of the exchange rate.

The second section of the chapter examines various policy measures aimed at influencing the exchange rate. First, we analyse some of the arguments in the fixed *versus* floating exchange rate debate and investigate the various types of exchange rate regimes. Secondly, we examine how governments might intervene in foreign exchange markets through the use of capital controls.

THEORIES OF EXCHANGE RATE DETERMINATION

Purchasing Power Parity

One of the oldest models of exchange rate determination is that of purchasing power parity theory. It can be traced back in some form to sixteenth-century Spain. It was popular amongst groups of Swedish, French and English bullionists[1] in the late eighteenth and early nineteenth century. In the twentieth century it is associated mainly with the Swedish economist Gustav Cassel.

There are two main forms of purchasing power parity (hereafter PPP) theory – absolute PPP and relative PPP. The absolute version of PPP is based on the 'law of one price' which is given in equation (3.1):

$$P_1 = EP_1^* \tag{3.1}$$

where P_1 is the price of good 1 in the domestic country, P_1^* is the price of good 1 in the foreign country and E is the exchange rate, expressed as the domestic currency price of a unit of foreign currency. We should note that throughout this chapter, we define the exchange rate as the domestic currency price of a unit of foreign currency. This is not the way exchange rates are usually quoted in the UK (where we use the foreign currency price of a unit of domestic currency). However, it is compatible with other countries' methods of quotation. It implies that a fall in the exchange rate is equivalent to an appreciation and a rise in the exchange rate is equivalent to a depreciation. If the domestic country is the UK and the foreign country is the US, then equation (3.1) says that the price of good 1 in sterling (P_1) must be equal to the sterling price of good 1 in the US (EP_1^*).

There are a number of assumptions which underlie this 'law'. First, it assumes no transport costs. Secondly, it assumes perfect information. Thirdly, it assumes there are no barriers to trade. Finally, it assumes that the good is homogeneous. Given these assumptions the equality represented in equation (3.1) will be brought about via arbitrage. If the sterling price of good 1 in the US is less than the sterling price in the UK, then it will be profitable for arbitrageurs to buy the good in the US and sell it in the UK.

From this 'law of one price' we can derive the absolute (or strong) version of PPP. The 'law of one price' refers only to one good. If we construct an index of the general price level in both the US and the UK, where each good has equal weight in both indices, then we can derive equation (3.2):

$$P = EP^* \tag{3.2}$$

where P is the general price level in the domestic country (the UK in our example) and P^* is the general price level in the foreign country (the US). Equation (3.2) represents the absolute version of the PPP theory. Rearranging equation (3.2), we derive:

$$E = P/P^* \tag{3.3}$$

which states that the exchange rate between two currencies is equal to the ratio of the general price levels between the two countries. Alternatively, we can say that price levels between the two countries, measured in the domestic currency, are equal, $P/EP^* = 1$.

In its relative (or weak) version, we replace equation (3.3) by (3.4a):

$$E = bP/P^* \tag{3.4a}$$

where b is some constant which reflects barriers to the operation of absolute PPP (e.g. transport costs, information costs, etc.). The relative version of PPP can be reinterpreted as saying that if b is constant the rate of change in the exchange rate between two currencies is equal to the difference between the rates of change in the price level in the two countries, that is:

$$\frac{dE}{E} = \frac{dP}{P} - \frac{dP^*}{P^*} \tag{3.4b}$$

Equation (3.4b) states the familiar proposition that if the domestic price level is rising faster than the foreign price level, the exchange rate is depreciating (that is, E will rise) and vice versa.

If PPP holds, this also implies that the real exchange rate of a country, which gives a measure of the country's competitiveness, should remain constant over time. The real exchange rate can be defined as:

$$R = EP^*/P \qquad\qquad (3.5)$$

i.e. the nominal exchange rate multiplied by the ratio of foreign to domestic prices. An appreciation of the real exchange rate or a decrease in R (due either to a decrease in E (appreciation), a decrease in P^* or an increase in P) is associated with a decline in competitiveness and vice versa. If changes in the nominal exchange rate (E) offset any differential change in prices, then clearly the real exchange rate (R) remains constant.

As it stands, PPP theory, in both its absolute and relative form, says nothing about causation. Under freely floating exchange rates, however, PPP becomes a theory of exchange rate determination. In the absolute version, the exchange rate will alter to ensure that the domestic and foreign price levels are brought into equality. In the relative version, exchange rate changes will offset differences in the rates of inflation across countries. While therefore the absolute version implies the relative version, the opposite is not necessarily true, as we have seen above.

There are a number of questions which arise when interpreting PPP as a theory of exchange rate determination. First, there is the question of what goods are included in the general price level of a country. Should PPP apply only to a basket of traded goods, or should it apply generally to all goods, both traded and non-traded? To apply to both traded and non-traded goods, we have to add the additional assumptions that there is a high degree of substitutability between these two kinds of goods (so that a change in the price of the traded good will cause price changes in the non-traded substitute), and that there are no productivity differences between the traded and non-traded goods sectors (otherwise, the relative price of traded goods to non-traded goods will change).

Secondly, there is the question of whether PPP holds in the short run as well as the long run or whether it can be considered only as a long-run theory of exchange rate determination. Stricter versions of the theory hold that PPP exists in the short run. Others, however, argue that it holds only in the long run. In the short run exchange rates can move away from PPP, but they always return to it in the long run.

Aside from the above problems of interpretation, there are a number of theoretical problems with PPP as a theory of exchange rate determination. We deal here with four criticisms which have often been cited in the literature. First, it is argued[2] that the existence of information costs, transport costs and trade barriers make it unlikely that PPP will ever hold. Information costs are important because of the way in which PPP is supposed to be brought about, that is, via commodity arbitrage. Information costs are usually incurred when discovering the prices in different countries. Transport costs are then incurred in actually transferring the goods from one country to another. Moreover, all this assumes that goods can actually be transferred from one country to another. Quotas, however, may prevent this. With tariffs, trade can take place, but there are costs involved in importing the good to the country where it is more expensive, possibly wiping out the arbitrage profit. These factors can all drive a wedge between prices in different countries.

The second theoretical criticism of PPP is that the direction of causality is unclear. We have interpreted it above as a theory of exchange rate determination – it is the exchange rate which changes in response to a disturbance to domestic or foreign prices. However, it could be that it is the exchange rate which determines prices. Indeed, some have argued that both exchange rates and prices are endogenously determined by variables unspecified by the PPP theory.[3] For example, the exchange rate and the price level may be determined by income levels, production capacity, product quality, wages and so on.

The third criticism relates to the implication of the theory that all disturbances are monetary, or at least that monetary disturbances are much more important than real disturbances. Samuelson (1964) and Officer (1976) have argued that real disturbances – the result, for example, of the discovery of a natural resource or an innovation which changes productivity in one country – necessitate a change in relative prices within the country and thus a change in the country's equilibrium real exchange rate. For example, let us assume that a country discovers it has vast reserves of a natural resource. This necessitates a rise in the real exchange rate since the country has discovered additional wealth which can positively contribute to exports. There is therefore a departure from PPP.

A final criticism of the PPP theory is that it essentially views the demand for foreign exchange as a demand that derives from the desire to purchase goods and services in other countries. As we noted in the introduction to this chapter, however, the growing integration of capital markets has resulted in a large demand for foreign exchange for the purchase of foreign assets. Frenkel (1981) argues that the demand for foreign assets is determined by expectations of the future. Thus 'exchange rates reflect expectations about *future* circumstances while prices reflect more *present* and *past* circumstances' (p. 162). This implies that fluctuations in exchange rates will not follow fluctuations in price levels; in other words, that PPP will not hold.[4]

If there are good theoretical reasons for believing that PPP will not hold and thus is an inadequate theory of exchange rate determination, then it is perhaps not surprising that empirical studies have found little evidence in its favour. We can divide the evidence on PPP into tests of commodity arbitrage, tests of the absolute version, and tests of the relative version. Within each group of tests, we are also interested in any differences between long-run and short-run results.

Looking at the issue of commodity arbitrage first. Most authors conclude that commodity arbitrage appears not to maintain the 'law of one price'. Isard (1977) examines manufactured goods from the US, Germany and Japan for the period 1970–75. He finds little evidence that the 'law of one price' holds. These findings are confirmed by Kravis and Lipsey (1978). Fraser, Taylor and Webster (1990) investigate whether the 'law of one price' holds in the long run. They use the econometric technique of cointegration, which allows them to test specifically for a long-run relationship, abstracting from short-term considerations. They conclude that there is little evidence that the 'law of one price' is valid. It is interesting to compare these results with those which test whether the 'law of one price' holds for primary goods as opposed to manufactured goods. Isard (1977) on the whole finds that it does.

Frenkel (1981) conducted tests of the absolute version of PPP using regression analysis. He compares the floating exchange rate period of the 1920s with that of the 1970s. Evidence from the 1920s is supportive of PPP. With respect to the 1970s, however, he finds little evidence in favour of PPP. Frenkel suggests that this is a consequence of the fact that disturbances in the 1920s tended to be monetary (in particular due to inappropriate monetary policy of the US Federal Reserve), whereas in the 1970s they tended to be real (for example, the oil price shock). As we explained above, monetary disturbances do not necessitate a change in the real exchange rate, whereas real disturbances do. However, Frenkel's evidence for the 1920s is contradicted by that of Krugman (1978), who uses a longer sample period and finds that his results are unfavourable to the PPP theory.

Tests of the relative PPP theory generally take one of two forms – either regression analysis or a simple plot of nominal and real exchange rates to test for independence. Frenkel (1981) uses regression analysis to test the relative PPP theory in the 1970s. He finds little support. Since relative PPP implies that real exchange rates remain constant, then a test of PPP might involve an investigation of the relationship between real and nominal exchange rates. Support for PPP would be forthcoming if the two exchange rates moved independently of each other. Instead, MacDonald (1988) shows that the two are not independent. This holds for sterling and Deutschemark exchange rates relative to the dollar for the period 1975–85.

Our brief discussion of the theory and evidence concerning the PPP theory has shown that as a theory of exchange rate determination it is clearly inadequate. At best, it identifies only one of a number of factors which affect exchange rates. PPP is frequently used as an assumption in more complete models of exchange rate determination. For example, it forms an important part of the monetary theory of the balance of payments which we discuss in Chapter 7.

Current Balance Model

The current account model of exchange rate determination views the exchange rate as the price of foreign exchange which equates the demand for and supply of foreign exchange arising from the purchase of imports or the sale of exports. More specifically, the demand for foreign exchange arises from the desire to purchase goods or services from abroad. The supply of foreign exchange comes from the export of goods and services produced domestically.

If the current account is in disequilibrium, this would be associated with disequilibrium in the market for foreign exchange. The exchange rate, that is the domestic price of foreign exchange, would therefore change in order to restore equilibrium at a zero current account. For example, let us assume that the current account is in deficit. This implies that the demand for imports exceeds the demand for exports, leading to an excess demand for foreign exchange. This causes the price of foreign exchange to rise, that is, the exchange rate to depreciate. As the exchange rate depreciates, the demand for imports falls, the demand for exports rises and, assuming the Marshall–Lerner conditions hold,[5] the current account improves. If the current account is in surplus then the current balance model says that the exchange rate will appreciate.

Isard (1978) notes that this model of exchange rate determination was particularly popular following the Second World War. He notes the fact that the International Monetary Fund (hereafter IMF) allowed exchange rate changes under the Bretton Woods system only in cases of 'fundamental disequilibrium' of the balance of payments. 'Fundamental disequilibrium' was usually taken to refer to the current account.

The elasticity and absorption approaches to the balance of payments, discussed in Chapter 5 and 6, focus on the current account of the balance of payments, albeit in more sophisticated models than the one presented here. However, in so far as the exchange rate enters into the import and export functions of both these approaches, they can be seen as models of exchange rate determination where the exchange rate responds, among other things, to the current account.

The main problem with theories of exchange rate determination which focus on the current account has already been touched upon in this chapter. The rise in the volume of capital movements has increased the importance of the asset demand for foreign exchange as a major determining factor of the exchange rate. Theories of exchange rate determination have therefore sought to take on board those factors which influence the movement of capital. It is to these factors and models based on the capital account which we now turn.

The Importance of Theories of Expectations Formation

Once exchange rate determination is extended to include considerations of the capital account, the role of expectations of the future exchange rate becomes important. The decision to invest overseas, leading to a capital outflow, crucially depends on expectations regarding movements in the exchange rate. If the domestic currency appreciates while an individual is holding foreign assets, then he/she will lose out. If, on the other hand, the domestic currency depreciates, then the individual will gain (see Chapter 1).

Theories of exchange rate determination often make different assumptions regarding the method of expectations formation, as we shall see later in the chapter. Here we propose to outline various theories of expectations formation[6] and what they imply in the context of exchange rates.

The simplest theory of expectations formation is to assume that expectations are static. The Mundell–Fleming model makes this assumption. If expected exchange rates are formed using static expectations, this implies that the expected value of the exchange rate is its current value. Thus there are no expectations of any change in the exchange rate. In this case, past values of the exchange rate provide no guide to its future value. Moreover, investors or speculators do not use any other information (such as differential interest rates, inflation rates etc.) in order to forecast the future course of the exchange rate.

A second method is that of extrapolative expectations. In this case, expectations are formed by extrapolating the trend of the exchange rate over the recent past. For example, if the exchange rate has been appreciating, then investors/speculators believe that it will continue to do so in the future. They will therefore buy the currency and if they do so in sufficient numbers (in other words, if a sufficient number of investors/speculators form their expectations in an extrapolative manner) then the exchange rate will rise and expectations will be self-fulfilling.

A third method of expectations formation is that of regressive expectations. Investors/speculators are assumed to have a view about what the long-run exchange rate is. If the current exchange rate has deviated from this long-run level, then it is expected that the exchange rate will appreciate or depreciate towards that level. For example, if we assume that the current sterling–dollar exchange rate is 75 pence to $1 and investors/speculators believe that the long-run exchange rate is 80 pence to $1, then they will expect that sterling will depreciate in the future. The Dornbusch overshooting model (see below) assumes that expectations are formed regressively.

Fourthly, expectations may be formed using an adaptive method. In this case, the expected exchange rate is a weighted average of present and past values of the exchange rate. It is usually assumed that the weights are such that observations for the more recent past and the present are given more weight than those of the distant past. The main criticism of this method of expectations formation is that it implies that individuals make systematic errors in their prediction of the future course of the exchange rate. For example, let us assume that the actual exchange rate takes the path given by the solid line

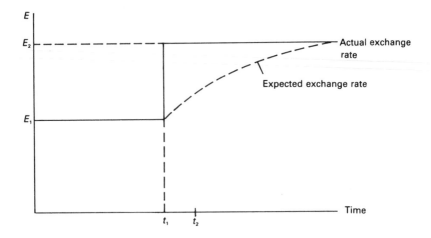

FIGURE 3.1   *Adaptive expectations*

in Figure 3.1. At time t_1, the exchange rate jumps from E_1 to E_2. If expectations are formed adaptively, then at time t_2, for example, the expected exchange rate will still be below the actual exchange rate, because expectations are formed by using exchange rates not only from the post-t_1 period, but also from the pre-t_1 period. The expected exchange rate converges only slowly on the actual exchange rate and individuals consistently underestimate its actual value. Consistently underestimating the exchange rate means that the individuals make systematic errors.

The fifth method of expectations formation, rational expectations, was developed partly as a response to this problem with adaptive expectations. If exchange rate expectations are formed rationally, then individuals use all information currently available to form their expectations of the future exchange rate. This information might include inflation rates, money supply growth, current account positions, interest rates and so on. However, this implies that behind rational expectations lies some theory of exchange rate determination. Only in this way can the information be used to form a view of future exchange rates.

Finally, the above methods of expectations formation are not necessarily mutually exclusive. Expectations may be formed using a mixture of the above methods. In the theoretical models which we shall examine here, however, only one method is usually employed. In empirical tests of exchange rate formation, such as those of

Frankel and Froot (1987), it is sometimes found that a mixture of methods is used.

The Mundell–Fleming Model

The Mundell–Fleming model was one of the first models to incorporate a major role for the capital account of the balance of payments. It was originally developed by Fleming (1962) and Mundell (1963). The version we present below is a modified account within an IS/LM/BP framework, which is discussed later in Chapter 8, where we are concerned with the question of external and internal balance and various policies to achieve it. Here we focus on the model mainly as a theory of exchange rate determination.

The Mundell–Fleming model makes a number of assumptions.

(i) It is a model of a small, open economy with unemployed resources. Prices are assumed to be fixed, so that an increase in aggregate demand will increase output and real income and reduce unemployment. In this sense, the model is essentially Keynesian in spirit.

(ii) It is assumed that there are four types of assets – domestic and foreign money and domestic and foreign bonds. Money is non-substitutable so that domestic money circulates only in the domestic economy and similarly for foreign money. Perfect capital mobility implies that domestic and foreign bonds are perfect substitutes for each other, that is, that returns are equalised for the given level of risk that they both possess.

(iii) Exchange rate expectations are assumed to be static. This implies that capital flows are a result of differential interest rates and not of expectations of exchange rate movements.

(iv) The balance of payments comprises the current account and the net capital inflow to the country. The current account (or net exports) is a component of aggregate demand. Depreciation is assumed to lead to an increase in net exports and hence in domestic demand (vice versa for appreciation).

With these assumptions we can express the model as follows:

$$M/P = Md(Y, i) \tag{3.6}$$

$$Y = AD = A(i, Y) + NX(EP^*/P, Y) + G \tag{3.7}$$

$$BP = NX(EP^*/P, Y) + K(i, i^*) = 0 \tag{3.8}$$

where:

M = nominal money supply
P = price level (assumed fixed)
Md = real demand for money
Y = real income
i = interest rate
AD = aggregate demand
A = absorption (consumption and investment)
NX = net exports
E = exchange rate (domestic currency price of a unit of foreign currency)
G = government spending
BP = balance of payments
K = capital account

Those variables with an * represent foreign country variables. The above equations represent three equilibrium conditions, with three endogenous variables – E, Y and i, since we are assuming flexible exchange rates.

Equation (3.6) represents money market equilibrium. Money demand is assumed to be positively related to income ($Md_y > 0$) and negatively related to the domestic interest rate ($Md_i < 0$). From this equation, we derive the LM curve in Figure 3.2. It is positively sloped because an increase in income increases the transactions demand for money, and therefore, with a fixed money supply, the interest rate must increase to reduce the speculative demand for money and maintain money market equilibrium.

Equation (3.7) represents goods market equilibrium. Aggregate demand (AD) is composed of absorption (consumption and investment), net exports (NX) and exogenous government spending (G). Absorption is positively related to income ($0 < A_y < 1$) and negatively related to the rate of interest ($A_i < 0$). An increase in the exchange rate (E), that is, a depreciation, and an increase in the foreign price level (P^*) increases net exports ($NX_E > 0$, $NX_{P^*} > 0$), as the country's competitiveness improves. The result that an increase in the exchange rate (i.e. a depreciation) increases net exports relies on assuming that the Marshall–Lerner condition holds (see Chapter 5). An increase in the domestic price level (P) and income (Y) decreases net exports ($NX_P < 0$, $NX_Y < 0$), since the rise in P reduces competitiveness and the rise in Y increases the demand for

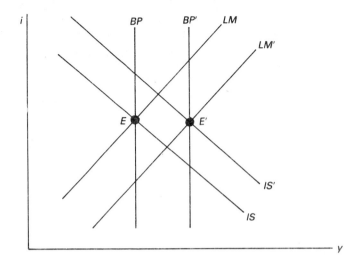

FIGURE 3.2 *The Mundell–Fleming model: zero capital mobility*

imports. From equation (3.7) we derive the *IS* curve in Figure 3.2. The IS curve is downward sloping, since, as the interest rate falls, so absorption is stimulated leading to a rise in income.

Equation (3.8) represents the balance-of-payments equilibrium condition. The balance of payments is divided into the current account (or net exports) and the capital account (or net capital inflows). Under flexible exchange rates, *BP* must equal zero. In other words, any deficit (surplus) on the current account must be offset by a surplus (deficit) on the capital account. The capital account is a positive function of the domestic interest rate ($K_i > 0$) and a negative function of the foreign interest rate ($K_i^* < 0$).

The slope of the curve representing the balance-of-payments equilibrium condition (*BP*) depends on the assumption we make about capital mobility. In Figure 3.2, we have drawn the *BP* curve under the assumption of zero capital mobility. With zero capital mobility, the balance-of-payments condition collapses to:

$$BP = NX(EP^*/P, Y) = 0 \qquad (3.9)$$

that is, the current account must be equal to zero. With P and P^* exogenous by assumption, for a given E this implies that income must be at a certain level to generate current account balance. The *BP* curve is thus vertical. What does this imply for exchange rate determination? The exchange rate will respond only to the current account situation. If the current account is in deficit, then the exchange rate will depreciate, and vice versa.

In particular, the Mundell–Fleming model shows how the exchange rate will respond to fiscal and monetary policy. Let us take the case of monetary policy to illustrate how the model works under zero capital mobility. Assume that the government seeks to increase the money supply in an attempt to stimulate aggregate demand and reduce unemployment. This causes the *LM* to shift to the right, to *LM'*. As income rises this increases the demand for imports and thus reduces net exports. The current account and the balance of payments as a whole move into an incipient deficit. This results in a depreciation of the domestic exchange rate (a rise in *E*). The BP curve moves rightwards to *BP'*, since a higher level of income can now be sustained along with balance of payments equilibrium. However, the depreciation also affects the *IS* curve. Net exports increase and this moves the *IS* curve to the right to *IS'*. The new equilibrium is established at *E'* where all three curves intersect. In the case of zero capital mobility, therefore, the exchange rate responds only to the current account and we are back to the current balance model presented above. We have essentially incorporated the current balance model into a macroeconomic model which allows us to examine monetary and fiscal policy effects.

The other two cases we examine here are arguably more interesting – those of perfect capital mobility and imperfect capital mobility. Once we introduce some degree of capital mobility, the exchange rate becomes dependent not only on the current account but also on the capital account. Looking first at the case of perfect capital mobility. This is represented in Figure 3.3. Perfect capital mobility, as we argued above, implies that individuals in the economy regard domestic and foreign bonds as perfect substitutes. This ensures that the following condition must hold:

$$i = i^* \tag{3.10}$$

If the domestic interest rate rises above the foreign interest rate, then we expect a large (and indeed, infinite) capital inflow. If the domestic interest rate falls below the foreign interest rate, then a large (indeed, infinite) capital outflow results. As a consequence, the *BP* curve is horizontal. Domestic interest rates cannot deviate from foreign

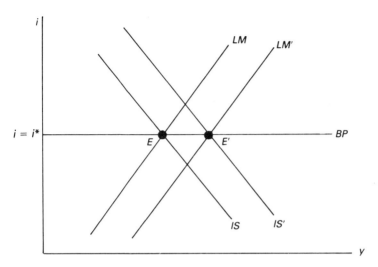

FIGURE 3.3   *The Mundell–Fleming model: perfect capital mobility*

interest rates, since only when they are equal will the balance of payments be in equilibrium. Any deviation will result in balance of payments disequilibrium, owing to the infinite capital inflows or outflows.

What happens if the government seeks to influence aggregate demand via monetary or fiscal policy? Taking the case of monetary policy first. An increase in the money supply moves the *LM* curve to the right to *LM'*. What happens to the balance of payments? The current account moves into incipient deficit since the rise in income has increased the demand for imports. The capital account also moves into incipient deficit, since there is downward pressure on domestic interest rates. Pressure from both the current and capital accounts thus cause the domestic currency to depreciate. This boosts net exports and shifts the *IS* curve to the right to *IS'*. Equilibrium is re-established at *E'* with the goods market, the money market and the balance of payments all back in equilibrium.

In the case of fiscal policy, the exchange rate again reacts to restore equilibrium. An increase in *G* shifts the *IS* curve to the right from *IS* to *IS'* (Figure 3.3). In this case, however, the impact on the balance of payments is conflicting. The current account moves into incipient deficit as before. The capital account moves into incipient surplus, because the increase in *G* generates a tendency for the domestic interest rate to rise. With perfect capital mobility, the

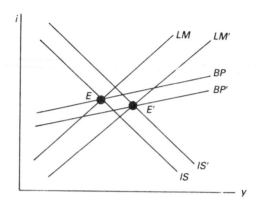

FIGURE 3.4   *The Mundell–Fleming model: a high degree of capital mobility*

capital inflow will more than outweigh the effect of the increase in aggregate demand on the current account. Thus the exchange rate falls (i.e. the domestic currency appreciates). This shifts the *IS'* curve back towards *IS*. Equilibrium is re-established at *E* and fiscal policy has had no effect on national income.

Figure 3.4 illustrates the case of a high degree of capital mobility. This can occur where investors view domestic and foreign bonds as imperfect substitutes. For example, there may be different risks associated with the two types of bonds. In this case, an interest rate differential can persist without a huge capital inflow or outflow, which completely swamps the current account. In terms of the *BP* curve, less-than-perfect capital mobility implies that it becomes positively sloped. If income increases and the current account goes into deficit, then a rise in interest rates will attract capital, allowing the deficit to be financed by a capital account surplus. The higher the degree of capital mobility, the smaller is the required rise in the interest rate and hence the flatter is the *BP* curve. The case of a high degree of capital mobility is presented in Figure 3.4. Assume that the govern-ment increases the money supply, shifting the *LM* curve to *LM'*. As income rises, so the current account moves into deficit. As the interest rate falls, capital flows out of the domestic economy. The combined current and capital account deficits cause the exchange rate to depreciate. This causes the *BP* curve to move to the right: for a given rate of interest, balance-of-payments equilibrium is now com-patible with a higher level of income. The *IS* curve also moves to the right as the depreciation stimulates net exports.

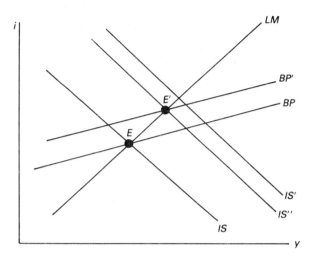

FIGURE 3.5 *The Mundell–Fleming model: a high degree of capital mobility*

The case of a fiscal policy expansion is shown in Figure 3.5. An expansion of government spending shifts the *IS* curve to *IS'*. As income increases, the current account moves into deficit. However, the capital account moves into surplus, since the rise in government spending has increased the interest rate. If capital mobility is high, as in Figure 3.5, the capital account effect will outweigh the current account. Overall there will be a balance-of-payments surplus and the exchange rate will appreciate. This moves the *BP* curve up to the left and the *IS* curve leftwards to *IS"*. Equilibrium is re-established at *E'*.

Thus what can we conclude about exchange rate determination in the Mundell–Fleming model? The above analysis has indicated that the more mobile capital is, the more likely that the exchange rate will be influenced by the capital account. Under zero capital mobility, the exchange rate responds only to the current account, as in the current balance model. As we move to greater degrees of capital mobility, so the capital account takes on increasing importance. Indeed, it eventually dominates the current account. Thus, for example, in the case of fiscal policy under a high degree of capital mobility, the exchange rate appreciates (due to the capital account surplus), even though the current account is in deficit. Thus, the exchange rate moves in the opposite direction from that implied by the current account and we can no longer rely on exchange rate changes to remove current account disequilibria.

The Mundell–Fleming model was the first model to introduce the capital account specifically into exchange rate determination questions. However, it does suffer from a number of problems. First, it assumes that exchange rate expectations are static. Thus capital flows are a function only of interest rate differentials, whereas as we argued in Chapter 1, we might also expect that the exchange rate (both spot and forward), and expectations of exchange rate movements, will also influence capital flows. Argy and Porter (1972) introduce regressive exchange rate expectations into the Mundell–Fleming model. This allows the domestic and foreign interest rates to differ from each other if the domestic exchange rate is expected to depreciate or appreciate. Under perfect capital mobility, the interest rate arbitrage condition changes from that given in equation (3.10) to:

$$i = i^* + \dot{E}_e = i^* + a(\bar{E} - E) \qquad (3.11)$$

where $\dot{E}_e$ is the expected rate of change of the exchange rate and $\bar{E}$ is the long-run equilibrium exchange rate.

This change modifies somewhat the conclusions of the ability of monetary and fiscal policy to affect income and unemployment. Monetary policy becomes less powerful under floating exchange rates and fiscal policy has some effect on national income when capital is perfectly mobile. We do not consider these effects further, since we examine the effect of exchange rate expectations on the determination of the exchange rate in the models considered below.

A second criticism of the Mundell–Fleming model is that it ignores the interaction between the current and capital accounts. In the Mundell–Fleming model, a country can continue to run a current account deficit indefinitely, so long as interest rates are such as to generate a capital inflow which covers the deficit. However, continuous capital inflows increase the stock of foreign debt of a country. At some time in the future, this will have to be repaid. Given that foreign debt repayment implies a capital outflow, it must be accompanied by a current account surplus. For this reason, the Mundell–Fleming model must be seen as short-run in outlook.

A related and final criticism of the model is that it assumes that a given interest rate differential will cause a permanent capital flow. It thus ignores the stock implications of capital flows. Assume the domestic interest rate is above the foreign one. In the Mundell–Fleming model this would lead to a continuous inflow of capital. However, as foreign investors put capital into the domestic economy, the stock of domestic assets which they hold increases. At some point, foreign investors will decide that the greater interest rate in the domestic economy does not warrant any further accumulation of domestic assets. The percentage of their portfolio which is invested in domestic assets is large enough and the benefits of portfolio diversification will be lost if more were invested in domestic assets. The capital inflow will then cease, even though the interest rate differential persists.

These last two criticisms essentially derive from the fact that the Mundell–Fleming model is a flow model which ignores stock considerations. Portfolio models which we consider later in the chapter seek to take on board these criticisms, by considering capital flows as a response to portfolio considerations.

In spite of the criticisms, the Mundell–Fleming model has been very influential. Although not primarily about exchange rate determination, if it is seen in that way it highlights the importance of the capital account. Indeed, where the capital and current accounts move in opposite directions (i.e. one into surplus and the other into deficit), the exchange rate is usually influenced more by the capital account. In this case, changes in the exchange rate can worsen the current account even further.

Exchange Rate Overshooting Models

The most well known of the overshooting models of exchange rate determination is that of Dornbusch (1976). Dornbusch's main aim in developing the model was to develop a theory which might go some way to explaining the large fluctuations in exchange rates which have been a feature of the floating exchange rate period. Overshooting refers to the tendency for the exchange rate to overshoot its new equilibrium level following some exogenous shock to the system. For example, assume that there is a shock which warrants a depreciation of the exchange rate to a new long-run level. In the short run, the exchange rate will tend to over-depreciate. The method by which overshooting is brought about in the model is through differential speeds of adjustment in the goods and asset markets. In particular, it is assumed that following a disturbance, the asset market moves rapidly to its new equilibrium. The goods market, by contrast, is characterised by sticky prices, and takes longer to adjust to a new equilibrium.

Aside from this overshooting aspect, the model has a number of advantages over the simple Mundell–Fleming model explained above. First, it does not assume that exchange rate expectations are static. Rather, expectations are assumed to be regressive. Secondly, the assumption of price fixity is removed. Instead prices in the goods market are assumed to be sticky in the short run.

Dornbusch (1976) sets out the formal model along the following lines.

(i) It is assumed that the country is a small, open economy. This allows us to assume that it faces a given world interest rate (i^*).

(ii) Perfect capital mobility and the assumption that domestic and foreign assets are perfect substitutes for each other ensures that uncovered interest parity holds continuously:

$$i = i^* + x \tag{3.12}$$

where i is the domestic interest rate, i^* is the foreign interest rate and $x = \dot{E}_e$ is the expected rate of depreciation of the domestic currency (i.e. the expected rate of increase of the domestic currency price of foreign exchange).

(iii) Expectations are formed according to equation (3.13):

$$x = \theta \, (\bar{e} - e) \tag{3.13}$$

where θ is the coefficient of adjustment ($\theta > 0$), e is the logarithm of the current exchange rate (the domestic currency price of a unit of foreign currency) and $\bar{e}$ is the logarithm of the long-run exchange rate.

Expectations are thus formed regressively. If the current exchange rate is above its long-run rate, then it will fall (i.e. appreciate) towards its long-run level and vice versa if the current exchange rate is below its long-run level. We can note that the assumption of regressive expectations is not inconsistent with rational expectations. For a certain value of θ, it can been shown that (3.13) is consistent with rational expectations.[7]

(iv) Money market equilibrium requires that real money demand equals real money supply. The money supply is assumed to be exogenous. Money demand is a negative function of the domestic interest rate and a positive function of real income. We can write the money market equilibrium condition in log-linear form:

$$m - p = \phi y - \mu i \tag{3.14}$$

where m is the logarithm of the domestic money supply, p is the logarithm of the domestic price level, y is the logarithm of domestic real income and i is the domestic interest rate. The model assumes that the economy is at full employment,[8] so that real domestic income is exogenous and given.

(v) The long-run exchange rate is determined by monetary factors and real factors. If domestic prices increase at a faster rate than foreign prices, then the exchange rate will depreciate to maintain a constant real exchange rate. In this sense, the model embraces PPP and money is assumed to be neutral in the long run. However, the long-run exchange rate is also determined by real factors, which may warrant a change in the real exchange rate (for example, real, full-employment income may change due to a natural resource discovery, higher productivity and such like).

(vi) Goods market equilibrium requires that aggregate demand equals aggregate supply. The demand for domestic output is a function of the real exchange rate, the domestic interest rate and real domestic income. In its log-linear version, aggregate demand is given by:

$$d = \alpha(e + p^* - p) - \sigma i + \gamma y \tag{3.15}$$

where d is the logarithm of the demand for domestic output.

Aggregate supply is fixed at its full employment level, y. If aggregate demand is greater than aggregate supply then prices will rise, and vice versa if aggregate demand is less than aggregate supply. This is reflected in the price adjustment equation:

$$\dot{p} = \delta[\alpha(e + p^* - p) - \sigma i + \gamma y - y] \tag{3.16}$$

Equations (3.14) and (3.16), i.e. the assets market equilibrium condition and the goods market equilibrium condition, form the heart of the Dornbusch model. Figure 3.6 shows a graphical representation of the model. The QQ schedule is derived from equation (3.14). If we substitute equation (3.12) and (3.13) into equation (3.14), we then get the following:

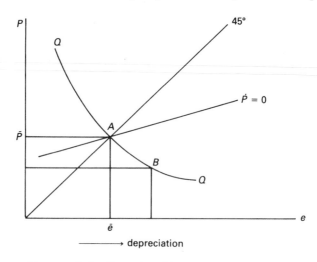

FIGURE 3.6   *Dornbusch's overshooting model*

$$m - p = \phi y - \mu[i^* + \theta(\bar{e} - e)] \qquad (3.17)$$

$$=> m - p = \phi y - \mu i^* - \mu\theta\bar{e} + \mu\theta e \qquad (3.18)$$

$$=> \mu\theta e = m - p - \phi y + \mu i^* + \mu\theta\bar{e} \qquad (3.19)$$

$$=> e = \bar{e} + (1/\mu\theta)\,[m - p - \phi y + \mu i^*] \qquad (3.20)$$

Equation (3.20) expresses the exchange rate and price level as a function of three exogenous variables: the real money supply, domestic real income and the foreign interest rate. For a given price level, the QQ curve tells us what the exchange rate has to be to ensure money market equilibrium. It slopes downward for the following intuitive reason. If p falls below $\bar{p}$ (Figure 3.6), then the real supply of money will have risen. The domestic interest rate will therefore have to fall to maintain money market equilibrium. However, if the domestic interest rate falls, then the interest parity condition (given by equation (3.12)) will be broken. The interest parity condition can be restored by creating an expected appreciation of the domestic currency, that is, a fall in x. This compensates investors for the fall in the domestic interest rate. Given the way exchange rate expectations are formed (that is, via equation (3.13)), if e is above $\bar{e}$, there is an expected appreciation (fall in e), since when e is above $\bar{e}$, it is depreciated relative to its long-run value. Thus a relatively high level of e (that is, an exchange rate depreciated relative to its long-run value) is required if p is low and the money market is to remain in equilibrium. To summarise, if p is low, this is associated with a lower domestic interest rate and therefore to restore interest parity, the exchange rate must be expected to appreciate. That is, a low p is associated with a high e (or an undervalued exchange rate). The negative slope of QQ is confirmed by equation (3.20) where e is a negative function of p. Thus point B in Figure 3.6 is associated with a price level below the long-run equilibrium level and an exchange rate above the long-run equilibrium level (i.e. undervalued).

The line $\dot{p} = 0$ in Figure 3.6 represents combinations of e and p which ensure that excess demand is equal to zero, that is, the goods market is in equilibrium. If we substitute equations (3.12) and (3.13) into (3.16) and set it equal to zero, we can derive the equation of this line:[9]

$$e = (1/(\alpha + \sigma\theta)) \, [\sigma(i^* + \theta\bar{e}) - \alpha \, (p^* - p) -$$
$$(\gamma - 1)y] \tag{3.21}$$

The $\dot{p} = 0$ curve is positively sloped, but is flatter than the 45° line. An increase in p above its equilibrium level has two effects on aggregate demand. First, it reduces the real value of the money supply leading to an increase in interest rates. This reduces investment and thus reduces aggregate demand (this is the 'Keynes' effect). The second effect of the rise in the price level is via its effect on competitiveness. A rise in domestic prices reduces competitiveness and thus the demand for the domestic country's exports falls. For both these reasons, aggregate demand falls below aggregate supply. In order to eliminate the excess supply in the goods market resulting from the price increase, the exchange rate, e, has to increase (i.e. depreciate) more than proportionately to the price increase. Not only does it have to counteract the decline in competitiveness, but it also has to compensate for the 'Keynes' effect. Thus the slope of the curve is less than that of the 45° line. The above analysis also explains why above $\dot{p} = 0$, there is an excess supply of goods and below an excess demand.

A key assumption in this model is that of differential market adjustment. On the one hand, it is assumed that the goods market adjusts only slowly toward equilibrium. In terms of Figure 3.6, this implies that the economy may not always be characterised by goods market equilibrium. In other words, we can be off the $\dot{p} = 0$ schedule. On the other hand, asset markets are assumed to clear continuously.

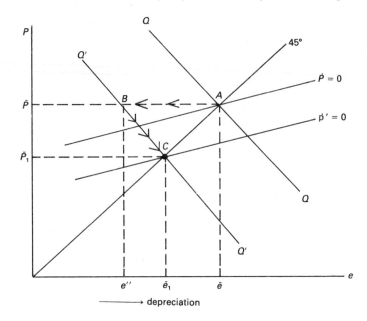

FIGURE 3.7   *A monetary contraction in the Dornbusch model*

In other words, the economy is always on the QQ schedule. The rationale for this assumption is that asset markets are usually seen as markets where prices (interest rates, exchange rates etc.) move quickly towards their equilibrium levels following some exogenous shock. On the other hand, goods markets are characterised by price stickiness and thus move more slowly towards equilibrium. It is notable in this model that goods markets do actually reach equilibrium, at full employment output in the long run. This is something which more Keynesian models might deny.

Let us now examine the impact of differential market adjustment following a contraction of the domestic money supply. This example is represented in Figure 3.7. The 45° line reflects the assumption that money is neutral in the long run. That is, changes in the supply of money have no long-run effect on the real economy. A given percentage increase (decrease) in the money supply will lead to the same percentage increase (decrease) in p and e. This can be seen to result from the fact that there is no money illusion or price stickiness in the long run in the model. Thus relative prices are unchanged by changes in the money supply.

Assume initially that the economy is in equilibrium at point A, with the exchange rate equal to $\bar{e}$ and the price level, $\bar{p}$. The decrease in the money supply causes the asset market equilibrium schedule to shift to the left (to $Q'Q'$). A decrease in the money supply causes the domestic interest rate to increase, disturbing the interest parity condition (equation (3.12)). Asset markets are now in disequilibrium. To restore equilibrium, an expected depreciation (i.e. a rise in e) is required. Thus for a given p, e has to be low (i.e. appreciated relative to its long-run value), for example at e''. At point B, there is also an excess supply of goods, because the contraction of the money supply has reduced aggregate demand. Thus for a given exchange rate, the price level must be lower to eliminate that excess supply, by increasing competitiveness and real money balances. The $\dot{p} = 0$ function thus shifts downwards to $\dot{p}' = 0$. A key point about Dornbusch's model is that it is easier to locate first the new long-run equilibrium and then analyse how the economy moves there. The new long-run equilibrium is given by point C, where the $Q'Q'$ schedule crosses the 45° line. Given that money is homogeneous of degree 1 (i.e. neutral), as argued above, in the long run a decrease in the money supply must lead to a proportional fall in the domestic price level and the long-run exchange rate (i.e. an appreciation). Thus the new equilibrium exchange rate is given by $\bar{e}_1$ and the price level by $\bar{p}_1$.

The long-run result is not the most interesting aspect of the model. Rather it is the short-run adjustment process by which the economy moves from point A to point C. The reduction in the money supply raises the domestic rate of interest for a given money demand in the short run. This arises because the reduction in the nominal money supply reduces the real money supply, since in the short run the price level is sticky. The rise in the domestic interest rate disturbs the interest rate parity condition (given by equation (3.12)). In particular, there is now an incentive for capital inflows. These cause the exchange rate to fall (i.e. appreciate). However, the exchange rate must fall (i.e. appreciate) beyond its new long-run equilibrium level, $\bar{e}_1$, so as to generate expectations of depreciation. Thus the exchange rate overshoots and this overshooting is necessary if asset market equilibrium is to hold continuously. If domestic interest rates have risen, then to restore interest rate parity, we must have expectations of a depreciation of the exchange rate back to its new long-run equilibrium level. Thus the economy moves from A to B in the short-run: with prices fixed, only the exchange rate can adjust to maintain asset market equilibrium.

How then does the economy move from *B* to *C*? At *B*, there is an excess supply of goods, since for the given price level, $\bar{p}$, the exchange rate has appreciated reducing the demand for net exports. This leads to price adjustment via equation (3.16). In particular, prices in the long run will fall. This increases the real money supply and causes interest rates to fall. As interest rates fall, an incipient capital outflow will develop, causing the exchange rate to depreciate to its new long-run level. The economy therefore moves down $Q'Q'$ from *B* to *C*.

In conclusion, therefore, in Dornbusch's overshooting model the exchange rate reacts to ensure asset market equilibrium. In this sense, it is the capital account which is its main determinant rather than the current account. Moreover, when the continuous clearing asset market is combined with slow adjustment in the goods market, the exchange rate can overshoot. In this way, Dornbusch's model can provide an explanation for the large fluctuations in exchange rates which have been observed in recent times.

Before going on to examine empirical tests of Dornbusch's model, we can highlight a number of criticisms which have been made of it. First, the assumption of full employment. Output is assumed to be constant at its full employment level. Dornbusch (1976) relaxes this assumption to allow for short-run output adjustments. The impact of this is that exchange rates no longer necessarily exhibit overshooting. For example, with a fall in the money supply and therefore income, money demand will also be reduced and interest rates may remain unchanged, or even fall. However, even with this modification, the supply side of the model is rather simplistic (MacDonald, 1988). In particular, MacDonald argues that there is no attempt to model wage–price interactions.

Secondly, residents are not allowed to hold foreign money, they can only hold domestic money. This non-substitutability between monies in the model is in sharp contrast to the assumption that domestic and foreign bonds are perfectly substitutable (Ingram, 1978). However, the implications of the lack of substitutability between monies are important. In our example, when the economy was moving from *B* to *C*, the exchange rate was expected to depreciate. If domestic and foreign money were perfect substitutes for each other, then holders of domestic currency would sell that currency and the exchange rate would depreciate to its new level immediately.

Thirdly, MacDonald (1988) shows that if we relax the assumption of perfect capital mobility and assume instead imperfect capital mobility, then exchange rates may undershoot. In other words, following a money supply decrease, for example, the exchange rate will appreciate only slightly in the first instance.

How does the overshooting model stand up to empirical tests? At the level of providing a possible explanation for specific instances of exchange rate overshooting, the model appears useful. Indeed, Dornbusch (1981) in evidence to the Treasury and Civil Service Committee attributed the sharp appreciation of sterling in 1980–81 to overshooting following the slowdown in the growth of the money supply. In other words, the example we gave above is illustrative of this case. However, in addition to a sharp monetary growth slowdown, which undoubtedly led to exchange rate appreciation, it is also argued that the exchange rate appreciated because of the fact that in 1980 the UK became self-sufficient in the consumption of oil.

The other way in which one can test the empirical validity of the model is through regression analysis. A regression is usually run where the exchange rate is a function of domestic money supply, the domestic price level, and domestic income. All variables usually appear both for the current period and lagged. Results however have been very disappointing. Work on the UK effective exchange rate by Hacche and Townend (1981) for the period 1972–80 finds evidence of overshooting. However, on the whole the equation is rather unsatisfactory with wrong signs, insignificant coefficients and structural instability. None the less, these poor econometric results could be caused by the difficulties of testing exchange rate models (e.g. simultaneous equation bias, the lack of well-specified dynamic structures). Given the poor performance of other models of exchange rate determination, as we shall see below, it is difficult to reject the overshooting model completely.

The Portfolio Model of Exchange Rate Determination

The distinguishing feature of portfolio models of exchange rate determination is that they place much more emphasis on the influence of asset markets. In particular, both the money and bond markets are key components of these theories. In the Mundell–Fleming model, the exchange rate is determined by both current account factors and asset markets; the latter, via the importance of the capital account. However, asset markets were only introduced in a simple way – the bond market, for example, was not specifically specified. In Dornbusch's overshooting model, only the money market is specified.[10] Thus the portfolio model can be seen as a broader model of exchange rate determination than either the Mundell–Fleming or Dornbusch models. Wealth-holders are assumed to hold a diversified portfolio. Changes in wealth affect the demand for assets, both foreign and domestic. Changes in the prices of the assets, in turn, as well as exchange rate changes, affect wealth. For example, an increase in the prices of foreign assets will increase wealth and vice versa. An appreciation of the domestic exchange rate reduces the domestic currency value of foreign assets, thereby reducing wealth. A depreciation of the domestic exchange rate increases wealth.

There are three main features of portfolio models which we wish to emphasise here. First, they model the exchange rate in a macroeconomic model of a small open economy. Along with asset markets (the markets for money and bonds), the real sector is modelled. One of the implications of this is that portfolio models can produce a variety of different results depending on the way in which the real economy is modelled. For example, some models assume price flexibility and full employment,[11] whereas others are more Keynesian in their conception.[12] Here we do not intend to present a full macroeconomic model, but rather want to try to pick out some of the more salient aspects.

A second feature of these models is the distinction between short-run and long-run exchange rate determination. Usually, the exchange rate in the short run is determined solely by wealth-holders' preferences for foreign and domestic assets. These preferences depend, among other things, on relative returns (that is, domestic and foreign interest rates) and expectations of future exchange rates. A number of models assume that exchange rate expectations are static,[13] since this simplifies the model considerably. However, Dornbusch and Fischer (1980) and Allen and Kenen (1980) introduce a variety of possible methods of expectations formation. Exchange rate expectations influence the demand for domestic and foreign bonds. For example, if the domestic exchange rate is expected to depreciate, then this will tend to increase the demand for foreign bonds and reduce the demand for domestic bonds. This is the result of the fact that a depreciation of the domestic exchange rate increases the domestic currency value of foreign assets.

The final feature of portfolio models is their emphasis on the distinction between stocks and flows. This distinction is incorporated into their models in two main ways. The first results from a criticism of the Mundell–Fleming model which we noted above. In the Mundell–Fleming model, capital flows are a function of the interest rate differential. If the domestic interest rate is lower than the foreign interest rate, then we expect a continuous capital outflow until the differential is eliminated. However, as capital flows out of the domestic economy, so domestic wealth-holders will build up the proportion of their wealth which they hold in foreign assets. In other words, the capital outflow has a stock implication – the domestic currency value of the stock of foreign assets will be increasing. The Mundell–Fleming model does not examine the implications of this. The portfolio model, on the other hand, does. In a portfolio model, the capital outflow would cease eventually, even if the interest rate differential persisted. This occurs because domestic and foreign assets are not considered to be perfect substitutes for each other, and therefore wealth-holders desire a diversified portfolio. If the capital outflow continued for long enough, then eventually almost all wealth would be held in foreign assets. This would not happen in the portfolio model because the benefits of diversification would then be lost. Interest rate differentials can persist in the portfolio model because assets are perceived to have different risks. For example, if foreign assets are considered to be more risky than domestic ones, then the foreign interest rate would be above the domestic one, with the difference compensating the wealth-holder for holding an asset which has a perceived higher risk. Thus in the portfolio model, capital flows are dependent not on the level of the interest rate differential, as in Mundell–Fleming, but rather on changes in the differential. For example, if the differential in favour of foreign assets rises, then, assuming no change in risks, we would anticipate a capital outflow.

The second stock-flow distinction in portfolio models relates to the implications of current account imbalance for asset accumulation. Current account deficits and surpluses are flow concepts, as explained in Chapter 1. However, they have stock implications. In particular, in portfolio theory, current account surpluses (deficits) imply an increase (decrease) in domestic holdings of overseas assets. Under a floating exchange rate regime, a current account surplus must accompany a capital account deficit (so that the balance of payments sum to zero). A capital account deficit or a capital outflow increases wealth-holders holdings of foreign assets (see Chapter 2). Thus in this way, the portfolio models include well-specified relationships between current and capital accounts.

In order to gain further insights into the conclusions which portfolio models make regarding exchange rate determination, we have to examine a particular model. Krueger (1983) offers a very simple version of a portfolio model which gives us a flavour of their distinctive aspects. In particular, her model abstracts from the real economy and the goods market, concentrating only on asset markets. The model assumes that domestic residents can distribute their wealth between three assets: domestic money, domestic bonds, and foreign bonds. Equilibrium in the three asset markets will be given when the supply of the three assets is equal to the demand. These conditions are given in the following equations:

$$M = m(i, i^* + \dot{E}_e)W \tag{3.22}$$

$$B = b(i, i^* + \dot{E}_e)W \tag{3.23}$$

$$EB^* = b^*(i, i^* + \dot{E}_e)W \tag{3.24}$$

where M is domestic money supply, B is the supply of domestic bonds, EB^* is the domestic currency value of net holdings of foreign assets, E is the domestic currency price of a unit of foreign currency, $\dot{E}_e$ is the expected rate of depreciation of domestic currency, i is the domestic interest rate and i^* is the foreign interest rate.

Krueger assumes that $\dot{E}_e = 0$, that is, she assumes that exchange rate expectations are static. While this is unsatisfactory, as we have mentioned above, it considerably simplifies the analysis. The demands for all three assets depend on wealth, the domestic interest rate, and the foreign interest rate. In particular, the demand for money is a decreasing function of both domestic and foreign interest rates. The demand for domestic bonds is an increasing function of the domestic interest rate and a decreasing function of the foreign interest rate. The demand for foreign bonds is a decreasing function of domestic interest rates and an increasing function of the foreign interest rate. Wealth affects all three demand functions in the same way: an increase in wealth leads to a proportionate increase in the demand for each asset. The demand functions are thus homogeneous of degree one in wealth.

Equation (3.25) states that wealth can be placed only in the three assets, such that:

$$W = M + B + EB^* \tag{3.25}$$

Thus m, b and b^* must sum to unity and equations (3.22), (3.23) and

(3.24) are not independent, that is if two of the markets are in equilibrium then the other must be also. Taking the market for foreign assets, it will be in equilibrium when demand equals supply, that is when:

$$EB^* = (1 - m - b)W = b^*(i, i^*)W \qquad (3.26)^{14}$$

Rearranging (3.26) we derive an equation for the exchange rate as:

$$E = b^*(i, i^*)W/B^* \qquad (3.27)$$

The exchange rate in this model ensures that equilibrium in all three markets is brought about. Any change in domestic or foreign interest rates, wealth or the supply of assets will bring about a change in the exchange rate which will restore equilibrium.

Let us take the example of an increase in the domestic money supply. Portfolio equilibrium is disturbed with an excess supply of money being accompanied by an excess demand for domestic and foreign bonds. As portfolio holders demand foreign exchange to purchase foreign bonds to restore portfolio equilibrium, the exchange rate will depreciate (i.e. E will rise). Money market equilibrium is restored via the impact of the depreciation on the domestic currency value of foreign assets. Depreciation increases the value of foreign assets and thus residents' wealth. As wealth increases, so does the demand for money thus helping to eliminate the excess supply. The depreciation of the domestic currency also reduces the excess demand for foreign bonds, as residents find that the proportion of their wealth they have invested abroad has increased. Finally, the excess demand for domestic bonds is reduced as the rate of interest falls as a result of the money supply increase. In this way, the exchange rate in the portfolio model alters to ensure that equilibrium is maintained in asset markets. Thus the exchange rate depreciates when the money supply increases, a conclusion similar to those of other models. However, here the mechanism by which adjustment is brought about is very different.

Another example is the effect of the imposition of capital controls which prevent domestic residents from holding foreign assets (either totally or partially). This is examined by Bond, Davis and Devereux (1987). Assume we are initially in portfolio equilibrium, with holdings of foreign assets above those allowed by the new controls. Following the imposition of the restrictions, there is a desire (or rather obligation) on the part of domestic residents to reduce their holdings of foreign bonds. There is therefore an excess supply of foreign bonds and an excess demand for domestic bonds and money. Given that the supplies of domestic bonds and money are fixed, non-residents have to be induced to reduce their holdings of these domestic assets, so that domestic residents can purchase them. Changes in the exchange rate ensure the new equilibrium is brought about. The initial imposition of controls causes domestic residents to sell their foreign securities and the repatriation increases the demand for domestic currency in the foreign exchange market. This causes the exchange rate to appreciate. An appreciation of the exchange rate increases the foreign currency value of non-resident holdings of domestic assets above its desired level: non-residents find that too great a proportion of their wealth is invested in foreign assets. They will therefore seek to sell some domestic assets, reducing the excess demand. At the same time an appreciation of the domestic exchange rate reduces the domestic currency value of foreign assets held by residents. The decrease in residents' wealth resulting from the exchange rate change also reduces the excess demand for domestic assets. As residents' funds are repatriated, they are used to purchase the domestic bonds which non-residents have sold.

In both these examples, exchange rate changes bring about equilibrium in the three asset markets following some disturbance. It is the effect which exchange rate changes have on the domestic currency value of foreign assets (and also on the foreign currency value of domestic assets) and therefore on wealth which ensure equilibrium is re-established.

How well does the portfolio model perform in empirical tests? Tests of the portfolio model are usually hindered by the lack of data on resident and non-resident holdings of bonds, securities and other assets. Data are often too aggregated to be useful for testing the portfolio model. For example, Branson, Halttunen and Masson (1979) test a reduced form portfolio model equation of the following type:

$$E = f(M, M^*, F, F^*) \qquad (3.28)$$

where F and F^* are domestic holdings of foreign bonds and foreign holdings of domestic bonds, respectively.

This equation is estimated for the Deutschemark–dollar exchange rate for the period 1971–8. Foreign assets (F) are estimated by taking cumulative current accounts, because of the unavailability of a direct measure. As MacDonald (1988) points out, this is unsatisfactory, because the cumulative current account surpluses include foreign assets held by residents of the US or Germany in third countries, which are largely irrelevant to the determination of the bilateral Deutschemark–dollar exchange rate. Although the results are supportive of the portfolio model, there were a number of econometric problems (in particular autocorrelation).

Bisignano and Hoover (1983) seek to improve these results by including domestic holdings of domestic bonds and foreign holdings of foreign bonds, two variables which Branson, Halttunen and Masson (1979) leave out. Their results are more successful and are again broadly supportive of the portfolio model.

With respect to forecasting, however, the portfolio models seem to perform very badly, as do the overshooting models. Meese and Rogoff (1983, 1984) test the forecasting power of a modified version of the portfolio model which includes real interest rate differentials.[15] However, success is limited, and the modified portfolio model did very badly at forecasting future exchange rates.

One can point to a number of problems which could explain this failure. Most are of an econometric nature – for example, poor data and poorly specified dynamics. In addition, however, MacDonald (1988) points to the unstable environment of the 1970s and 1980s. For example, exchange rates have been affected significantly by the two oil price shocks and the international debt crisis. Such shocks are difficult to incorporate easily into econometric models yet are clearly very important. On the whole, therefore, it is difficult to come to any firm conclusion about the validity of the portfolio approach. Its contribution, however, has been to highlight the importance of asset demands and supplies as determinants of the exchange rate.

Speculative Bubble Models of Exchange Rate Determination

Speculative bubble models of exchange rate determination seek primarily to explain why exchange rates appear to exhibit so much volatility. They differ from the models above in the sense that the exchange rate is not determined only by fundamental economic variables such as asset preferences, the desire to import, the attractiveness of a country's exports, the growth of the money supply and so on. In addition, these models include the idea that the exchange rate can rise or fall due to speculative activities and according to the whims of foreign exchange dealers. In this way the exchange rate might be subject to bandwagon type effects. These models became particularly popular in the 1980s following the long and sustained rise in the dollar between 1980 and 1985.

There are a number of speculative bubble models in the literature, applying to all kinds of financial markets. Here we want to examine two types of models, one based on extrapolative expectations, the other on rational expectations.

Extrapolative expectations imply, as we argued above, that if the exchange rate depreciated (appreciated) in the last period, we might expect it to do the same in this period. These kind of models of speculative bubbles are a simple bandwagon effect and can be explained by crowd psychology arguments.

Frankel and Froot (1987) examine the hypothesis that exchange rate expectations can exhibit bandwagon effects by examining survey data. The data are collected and published by the *American Express Banking Corporation*, the *Economist Financial Report* and *Money Market Services (US) Inc*. Each source represents the views of a number of economists, bankers and corporate treasurers who are asked how they expect a number of exchange rates to move over the next three, six or twelve months. The data are for a number of exchange rates *vis-à-vis* the dollar – sterling, Deutschemark, Swiss franc, Yen and French franc. Frankel and Froot analyse data from these surveys for the first half of the 1980s. Their results show that there is no evidence of bandwagon effects, that is, a depreciation (appreciation) of the exchange rate over the past period, does not lead to expectations of further depreciations (appreciations). The results of Frankel and Froot conflict with those of MacDonald and Torrance (1988). They use survey data produced by *Money Market Services (UK)* for the period 1985–6. They find that the Deutschemark–dollar exchange rate does show evidence of bandwagon effects, although they add the caveat that their results are not highly significant statistically.

Despite the lack of evidence in favour of bandwagon effects in foreign exchange markets, Frankel and Froot (1987, p. 142) conclude that 'it may still be true that psychological factors are important in foreign exchange markets. The absence of bandwagon effects in the data does not rule out the possibility of speculative bubbles'. This leads us to our second type of bubble model, which seeks to explain why a speculative bubble can occur, even if we assume rational expectations.[16]

In rational speculative bubbles models, the price of foreign exchange is a function not only of economic fundamentals, but also of expected changes in the exchange rate. It is the inclusion of this latter variable which generates the potential for a speculative bubble. We can illustrate its importance by the following example. Let us assume that we have a country with a large trade surplus. In terms of economic fundamentals, we might therefore expect the exchange rate to appreciate in the future. Foreign exchange market operators may believe this to be the case. The exchange rate begins to appreciate as speculators are buying the domestic currency to force the exchange rate towards its long-run equilibrium value (as Friedman argues, see Chapter 1). However, it is unlikely that the exchange rate will stop appreciating at the exact long-run exchange rate, because there are a large number of speculators whose actions are all uncoordinated. Hence the exchange rate could overshoot, that is appreciate beyond its long-run equilibrium level. All speculators know that at some time the exchange rate will have to depreciate, but the question is when. They may believe it will not depreciate immediately. They will therefore be willing to continue to buy the currency in question, in the belief that they can make a profit before economic fundamentals again dominate exchange rate determination and the exchange rate begins to depreciate. In other words, rational speculators can still make a profit even though the exchange rate is deviating from its long-run equilibrium value. If enough foreign exchange market operators expect that the exchange rate will appreciate, their expectations will be self-fulfilling, and the exchange rate will appreciate. The point to note about this behaviour is that it is not irrational.

Evidence concerning the existence of such rational bubbles is difficult to interpret. Let us take one recent example of an empirical test in order to understand some of the difficulties involved. Pittis (1989) tests for bubbles for the period 1975–86 for the Deutsche Mark, Yen and sterling exchange rates *vis-à-vis* the dollar. His results suggest that we cannot rule out the possibility of the existence of bubbles. The main problem of tests for bubbles arises from the fact that the economic fundamentals which influence the exchange rate have to be specified. Pittis uses a Dornbusch-type overshooting model with bubbles. However, one could have chosen some other model (for example, the Mundell–Fleming model or the portfolio model) and the results may have been different. The method used to identify bubbles examines whether or not the exchange rate and the economic fundamentals which influence it move together over time (in econometric terms, this implies that we examine whether or not the exchange rate and the economic fundamentals are cointegrated). If they do move together then this suggests the absence of bubbles. If they do not move together, that is, they tend to drift away from each other over time, then this is consistent with the existence of a speculative bubble. It is the bubble which may be moving the exchange rate away from what is implied by the fundamental economic factors. However, the problem with this conclusion is that the equation may simply be mis-specified. In other words, it may be that we have chosen the wrong economic fundamentals. In view of the fact that most models of exchange rate determination show poor empirical performance, this is the most likely explanation. Indeed, it is not clear how this criticism of empirical tests, which seek to determine whether or not bubbles exist, could ever be overcome.

In spite of the problems associated with identifying the existence of speculative bubbles, the theory behind them tends to capture a widely-held belief that speculators are important in the determination of exchange rates and that they need not necessarily act in a stabilising manner.

Exchange Rate Determination: What Have We Learnt?

We have examined a number of different models of exchange rate determination. All these models produce different results for two main reasons. First, each model makes different assumptions about the way in which macroeconomic aspects of the economy work. For example, in the Mundell – Fleming model, prices are fixed, so that any expansion of aggregate demand will lead to an increase in national income. In the Dornbusch model, on the other hand, prices are sticky in the short run but fully flexible in the long run. In the long run, therefore, an increase in the money supply has no effect on national income, which remains at its full employment level. Secondly, different assumptions are made about what factors determine the exchange rate. For example, in the portfolio model, changes in interest rates and wealth affect the desire to invest abroad. In the Mundell–Fleming model, the current account can play a major role in determining exchange rates when capital is not highly mobile. When capital flows are significant, the interest rate level is important (in contrast, to *changes* in interest rates in the portfolio model). Similarly the role played by exchange rate expectations differs between models. In the Mundell – Fleming model, we made the simple assumption that exchange rate expectations were static. However, as we pointed out, this is unsatisfactory and the Dornbusch overshooting model makes some attempts to incorporate a more realistic role for exchange rate expectations.

A number of authors (Krueger, 1983; Bird, 1987) seek to provide a possible reconciliation of these differing theories, by arguing that different models can be applied to different time periods. For example, a short-run theory of exchange rate determination may place a lot of emphasis on exchange rate expectations, speculative factors and portfolio aspects. In the medium term, the current account and the real side of the economy could assume a greater role. Finally, in the long run, purchasing power parity is often assumed to be a major influence on exchange rate movements. However, the extent to which one can reconcile the models in this way is limited. For example, the Mundell–Fleming model's assumption of fixed prices suggests that it is more relevant to a short time horizon. It is not clear, however, how this is reconciled with its view that the current account can be an important determinant of exchange rates.

One method of discriminating between different models is via empirical investigation. Here, however, we have shown that the results are very disappointing. No model seems to perform particularly well. A number of reasons can be highlighted which might explain this. First, it is important to note that exchange rates are very volatile, much more volatile than any of the possible determinants which the models have identified. Thus it is perhaps not surprising that empirically, exchange rate determination models have done rather badly. Secondly, there are a variety of econometric problems associated with modelling exchange rates, for example, simultaneous equation bias and poor dynamic specification. Thirdly, while it is conceptually easy to see how exchange rate expectations might influence actual exchange rate movements, it has not been easy to incorporate them into exchange rate determination models. Finally, there have been a number of factors which have contributed to structural instability during the floating exchange rate period, such as the two oil price shocks.

What we can perhaps conclude is that exchange rates appear to be driven by factors other than simply economic fundamentals such as interest rates, money supplies, wealth, and current accounts. There appears to be some evidence that foreign exchange markets are characterised by bubbles and that exchange rates can often over-react to changes in fundamentals, appreciating or depreciating beyond their implied new equilibrium level. This may go some way to explaining the large volatility characteristic of exchange rates. Finally, one aspect which has been clearly demonstrated in both theoretical and empirical models of exchange rate determination is the importance of the capital account, which can and often does far outweigh any influence the current account may have on exchange rates.

EXCHANGE RATE SYSTEMS AND POLICIES

In the previous section, we noted that exchange rates have been highly volatile during the period of floating exchange rates. We argued that the exchange rate is determined to a large extent, at least in the short to medium run, by capital flows which are independent of trade in goods and services. Thus the capital account can often dominate exchange rate determination. In this way, the exchange rate can no longer always be relied upon to correct current account imbalances, something which is perhaps supported by the increase in current account deficits and surpluses throughout the period of floating exchange rates.

In this section, we examine some policy aspects associated with exchange rates. In particular, we want to analyse possible methods by which the monetary authorities might intervene in foreign exchange markets and thereby mitigate some of the problems which flexible exchange rates appear to have generated. We highlight two main types of intervention.

First, a country can choose not to have a pure floating exchange rate, but rather to intervene to some degree in the foreign exchange market. In order to understand the factors which might influence a country's decision, we examine the fixed *versus* flexible exchange rate debate. We then discuss the types and history of exchange rate systems, in order to highlight the variety of choices available to a country.

The second method by which governments might seek to intervene in foreign exchange markets is through placing restrictions on capital movements. The explicit aim of such controls is to reduce the volume of speculative, short-term capital flows, and thus help to reduce exchange rate volatility. We examine the role that capital (or exchange) controls have played in countries in the past, taking as examples, the UK and some of the countries of the European

Monetary System. We conclude the chapter with some thoughts on exchange rate policies for the 1990s.

Fixed Versus Flexible Exchange Rates

We can define flexible (or floating) exchange rates with reference to equation (3.29):

$$BP = \text{trade account} + \text{capital account}$$
$$+ \text{ official financing} \tag{3.29}$$

In theory, when the exchange rate is cleanly floating, official financing must be equal to zero; that is, there is no government intervention in the foreign exchange market. The case for flexible exchange rates was strongly advocated in the 1950s by Friedman (1953), and later by Johnson (1970), among others. They outlined five main arguments in favour of flexible exchange rates.

First, flexible exchange rates provide some method of external adjustment to balance-of-payments disequilibrium. In this way, they remove the external constraint and allow governments to use monetary and fiscal policy to achieve other targets, such as full employment, low inflation, and growth. This is in contrast to the situation under fixed exchange rates, where a key problem is the method by which adjustment to balance-of-payments equilibrium is brought about. If the balance of payments falls into deficit, the exchange rate can no longer act to restore equilibrium. Instead the government must either deflate the economy to reduce the demand for imports and/or raise interest rates to finance the deficit. Both these policies are likely to lead to an increase in unemployment, or to slow down the rate of growth. Flexible exchange rates are therefore seen as a mechanism by which governments may be released from the constraints of the balance of payments.

Secondly, flexible exchange rates allow a country monetary autonomy. Under fixed exchange rates, the money supply is completely endogenous, as we can show from equation (3.30):

$$HPM = D + F \tag{3.30}$$

where *HPM* is high-powered money or the monetary base, *D* is the domestic component of the monetary base, i.e. notes and coins plus reserves held by commercial banks at the central bank, and F is the foreign component of the monetary base, i.e. foreign exchange reserves of the central bank.

If exchange rates are fixed, then the government is intervening in the foreign exchange market and the foreign component of the monetary base will be changing. For example, let us assume that there is a deficit on the balance of payments. In this case, at the fixed exchange rate, the supply of pounds in the foreign exchange market is greater than the demand. There is therefore pressure on the exchange rate to depreciate. The government has to intervene in the foreign exchange market to buy up the excess supply of pounds if the exchange rate is to remain fixed. It purchases the pounds with foreign exchange held in its reserves. F therefore falls and this decreases the monetary base. We can see why foreign exchange reserves are a component of the monetary base by the following example. Assume an importer requires Deutschmarks to buy German goods. The importer will sell sterling to purchase deutschmarks. There is pressure on the pound to depreciate and the Bank of England has to buy the pounds (reducing their supply) and supply deutschmarks (reducing F). If the balance of payments is in surplus, then F will be increasing. By contrast, when exchange rates are fully flexible, the government is not intervening in the foreign exchange market and hence there is no change in F. The government can then control D in order to control the monetary base. If the balance of payments is in deficit, the exchange rate would simply depreciate to restore equilibrium. For monetarists, like Friedman, who place much weight on the control of the money supply, clearly flexible exchange rates are important.

The third argument put forward in favour of flexible exchange rates is that monetary policy would become more effective if exchange rates are flexible. This derives from two results of the Mundell–Fleming model:

(i) With high capital mobility, monetary policy is more effective under flexible exchange rates than under fixed exchange rates;
(ii) With high capital mobility, monetary policy is more effective than fiscal policy under flexible exchange rates.

The first result can be shown with the following example. Let us assume that the government increases the money supply in an attempt to boost national income and reduce unemployment. The rise in the money supply, for a given money demand, reduces the rate of interest. On the current account, the increase in aggregate demand resulting from reduction in the rate of interest increases the demand for imports and hence the current account moves into deficit. On the capital account, the fall in the domestic interest rate leads to a large capital outflow (since capital is highly mobile). The combined current and capital account deficits lead to exchange rate depreciation under flexible exchange rates. This further boosts income. Under fixed exchange rates, by contrast, intervention by the government to prevent depreciation leads to a fall in F (equation (3.30)), a fall in the money supply and income is reduced to its original level. The second result is clear if we contrast the above case of a money supply increase under flexible exchange rates with that of an increase in government expenditure under flexible exchange rates. An increase in government expenditure leads to a rise in the interest rate. Since the government sells bonds to finance the expenditure, it has to raise the interest rate to induce people to hold them. A rise in the interest rate causes a large capital inflow, which, if capital is highly mobile, will offset the current account deficit. There is therefore an overall balance-of-payments surplus. The exchange rate appreciates, reducing demand for exports and thus lowering income. This is in contrast to the monetary expansion which causes exchange rate depreciation, which gives a further boost to national income.

Fourthly, it is claimed that flexible exchange rates will lead to a reduction in the demand for international reserves. If the government does not intervene in the foreign exchange market, then its need for international reserves is limited. However, if the exchange rate is fixed and strong speculative pressure against the domestic currency develops, then the government requires large foreign exchange reserves in order to intervene and maintain the value of the currency. Flexible exchange rates will avoid this. Indeed, as we indicated before, the theoretical expectation is that in a system in which the exchange rate is free to vary, speculation will, on balance, be stabilising (see Chapter 1). Any initial depreciation, it is claimed, will induce private speculators to move funds into the depreciating currency. This serves to limit speculation against the currency and to arrest the depreciation. There is therefore a saving in foreign exchange reserves.

The final argument put forward by proponents of flexible exchange rates is that flexible exchange rates insulate a country from instability in other countries. Again the Mundell–Fleming model can serve to illustrate this point. Assume that there is a reduced demand for exports from the domestic country as a result of a recession in the rest of the world. Will this recession be transmitted to the domestic country or will it be insulated from its effects? Under flexible exchange rates, the resulting balance-of-payments deficit will be corrected by exchange rate depreciation, with no effects on domestic income. Flexible exchange rates in this way provide insulation. Under fixed exchange rates by contrast, the balance-of-payments deficit will require the government to intervene in the foreign exchange market and buy up the domestic currency which is in excess supply. This reduces the foreign component of the money supply and thus has a contractionary effect on national income. In this case, the domestic country is not insulated from the recession in the rest of the world.

Thus flexible exchange rates are supposed to offer a country the advantages of the removal of the external constraint, monetary autonomy, increased effectiveness of monetary policy, a reduction in the demand for international reserves and insulation from changes in economic activity in the rest of the world. The experience with flexible exchange rates in the 1970s and 1980s suggests that some of these advantages have not been realised. This has led to calls for a return to greater fixity of exchange rates. We càn outline four main reasons which have been put forward in favour of fixed (or more fixed) exchange rates.

First, it is sometimes claimed that, whereas flexible exchange rates will encourage inflation, fixed exchange rates will help to maintain low inflation. Flexible exchange rates tend to be inflationary, for the following reason. In countries experiencing exchange rate depreciation, the domestic price of imports will rise, which increases costs directly and indirectly, and hence domestic prices, to the extent that prices are based on costs. Admittedly countries experiencing exchange rate appreciation should find their import prices falling, but domestic prices are notoriously sticky downwards. Thus there tends to be asymmetry in the system with costs and prices rising more in countries whose exchange rates are depreciating than they fall in countries whose exchange rates are appreciating. Flexible exchange rates can therefore be inflationary overall. Moreover, under fixed exchange rates, a country which has a higher inflation rate than the countries with whom it trades will suffer a deterioration in its competitiveness and the balance of payments will move into deficit. Since foreign exchange reserves are in limited supply, it cannot run this deficit indefinitely. Eventually it will be forced to undertake deflationary policies which will reduce the balance-of-payments deficit and inflation. It is the dominance of low-inflation Germany within the European Monetary System (EMS), which has tempted a number of European Community (hereafter EC) countries to join the exchange rate mechanism. We discuss this in more detail later in the chapter.

A second argument often put forward in favour of fixed exchange rates is that they reduce uncertainty. Exporters and importers, it is argued, can benefit from knowing the price at which their good will sell in foreign markets. If exchange rates are flexible, then the foreign price of exports will be volatile. This makes it more difficult to plan output and the uncertainty therefore results in a reduction in trade. Tests of exchange rate volatility in the period of floating exchange rates suggest that not only has volatility increased relative to the fixed exchange rate period, but also that it has increased as experience with floating exchange rates has matured (Williamson, 1983). There are two arguments which are usually used to counter the above hypothesis. First, it is argued that exporters and importers can use the forward exchange market in order to reduce the uncertainty. They can buy or sell foreign currency forward at a fixed price thus guaranteeing them a fixed amount of domestic currency. However, forward markets in some countries are underdeveloped and it is not always possible to reduce the uncertainty significantly. Secondly, there is not much evidence which supports the argument that uncertainty over exchange rates reduces international trade.

A third argument in favour of fixed exchange rates is the tendency for floating exchange rates to lead to large misalignments. Williamson (1983) defines an exchange rate misalignment as a persistent departure of the exchange rate from its long-run equilibrium level. The long-run equilibrium level is given by the exchange rate which ensures that the current account plus the long-term capital account is in equilibrium. For example, Williamson calculates that in 1983 the US dollar was around 18 per cent overvalued and sterling around 11 per cent overvalued. Such misalignments have significant costs. A large period of overvaluation reduces the profitability of exports (since the foreign currency price of exports rises, decreasing demand). This reduces demand for resources used to produce exports, and capital and labour are made redundant. Thus a sustained period of misalignment can lead to unemployment. However, misalignment can also result in firms reducing their productive capacity or even closing down altogether. In this way misalignment can cause 'deindustrialisation', a phenomenon we examine in more detail in Chapter 15. The costs associated with misalignments thus provide Williamson with a case for greater management of exchange rates. We discuss his suggested reforms later in the chapter.

A final argument in favour of fixed exchange rates follows from the experience of flexible exchange rates in the 1970s and 1980s which suggests that they have not given the benefits which their proponents claim. First, with respect to external adjustment, balance-of-payment disequilibria have not been removed and governments have certainly not been able to concentrate solely on the pursuit of faster growth without unemployment and inflation. Instead, demand management policies have also had to be directed at the balance of payments. Secondly, it is not clear that flexible exchange rates have allowed greater monetary autonomy. Some have argued that the money supply is endogenous and therefore it is not easy to control it, whilst others have debated over which monetary aggregate should be targeted. Finally, floating exchange rates do not appear to have insulated small open economies from the international business cycle. On the contrary, the world economy is now much more interdependent and business cycles tend to coincide.

In conclusion, therefore, there are good reasons for believing that floating exchange rates have not delivered the advantages which their proponents emphasised. However, this does not necessarily mean that rigidly fixed exchange rates are preferred. In reality, a whole spectrum of possible systems can be identified. Indeed, historically, we can identify a number of exchange rate regimes which have operated. It is to a discussion of these which we now turn.

Types of Exchange Rate Regime

In reality we rarely see either completely fixed or floating exchange rates. Indeed, governments are usually very reluctant to allow completely floating exchange rates as we defined them above. The history of exchange rate systems has been dominated by some form of intervention. An examination of that history highlights two things. First, it illuminates some of the theoretical aspects of the fixed *versus* flexible exchange rates debate and shows the impact of this on the way in which systems have worked historically. Secondly, we can see how some of the tensions of either fixed or floating exchange rates led to the breakdown of systems in the past.

Five main types of exchange rate regime can be distinguished, all of which have operated at some time in one form or another. Proposals for alternative exchange rate regimes fall within one or other of the five main categories of regime distinguished, though some schemes comprise features of more than one of the main types. The five main types of regime that we shall discuss briefly are as follows:

(i) Rigidly fixed exchange rates epitomised by the old gold bullion standard;
(ii) Pegged exchange rates, an example of which was the adjustable peg, or par-value, system which governed international monetary relations between 1944 and the early 1970s and was referred to as the gold exchange standard. Many countries still peg their currency to another currency or to a basket of currencies; The Exchange Rate Mechanism (ERM) is essentially a pegged exchange rate system.
(iii) Managed exchange rate flexibility, which is the exchange rate system normally practised by countries which do not peg;
(iv) Freely floating exchange rates, and
(v) Multiple exchange rates, of which dual exchange rates are a special case.

(i) Rigidly Fixed Exchange Rates: the Gold Bullion Standard

Under a fixed exchange rate system, the use of exchange-rate changes for balance-of-payments adjustment is ruled out by definition. Balance-of-payments adjustment must take place through price and income adjustments in the domestic economy. The gold bullion standard, which was in operation in its purest form between 1880 and 1914, was a fixed exchange rate system under which balance-of-payments adjustment was supposed to be achieved automatically through internal adjustment provided certain rules were adhered to. Under the gold bullion standard each country fixed its currency in terms of gold, each country's currency was convertible into gold[17], and international settlements were made in gold. The exchange rate between two countries could not vary outside the so-called 'gold-export points' determined by the cost of shipping gold from one country to another. Suppose, for example, that the same amount of gold is bought and sold by the monetary authorities in country X for \$2 and in country Y for £1. The exchange rate between country X and country Y would then be \$2 to £1. Now suppose that country Y is in balance-of-payments deficit and there is an excess supply of pounds. There will be a tendency for the exchange rate to fall below \$2 to £1. But the movement cannot go far since people in country Y with debts to pay to creditors in country X could always take £1 to their own monetary authority, obtain gold with it, export it to country X and get \$2 for it. There are costs involved in doing this, however, so that it would only be profitable to export gold from Y to X if the exchange rate falls outside the 'cost margin' around the fixed rate. For example, suppose the cost of obtaining gold in Y, shipping it to X and converting it into dollars is 2 cents per \$2 of gold. It would then pay to export gold to obtain dollars only if the rate of exchange fell below \$1.98 to £1. Otherwise more dollars could be obtained per pound by converting pounds into dollars directly. \$1.98 is referred to as country Y's gold-export point or X's gold-import point. Similarly, if it cost 2 cents per \$2 to export gold from X to Y, it would pay to export gold to obtain pounds only if the rate of exchange rose above \$2.02 to £1. This would be X's gold-export point or Y's gold-import point. Thus under the gold standard the exchange rate may vary within the gold points. Outside these points, however, there will be no variation in the exchange rate; instead, gold will flow to accommodate any surplus or deficit on the balance of payments.

Then, according to the rules of the gold standard, if country Y is in balance-of-payments deficit, gold should flow from country Y to country X, causing first a contraction of the money supply in Y and an expansion of the money supply in X. As a consequence interest rates should rise in Y, and wages and prices fall, while interest rates should fall in X, and wages and prices rise, until external equilibrium is achieved. External equilibrium does not, of course, guarantee internal balance in the sense of full employment unless there is an appropriate downward adjustment of the money-wage rate in relation to the price level in the deficit country. For both external and internal balance in the deficit country, a reduction in real wages is required. The gold standard mechanism uses, in effect, financial policy for external balance and wage flexibility for internal balance.

The workings of the gold standard were never perfect and were modified through time by several factors. Research shows that actual gold movements in relation to the size of balance-of-payments deficits were very small. First, there was never a one-to-one correspondence between changes in the supply of gold and changes in a country's money supply. There never could be except under a strict gold specie system where the money supply itself consists of gold, or where the money supply is backed 100 per cent by gold. In practice small changes in gold brought about large changes in the money supply, explaining why large balance-of-payments deficits were accompanied by gold movements which were very small in comparison. Second, income adjustments frequently took place, at times of bad harvests for example, reducing or eliminating deficits that would otherwise have arisen and necessitated the export of gold. Third, larger and larger capital flows occurred in response to interest-rate differences, helping to finance balance-of-payments deficits on current account without the export of gold.

The fixed exchange rate system imposed by the old gold standard ultimately broke down in 1931, largely because the rules of the gold standard were not being adhered to.[18] Countries such as the United States and France which were accumulating gold were not pursuing sufficiently expansionary policies, and Britain, which was losing gold, was not willing to pursue further deflationary action to stop the gold outflow. With her gold reserves virtually exhausted, Britain suspended the gold standard, and for a time some of the major currencies floated against each other. The period was one of the great international economic turmoil characterised by world depression, a lack of international liquidity and acceptable reserve currencies for countries to finance balance-of-payments disequilibrium, and trade restrictions for balance-of-payments protection which worsened the world depression. It was to overcome these features of the international economy of the 1930s which led to the Bretton Woods agreement and the establishment of the International Monetary Fund in 1944.

(ii) Pegged Exchange Rates

An exchange rate is said to be pegged if the authorities accept an obligation to prevent the market rate from deviating by more than a specified amount from the peg (called a *margin*). Twice the margin gives the *band* - or maximum range within which the exchange is allowed to move without a change in the peg (or central rate).

The adjustable peg or par-value system

The agreement at Bretton Woods in 1944 re-established fixed (but adjustable) exchange rates between currencies in the form of so-called 'par values', defined in terms of gold. Countries were obliged to intervene in the market to maintain the exchange rate within 1 per cent either side of its par value. Provision was made, however, that par values could be adjusted by up to 10 per cent without permission of the IMF and by more than 10 per cent if it was convinced that the balance of payments of the country concerned was in fundamental disequilibrium. Fundamental disequilibrium was never defined precisely. The system evolved was a gold exchange standard in which domestic currencies were not convertible into gold as under a gold bullion standard, but in which the monetary authorities undertook to buy and sell the currency of another country which was itself operating a gold bullion standard. Under the Bretton Woods system national currencies were convertible into the dollar, and the dollar itself was convertible into gold at $35 per ounce. The par value of sterling in relation to the dollar was $4.03 to £1. In effect the dollar replaced gold as the reserve asset of the international monetary system.

In theory balance-of-payments adjustment under a gold exchange system is supposed to work in the same way as under the gold standard, with deficit countries allowing prices to fall and interest rates to rise, while surplus countries allow prices to rise and interest rates to fall. In the Articles of Agreement of the Bretton Woods system, however, it was clearly recognised that internal price flexibility could not be relied on and that if provisions were not made it would be income and employment that would bear the brunt of adjustment, as in the inter-war years. Two provisions were made to safeguard full employment. First, a country in temporary disequilibrium could borrow from the IMF to tide it over its difficulties without having to pursue internal adjustment policies which threatened employment. Second, provision was made for exchange-rate adjustment – in practice this was rarely used. Here we cannot go into the many reasons, some no doubt of a political and psychological nature, why countries were reluctant to alter the par value of their currencies – which was quite permissible under the IMF Articles of Agreement. Perhaps, however, their economic instinct and judgement against adjustment was correct, for variable exchange rates can only rectify payments disequilibrium without sacrificing employment if there is sufficient flexibility of the real-wage rate, i.e. wage-earners must accept a cut in real wages which a reduction in the real terms of trade through devaluation implies. If money wages chase prices upwards, there can be no change in the real terms of trade and the balance-of-payments disequilibrium remains. Despite the criticisms levelled against countries in the 1950s and 1960s for maintaining fixed exchange rates at the apparent sacrifice of domestic employment, the movement from fixed to flexible exchange rates in the world economy has not been conspicuously successful in reconciling payments balance with full employment and has undoubtedly exacerbated inflation.

The workability of a gold exchange standard depends both on the maintenance of confidence in the currency that is being used as the reserve asset, and also on convertibility into gold. Under the Bretton Woods system the dollar became the key currency, and because of a general shortage of world liquidity it was convenient for the rest of the world to allow the United States to run payments deficits to augment the supply of international reserves. As dollar liabilities began to mount, however, increasingly the ability of the United States to maintain the convertibility of the dollar into gold became doubted. The loss of confidence in the dollar eventually became such that on 15 August 1971 the convertibility of the dollar into gold was suspended and the gold exchange standard that had governed international monetary transactions for over twenty-five years was formally ended. For a short time currencies floated against each other until par values were restored again by the Smithsonian Agreement in December 1971 which raised the price of gold to $38 per ounce and devalued the dollar correspondingly by approximately 8 per cent, and widened the permissible fluctuations around the par values from 1 per cent to 2.25 per cent. The wider bands, however, were not sufficient to stop speculation against the weak currencies, particularly sterling, and an era of floating exchange rates was ushered in in 1972 with the United Kingdom's decision to float the pound. Other countries followed rapidly, and by mid-1973 most of the major currencies were floating against each other.

In a world of capital movements one of the intrinsic problems of an adjustable peg system with little flexibility is containing speculative pressure against a currency which traders feel will ultimately have to be devalued. Speculators are provided, in effect, with a system in which they can hardly lose if the pressure becomes so great: a so-called 'one-way option' for speculators. Whatever stability a fixed exchange-rate system might give to international monetary relations, it has to contend with this fundamental drawback and the problem it poses for confidence in the reserve currencies of the system.

In an attempt to preserve the virtues of pegged exchange rates, while avoiding the speculative pressure that can build up with the threat of devaluation, several schemes have been developed by economists which might make the adjustable peg system workable by introducing more flexibility into it. One such scheme, attributed to Professor Machlup of Princeton University and developed by Williamson (1965), is the *crawling peg*. Under the crawling peg a country would maintain its pegged exchange rate within agreed margins at a level equal to the moving average of the market exchange rate over an agreed previous time period. This would allow a country's currency to drift gradually lower if circumstances warranted, and at the same time would avoid both the upheaval of devaluation under the adjustable peg system and the possibility of excessive depreciation under free floating. To avoid speculation against the currency the interest rate could be raised by a margin equal to the permitted rate of depreciation.

Other objective indicators, other than a moving average of the past rates of exchange, could be used to introduce more flexibility into exchange rates while preserving some semblance of order. Changes in the level of reserves, the domestic rate of inflation, the level of employment, etc., could all be used to trigger off exchange-rate changes according to agreed rules (Kenen, 1975; Machlup, 1973; Williamson and Miller, 1987). All the proposals here would involve automatic adjustment of a pegged rate according to some agreed formula.

Choice of peg

Apart from the degree of peg flexibility, the other major issue, particularly in a world of generally floating rates among the major currencies, is *what* a country should peg its currency to. This is particularly an issue for developing countries, which for various reasons may be averse to floating themselves and wish to anchor their currency to another. This is the issue of what is called in the literature the *optimal peg*. There are 3 broad choices of peg: (i) pegging to a single currency such as the dollar, pound or franc, etc.; (ii) pegging to an individually tailored basket of currencies reflecting the trade of the country concerned; and (iii) pegging to a common basket of currencies such as the SDR (Special Drawing Rights). The choice depends on the objective function to be maximised. As of 1990, 49 countries had exchange rates pegged to a single currency; 33 to a basket of currencies, and 6 to the SDR. Fifty-two countries had other exchange rate arrangements including managed floating; floating according to a set of indicators, or independent floating.

There is now a large literature on the optimal peg. The major conclusions that seem to have emerged are as follows (Williamson, 1982b): First, there is a consensus that pegging against *one* currency will not be optimal if macroeconomic stability is the objective, since movements in a country's exchange rate will bear no necessary relation to its own balance of payments (but instead will move according to the balance of payments of the intervention currency). Secondly, that the choice of peg cannot eliminate the need for structural change and shifts in resources resulting from changes in bilateral rates against other countries – if pegging is to one or to a basket of currencies. Thirdly, there seems to be agreement that the aim should be to *stabilise* something rather than to *optimise* something. Targets for stabilisation include: minimising the variance of traded goods prices; minimising the variance of the balance of trade; minimising terms of trade instability, and minimising the variability of inflation. Different pegs (and different weights used in constructing the pegs) reflect differences in the objective function suggested and the characteristics of the countries concerned (e.g. whether they are small dependent economies and price takers, or whether they are price makers in world trade).

Williamson (1982b, 1983) argues that there is a strong case for taking as the objective *Continuous Internal Balance* which was the normative guiding principle of the IMF: in other words that the pegs should be chosen to preserve internal balance: The implication of this simple objective function is that the peg should be chosen to stabilise what may be called the *effective exchange rate*, i.e. that rate which will balance out the effect of individual *bilateral* exchange rate changes over the economy as a whole and so not disturb macroeconomic equilibrium. The question then is how should all the currencies in the peg be weighted with the potential of stabilising the effective exchange rate? The consensus here is that the weights should reflect the direction and elasticity of *total* trade between the country and its trading partners (taking both imports and exports). Finally, the long term questions of neutralising the effect of inflation differentials, and achieving payments adjustment, should be handled by changing the value of the peg rather than by influencing the unit to which the currency is pegged.

There is a third possibility of countries pegging their currency to a common peg, the SDR, which now is a weighted basket of five major currencies. The interesting question then is: would the SDR peg stabilise the effective exchange rate? Some studies have been done of this question with the general conclusion that firstly, an SDR peg produces less instability of the effective exchange rate than any single currency peg; but secondly, that the SDR peg probably gives more instability of the effective exchange rate than an individually tailored basket of currencies. On the other hand there would be compensating advantages of the SDR peg, particularly if all countries adopted it. For example, cross rates against all other currencies would be stabilised, which would be a stimulus to intra-regional trade compared with countries pegging to different baskets and cross rates varying. Secondly, there would be less uncertainty for foreign investors. There remains the problem with the SDR, however, that it is still not recognised as an intervention currency, to be bought and sold in the same way that normal currencies can be bought and sold to influence exchange rates.

The exchange rate mechanism of the European Monetary
System (EMS)

The EMS is a contemporary example of the adjustable peg system. In this section, we look at some of the reasons why the UK took so long to join the exchange rate mechanism of the EMS and what its prospects are now it has joined. In doing so, we highlight some of the theoretical aspects of the way the system has functioned.

The EMS was not the first attempt at some form of exchange rate system within the EC. In 1972, following the breakdown of the Bretton Woods system, a number of European countries formed 'the Snake', which sought to keep exchange rates within margins of 2.25 per cent either side of the central parity rate with the dollar. However, it was not particularly successful and was abandoned as many EC countries decided to move towards a floating exchange rate (for example, sterling was in the system for only six weeks, the French franc left at the beginning of January 1974).

The EMS, set up in 1979, has four main components: the ECU, credit facilities, the European Monetary Cooperation Fund (EMCF) and the exchange rate mechanism (hereafter ERM). The ECU is composed of a certain amount of all EC currencies and its value therefore changes as the values of the currencies of which it is composed fluctuate. Credit facilities are provided to members of the EMS for intervention in foreign exchange markets and to finance balance-of-payments deficits for short periods while economic policies to facilitate balance-of-payments adjustment are implemented. The EMCF is responsible for the ERM and for short-term credit facilities. Members deposit 20 per cent of their gold and foreign exchange reserves with the EMCF and in return they receive ECUs.

Members of the ERM set central exchange rates for their currencies *vis-à-vis* all other currencies within the system and thereby fix

TABLE 3.1
ERM realignments

Percentage devaluations (–) or revaluation (+)

Date	Deutsche-mark	French Franc	Dutch Florin	Belgian/ Luxembourg Franc	Italian Lire	Danish Kroner	Irish Punt
24.9.79	+2					−3	
30.11.79						−5	
23.3.81					−6		
5.10.81	+5.5	−3	+5.5		−5		
22.2.82				−8.5			
14.6.82	+4.25	−5.75	+4.25		−2.75		
21.3.83	+5.5	−2.5	+3.5	+1.5	−2.5	+2.5	−3.
22.7.85	+2	+2	+2	+2	−6	+2	+2
7.4.86	+3	−3	+3	+1			
4.8.86							−8
12.1.87	+3		+3	+2			
8.1.90					−3		

Source: Eurostat, *Money and Finance*.

the central rate *vis-à-vis* the ECU. The exchange rate can fluctuate up to 2.25 per cent on either side of this central rate. In the case of the UK and Spain the margins are plus or minus 6 per cent. This was also the case for Italy until 1 January 1990, when it moved to the narrower margins. Changes in the central rate are mutually agreed by all members.

There have been 12 changes in central rates, or realignments up to June 1991 (see Table 3.1). We can note that realignments became less frequent in the later 1980s. In spite of the frequency of early realignments, evidence suggests that the system has been successful at reducing exchange rate volatility. Artis and Taylor (1988), for example, find that bilateral intra-EC exchange rates were less volatile in the post-1979 period than in the pre-1979 period. This is in contrast to bilateral dollar exchange rates which experienced increased volatility post-1979. With respect to effective exchange rates of ERM members, the reduction in volatility was less significant. Artis and Taylor also investigate whether this reduced exchange rate volatility has resulted in increased interest-rate volatility. When exchange rates come under pressure to appreciate or depreciate in an adjustable peg system, then it is likely that interest rates will be altered. A rise in interest rates, by attracting capital inflows, reduces the pressure for a currency to depreciate (vice versa for a decrease in interest rates).

However, they find no evidence of increased interest rate volatility, although they attribute this largely to the role which capital controls have played in the ERM, something we discuss later in the chapter. In addition to reducing volatility, the ERM has not been associated with large misalignments. Williamson (1983) calculates that the deutschmark and French franc did not exhibit any large misalignments, in contrast to sterling, the dollar and the Yen (see Williamson, 1983, Figures A6–A10). Thus the ERM has tended to contribute to stability within the EC.

Having explained the main features of the EMS and the functioning of the ERM, we can turn to the question of why the UK did not join the ERM until 8 October 1990. Interestingly, the reasons given for this delay have differed.[19] In 1978, the Labour government took the decision not to join the system at its inception. The main reason they gave was that they thought the system would be dominated by Germany and would therefore tend to be deflationary. This results from the fact that adjustable peg exchange rate systems tend to operate asymmetrically. To see this, let us assume that there is one country within the ERM (call it country A) whose inflation rate is higher than other ERM countries. If the exchange rate between A and the rest of the ERM countries is not altered, then country A's competitiveness will decline, since the prices of its exports and import substitutes rise faster than those of the other ERM countries. As a result, country A's current account tends to move into deficit. Pressure then builds up for its exchange rate to depreciate and it is required to intervene in the foreign exchange market in order to buy up the excess supply of its currency. It purchases its currency by using its foreign exchange reserves. Since these reserves are limited, eventually country A will have to deflate its economy to lower inflation and remove the current account deficit. We know, however, that if one country has a deficit, then this must be matched by a surplus in another country (or group of countries). Why should the surplus countries not be the ones to experience pressure to reflate their economies? Surplus countries experience pressure for their exchange rates to appreciate. They are therefore accumulating foreign exchange reserves, and can continue to do so for a much longer period than the deficit country can run down its reserves. Pressure therefore usually falls on the deficit country to adjust. Within the ERM, there are currencies which have traditionally been weak currencies (for example, the French franc and the Italian lire) and those which have been strong currencies (for example, the deutschmark). The

Labour Party's objection in 1978 was that inflation rates in France and Italy and the UK, if it were to join, would be forced to converge on German levels. In this way they argued the ERM may be deflationary and they were therefore unwilling to allow sterling to join. Instead, the Labour Party wanted some convergence of economic policy between member countries before they would consider joining.

A second reason for the Labour Party's reticence to join the ERM stemmed from the reluctance to give up a policy instrument such as devaluation. There are a number of reasons why such an instrument is useful. Within the EC, it is clearly the case that the greater the divergence between members' economic policies, the greater the need for an extra offsetting instrument such as devaluation. Moreover, devaluation is also useful to offset country specific economic shocks. Labour's view in 1978 can be explained therefore as a reluctance to surrender a potentially useful instrument of policy.

When the Conservative Party came to power in 1979, they were also reluctant to take the UK into the ERM. However, the reasons they gave were very different. First, their economic policy placed much emphasis on the setting of monetary targets in order to eliminate inflation. As we argued earlier in the chapter, when exchange rates are fixed, control over the money supply is lost and therefore it is not possible to implement monetary targets. Secondly, the UK became a major oil producer – by 1980 it was self-sufficient in the consumption of oil. Sterling therefore would tend to appreciate following a rise in the price of oil and depreciate if the price of oil fell. This movement would mirror the effect of changes in oil prices on all other ERM members, who, with the exception of the Netherlands, are not oil producers. Thus it was argued that if the UK entered the ERM, the system would come under much pressure when the price of oil changed as sterling moved in the opposite direction to all other member currencies.

However, the experience with monetary targets changed the attitude towards the ERM of some members of the UK government (for example, Nigel Lawson, the Chancellor of the Exchequer). On the one hand monetary targets overshot in the early 1980s. On the other hand, it was clear that the policy was severely deflationary. Inflation fell and unemployment rose. Indeed, it was argued that the strength of deflation could be seen in the rapid appreciation of the exchange rate. In this way, the exchange rate came to be seen as a better indicator of monetary tightness than movements in monetary aggregates themselves. Thus some now argued that an exchange rate target, where the exchange rate was linked to some low inflation country, could more easily ensure a reduction in inflation.

In addition, pegging sterling to a low inflation currency such as the Deutschemark was seen to add credibility to the fight against inflation. The very fact that the ERM tended to operate asymmetrically (Labour's main objection to it) was now seen to be a virtue of the system. The credibility argument runs as follows. If a country (say the UK) pegs its exchange rate to a low inflation country (say Germany), then if the UK is to maintain its competitiveness, it must lower inflation. In particular, employers and trade unions should no longer negotiate wage increases which are higher than those in Germany. Wage increases which are larger than those in Germany will increase the price of UK goods and lower its competitiveness. Since the exchange rate can no longer alter in order to offset the impact of relatively higher wage increases, wage increases must be lowered, if deteriorating competitiveness (and thus ultimately increasing unemployment and low growth) are not to result. Joining the ERM thus helps to lower inflation and alter expectations.

The importance of altering expectations can be seen within a Phillips curve framework. In Figure 3.8, PC_1 and PC_2 are short-run expectations-augmented Phillips curves. PC_1 is associated with a zero expected inflation rate. PC_2 is associated with a positive expected inflation rate. The aim is to move the economy from point A where inflation is positive (i.e. relatively high) to point B where inflation is zero (i.e. relatively low). One way to move from A to B is to announce tight monetary targets, as was done in the UK in the 1979–81 period. The alternative we have been discussing is to announce an exchange rate target (i.e. join the ERM). In order to examine the impact of ERM entry on the disinflation process, let us first analyse what would happen if ERM entry had *no* effect on expectations. As a high exchange rate exerts a deflationary impact on the economy, the Phillips curve analysis predicts that the economy will move from A to B via a point such as D. In other words, as inflation falls, unemployment will initially rise. This occurs because employees are slow to alter their expectations of inflation and therefore continue to ask for wage increases assuming inflation is still high, when it has in fact fallen. We therefore move rightwards along PC_2 and unemployment rises as a result of the fact that real wages have risen (wage increases have been higher than price increases). Over time, employees will alter their expectations of inflation, reduce their demands for wage increases and the economy will move to B.

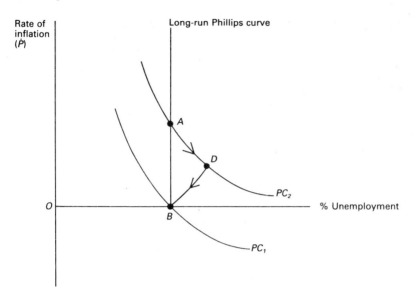

FIGURE 3.8   *Credibility and the EMS*

However, the impact of joining the ERM, it is claimed, *will* alter expectations and thus will make the process of disinflation much less costly in terms of unemployment. To take an extreme case, let us assume that expectations of inflation adjust immediately. The economy will then move from A to B directly. The act of fixing the exchange rate immediately reduces inflationary expectations and the short-run Phillips curve immediately shifts down to PC_1. Since employees are no longer asking for wage increases (since inflation is zero), their real wages will not rise and therefore unemployment will not increase above B. More generally, we can argue, the quicker expectations adjust, the less the impact of disinflation on unemployment and hence the less costly it is. It is this argument that has prevailed and led to the decision by the UK to join the ERM in October 1990.[20]

Now that the UK has taken the decision to join the ERM, what are the prospects for the 1990s? First, how convincing is the credibility argument? We can look at the experience of France and Italy, which both had high inflation rates when they joined the ERM. Between 1973 and 1980 Italy had an average annual inflation rate of 17.6 per cent and France of 10.7 per cent. This compares with the German average of 4.8 per cent. By 1988, German inflation had fallen to 1.5

per cent, French inflation to 3.2 per cent and Italian inflation to 5.9 per cent.[21] Thus inflation certainly appears to have been successfully reduced within the ERM. However, over the same period, a number of other OECD countries also succeeded in reducing inflation. The credibility argument states that ERM countries were able to disinflate at a lower cost in terms of unemployment. Davies (1989) argues that evidence on this is not so clear-cut. France and Italy both experienced rises in unemployment during the 1980s, suggesting that credibility was not something that was achieved simply by joining the ERM. Instead, France and Italy found that they had to convince economic agents that they were unwilling to realign within the ERM (that is, accommodate inflationary wage and price increases by devaluing the currency). In other words, as Davies (1989) concludes, joining the ERM may be costly in the short run, but it can have some benefits in the long run since the reduction in inflation has been much more durable. This can be contrasted with the UK experience where the initial success against inflation in the first half of the 1980s (albeit with high unemployment) was reversed from the mid-1980s onwards.

Secondly, British prospects will depend on how costly is the loss of one policy instrument (i.e. devaluation). Of course, the ERM is not a totally fixed exchange rate system and reaignments are possible. However, too frequent realignments clearly unc' 'rmine the potential credibility given by the ERM. Furthermore, if the EC does move towards greater economic and monetary union, then clearly realignments will become less frequent. In this case, the prospects for the British economy will depend on the extent to which various EC policies (coordinated macroeconomic policy, regional policy) can replace the lost instrument.

(iii) Managed Floating

Under managed floating there are no pegs and no parities that the authorities are obliged to preserve. Instead the currency is free to float but the authorities intervene to avoid what they regard to be undesirable consequences of excessive appreciation or depreciation. A weak currency may lead to excessive depreciation which the authorities may wish to avoid because of its repercussions on the domestic price of imports and the internal cost structure. Alternatively, countries with a strong currency may wish to avoid appreciation if they want to accumulate reserves and are not unduly worried about the effect of reserve changes on the money supply. A country may even wish to engineer the depreciation of its currency that would otherwise appreciate if the foreign exchange market were left to operate freely. Such examples are sometimes referred to as 'leaning against the wind'. Another example of managed exchange rates would be setting target zones for exchange rate movements but with 'soft bands' – as opposed to rigid bands under pegged rates. To operate a managed float requires that the monetary authorities add to the supply of or demand for foreign exchange as circumstances warrant in order to achieve the exchange rate desired. The limits to which a country can manage a floating rate depends on the volume of reserves it has (to defend a depreciating currency), and its ability to control the money supply, if need be, as it accumulates reserves (to prevent an appreciating currency). Countries may also experience international pressure to let the market operate freely, particularly surplus countries that accumulate reserves instead of allowing the exchange rate to appreciate.

Perhaps reflecting some of the disappointment with floating exchange rates, which we have discussed, in the second half of the 1980s there were some moves towards greater coordination and management of the exchange rates of major world currencies. These moves resulted in the main from the experience of dollar misalignment in the early 1980s. The dollar appreciated sharply, in spite of a growing and large current account deficit as Table 3.2 shows. The question was asked why the dollar was continuing to rise, when economic fundamentals (the current account) were deteriorating.

The dollar began to fall in 1985 and continued to do so throughout the rest of the 1980s. However, an agreement between the major industrialised countries in September 1985, the so-called Plaza Agreement, aimed at intervening in foreign exchange markets in order to induce dollar depreciation. This was followed in February 1987 by the Louvre agreement. This stressed the need for governments to continue to intervene in the foreign exchange markets, in particular to control the pace at which the dollar depreciated. There was a general fear that if the dollar depreciation was to be left to the market then it might fall too quickly, leading to a large collapse of confidence and further unwarranted depreciation. In addition to controlling the pace of dollar depreciation, the major industrialised countries agreed to a greater degree of coordination of their economic policies. These agreements reflected some recognition that countries could no longer operate in isolation and that if they did, this would be to the detriment of growth in the world economy.

TABLE 3.2
US exchange rate and current account, 1979–85

Year		Effective exchange rate (1980 = 100)	Current account (US$ billion)
1979		99.0	−0.97
1980		100.0	1.84
1981		112.7	6.37
1982		125.9	−8.03
1983		133.2	−40.86
1984		143.7	−101.60
1985	(Quarter 1)	160.0 ⎫	
	(Quarter 2)	155.7 ⎬	−148.90
	(Quarter 3)	147.6 ⎭	

Source: Bliss, C. (1985), 'The Rise and Fall of the Dollar', *Oxford Review of Economic Policy*, Winter.

It has to be said that, while this intervention represented a shift away from the views prevalent in the early 1980s that intervention in markets should be kept to a minimum, the extent to which exchange rates were managed was still quite small. Williamson (1983) has emphasised the need for a greater degree of exchange rate management if the misalignments of the early 1980s are to be avoided in the future. In particular, he has stressed the need for target zones. He defines a target zone as being closer to a form of floating exchange rates than to an adjustable peg system. 'Target zones have "soft margins" which the authorities are *not* committed to defending' (Williamson, 1983, p. 65, his emphasis). Having taken the decision to opt for target zones, there are a number of decisions about the form the target zone will take.

Initially, there is the question of how wide the target zone should be. Williamson opts for a minimum target zone of ±10 per cent around the central rate. There are two main reasons for this. First, wide margins allow central rates to be altered without precipitating speculative crises. Figure 3.9 illustrates this principle. At time t_1, the central rate is altered by a large amount, such that the new central rate is outside the old bands, e_1e_2. As a result, the actual exchange rate has to make a discrete jump on the day the central rate is changed. This generates large returns for speculators who can usually guess whether the exchange rate is going to appreciate or depreciate.

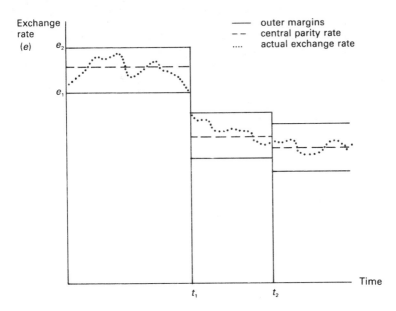

FIGURE 3.9 *Changing the central rate in a target zone*

This situation contrasts with the change in the central rate illustrated at time, t_2. Here the new band overlaps the old band. The exchange rate no longer has to make a discrete jump, thus limiting the potential for a large speculative crisis. Secondly, Williamson argues that large margins are required because of the difficulty of estimating the central rate. Williamson believes this rate should be the fundamental equilibrium exchange rate, that is, that rate which would ensure that the current account plus the long-term capital account equals zero. Since he believes that his calculations have a margin of error of ± 10 per cent, so the margins of the target zone should be at least that.

Secondly, there is the question of when the central rate should be changed. Williamson argues that changes must reflect inflation differentials and any underlying need to alter the real exchange rate to maintain a country's competitiveness and promote balance-of-payments adjustment. Moreover, the central rate should be changed continuously in order to minimise the extent to which speculative crises can occur.

The third question concerns whether the target zones should be announced. The problem with announcing the central rate and the margins is that if the exchange rate moves outside the band, then the authorities can lose credibility. Williamson, however, opts for publication since he believes that it encourages the authorities to be honest and allows the market to have greater access to information.

Finally, there is the question of what policy instruments should be used in order to manage the exchange rate within its band. He suggests that monetary policy is the best option because changes in the rate of interest have a quick and easily predictable effect on the exchange rate.

(iv) Freely Floating Exchange Rates

Under freely floating exchange rates the exchange rate is left to find its own level in the market without any official intervention. Balance-of-payments equilibrium is supposed to be achieved automatically, but only in a net currency flow sense. In an economic system in which the authorities are indifferent to the exchange rate, there is no need for international reserves. In practice, however, countries are not indifferent to the value of their currency in relation to others, and in the recent past free floating has never been adopted for any length of time as an exchange-rate regime. It stands at the other end of the spectrum to the rigidly fixed parities of the old gold standard, and probably neither of these extremes will ever be adopted in the future.

(v) Multiple Exchange Rates

Multiple exchange rate systems imply different exchange rates for different transactions either on current or capital account. The IMF's official definition of a multiple (more than one!) exchange rate is 'an effective buying or selling rate which, as a result of official action, differs from parity by more than 1%'. The IMF have been traditionally hostile to multiple exchange rate practices, seeing them as an interference with a free market in goods and capital, but they are perhaps to be preferred to more direct means of control which have typically been resorted to when multiple exchange rates have been abandoned. Multiple exchange rates can be viewed both as a form of exchange control (particularly over capital transactions) and as a rational response to the fact that different classes of goods have different price elasticities in world trade. Take the case, for example, of a dualistic developing country producing and exporting primarily agricultural commodities or raw materials, which wishes to develop an industrial sector, keeping input costs low and discouraging unnecessary imports. An exchange rate appropriate to the needs of the nascent industrial sector may not be the appropriate rate for the agricultural sector. If a country is a price taker in agricultural markets, a devalued rate to encourage industry will cause domestic inflation, and raise domestic input costs. If a country is a price maker in agricultural markets, and demand is price inelastic, a devalued rate will lower foreign exchange earnings. One (high) rate for agricultural exports (and necessary imports) and a lower (devalued) rate for industrial exports (and unnecessary imports) would be a sensible exchange rate system if it can be managed. Many countries, including the United Kingdom in the past with the 'dollar premium', charge a higher domestic price for foreign currency than the prevailing market rate for investment abroad in capital assets such as shares and property. This acts as a form of exchange control. We discuss controls over capital movements in the next section.

Controls on Capital Movements

Exchange (or capital) controls seek to prevent the free movement of capital, either capital inflows or outflows. They can apply to different kinds of capital flows. For example, it is often the case that controls apply more stringently to short-term capital and portfolio flows, whereas direct foreign investment is completely free. There are a variety of different kinds of controls – dual exchange rate systems, quantitative controls or taxes on capital movements. We discuss the advantages and disadvantages of these various kinds of controls later in the section.

The main argument against controlling capital movements is that this prevents an optimal allocation of resources. Let us assume that we have two countries, A and B. The productivity of capital is higher in A than in B. Following the liberalisation of capital movements, capital would move to where it is most productive, that is to country A. What effect does this have on the welfare of both A and B? The inflow of capital to country A will increase the productivity of labour (which becomes relatively scarcer) and lowers the productivity of capital (which becomes relatively more plentiful). Wage earners in A therefore gain and capital holders lose. Overall, however, it can be shown that the gains outweigh the losses, and the country's national income increases. In country B the outflow of capital has the reverse effect. The productivity of capital rises (as capital becomes relatively scarcer) and the productivity of labour falls (as labour becomes relatively more plentiful). Thus wage earners lose and capital holders gain, but overall the country's national income increases. The intuitive reason why both countries gain from the removal of capital controls is that their removal allow capital to be better allocated to where it is most productive.

There are a number of criticisms which we can make about this argument. First, Basevi (1988) notes that the gains from liberalisation will only be achieved if there are no other distortions and market failures. The above account of the gains from liberalisation is only valid within a perfectly competitive, neoclassical world. Exchange controls are the only distortion and therefore their removal is beneficial. However, the theory of second best argues that where there are a number of distortions (for example, monopoly power, rigidities in the labour market) the removal of one does not necessarily lead to an improvement in welfare.

Secondly, following the liberalisation of capital movements, capital may not flow to the country where it can do the most good. In the model outlined above, capital flows to where it is scarce relative to labour, since its scarcity generates higher returns. In order to see why this may not occur, let us assume that our two countries are in fact two parts of the UK, Scotland and the south-east of England. Capital is scarce in Scotland relative to labour and relatively plentiful in the south-east of England. We would thus expect capital to flow towards Scotland since there are not controls which prevent it. However, it is often difficult to attract capital to Scotland, because it benefits from remaining in areas which are already highly developed (i.e. the south-east of England). There are external economies associated with remaining in an area with good infrastructure, education, financial services and so on. It is on these grounds that the case for regional policies has often been based.[22]

The final criticism of the resource allocation argument is that, as we saw when we discussed exchange rate determination, capital movements are often speculative in nature. Capital movements depend on exchange rate expectations and nominal interest rates. These may not always reflect underlying real returns.

Thus it is not clear that the removal of exchange controls leads to an optimal allocation of resources. In addition, we can point to three main advantages which exchange controls (on short-term capital flows and portfolio flows) can confer on an economy. First, they reduce the influence which speculative capital flows have on the exchange rate. In this way, the exchange rate will be determined by the current account and the long-term capital account, increasing the likelihood that equilibrium can be achieved via exchange rate movements.

The second advantage of capital controls is that they help to reduce speculative attacks on currencies. This role has been particularly useful in the operation of the ERM of the EMS. Gibson and Tsakalotos (1990) have shown that speculative capital outflows from a number of European countries have been triggered by differential interest rates, expectations of devaluations and differential political risks. When interest rates are higher abroad or when the exchange rate is expected to be devalued, capital tends to flow out of a country. In addition, speculative capital flows can occur in response to changing political circumstances. The case of France is instructive here. Following the election of a socialist government (under Mitterrand) in 1981, there was a large capital outflow, because wealth-holders feared that the economic programme might be harmful to their interests (for example, by involving greater taxation of wealth). This can be contrasted with the imposition of a more orthodox 'stabilisation programme',[23] following the U-turn of the Mitterrand government in March 1983. At that time, there were capital inflows. How exactly did the existence of capital controls help to contain such crises, especially within the context of the EMS? Assume we are in one of the periods when there was downward speculative pressure on the French franc (for example, in 1981). If the French monetary authorities wanted to maintain the central parity of the French franc within the ERM they had to do one of two things: increase interest rates to attract capital back (or prevent it from leaving) or allow capital controls to operate. In the case of France the evidence suggests that the latter option was the preferred one during the first half of the 1980s. Wyplosz (1988) examines what would have happened to domestic interest rates had there been no capital controls. He uses the offshore–onshore interest rate differential. The offshore interest rate is given by the Euro-FrenchFranc interest rate. This rate prevails on bank accounts in French francs which are held abroad (i.e. outside France) and it is representative of the interest rate which would have prevailed in France had there not been capital controls. The onshore interest rate is simply the domestic interest rate. Before a devaluation of the French franc within the ERM, the offshore interest rate rose to very high levels, much higher than the domestic interest rate. This increase was to compensate holders of French Franc bank accounts abroad for the loss they would incur if the franc was devalued. However, those holding French Francs within France were not compensated, because interest rates were not raised. If there had been no controls on capital movements, then the expected devaluation would have led to much larger capital outflows than actually occurred, as French residents moved their wealth from domestic banks and assets to offshore assets (in the Euro-FrenchFranc market). The existence of these interest rate differentials is some evidence that exchange controls were effective. The great advantage of the controls was that they limited speculative outflows and allowed the French authorities to devalue the French Franc in an orderly manner. Given that a number of other European countries had controls on capital movements, it has been argued (for example by Wyplosz (1988) and Artis and Taylor (1988)) that they were important to the successful operation of the ERM at times when there was little policy convergence.

The third and final advantage of exchange controls is that they do allow a country some monetary independence, even if exchange rates are either fixed or being highly managed. Gibson (1989) analyses the impact of the removal of exchange controls on the independence of UK monetary policy. As described in Chapter 2, the UK had extensive controls over capital outflows until October 1979. Figure 3.10 shows the Eurosterling interest rate and the domestic sterling interest rate (represented here by the Local Authority loan rate, LA rate) between 1974 and 1984. Up until 1979, the offshore rate (the Euro-sterling rate) was persistently above the domestic interest rate. If residents of the UK had been able to transfer funds to the offshore market (something which was prevented by the existence of the exchange controls), then they would have done so, forcing domestic interest rates to rise. This pre-1979 period can be contrasted with the post-1979 period, when the two interest rates were very close. What does all this imply for monetary independence? The possibility of having an interest rate which is different from the offshore interest rate is evidence of some monetary independence, since offshore sterling interest rates are strongly influenced by US interest rates. In an examination of monetary policy in the UK in the period 1974–84, Gibson (1989) concludes that policy was influenced by two main factors – exchange rate policy and the existence or otherwise of exchange controls. Exchange rate policy is important, because if governments are seeking to manage the exchange rate, then the

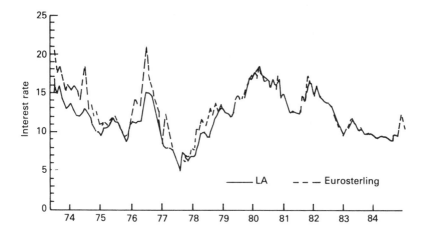

FIGURE 3.10 *Onshore–offshore sterling interest rate differential*
Source: H.D. Gibson, *The Eurocurrency Markets, Domestic Financial Policy and International Instability* (London: Macmillan, 1989).

money supply becomes endogenous, as we explained above. Up until 1977, the UK government was actively intervening in the foreign exchange markets. Policy independence was thus limited, although the existence of exchange controls did allow domestic UK interest rates to be insulated somewhat from movements in US interest rates. After the removal of exchange controls, even though the government was intervening to a smaller extent in the foreign exchange markets, monetary policy independence was much reduced and changes in US interest rates frequently led to expectations of changes in UK interest rates. Thus without capital controls, the interest rate required for external balance may diverge considerably from that required for internal balance, for example to stimulate investment for growth and full employment.

In conclusion, therefore, there is some evidence that exchange controls can moderate speculative attacks against a currency and provide the monetary authorities with some policy independence. However, critics of exchange controls often point to a number of practical problems. First, they generate incentives for investors to engage in activities which are not socially productive, but are aimed merely at avoiding the controls. Such activities are not beneficial from the point of view of the economy's welfare. Secondly, they argue that exchange controls are administratively expensive and lead to the creation of black markets which allow circumvention. While, there is no doubt that exchange controls are circumvented (in the same way that some people evade income tax), the evidence presented above suggests that they are not wholly useless. Moreover, the ability to circumvent controls and the administrative costs of controls varies according to which kind of exchange controls are in place.

A first possible option is quantitative controls on capital movements. These prevent any capital movements of certain types, for example portfolio flows or short-term flows, and are the kind of controls which most European countries have had at some time during the post-war period. Such controls are usually administratively complex. In order to prevent those who have access to foreign exchange legitimately (for example, importers and exporters) from using the foreign currency for speculative purposes, importers and exporters have to apply for special permission to get access to foreign exchange, they have to surrender the foreign exchange they receive from transactions within a certain period and so on. The disadvantage of these quantitative controls is that they are administratively expensive.

A second possible method of controlling capital movements has been proposed by Tobin (1978). He argues that transactions across currencies should be subject to an international transfer tax. It is a well-known proposition of microeconomic theory that if a certain activity is taxed, its volume will decline (the most obvious example is a tax on an activity which leads to pollution). Tobin suggests that short-term capital movements should be subject to a fixed tax. One way in which this could be achieved is by taxing all outflows and inflows if they are repatriated within, say, one year. This would increase the cost of such transactions and therefore they would only be undertaken if they were highly profitable. The advantage of this policy is that it does not prohibit all short-term capital movements, only those which are mostly speculative (i.e. for a short time period).

A third possible method of controlling capital movements is via a dual exchange market. Belgium and Luxembourg operate a dual exchange market, and the investment currency market which existed in the UK (see Chapter 2) was a kind of dual system. A dual exchange market works in the following way. There are two exchange rates, one for current account transactions and the other for purely capital account transactions (usually known as the official and the financial exchange rates respectively). These exchange rates may differ. For example, if there is a large capital outflow the financial rate will depreciate, while the official rate will be unaffected. In the case of the Belgian-Luxembourg system, the financial rate has often been depreciated by up to 10 per cent relative to the official rate. As the financial rate depreciates, so the incentive for capital outflows is reduced. Alternatively, if the country experiences strong capital inflows, the financial rate will begin to appreciate above the official rate, thus reducing the inflow. Thus the difference between the two exchange rates acts as a tax on capital outflows when the financial rate depreciates below the official rate and as a subsidy on outflows when the financial rate appreciates above the official rate. In this sense, a dual exchange rate system is like a variable Tobin tax. It can act to discourage either net capital outflows or inflows at times when speculative pressure on a currency is strong. At other times, the two exchange rates will tend to move together. The dual exchange market is often criticised because there might be some circumvention of controls, that is the channelling of capital account transactions through the current account market and vice versa. Over time therefore the system may become ineffective. This, however, is not the experience of the Belgian-Luxembourg system (Steinherr and De Schrevel, 1988).

In conclusion, therefore, there are clearly costs and benefits associated with the imposition of controls on capital movements. However, it does appear that some kind of tax (either the Tobin tax or a dual exchange market) would provide some benefits in terms of increased monetary independence and the ability to control speculative attacks against a currency, without imposing too high a cost.

Exchange Rate Policies in the 1990s

Exchange rate policy in the 1990s tends to be moving further away from the floating exchange rates of the 1970s and 1980s. In this regard, the most important developments are taking place in Europe. The first stage of the Delors Plan involves all countries becoming members of the ERM within the narrow band, the removal of exchange controls,[24] and moves towards greater monetary cooperation, in an attempt to integrate the capital markets of the EC more closely. The second stage of the Delors plan involves greater monetary cooperation, strengthened and institutionalised with the creation of a European central bank. Furthermore, realignments would only be made in exceptional circumstances. The third stage involves irrevocably fixing exchange rates, as a prelude to full monetary union and a single currency.

The main problems associated with completely fixed exchange rates (or a single currency) is that it eliminates a possible policy which can be used to negate adverse trends or the impact of a negative shock on one country within the EC. For example, assume a large negative shock to one country within the EC which reduces the demand for one of its main products. If exchange rates are flexible, then this negative shock can, to some extent, be reduced by the depreciation of its exchange rate relative to other EC countries, moderating the impact of the shock. However, if exchange rates are fixed or there is *one* currency, then that EC country would become a depressed region. One possible policy which could help to mitigate the impact of a negative shock has been lost.

It is for this reason that moves towards European Monetary Union (EMU) must be accompanied by the establishment of large regional funds, with budgetary transfers being made to the weaker and more depressed regions/countries of the Community. Thus while the movement towards fixed exchange rates in the EC will bring a new set of problems, there are possible steps which can be taken to mitigate these effects.

Exchange rate policy outside the EC in the 1990s is more difficult to predict. In particular, it is not clear what the relationship will be between the EMS and the other major world currencies, the dollar and the Yen. In the 1980s, we witnessed moves towards a greater management of exchange rates, as shown in the Plaza and Louvre agreements. It is certainly likely that this kind of cooperation will continue into the 1990s, but whether it will develop into something stronger is an open question.

4
The Balance of Payments and the National Economy[1]

THE INTEGRATION OF THE BALANCE OF PAYMENTS INTO THE NATIONAL ACCOUNTS

In a closed economy with government activity there are three types of expenditure which generate income – private consumption, private investment and government expenditure – and three ways in which income may be disposed of – by consumption, saving and tax payments. In a closed economy total expenditure can fall short of income but cannot exceed it.

In an open economy income is generated by consumption, investment, government expenditure and exports, each of which may have an import content which will not generate income domestically. Hence

$$Y = C + I + G + X - M \tag{4.1}$$

where Y is income, C is private consumption, I is private investment, G is government expenditure, X is exports and M is imports. The disposal of income may be written as

$$Y = C + S + T \tag{4.2}$$

where S is saving and T is tax payments. Combining equations (4.1) and (4.2) gives the condition for income equilibrium:

$$S + T + M = I + G + X \tag{4.3}$$

In an open economy expenditure may exceed domestic income if imports exceed exports. By the use of these three equations the relationship of the balance of payments to the functioning of the economy may be seen. Let us give some simple examples. Suppose that the government's budget is balanced so that $G = T$; then the plans of the private sector to invest in excess of saving would lead to an excess of imports over exports and the plans could be realised by a balance-of-payments deficit financed by foreign borrowing. Alternatively, suppose the private sector is in balance ($I = S$); then the plans of government to spend in excess of taxation would also lead to a balance-of-payments deficit and the plans could be realised if the deficit can be financed. This was the basis of the so-called New Cambridge theory which ascribed the UK's balance-of-payments deficits in the 1960s and early 1970s to government budget deficits, basing the theory on the empirical observation that the private sector of the economy stays roughly in balance.[2] No sooner had the theory been expounded, however, than it was confounded by contrary empirical evidence, and the theory died a quick death. It remains true, however, that the performance of the current account of the balance of payments will be a function of expenditure decisions in both the private and public sectors of the economy; and, of course, in an accounting sense the difference between imports and exports must be equal to the difference between saving plus taxation and investment plus government spending.

In this chapter we shall be concerned with three main questions. First, we shall consider the conflict between balance-of-payments equilibrium and the achievement of other goals of economic policy. Second, we shall be concerned with how trade alters the condition for income equilibrium in the macro economy, and how, through the foreign-trade multiplier, fluctuations in income may be transmitted from one country to another. Here a departure is made from the traditional approach to the determination of income equilibrium in an open economy, which relates imports to income via the marginal propensity to import. Following the approach developed by Kennedy and Thirlwall (1979a, 1979b), imports will be related to expenditure. Relating imports to income assumes implicitly either that all expenditures have the same ratio of imports to expenditure or that all imports are consumption goods. Only on these assumptions will the marginal propensity to import be independent of the type of expenditure which generates the multiplier process. In practice, however, it is extremely unlikely that the ratio of imports to expenditure will be the same for all items of expenditure, or that all imports will be consumption goods, so that relating imports to income may be a serious mis-specification of the income multiplier. This is the only textbook to present a simple exposition of the income multiplier which relates imports to expenditure, which, given its greater realism, ought to be more widely taught. The model is also extended to the two-country case to examine the condition for equilibrium when foreign repercussions are considered. Finally, a brief introduction will be given in this chapter to the theory of balance-of-payments adjustment before considering more fully the major approaches to balance-of-payments adjustment policy in later, separate chapters.

THE CONFLICT BETWEEN BALANCE-OF-PAYMENTS EQUILIBRIUM AND OTHER OBJECTIVES OF ECONOMIC POLICY

The discussion here abstracts from the possibility of exchange-rate changes and the adoption of policies to improve the capital account of the balance of payments. These considerations are taken up in subsequent chapters.

Balance-of-payments equilibrium, however defined, is not desired for its own sake. There is nothing particularly virtuous or conducive to welfare in balance-of-payments equilibrium itself. Balance-of-payments equilibrium is an intermediate objective, along with others, towards the final objective of most economic societies of maximising welfare per head. The other main macroeconomic objectives along with balance-of-payments equilibrium are full employment, faster growth and stable prices – the 'magic quadrilateral', as Joan Robinson once described them. A balance-of-payments surplus means that residents of a country are forgoing immediate welfare by exporting more goods and services than they import, thus in effect transferring welfare to other countries. A balance-of-payments deficit, while it may lead to a temporary increase in welfare, will require rectification in the long run which may mean the sacrifice of other domestic goals. There is no conflict between balance-of-payments equilibrium and stable prices, but there may be a conflict between balance-of-payments equilibrium and both full employment and faster growth.

If full employment and balance-of-payments equilibrium conflict, full employment may have to be sacrificed to achieve balance-of-payments equilibrium if other policy measures are ruled out or fail. Economic-policy discussion to improve the UK balance of payments has been dominated, under fixed and floating exchange rates, by the consideration of policies to reconcile the conflict between full employment and balance-of-payments equilibrium. Assuming fixed exchange rates, a conflict may exist for the following reasons. The level of employment is determined by the relationship between national expenditure and the output capacity of an economy. The higher the level of expenditure in relation to capacity output, the higher the level of employment. As expenditure increases, however, and the level of output approaches capacity, imports are likely to rise. Some imports, mainly those without domestic substitutes, will tend to be required in some fixed proportion to domestic expenditure, and these will rise as expenditure and employment rise. Other imports, which have domestic substitutes, will rise slowly at first but then will become increasingly sensitive to the pressure of demand because at full employment domestic output reaches its capacity level and demand can only be met by imports. At the same time exports may fall, or at least not match the increase in imports, because production for the home market becomes more profitable. Thus, as the economy moves towards full employment, the balance of payments may be expected to deteriorate, with the possibility that at the level of full employment (however a country defines this elusive concept) there may be a balance-of-payments deficit. The conflict may be represented by a trade-off curve, the slope of which shows how much the balance of payments deteriorates as the level of employment increases and the unemployment rate falls. A hypothetical curve is shown in Figure 4.1. In this particular example the trade-off curve has been drawn cutting the horizontal axis at 5 per cent unemployment. This means that if full employment were to be defined as 2 or 3 per cent unemployment, a conflict would exist between full employment and balance-of-payments equilibrium. At this level of unemployment the balance of payments would move into deficit. Cutting expenditure to achieve balance-of-payments equilibrium would mean a sacrifice of full employment.

What this trade-off looks like for the UK is shown in Figure 4.2. Here, the current account is measured as a percentage of GDP, and unemployment is measured in millions. The quarterly observations over the 30 years 1958 to 1988 show the trade-off between unemployment and balance-of-payments equilibrium worsening through time. The level of unemployment consistent with current account balance now appears to be approximately 3 million compared with only one-half a million 30 years ago.

It may, of course, be possible to shift the trade-off curve inwards to

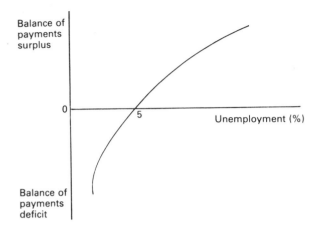

FIGURE 4.1

reconcile the conflict. Devaluation is supposed to act in this way. Ruling out exchange-rate changes, however, such policies as the better marketing of exports, improved productivity, import tariffs and export subsidies could all potentially improve the balance of payments at a given level of unemployment. It can also be shown that the position of the trade-off curve will depend on the degree of demand disequilibrium between markets in the economy. If some markets have excess demand, and others have excess supply, and if imports are increasingly sensitive to the pressure of demand, the aggregate level of imports will be higher for any given level of aggregate demand (or unemployment) than if all markets were in equilibrium at the given level of aggregate demand (see Thirlwall and White, 1974; and Hughes and Thirlwall, 1979). In Chapter 10 evidence is given to suggest that bottlenecks in particular sectors of the UK economy may have raised the import bill in the 1960s and 1970s by up to £1 billion per annum (at 1970s prices) at the pressure of demand prevailing.

The conflict between faster growth and balance-of-payments equilibrium, again assuming fixed exchange rates, arises for the same type of reasons as the conflict between full employment and balance-of-payments equilibrium. The attempt to grow faster from a position of below full employment increases the import bill, and the attempt to raise the capacity growth rate by expanding demand in excess of the capacity growth rate, in the hope that this will encourage investment,

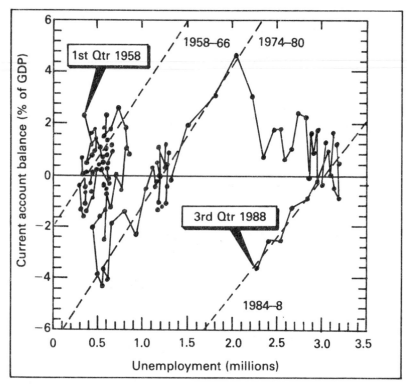

FIGURE 4.2

Source: T. O'Shaughnessy, *Financial Times*, 1 February 1989.

will increase the import bill even more. There are only two ways in which expenditure in excess of output in the domestic economy can be eliminated, either by prices rising to equilibrate demand and supply, or by imports rising (or exports falling). One of the reasons why a country may want to grow faster, and certainly why the United Kingdom has suffered a growth neurosis since the Second World War, is that its growth rate is inferior to that of other countries. Whether a country can grow at the rate of other countries without running into balance-of-payments difficulties depends primarily on the income elasticity of demand for its imports and exports. The income elasticity of demand for imports measures the proportional change in demand for imports with respect to a proportional change in the country's income. The income elasticity of demand for exports measures the proportional change in the demand for a country's exports with respect to a proportional change in other countries' incomes. If a country's income elasticity of demand for imports is no greater than the income elasticity of demand for its exports, it is possible (other things remaining the same) for a country to grow at the same rate as other countries without imports growing faster than exports and the balance of payments deteriorating. If, however, a country's import elasticity is higher than its export elasticity, it cannot grow faster than other countries without the balance of payments deteriorating, even if it possessed the capacity to do so. For example, suppose that other countries are growing at 5 per cent per annum, that the income elasticity of demand for a country's exports is unity, and the country's income elasticity of demand for imports is 2. The country's exports will be growing at 5 per cent (5×1), but if the country's growth of output is 5 per cent, its imports would grow at 10 per cent (5×2). To keep the growth of imports in line with exports the growth of output would need to be constrained to equal the growth of exports divided by the income elasticity of demand for imports, i.e. to $5 \div 2 = 2.5$ per cent per annum. This illustrative example is not far removed from the experience of the United Kingdom in the years since the Second World War. The rest of the world has been growing roughly twice as fast as the UK economy, and the UK growth rate has had to be constrained to an average of about 2.5 per cent per annum in order to maintain balance-of-payments equilibrium. The capacity growth rate of the UK economy has been slightly above 2.5 per cent, but this higher rate has not been sustainable over a long period because of the balance-of-payments consequences. The result has been a slow but steady rise in the underlying rate of unemployment. In one sense it is fortunate that the United Kingdom has not possessed the capacity to grow at the rate of other countries, because if it had the potential growth of output would not have been achievable and there would have been more unemployment. Instead of the gap between the growth of actual and potential output being, on average, 0.5 per cent it would have been closer to 2.5 per cent, with the consequence of much greater surplus capacity. In Chapter 12 it is shown how closely the growth rate of several industrial countries approximates to their rate of growth of exports divided by their income elasticity of demands for imports, and throughout the book the thesis is argued that at the heart of the

United Kingdom's inability to grow faster, and its weak balance of payments, is its slow rate of export growth associated with the low income elasticity of demand for UK exports in world markets.

INCOME EQUILIBRIUM IN AN OPEN ECONOMY AND THE OPEN ECONOMY MULTIPLIER

Earlier we presented the equations which integrate the balance of payments with the functioning of the national economy. In using these equations for the determination of the equilibrium level of income, all the magnitudes must be interpreted in an *ex ante* sense. The expenditures and disposals of income are planned (p). For simplicity, government spending and taxation are now ignored:

$$Y = C_p + I_p + X_p - M_p \tag{4.4}$$

and

$$Y = C_p + S_p$$

In a closed economy (with no exports and imports) the condition for income equilibrium is the familiar Keynesian condition $I_p = S_p$. In an open economy the condition for income equilibrium becomes

$$S_p = I_p + X_p - M_p \tag{4.5}$$

or

$$S_p + M_p = I_p + X_p \tag{4.6}$$

In words, plans to save and import must equal planned investment plus export demand. If plans to save and to buy foreign goods (the purchase of which does not generate income at home) exceed plans to invest and for foreigners to buy home goods (the purchase of which does generate income at home), income will fall, thus reducing saving and imports, until plans to save and import equal once again plans to invest and export. Conversely, if plans to save and import fall short of plans to invest and export, income will rise, raising saving and imports, until plans to save and import are equal once again to plans to invest and export. The mechanism by which plans to save and import are brought into line with plans to invest and export, once a disturbance takes place, is the so-called *multiplier* mechanism, which is the relationship between a change in planned (autonomous) expenditure and the corresponding change in income. To derive the multiplier we first have to derive an expression for the equilibrium level of income in the open economy. The usual method of approach is to assume that planned investment and exports are autonomous (i.e. not dependent on income), and that planned saving and planned imports are both functions of income.[3] Thus for equation (4.6) we have:

$$I_p = \bar{I}_p \tag{4.7}$$

$$X_p = \bar{X}_p \tag{4.8}$$

$$S_p = \bar{S}_{ap} + sY \tag{4.9}$$

and

$$M_p = \bar{M}_{ap} + mY \tag{4.10}$$

where a bar over a variable denotes 'autonomous', s is the marginal propensity to save, m is the marginal propensity to import, and $\bar{S}_{ap}$ and $\bar{M}_{ap}$ represent autonomous saving and imports, respectively. Substituting equations (4.7) to (4.10) into equation (4.6) gives:

$$\bar{S}_{ap} + sY + \bar{M}_{ap} + mY = \bar{I}_p + \bar{X}_p \tag{4.11}$$

Rearranging, and solving for the equilibrium level of income:

$$Y = \frac{\bar{I}_p + \bar{X}_p - \bar{S}_{ap} - \bar{M}_{ap}}{s + m} \tag{4.12}$$

The multiplier, which is defined as the relation between a change in autonomous expenditure and the resulting change in income, can be derived with respect to any of the elements of autonomous expenditure in the numerator of equation (4.12). For the same increase in investment or export demand, for example, the change in income is

$$\frac{\Delta Y}{\Delta \bar{I}_p} = \frac{\Delta Y}{\Delta \bar{X}_p} = \frac{1}{s + m} \tag{4.13}$$

For an increase in autonomous saving or imports (which would exert a negative effect on income):

$$\frac{\Delta Y}{\Delta \bar{S}_p} = \frac{\Delta Y}{\Delta \bar{M}_p} = \frac{-1}{s + m} \qquad (4.14)$$

$1/(s + m)$ is called the income multiplier. It contrasts with the multiplier for a closed economy of $1/s$ (which can be derived from equation (4.11), eliminating imports and exports from the equation). Since $0 < m < 1$, the multiplier with foreign trade will be less than the multiplier without foreign trade. The explanation is that some additional income leaks into imports (as well as into saving), and this does not generate any further income at home. To show how the multiplier process brings income back into equilibrium following an autonomous disturbance, let us work a simple numerical example. Suppose $s = 0.1$ and $m = 0.1$, giving an income multiplier of $1/0.2$ (= 5). Start with income in equilibrium at £100m and then assume an autonomous increase in investment of £1m raising planned investment plus export demand in excess of planned saving plus imports. With a multiplier of 5, an increase in investment of £1m will increase income by £5m. Out of the £5m increase in income, however, there will be increased saving of £5m × 0.1 = £0.5m. and increased import demand of £5m × 0.1 = £0.5m so that the total level of planned saving plus imports increases by £1m – exactly equal to the planned increase in autonomous expenditure. Income will remain at a new equilibrium level of £105m where planned saving and imports equal planned investment and exports, until equilibrium is again disturbed. In practice the propensity to save in the United Kingdom is about 0.15 (in the long run) and the propensity to import is about 0.2. These values would give a closed-economy multiplier of 6.6 and an open economy multiplier of 2.9, a substantial difference. The multiplier in reality is much lower than 2.9 because additional income also leaks into taxation (the sensitivity of tax revenue to national income is about 0.2).

In practice, also, the multiplier will vary according to the magnitude of the import content of the initial autonomous expenditure change, but this is ignored by the traditional approach to the foreign-trade multiplier which relates imports to income. For example, suppose that there is an increase in autonomous investment of £100m but £50m of this expenditure is on investment goods imported from abroad. The initial stimulus to the domestic economy is only £50m.

Compare this with an increase in the demand for exports of £100m which has an import content of only £10m. In this case the initial stimulus to the domestic economy is £90m and the total effect on income via the multiplier will be greater than for an equal increase in investment.

To cope with this weakness of the traditional approach to the open economy multiplier, however, it is not sufficient simply to subtract the proportion of imports in autonomous expenditure from the numerator of the multiplier formula and work on in the same way. The denominator of the multiplier must also be changed. The induced leakage of income into imports which dampens the process of income generation is, strictly speaking, the import content of induced consumption, and only by chance will m, the marginal propensity to import, be a measure of this when imports are related to the different components of expenditure which generate income. A complete overhaul of the presentation of the open economy multiplier is called for in which imports are related to the different components of expenditure. It can be shown that the two approaches of relating imports to income and imports to expenditure are only equivalent in the very special case of all items of autonomous expenditure having the same ratio of imports to expenditure (i.e. the same import coefficient). A special case of this, in turn, would be if autonomous expenditure had no import content, in which case the import coefficients would be zero and all imports would be induced consumption-good imports. In developing the new open economy multiplier the model will also be extended to the two-country case where changes in income in one country affect activity in the other, which in turn affects activity in the first country. The multiplier and the condition for income equilibrium will be affected.

THE OPEN ECONOMY MULTIPLIER RELATING IMPORTS TO EXPENDITURE

We start with the income equation:

$$Y = C + I + X - M \qquad (4.15)$$

Let consumption (like saving earlier) be partly autonomous ($\bar{C}$) and partly dependent on income (cY), where c is the marginal propensity to consume. Let I and X be autonomous, as before. Now make imports a function of expenditure (not income) and assume, as is the case in practice, that each type of expenditure has an import content. The import function can then be written as

$$M = \bar{M} + \lambda_{ac}\,\bar{C} + \lambda_c\,cY + \lambda_i\,\bar{I} + \lambda_x\,\bar{X} \qquad (4.16)$$

where $\bar{M}$ is autonomous imports, λ_{ac} is the import coefficient of autonomous consumption, λ_c is the import coefficient of induced consumption, λ_i is the import coefficient of investment, λ_x is the import coefficient of exports, and the import coefficient (λ) is defined generally as the ratio of imports to expenditure.

Substituting equation (4.16) into (4.15) gives the expression for income of

$$Y = \bar{C} + cY + \bar{I} + \bar{X} - \bar{M} - \lambda_{ac}\,\bar{C} - \lambda_c\,cY - \lambda_i\,\bar{I}$$
$$- \lambda_x\,\bar{X} \qquad (4.17)$$

or

$$Y = \frac{-\bar{M} + (1 - \lambda_{ac})\bar{C} + (1 - \lambda_i)\bar{I} + (1 - \lambda_x)\bar{X}}{1 - c(1 - \lambda_c)} \qquad (4.18)$$

The income multiplier with respect to any change in autonomous expenditure in the numerator of equation (4.18) can be derived in the normal way. With respect to a change in autonomous investment we have:

$$\frac{\Delta Y}{\Delta \bar{I}} = \frac{1 - \lambda_i}{1 - c(1 - \lambda_c)} \qquad (4.19)$$

Equation (4.19) contrasts with the conventional open economy multiplier in which imports are related to income through the marginal propensity to import, of (see equation (4.13)):

$$\frac{\Delta Y}{\Delta \bar{I}} = \frac{1}{1 - c + m} \qquad (4.20)$$

where $1 - c = s$.

The result in equation (4.20) ignores the import content of the autonomous expenditure, or, as we shall prove below, assumes the import coefficient of investment and consumption to be the same.

Note also from the more realistic formulation of the open economy multiplier that it is clearly wrong to treat the effect of an autonomous increase in imports as the exact obverse of an autonomous increase in exports which is what the conventional approach assumes. From equation (4.18) the multiplier with respect to an autonomous change in imports is

$$\frac{\Delta Y}{\Delta \bar{M}} = \frac{-1}{1 - c(1 - \lambda_c)} \tag{4.21}$$

while the multiplier with respect to an autonomous change in exports is

$$\frac{\Delta Y}{\Delta \bar{X}} = \frac{1 - \lambda_x}{1 - c(1 - \lambda_c)} \tag{4.22}$$

The effect of an equal change in autonomous exports and imports on income is not zero as one would be led to suppose from the conventional multiplier formulation. For an equal increase in autonomous exports and imports, income will fall by $- \lambda_x/[1 - c(1 - \lambda_c)]$ times the equal change in exports and imports; and for an equal decrease in autonomous exports and imports, income will rise by $\lambda_x/[1 - c (1 - \lambda_c)]$ times the equal change in exports and imports.

The conventional open economy multiplier result with respect to a change in autonomous expenditure will be equivalent to our more realistic result *if and only if* all components of autonomous expenditure have the same import coefficient and there is no change in autonomous imports. A special case of this would be if all the import coefficients attached to autonomous expenditures are zero, in which case all imports would be induced consumption-good imports. The proof is as follows. Totally differentiating equation (4.16) and assuming $d\bar{M} = 0$, we have:

$$dM = \lambda_{ac} d\bar{C} + \lambda_c \, cdY + \lambda_i d\bar{I} + \lambda_x \, d\bar{X} \tag{4.23}$$

and dividing through by dY:

$$\frac{dM}{dY} = m = \frac{\lambda_{ac} \, d\bar{C} + \lambda_i d\bar{I} + \lambda_x d\bar{X}}{dY} + \lambda_c c \tag{4.24}$$

Now from equation (4.18) we have by total differentiation (assuming $d\bar{M} = 0$):

$$dY = \frac{(1 - \lambda_{ac})d\bar{C} + (1 - \lambda_i)d\bar{I} + (1 - \lambda_x)d\bar{X}}{1 - c(1 - \lambda_c)} \qquad (4.25)$$

Substituting (4.25) into (4.24) gives:

$$m = \frac{\lambda_{ac}d\bar{C} + \lambda_i d\bar{I} + \lambda_x d\bar{X}}{(1 - \lambda_{ac})d\bar{C} + (1 - \lambda_i)d\bar{I} + (1 - \lambda_x)d\bar{X}}\,[1 - c(1 - \lambda_c)] + \lambda_c c \qquad (4.26)$$

m will be independent of $d\bar{C}$, $d\bar{I}$ and $d\bar{X}$ *if and only if*

$$\lambda_{ac} = \lambda_i = \lambda_x = \lambda \text{ (say)} \qquad (4.27)$$

On that assumption we have:

$$m = \frac{\lambda}{1 - \lambda}\,[1 - c(1 - \lambda_c)] + \lambda_c c \qquad (4.28)$$

If equation (4.28) is substituted for m in the conventional formulation of the multiplier – equation (4.20) – we obtain, after simplification:

$$\frac{1}{1 - c + m} = \frac{1 - \lambda}{1 - c(1 - \lambda_c)} \qquad (4.29)$$

which is the formulation of the multiplier which results from relating imports to expenditure. In the special case of autonomous expenditure having no import content, so that $\lambda = 0$, it is clear from equation (4.28) that the conventional multiplier result would also be obtained since $m = \lambda_c c$, so that the multiplier $(1 - \lambda)/[1 - c(1 - \lambda_c)]$ would reduce to $1/(1 - c + m)$. Many treatments of the traditional open economy multiplier which relate imports to income say explicitly that the assumption is being made that all imports are consumption goods. It has not been explicitly recognised, however, that the same result would obtain if the import coefficients attached to all items of autonomous expenditure were the same. In practice neither circumstance is likely to prevail, and there must therefore be strong grounds for discarding the traditional approach in favour of relating imports to expenditure, particularly as it is so easy to do. The difference made to the value of the multiplier could be very great in countries, such as developing ones, where the import coefficients differ substantially. Typically in a developing country the import coefficient of investment expenditure, for example, is very high, while the import coefficient of other expenditures might be much lower.

A study of Tsegaye (1981) of 14 developing countries (including Israel and South Africa) gives some interesting calculations, reported in Table 4.1. Section A gives values of the multiplier adopting the conventional approach of relating imports to income via the marginal propensity to import. Section C gives values for the multiplier depending on the initial injection of autonomous expenditure based on estimates of the import coefficients of the various components of expenditure derived from input–output tables, and shown in Section B. Let us take Peru as an example, where the estimated import coefficient of consumption is only 0.14, while the import coefficient of investment is 0.75. The conventional open economy income multiplier is 2.62, but the input–output approach shows that the income multiplier with respect to a change in investment is only 0.93, while for a change in consumption it is 3.19 – a big difference.

In the case of the United Kingdom, the difference made is not that great because different components of expenditure have roughly similar import coefficients. Turning to the 'Input-Output Tables for the United Kingdom (1984)' we find $\lambda_{ac} = \lambda_c = 0.25$, $\lambda_i = 0.26$, $\lambda_x = 0.14$, and that the import coefficient of total final expenditure (including public expenditure and expenditure on stocks) is 0.23. Using the traditional open economy multiplier with $c = 0.8$ and $m = 0.21$ gives an income multiplier of 2.44. Relating imports to expenditure the following multipliers are obtained:

$$\frac{\Delta Y}{\Delta \bar{C}} = 1.86; \quad \frac{\Delta Y}{\Delta \bar{I}} = 1.85; \quad \frac{\Delta Y}{\Delta \bar{X}} = 2.15$$

While the difference is not large between the traditional and the new results, or between the various expenditure multipliers, even an error of 0.2 in the assumed value of the multiplier could mean a vast absolute difference in the prediction of the change in income resulting from a forecast change in some item of expenditure. It can also be shown (Kennedy and Thirlwall, 1979a) that the new formulation of the multiplier is more stable than the conventional formulation with respect to variations in common parameter values. For purposes of

TABLE 4.1

The conventional and input-output multipliers compared

	Sri Lanka	Israel	Peru	Sudan	Panama	Trinidad and Tobago	Guyana	Indonesia	Jamaica	Malaysia	Brazil	Tanzania	Egypt	S. Africa
	1958	1959												
Section A: Conventional multiplier values														
c^{*}	0.93	0.81	0.85	0.66	0.80	0.83	0.70	0.78	0.80	0.68	0.84	0.88	0.97	0.71
$m^{\dagger}$	0.23	0.13	0.23	0.22	0.57	0.61	0.67	0.23	0.60	0.59	0.08	0.23	0.35	0.23
Multiplier value	3.33	3.13	2.63	1.79	1.30	1.28	1.03	2.27	1.25	1.10	4.17	2.86	2.63	1.92
Section B: Estimated import coefficients*														
λ_c	0.20	—	0.14	—	—	—	—	0.53	—	—	—	—	—	—
λ_{pc}	0.19	0.24	—	0.14	0.45	0.29	0.35	—	0.18	0.27	0.04	0.21	0.14	0.20
λ_{gc}	0.09	0.46	—	0.14	—	0.31	0.28	0.03	0.23	0.16	0.07	0.18	0.12	0.12
λ_i	0.20	0.41	0.75	0.61	0.12	0.22	0.27	0.37	0.21	0.42	0.12	0.33	PI=0.37 GI=0.11	0.35
$\lambda_{\Delta s}$	0.29	0.30	—	—	0.62	0.22	—	0.02	—	0.52	—	—	0.09	0.32
λ_x	0.07	0.18	0.05	—	—	0.22	0.28	0.04	0.17	0.20	0.03	0.10	0.07	0.16
λ	0.16	0.30	0.19	0.19	0.36	0.31	0.31	0.17	0.20	0.26	0.07	0.20	0.14	0.21
Section C: Input-output income multipliers with respect to autonomous expenditure of:														
Total consumption	—	2.29	3.19	—	—	—	—	0.75	—	—	—	—	—	—
Private consumption	3.24	2.00	—	2.00	0.98	1.73	1.20	1.54	2.41	1.46	5.05	2.63	5.05	1.86
Government consumption	3.64	1.42	—	2.00	—	1.68	1.33	1.00	2.26	1.68	4.89	2.73	5.18	2.05
Investment	3.20	1.55	0.93	0.91	1.57	1.90	1.35	1.00	2.32	1.16	4.53	2.23	PI=3.71 GI=5.24	1.51
Δ Stocks	2.84	1.84	—	—	—	—	—	1.56	—	0.96	—	—	5.35	1.58
Exports	3.72	2.16	3.52	—	0.68	1.90	1.33	1.52	2.44	1.60	5.11	3.00	5.47	1.95
Total final expenditure	2.96	1.84	3.00	1.88	1.45	1.68	1.28	1.32	2.35	1.48	4.89	2.67	5.06	1.84

* c = marginal propensity to consume.
† m = marginal propensity to import.
PI = private investment.
GI = government investment.
Source: Tsegaye (1981).

policy-making and prediction it is always better to work with a relation which is as stable as possible so as to minimise the effects of errors in the parameters.

THE 'NEW' OPEN ECONOMY MULTIPLIER WITH FOREIGN REPERCUSSIONS

Up to now we have considered the open economy multiplier without regard to the fact that countries are linked together by trade and that income changes in one country will affect income in other countries, which in turn will feed back on the country experiencing the initial income change. Consider a two-country model in which the exports of country a are the imports of country b, and the exports of country b are the imports of country a. The expressions for the equilibrium level of income, and the income multiplier, must be modified. We now have a household sector for both countries and a firm sector for both countries disaggregated into the production of consumption goods, investment goods and exports. The export function of both countries has two components: an autonomous component equivalent to the autonomous import term of the other country; and an 'induced' component related to expenditure in the other country. We will show that in the case of foreign repercussions, the multiplier with respect to an autonomous increase in exports is not the same as the multiplier with respect to an autonomous increase in investment. The model is as follows.[4] For country a:

$$Y_a = (1 - \lambda_{ca}) C_a + (1 - \lambda_{ia}) I_a + (1 - \lambda_{xa}) X_a - \bar{M}_a \tag{4.30}$$

$$C_a = \bar{C}_a + c_a Y_a \tag{4.31}$$

$$I_a = \bar{I}_a \tag{4.32}$$

$$X_a = \bar{X}_a + \lambda_{cb} C_b + \lambda_{ib} I_b + \lambda_{xb} X_b \tag{4.33}$$

For country b:

$$Y_b = (1 - \lambda_{cb}) C_b + (1 - \lambda_{ib}) I_b + (1 - \lambda_{xb}) X_b - \bar{M}_b \tag{4.34}$$

$$C_b = \bar{C}_b + c_b Y_b \tag{4.35}$$

$$I_b = \bar{I}_b \tag{4.36}$$

$$X_b = \bar{X}_b + \lambda_{ca} C_a + \lambda_{ia} I_a + \lambda_{xa} X_a \tag{4.37}$$

Rearranging equations (4.30) to (4.37), and solving simultaneously (by matrix methods), expressions for Y_a and Y_b can be obtained which incorporate the feedback effects from one country to another arising from the fact that the exports of one country are the imports of the other. Taking country a, the multiplier can then be derived with respect to any change in autonomous expenditure in the system. With respect to a change in investment in country a we obtain:

$$\frac{\Delta Y_a}{\Delta I_a} = \frac{(1 - \lambda_{ia}) - \dfrac{(\lambda_{xa} - \lambda_{ia})[\lambda_{xb} + c_b(\lambda_{cb} - \lambda_{xb})]}{1 - c_b(1 - \lambda_{cb})}}{1 - c_a(1 - \lambda_{ca}) - \dfrac{[\lambda_{xa} + c_a(\lambda_{ca} - \lambda_{xa})][\lambda_{xb} + c_b(\lambda_{cb} - \lambda_{xb})]}{1 - c_b(1 - \lambda_{cb})}} \tag{4.38}$$

This multiplier is extremely complex to interpret, but note that if the import coefficient of the different components of expenditure is the same, the result reduces to

$$\frac{\Delta Y_a}{\Delta I_a} = \frac{1 - \lambda_{ia}}{1 - c_a(1 - \lambda_{ca}) - \dfrac{\lambda_{xa}\lambda_{xb}}{1 - c_b(1 - \lambda_{cb})}} \tag{4.39}$$

This result differs from the earlier investment multiplier result without foreign repercussions (equation (4.19)) by an additional term in the denominator. Since all the coefficients that comprise the term lie between zero and unity, and the term has a negative sign attached, the effect of the additional term is to increase the value of the multiplier – as one would expect. The new multiplier with foreign repercussions may be compared with the conventional result using the marginal propensity to import, as (for example) in Brooman (1970), which is:

$$\frac{\Delta Y_a}{\Delta I_a} = \frac{1}{1 - c_a + m_a - \dfrac{m_a m_b}{1 - c_b + m_b}} \tag{4.40}$$

where m_a and m_b are the marginal propensities to import in the two countries. It can be readily shown that the conventional open economy multiplier result with foreign repercussions will only be equal to the new formulation if all components of autonomous expenditure have the same import coefficient, λ.[5]

The case of an autonomous increase in exports in country a will give a different multiplier result from that in equation (4.38), even if the import coefficient attached to autonomous exports is the same as that attached to autonomous investment. The reason is that an autonomous increase in a's exports means an autonomous increase in b's imports, i.e. $\Delta \bar{X}_a = \Delta \bar{M}_b$. This reduces b's income directly, and thus the feedback effects on a's exports and income will be less than in the case of an autonomous increase in investment in country a. Using the same system of equations as before, the change in income in country a with respect to a change in autonomous exports in a is

$$\frac{\Delta Y_a}{\Delta \bar{X}_a} = \frac{\partial Y_a}{\partial \bar{X}_a} + \frac{\partial Y_a}{\partial \bar{M}_b}$$

$$= \frac{(1 - \lambda_{xa}) - \dfrac{(1 - \lambda_{xa})\lambda_{cb}\, c_b}{1 - c_b(1 - \lambda_{cb})}}{1 - c_a(1 - \lambda_{ca}) - \dfrac{[\lambda_{xa} + c_a(\lambda_{ca} - \lambda_{xa})][\lambda_{xb} + c_b(\lambda_{cb} - \lambda_{xb})]}{1 - c_b(1 - \lambda_{cb})}}$$

$$(4.41)$$

Note again that if the import coefficient of different components of expenditure is the same, the result reduces to

$$\frac{\Delta Y_a}{\Delta \bar{X}_a} = \frac{\partial Y_a}{\partial \bar{X}_a} + \frac{\partial Y_a}{\partial \bar{M}_b} = \frac{(1 - \lambda_{xa}) - \dfrac{(1 - \lambda_{xa})\lambda_{cb}\, c_b}{1 - c_b(1 - \lambda_{cb})}}{1 - c_a(1 - \lambda_{ca}) - \dfrac{\lambda_{xa}\,\lambda_{xb}}{1 - c_b(1 - \lambda_{cb})}} \qquad (4.42)$$

This may be compared with the conventional result, as in Brooman (1970), of

$$\frac{\Delta Y_a}{\Delta \bar{X}_a} = \frac{1 - \dfrac{m_b}{1 - c_b + m_b}}{1 - c_a + m_a - \dfrac{m_b \, m_a}{1 - c_b + m_b}} \qquad (4.43)$$

Both the new and the conventional results give a lower value for the multiplier with respect to an autonomous change in exports than with respect to an autonomous change in investment, as predicted. There is now an additional negative term in the numerator. It is no longer true, however, that the conventional result will be equal to the new result even if all items of autonomous expenditure have the same import coefficient. Even under these restrictive assumptions equations (4.42) and (4.43) will differ by the term c_b in the second expression of the numerator of equation (4.42). Since $0 < c_b < 1$, the multiplier using the new formulation will be higher than that given by the conventional treatment of imports, as in Brooman (1970) for example. The reason is that as autonomous imports rise in country b, consumption in b falls less than income in b, and therefore the second- and subsequent-round effects on a's exports are less than they would be if b's imports and a's exports were linked to income in b rather than to expenditure in b. This is a new insight derived from the new multiplier formulation.

BALANCE-OF-PAYMENTS ADJUSTMENT

We conclude this chapter with an introductory discussion of different approaches to the theory of balance-of-payments adjustment, as a prelude to a fuller discussion of the different approaches in the chapters to follow. In the earlier discussion it was argued that under fixed exchange rates balance-of-payments difficulties may require internal price and income adjustments involving the sacrifice of domestic goals. Internal price and income adjustment is just one of several methods of adjustment to balance-of-payments disequilibrium. Exchange-rate variation is another possible adjustment mechanism. For a long time after the collapse of the international gold standard in 1931, economic analysis of the balance of payments was dominated by the so-called *elasticity* approach to balance-of-payments adjustment, with attention centred on the effect of exchange-rate changes and the price elasticities of demand for exports and imports in international trade. When Keynesian theory brought income analysis to the fore, models of balance-of-payments adjustment were developed incorporating both the price and income effects of changes in exchange rates. There was, however, a general dissatisfaction with the partial-equilibrium framework of the elasticity approach, and in response the absorption approach to balance-of-payments adjustment was developed, and this argued that movements in the balance of payments can only be understood in relation to how policies affect the total functioning of the economy – specifically how expenditure is affected relative to output. In recent years, although balance-of-payments policy in the United Kingdom and other countries has been dominated by exchange-rate changes, the professional literature has come to be dominated by the so-called 'monetary' approach to the balance of payments, which is essentially an extension of the absorption approach, stressing balance-of-payments deficits as a monetary phenomenon to be corrected by monetary means. After a brief survey of the different approaches to balance-of-payments adjustment, we shall look more closely at the elasticity approach, the absorption approach and the monetary approach in separate chapters. We shall be critical of the assumptions of the elasticity approach, and cast doubt on whether the monetary approach is useful for the study of balance-of-payments problems that originate in the real economy. We conclude that the absorption approach is probably the most useful and versatile. However, these approaches to balance-of-payments adjustment do not come to grips with permanently improving the balance of payments in a growing economy or raising permanently a country's balance-of-payments equilibrium growth rate, which is the fundamental problem facing the UK economy. The reason why these approaches do not cope with the fundamental problem is that they do not focus on the non-quantifiable adjustments in the real economy which are needed to raise the income elasticity of demand for exports in order to raise the rate of growth of exports. The approaches either stress price adjustment through exchange-rate changes or monetary adjustment, and these do not offer a solution to raising permanently the rate of growth of exports, unless they induce structural change and enable producers to break into fast-growing markets.

THE CLASSICAL PRICE-SPECIE FLOW MECHANISM

The classical price-specie flow mechanism describes the automatic adjustment that is supposed to have taken place as a result of payments imbalance under the gold standard. A key part of the mechanism is the assumed rise and fall of the price level according to whether the balance of payments is in surplus or deficit. A surplus would lead to the accumulation of gold and an expansion of the domestic money supply, causing prices to rise and the balance-of-payments surplus to be reduced. A deficit would lead to a loss of gold and a contraction of the domestic money supply, causing prices to fall and the balance-of-payments deficit to be improved. David Hume used this mechanism to refute the mercantilist belief that a country could achieve a persistent balance-of-trade surplus by the mercantilist policies of trade protection and export promotion.

The classical monetary theory assumed a system of fixed exchange rates, the rates being fixed by the gold points (as discussed in Chapter 1). The theory is the classical precursor of the new monetary theories of the balance of payments which analyse the balance of payments in terms of the relation between the supply of and demand for money. The classical approach to balance-of-payments adjustment contained no analysis, however, of the effect of exchange-rate changes as a substitute in a fixed-price world for flexible domestic prices, which was more relevant to the period after 1931 when the gold standard collapsed as a system of international payments.

THE ELASTICITY APPROACH

The elasticity approach to balance-of-payments adjustment was developed in the 1930s largely by Joan Robinson (1937) in response to the need for a theory of balance-of-payments adjustment under flexible exchange rates. The elasticity approach and the Keynesian multiplier extension of it are concerned with three questions: What are the conditions for currency depreciation (devaluation) to improve a country's balance of payments on current account? What will be the effect of currency depreciation on the level of domestic activity, and how will this affect the balance of payments and the conditions for depreciation to be successful? Finally, what will be the effect of devaluation on the terms of trade of the devaluing country?

The question of whether devaluation will rectify a balance-of-payments deficit is conducted within the framework of partial-equilibrium analysis focusing on the price elasticities of demand for exports and imports. At the simplest level the elasticity of supply of exports and imports is assumed infinite and income is held constant. Within this framework the so-called Marshall-Lerner condition for a successful devaluation can be derived, and it states that the sum of the price elasticities of demand for exports and imports (measured in a common currency) should exceed unity. Despite its shortcomings as a method of approach, and the unreal assumptions on which the analysis is based, those who defend the use of currency depreciation to rectify balance-of-payments deficits still cling strongly to favourable evidence relating to the price elasticities of demand for exports and imports in support of their case. We shall consider in detail in Chapter 5 the derivation of the Marshall–Lerner condition, the shortcomings of the elasticity approach, and the unfavourable effects that devaluation can have on the domestic economy, especially on the rate of inflation.

Devaluation not only alters the relative price of traded and non-traded goods, by making exports cheaper in foreign currency and imports dearer in domestic currency, but also raises income by a multiple of the net expansion of demand if devaluation switches demand from foreign to home-produced goods. Traditional elasticity analysis assumed no change in domestic income, or assumed that income was stabilised by the monetary authorities. Neither assumption was satisfactory. The immediate reaction in the light of Keynesian theory was to add a multiplier effect to the initial impact effect of the exchange-rate change. This does not alter the Marshall-Lerner condition for a successful devaluation, holding autonomous expenditure constant in money terms, but weakens the magnitude of the impact of the exchange-rate change. In Chapter 5 there is a more detailed discussion of this point.

Tagging the income effects of devaluation on to the elasticity approach, however, does not come to grips with the fundamental weakness of the elasticity approach, which is that it is partial-equilibrium analysis and confines attention to the effect of exchange-rate changes within the markets for exports and imports alone. But price changes in these two markets will have ripple effects throughout the economic system which will feed back to the export and import markets. The operation of the income multiplier will itself have relative price effects. Monetary effects are also ignored. It was increasingly recognised that the balance of payments is an aggregate phenomenon and that partial-equilibrium analysis is an inadequate framework for understanding aggregate phenomena in general. The response to this major worry was the development of the absorption approach to the balance of payments pioneered by Alexander (1952), but suggested earlier by Harrod (1947).

THE ABSORPTION APPROACH

Alexander's argument, and the essence of the absorption approach to the balance of payments, is that the most fruitful way to diagnose the balance of payments and to evaluate policies to rectify surpluses and deficits is to consider the relation between imports and exports and the functioning of the economy as a whole. In fact if the elasticities used by the elasticity approach are defined as total elasticities and not partial elasticities (because other things do not remain constant outside the foreign-trade sector when exchange rates change), this is what the elasticity approach also amounts to. The absorption approach views the balance of payments as the outcome of the difference between a country's expenditure and its income, and states that balance-of-payments policy will only improve the balance of payments if expenditure is reduced relative to income (or income is raised relative to expenditure). At the heart of the absorption approach is the accounting identity which we have already come across in Chapter 1, i.e. $B = X - M = Y - E$, where E is total domestic expenditure. Since the approach deals with an accounting identity, care must be exercised in deducing the *cause* of balance-of-payments deficits. Because a deficit must mean that expenditure exceeds income, this does not imply that the deficit is caused by decisions to spend in excess of income – as a result, for example, of excessive monetary expansion. The cause of the deficit may be the result of a gradual deterioration in the quality or relative price of exports, which would also show up in the accounts as expenditure in excess of income, but the cause would be a fall in output. A belief in the usefulness of the absorption approach to an understanding of balance-of-payments difficulties and for evaluating the efficacy of corrective policies does not imply a belief that balance-of-payments deficits are necessarily a monetary phenomenon caused by excessive monetary expansion, which is the argument propounded by Johnson (1958) in his elaboration of the absorption approach. The absorption approach, or rather his elaboration of it, is indeed the precursor of the monetary theories of the balance of payments and of the monetary approach to balance-of-payments adjustment.

THE MONETARY APPROACH

A clear statement of the monetary approach to the balance of payments is not easy because disciples of the approach do not all propound the same gospel. The essence of the approach would seem to be, however, that the balance of payments must be looked at as a whole (the current plus the capital account) and that international monetary movements must be considered as the outcome of stock disequilibrium between the supply of and demand for money within a country; an excess demand for money leading to an inflow of international reserves and a balance-of-payments surplus, and an excess supply of money leading to a loss of reserves and a balance-of-payments deficit. Thus, according to Johnson (1977b):

> the essential difference between the monetary approach and the other post-Keynesian approaches . . . is that the monetary approach formulates the problem of the balance of payments as a monetary phenomenon to be analysed with the tools of monetary theory, whereas the other approaches formulate it as a residual difference between real flows determined by other flows and real relative prices.

This leads Johnson (1977a) to assert:

> all balance of payments disequilibria are monetary in essence. So-called 'structural' deficits or surpluses simply cannot exist. . . . Similarly any assertion that real changes cause balance of payments deficits is correct only if the real change in question is accompanied by policies involving either the running down of reserves or borrowing on commercial terms.

These are challenging statements and will be scrutinised in Chapter 7. The policy implications that Johnson lists are then as follows. Since balance-of-payments deficits represent a monetary stock disequilibrium between the supply of and demand for money, balance-of-payments disequilibrium must inevitably be transitory because ultimately there must be self-correcting monetary consequences. If the natural adjustment processes cannot be allowed to work themselves out, there must be deliberate monetary contraction. Devaluation, tariff policy and other expenditure-switching policies are simply substitutes for monetary contraction and will improve the balance of payments only if they increase the demand for money, for example through a real-balance effect,[6] by raising the domestic price level. All balance-of-payments policies, it is argued, must be analysed in terms of their effect on reducing monetary disequilibrium. In this monetary framework the effect of devaluation does not depend directly on the elasticities of demand for exports and imports but on whether the price effects of devaluation produce a reduction in real expenditure relative to income by increasing the nominal demand for money. It also follows from the monetary approach that the effects of balance-of-payments policies, as well as balance-of-payments disequilibrium itself, must be transient in nature, unless stock disequilibrium is continually recreated by domestic credit changes.

5
The Elasticity Approach to the Balance of Payments

THE MARSHALL–LERNER CONDITION DERIVED

As indicated in the last chapter the elasticity approach to the analysis of balance-of-payments adjustment based on the Marshall–Lerner condition rests on several restrictive assumptions. First, the analysis is founded upon partial equilibrium in the sense that it considers only the effect of exchange-rate variations in the market for exports and imports, and everything else is held constant, so that the position of the demand curves for exports and imports themselves are held constant. In practice everything else will not remain constant. Exchange-rate changes will have price effects elsewhere in the system which will shift the demand curves for exports and imports. Income will also change, affecting the demand curves for exports and imports. A second restrictive assumption is that all relevant elasticities of supply of output are assumed to be infinite so that the price of exports in the home currency does not rise as demand increases, the price of foreign goods that compete with exports does not fall as demand for them falls, the price of imports in foreign currency does not fall as the demand for imports falls, and the price of domestic goods competing with imports does not rise as the demand for import substitutes increases. There are four elasticities of supply to consider: the elasticity of supply of exports; the elasticity of supply of foreign goods that compete with exports; the foreign elasticity of supply of imports; and the elasticity of supply of home goods that compete with imports. The basic Marshall–Lerner condition for a successful currency depreciation assumes all four supply elasticities to be infinite. The simple formula can be modified to incorporate the elasticity of supply of imports and exports, but the elasticity of supply of goods that compete with imports and exports is still assumed to be infinitely elastic. Third, the elasticity approach ignores the monetary effects of exchange-rate changes. Finally, it is assumed that trade is initially balanced and that the change in the exchange rate is a small one. The Marshall–Lerner condition is easily modified to cover the case where trade is initially unbalanced, but the small-change assumption is necessary so that second-order interaction terms arising from changes in multiplicative variables can be ignored.

On the above assumptions the Marshall–Lerner condition states that devaluation will improve the balance of payments on current account if

$$E_m + E_x > 1 \tag{5.1}$$

where E_m is the price elasticity of demand for imports, and E_x is the price elasticity of demand for exports.

The Marshall–Lerner condition can be derived in a number of ways, and with respect to measurement in foreign or domestic currency. Since the essence of a balance-of-payments problem is a shortage of foreign currency, it is more appropriate to conduct the analysis measuring exports and imports in units of foreign currency. If the focus of attention were on the impact of exchange-rate changes on domestic income and employment, it might be more appropriate to work with units of domestic currency. A simple formal proof of the Marshall–Lerner condition is as follows. Let

$$B = pX - M \tag{5.2}$$

where B is the balance of payments measured in foreign currency, X is exports measured in domestic currency, p is the exchange rate, i.e. the foreign price of a unit of domestic currency, and M is imports measured in foreign currency. Devaluation will improve the balance of payments if $dB/dp < 0$ that is, if a *fall* in the foreign price of domestic currency *raises* B. Differentiating equation (5.2) with respect to a change in p (i.e. taking a small change in the exchange rate):

$$\frac{dB}{dp} = X + p\,\frac{\partial X}{\partial p} - \frac{\partial M}{\partial p} = X\left(1 + \underbrace{\frac{p}{X} \times \frac{\partial X}{\partial p}}_{E_x} - \underbrace{\frac{\partial M}{\partial p} \times \frac{p}{M} \times \frac{M}{pX}}_{E_m}\right) \tag{5.3}$$

Now $-[(p/X) \times (\partial X/\partial p)]$ measures the price elasticity of demand for exports (E_x) assuming that the domestic price of exports remains unchanged. $E_x > 0$ if exports respond positively to a fall in the exchange rate. Similarly, $[(p/M) \times (\partial M/\partial p)]$ measures the price elasticity of demand for imports (E_m) assuming that the foreign price of imports remains the same. $E_m > 0$ if imports fall with a fall in the exchange rate. As long as trade is initially balanced with $M = pX$, we have, from (5.3).

$$\frac{dB}{dp} = X(1 - E_x - E_m) \qquad (5.4)$$

so that $dB/dp < 0$ if $E_x + E_m > 1$. In words, the balance of payments will improve with a fall in the exchange rate if the sum of the price elasticities of demand for imports and exports exceeds unity.

The result can be grasped intuitively by appreciating that if export volume were to rise proportionately with a reduction in the foreign price of exports $(E_x = 1)$, the balance of payments would remain unchanged, and any reduction in imports as a result of a higher domestic price of imports $(E_m > 0)$ would be sufficient to improve the balance of payments. Under the conditions of the theorem, any combination of export and import demand elasticities is sufficient provided their sum exceeds unity.

The Marshall–Lerner condition can also be illustrated diagrammatically. Take the two-country model of the United Kingdom and the United States used in Chapter 1. Figure 5.1 represents the supply of and demand for UK exports in relation to the dollar price of exports. The supply is assumed infinitely elastic, and the demand negatively related to the dollar price. Assume that trade is initially balanced at the prevailing exchange rate. Devaluation reduces the dollar price of exports from P to P_1, causing a shift in the supply curve from SS to S_1S_1 and a movement along the demand curve from A *to* B. The level of dollar receipts from exports before devaluation is $OPAQ$, after devaluation it is OP_1BQ_1. Whether the new level of foreign-exchange receipts is greater than the old depends on the price elasticity of demand for exports. If $E_x < 1$, receipts go down; if $E_x = 1$, receipts stay the same; and if $E_x > 1$, receipts increase.

Figure 5.2 represents the supply of and demand for UK imports. The supply is assumed infinitely elastic and the demand negatively related to the dollar price. Devaluation itself does not alter the dollar

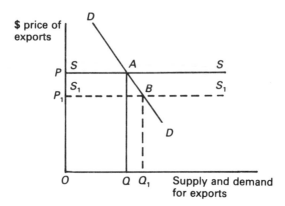

FIGURE 5.1

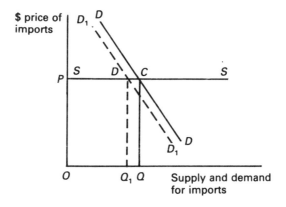

FIGURE 5.2

price of imports but will raise the sterling price. The effect of devaluation is thus to reduce the demand for imports at any given dollar price provided demand with respect to the sterling price is not totally inelastic. The demand curve shifts leftwards from DD to D_1D_1 and the quantity of imports demanded falls from Q to Q_1. Dollar expenditure on imports will fall from $OPCQ$ to $OPDQ_1$. The total change in foreign-exchange receipts depends on the behaviour of both exports and imports. If the demand for exports is totally inelastic, the demand for imports would have to be of at least unitary elasticity for the loss of foreign-exchange earnings from exports to be offset. At the other extreme, if the demand for imports is totally inelastic, the demand for exports would have to be of at least unitary elasticity to prevent foreign-exchange earnings from falling. Any combination of export and import elasticities in between is possible provided their sum exceeds unity.

The percentage improvement in foreign-currency receipts resulting from devaluation will be approximately equal to the sum of the percentage increase in the volume of exports plus the percentage decrease in the volume of imports minus the percentage decline in the foreign price of the domestic currency. This may be expressed as

$$\frac{\mathrm{d}p}{p} \left(\frac{\mathrm{d}X/X}{\mathrm{d}p/p} + \frac{\mathrm{d}M/M}{\mathrm{d}p/p} - 1 \right) 100 \tag{5.5}$$

For a small (1 per cent) devaluation of the exchange rate, the Marshall–Lerner condition for an improvement in foreign-exchange receipts is easily seen as $E_x + E_m - 1 > 0$, or $E_x + E_m > 1$.

If the balance of payments is not initially balanced, it is clear from equation (5.3) that the Marshall–Lerner condition must be modified. Measured in terms of foreign currency, the condition for a successful devaluation starting from imbalance is

$$E_x + E_m \left(\frac{M}{pX} \right) > 1 \tag{5.6}$$

Thus the larger the initial deficit $(M > pX)$, the less stringent is the elasticity condition for a successful devaluation.[1]

As indicated above, the Marshall–Lerner condition also hinges crucially on the assumption that four elasticities of supply are infinite. Robinson (1937) has incorporated the elasticity of supply of exports and imports into the Marshall–Lerner condition. The algebra is tedious and we will simply give the result. The condition for the balance of payments to improve, following a devaluation, is

$$(pX)\frac{S_x (E_x - 1)}{S_x + E_x} + (M)\frac{E_m (S_m + 1)}{E_m + S_m} > 0 \tag{5.7}$$

Equation (5.7) reduces to the Marshall–Lerner condition of $E_x + E_m > 1$ if $S_x = S_m = \infty$, and $pX = M$.[2] If the elasticity of supply of foreign goods that compete with domestic exports and the elasticity of supply of domestic goods that compete with imports are not infinite, the demand curves for imports and exports themselves will be affected, and this remains a limitation of the Marshall–Lerner condition along with other *ceteris paribus* assumptions. The importance of holding the supply and demand curves for foreign currency constant in deriving the elasticity conditions for a successful devaluation was shown in Figure 1.6 in Chapter 1.

In conditions when resources are unemployed, as (for example) in the 1930s when the elasticity approach was first formulated, it may not be unreasonable to assume that supply elasticities are infinite. In conditions close to full employment the assumption is much more questionable. Also, in conditions of unemployment devaluation will raise income in the devaluing country, which will then increase the demand for imports, and decrease the demand for exports if income falls in the non-devaluing countries. To incorporate income effects into the Marshall–Lerner condition it is necessary to make imports and exports not only a function of variations in the exchange rate but of income too. The incorporation of the income effects of depreciation does not alter the Marshall–Lerner condition for a successful devaluation, but it will lower the magnitude of the effect of depreciation on the balance of payments. To show this let:

$$Y = A + (1 - s)\, Y + B/p \tag{5.8}$$

where Y is money income; A is autonomous expenditure in money terms; B is the balance of payments measured in foreign currency and is converted into domestic currency by the exchange rate, p; and s is the marginal propensity to save. From equation (5.4) let:

$$dB = X(1 - E_x - E_m)\, dp - m(dYp) \tag{5.9}$$

where m is the marginal propensity to import in the devaluing country. Now assuming no change in the money value of autonomous expenditure ($dA = 0$), we have from equation (5.8): $dY = dB/sp$. Substituting this result into (5.9) gives:

$$dB = \frac{s}{s + m}\, X(1 - E_x - E_m)\, dp \tag{5.10}[3]$$

The sign condition for the price elasticities to improve the balance of payments is clearly not affected (the price elasticities must still sum to greater than unity), but since $s/(s + m)$ is a fraction, the magnitude of the change in dB will be smaller than if the expansionary effects are ignored. The Marshall–Lerner condition could not be more stringent (holding A constant) since if the income effects outweighed the 'elasticity' effects, so as to worsen the balance of payments, the depreciation of the currency could not be expansionary.

A seemingly contrary result has been derived by Harberger (1950) and Stern (1973), among others, which suggests that the income effects of devaluation alter the Marshall–Lerner condition, making it more stringent. The explanation is that these models hold real autonomous expenditure constant allowing autonomous expenditure in money terms to vary in response to devaluation, so that, in a two-country model, money expenditure rises in the devaluing country and falls in the non-devaluing country. This raises imports in the devaluing country and reduces the exports of the devaluing country to the non-devaluing country. Allowing for these effects, it can be shown (e.g. see Stern (1973)) that the condition for depreciation to improve the balance of payments (starting from equilibrium) becomes:

$$E_x + E_m > 1 + m_1 + m_2 \qquad (5.11)$$

where m_1 is the marginal propensity to import in the devaluing country and m_2 is the marginal propensity to import in the other country.

Thus while the traditional result derived by Robinson (1937) and Brown (1942) holds autonomous expenditure constant in money terms, the result above holds real expenditure constant and allows money expenditure to vary. It is not obvious which specification should be preferred *a priori*, or which is the most realistic. Presumably if the government wishes the devaluation to be as successful as possible it will try to prevent money expenditure from rising, in which case the traditional result would hold. On the other hand, if a successful devaluation is interpreted to mean a devaluation which improves the balance of payments without real income falling, the Harberger–Stern condition would have to be satisfied.

DEVALUATION AND THE RESPONSE OF FIRMS

What actually happens to the volume of exports and imports in practice as exchange rates change depends very much on the feasibility of a supply response to meet greater export demand and the demand for import substitutes, and how manufacturers respond to a change in the value of the currency with respect to the pricing of their products. For devaluation to increase exports, either the foreign price must be lowered or the home price raised to encourage firms to produce more for export given the increase in the profitability of exports. For devaluation to lower imports the sterling price of imports must be raised, or foreign supply discouraged. A number of factors, however, may prevent the adjustment of prices and may nullify the effectiveness of exchange-rate changes. The structure of the market in which firms operate may make it unwise to alter prices; for example, under oligopoly if firms are uncertain about rivals' reactions. Commodities may be subject to international price agreements and cartel arrangements. There are costs associated with altering prices; accounting costs and loss of goodwill. There may be fear by exporters that other countries will retaliate. Exports and imports may be traded on the basis of long-term contracts signed in terms of domestic currency. This is particularly likely to be true in the case of heavy capital goods, with the unfortunate side-effect that if there is the expectation by manufacturers of higher home costs as a result of devaluation, this will result in a much higher contract price for exports than would otherwise have been the case. According to many industrialists, devaluation reduces competitiveness on a continuous basis for a substantial proportion of UK exports.[4] Another factor to bear in mind is that exporters may invoice orders in the home currency leaving overseas agents to price the product in foreign currency. In this case, which is said to be the typical practice in UK industry, the gain to the firm in terms of profits or greater sales volume becomes very uncertain.

A survey in *The Banker* (September 1976) reported that 81 per cent of UK goods are denominated in sterling. If this is so, and the prices of goods are held constant in foreign currency, the retailers, wholesalers, importers and agents will share the profits from devaluation. This will have beneficial consequences if it encourages the stocking of UK goods but the supply response may be weaker than if the extra profit accrued to the firms themselves.

It is clear that there may be a clash between the national interest and the interests of the firm in the firm's reaction to a devaluation. If conditions are such that it is most profitable to keep the foreign price of the product the same and to raise the home price, this will not increase exports directly – only indirectly to the extent that the higher profitability of exports induces a greater export effort. The effort may not be forthcoming, however, if there are supply difficulties, with the domestic economy so buoyant that the profitability of home sales is still greater than the profitability of exports. In a study of UK firms by Gribbin (1971), it was found that prior to the 1967 devaluation of sterling, the profit rate on export sales was lower than on home sales for a significant proportion of firms in the sample, owing largely to tougher price competition in foreign markets. No relation was found, however, between differences in the rate of profit on home and export sales and the rate of growth of exports of firms.

Let us consider in more detail the theoretical expectation of the response of firms to devaluation in different market conditions, and then examine some of the empirical evidence. We shall draw largely on the work of Hague, Oakeshott and Strain (1974), based on the 1967 devaluation, and of Holmes (1978). Assume that firms attempt to maximise profits and that they export all their output to one market, and consider how a firm will set its export prices after a devaluation under the four different market structures of perfect competition, monopoly, monopolistic competition and oligopoly.

Under perfect competition there is no pricing decision for the firm to make. The demand curve facing the firm is perfectly elastic at the given world market price. The firm should raise the home price of the product by the full amount of the devaluation and increase the volume of exports to profit from the increase in the home price. According to the Marshall–Lerner condition incorporating supply elasticities (equation (5.7)), the greater the demand elasticity, the greater the supply elasticity should be for a successful devaluation.

Under a monopoly in the export market the pricing decision is complicated. In Figure 5.3 the curves labelled '1' represent the average and marginal revenue curves from exports before devaluation, and the curves labelled '2' represent the average and marginal revenue curves after devaluation. To simplify the analysis we assume constant average costs. Before devaluation the firm maximises export profits at X_1 at price P_1 (in home currency), where marginal revenue (MR_1) equals marginal cost (MC). Devaluation raises the home price of foreign currency, and therefore increases the home-price equivalent of each foreign price. With no increased foreign competition

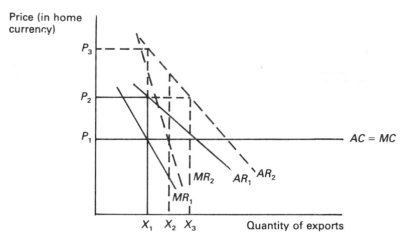

FIGURE 5.3

this shifts the average and marginal revenue curves upwards by the full amount of the devaluation to AR_2 and MR_2 respectively. The firm now has a choice: it could maximise profits with an export level of X_2, raising the home price from P_1 to P_2 which is not equal to the full amount of the devaluation; or it could keep the level of exports the same at X_1 and raise the home price by the full amount of the devaluation to P_3 (which would not maximise profits). Alternatively, it could keep price at P_1 and increase the quantity of exports to X_3 (which would not maximise profits either). If the monopolist is uncertain about demand conditions and believes that the demand curve facing him is very inelastic, he may well prefer to do nothing and stay at X_1 with a home price of P_3. The sacrifice of profits would be minimal. According to equation (5.7), the lower the demand elasticity, the lower the supply elasticity should be for a successful devaluation. Any export volume response should take the form of firms attempting to sell more at the same foreign currency price by improved design, marketing, delivery and so on.

Under monopolistic competition in the export market, with no increase in foreign competition, the choices facing firms will be the same as those in the case of the monopolist discussed above. How one firm reacts will largely depend on how other firms react. If one or two firms decide to increase exports, others might try to follow suit, and there may be a general price-cutting war. On the other hand, if the profitability of exports before devaluation was unsatisfactory, firms may decide to raise the home price of exports, though not by the full extent of the devaluation.

Under oligopoly, because of the strong interdependence between producers and the uncertainty among producers over how others will react if one firm alters price, foreign currency prices are likely to be sticky and oligopolists will take the benefit of devaluation in higher home prices, leaving output unchanged.

In none of the cases examined can we necessarily expect a strong quantity response to devaluation, and in some cases it would not be desirable. In most cases it would seem to pay firms to raise the home price of their exports and reap the benefits of devaluation in the form of a higher profit per unit of exports. This will only benefit the balance of payments to the extent that the desire of firms to export is increased and more can be sold without lowering the foreign price. Apparently, however, many firms regard the difference between the profitability of exports and home sales as a meaningless distinction. For most firms, production for one market supports production for the other, in the sense of helping to keep average costs of production down, and therefore the profitability of sectors is interdependent. The comparative profitability of exports is irrelevant to the export decision. This conclusion emerges strongly from a study by Hovell (1968) of 50 UK companies producing agricultural machinery, mechanical handling equipment and textile machinery.

As far as pricing is concerned, Hague, Oakeshott and Strain (1974) found in their study of nineteen firms following the 1967 UK devaluation that the majority of the firms contemplated only the two extreme policies of either no change in price or the full change equal to the percentage devaluation, when a compromise would probably have been optimal depending on the demand elasticity for the output and the capacity to supply. Most firms, however, appeared to be ignorant of the elasticity of the demand curve facing them and had little idea about competitors' reactions. In over one-half of the firms the same decision following devaluation was taken with respect to all export markets, regardless of differences between markets. Only two firms had worked out a plan of action in anticipation of devaluation and none seemed quite sure what the national interest required, whether to reduce foreign prices or to raise sterling prices. On the import side it appears that none of the firms practised import substitution as a result of the increase in the home price of imports mainly because of a lack of domestic substitutes and because import substitutes were also raised in price by home suppliers.

In another study of 29 firms in the electrical and mechanical engineering industries conducted by Rosendale (1973) at the National Institute of Economic and Social Research, 17 firms claimed that they benefited from the 1967 devaluation in terms of higher sales revenue for periods of one to three years, after which rising costs eliminated the advantage: 30 per cent of the 41 products distinguished were raised in price by the full amount of the devaluation (i.e. there was no direct volume response), and in 50 per cent of cases there was no rise in sterling prices.

A study by Holmes (1978) considers the behaviour of 54 large companies and their pricing behaviour following the 1967 devaluation and exchange depreciation since 1972. Many of the large exporters operate in oligopolistic markets, and his findings accord with our earlier theoretical prediction that where this is so foreign prices will not be cut for fear of retaliation. Supply constraints also militate against cutting foreign prices.

LAGS AND THE *J*-CURVE EFFECT

Even if a volume response is forthcoming, and the Marshall–Lerner condition is ultimately satisfied, there may be a long lapse of time before the quantities adjust sufficiently to offset the change in the price of foreign exchange, making the balance of payments worse before it gets better. As the balance of payments worsens, domestic policy and the achievement of other goals may be upset considerably. In the first place devaluation may not immediately affect the relative prices of traded and non-traded goods if foreign trade is subject to forward contracts. If export prices are fixed in sterling and imports in foreign currency, under contract for some months ahead, foreign-exchange receipts will suffer as a result of devaluation and the balance of payments will worsen. Once relative prices have changed (if they change) there will still be recognition lags, decision lags, delivery lags and production lags, all of which may produce in the short term a less than proportionate response in exports and imports to the fall in the value of the currency. Artus (1973) has calculated the average export delivery delays from three countries in the fourth quarter of 1971 to be: for machinery, 400 days for West Germany, 297 days for the United Kingdom, and 107 days for the United States; and for machine tools, 308 days for the United Kingdom and 217 days for the United States. In the work of Junz and Rhomberg (1973) exchange-rate changes only seem to affect export-market shares significantly after a lag of some three years. The experience of the

United Kingdom will be discussed more fully later in the empirical chapters. There is also the phenomenon of physical leads and lags (in addition to the monetary leads and lags discussed in Chapter 1). If devaluation is seen by traders as a prelude to further devaluation (or currency depreciation is seen as a prelude to further depreciation under a system of floating exchange rates), domestic importers will accelerate orders through fear of having to pay more for goods in the home currency later, while foreign importers delay their orders for the exports of the devaluing country in the hope of buying them more cheaply later in terms of their own currency. This will cause the volume effect from devaluation (at least in the short term) to be perverse, worsening the balance of payments.

The short-term worsening of the balance of payments resulting from devaluation for the reasons mentioned above is sometimes described as the *J*-curve effect since the plotting of the balance of payments against time traces out such a shape (see Figure 5.4).[5]

The time span that elapses before the perverse effects of devaluation are overcome could be quite long. There is not only the time taken for the balance of payments to register improvement to be taken into account (*A* to *B*) but also the time taken for the losses of devaluation between *A* and *B* to be recouped (*B* to *C*). Estimates for the United Kingdom by the Treasury suggest that the initial deterioration in the current account lasts about two quarters (*A* to *D*) and that the cumulative loss is eliminated within a year. Masera's study (1974) of the 1967 UK devaluation, discussed in more detail in Chapter 9, suggests about six to seven quarters for losses to be made good. But moving up the curve cannot be guaranteed. In the context of the elasticity approach to the balance of payments, the deficit will

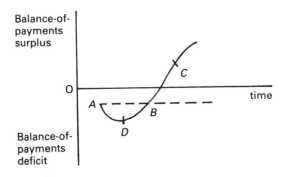

FIGURE 5.4

not improve if the Marshall–Lerner condition is not satisfied. It will not improve either if the rise in the home price of imports so affects the internal price level that the competitive advantage conferred by devaluation is completely offset or turned into a competitive disadvantage. There are a number of plausible models which predict that in the absence of strong counter-inflationary domestic policy the internal price level may rise by the full amount of the devaluation. The models which predict this outcome come from quite diverse schools of economic thought, from Keynesians on the one hand to international monetarists on the other. Two representative models of devaluation and inflation are considered below.

DEVALUATION AND INFLATION

The model to be developed first is an elaboration of a model presented by Wilson (1976) which starts by making the average price of final output equal to the sum of wage costs, profits and import costs per unit of output:

$$P = \frac{W + R + M}{Q} \tag{5.12}$$

where P is price, W is total wage costs, R is profit, M is total import costs and Q is output. Totally differentiating equation (5.12) and dividing by P gives

$$\frac{dP}{P} = \frac{d(W/Q)}{(W+R+M)/Q} + \frac{d(R/Q)}{(W+R+M)/Q} + \frac{d(M/Q)}{(W+R+M)/Q} \tag{5.13}$$

Now

$$\frac{W+R+M}{Q} = \frac{W}{Q} \times \frac{W+R+M}{W} = \frac{R}{Q} \times \frac{W+R+M}{R} = \frac{M}{Q} \times \frac{W+R+M}{M}$$

so that

$$\frac{dP}{P} = \frac{d(W/Q)}{W/Q} \times \frac{W}{W+R+M} + \frac{d(R/Q)}{R/Q} \times \frac{R}{W+R+M}$$

$$+ \frac{d(M/Q)}{M/Q} \times \frac{M}{W+R+M} \tag{5.14}$$

or

$$\frac{dP}{P} = \frac{dw}{w} \times \frac{W}{O} + \frac{dr}{r} \times \frac{R}{O} + \frac{dm}{m} \times \frac{M}{O} \qquad (5.15)$$

where dw/w is the rate of change of wage costs per unit of output, dr/r is the rate of change of profits per unit of output, dm/m is the rate of change of import costs per unit of output, and O is the money value of total output. Thus the domestic rate of inflation is equal to the weighted sum of the rates at which the different 'costs' of output rise, where the weights are the proportional shares of those costs in the money value of total output.

The initial effect of devaluation (which raises the home price of imports) is to raise internal prices by

$$\frac{dm}{m} \times \frac{M}{O} \qquad (5.16)$$

This is the first-round effect. The relationship between the magnitude of devaluation and the rise in import prices is discussed later. For the moment it is assumed to be equiproportional.

Now assume that wages chase prices upwards and that the profit margin is a fixed proportion of import costs and wages so that profits per unit of output remain unchanged. The second-round effect on prices is then

$$\frac{dw}{w} \left(\frac{W + R}{O} \right) = \frac{dm}{m} \times \frac{M}{O} \left(\frac{W + R}{O} \right) \qquad (5.17)$$

If wages then chase second-round price effects, the third-round effect on prices is

$$\left[\frac{dm}{m} \times \frac{M}{O} \left(\frac{W + R}{O} \right) \right] \left(\frac{W + R}{O} \right) \qquad (5.18)$$

and so on. The ultimate rate of increase in prices arising from the increase in import prices is

$$\frac{dP}{P} = \frac{dm}{m} \times \frac{M}{O} \left[1 + \frac{W + R}{O} + \left(\frac{W + R}{O} \right)^2 \cdots + \left(\frac{W + R}{O} \right)^n \right]$$

(5.19)

$$= \frac{dm}{m} \times \frac{M}{O} \left[\frac{1}{1 - (W + R)/O} \right]$$

(5.20)

$$= \frac{dm}{m} \times \frac{M}{O} \left[\frac{1}{M/O} \right]$$

(5.21)

Therefore

$$\frac{dP}{P} = \frac{dm}{m}$$

(5.22)

that is, the internal price level increases by the same amount as the rise in import prices.

Whether the internal price level rises in the same proportion as the devaluation itself depends on two factors: first, the extent to which import prices rise with respect to the devaluation; and second, on whether wage increases match price increases equiproportionately. The home price of imports will rise in the same proportion as the rise in the home price of foreign currency if (i) other countries do not alter their exchange rate, (ii) suppliers do not alter the foreign price of imports, and (iii) either the own price elasticity of demand for imports is zero or the own price elasticity of supply of imports is infinite. Thus

$$\frac{dm}{m} = K \left(\frac{dk}{k} + \frac{dP_f}{P_f} \right)$$

(5.23)

where k is the exchange rate expressed in home currency per unit of foreign currency, P_f is the foreign price, and $K = [1 - (e_m/s_m)]^{-1}$, where e_m is the own price elasticity of demand for imports and s_m is the own price elasticity of supply of imports, and $0 < K < 1$ (see Goldstein, 1974; and Branson, 1972). The relation between dm/m and dk/k is ultimately an empirical issue. To allow for the fact that the relation may not be equiproportional, let $dm/m = \lambda \, (dk/k)$ for substitution in equation (5.16).

Also, how much domestic prices change depends on the precise response of wages to prices. Ultimately this is also an empirical issue. To allow for the fact that the relation may not be equiproportional let $dw/w = \gamma [(dm/m) (M/O)]$ for substitution in equation (5.17). Using the substitutions for dm/m and dw/w in equations (5.16) and (5.17) and computing the price effects round by round gives the ultimate rate of increase in prices arising from devaluation of

$$\frac{dP}{P} = \lambda \frac{dk}{k} \times \frac{M}{O} \left\{ 1 + \gamma \left(\frac{W + R}{O} \right) + \left[\gamma \left(\frac{W + R}{O} \right) \right]^2 \cdots \right.$$

$$\left. + \left[\gamma \left(\frac{W + R}{O} \right) \right]^n \right\} \qquad (5.24)$$

Thus

$$\frac{dP}{P} = \lambda \frac{dk}{k} \times \frac{M}{O} \left[\frac{1}{1 - \gamma(1 - M/O)} \right] \qquad (5.25)$$

If $\lambda = \gamma = 1$, equation (5.25) reduces to equation (5.22). From the model more or less pessimistic conclusions can be drawn about the inflationary consequences of devaluation depending on the actual values attaching to λ and γ. As far as λ is concerned, there is no reason why import prices should rise more than the devaluation, so that $0 < \lambda \leqslant 1$. It is possible, however, that γ may be greater than unity, causing domestic prices to rise by more than in proportion to the devaluation. For example, suppose that wage-earners gear their wage demands not to the over-all increase in prices resulting from devaluation but to the price of food, which may rise by more because the proportion of total food imported is higher than the proportion of total output imported. In that case γ will be greater than unity and, depending on λ, values of γ not far above unity could make inflation 'explosive'. Inflationary expectations may also cause γ to exceed unity. Progressive taxation may also push γ above unity, since to protect net income against a rise in prices the demand for gross income has to be greater than the rise in prices. On the other hand, employers may not give in to wage demands, which will act as a moderating influence. Wages policy may also temporarily dampen wage claims, or the monetary authorities may refuse to finance excessive wage claims so that claims are moderated through the fear of unemployment.

The evidence for the United Kingdom following the 1967 devaluation, which raised the sterling price of the dollar by 16.7 per cent, is that import prices rose over all by between 13 and 14 per cent. Barker (1968) estimates a 13.9 per cent increase over all using an input–output framework, and the National Institute of Economic and Social Research (1972) estimated an over-all increase of 13.5 per cent. This would imply an estimate for λ of 0.8. Estimates of γ, in variously specified wage-price equations, generally centre around a value of between 0.7 and unity, rarely exceeding unity. If it is assumed that $\lambda = 0.8$ and $\gamma = 1$, prices would ultimately rise by 80 per cent of the devaluation. If γ is not equal to unity, it can be seen from equation (5.25) that the rate at which prices rise as a proportion of the devaluation will depend on import costs as a proportion of the value of output (M/O). Goldstein (1974) has attempted to estimate empirically the effect of exchange-rate changes on aggregate wage and price behaviour in the United Kingdom using a simple two-equation model which incorporates the relationships outlined in the model above, namely: the effect of a change in import prices on domestic prices (assuming that import prices rise by the full amount of the devaluation, $\lambda = 1$); the effect of prices on wages; and the effect of wages on prices. The two-equation model is

$$\frac{\mathrm{d}w}{w} = a_0 + a_1\, U + a_2 \frac{\mathrm{d}P}{P} \tag{5.26}$$

and

$$\frac{\mathrm{d}P}{P} = b_0 + b_1 \frac{\mathrm{d}w}{w} + b_2\, Q + b_3 \frac{\mathrm{d}m}{m} \tag{5.27}$$

where U is the percentage level of unemployment, Q is productivity growth, and the other variables are as defined above. The relationship between the change in import prices and the rate of inflation is given by

$$\frac{\partial\, (\mathrm{d}P/P)}{\partial\, (\mathrm{d}m/m)} = \frac{b_3}{1 - a_2 b_1} \tag{5.28}$$

In our model elaborated above b_3 is constrained to the value of the ratio M/O (see equation (5.16)), and b_1 is constrained to the value of

$(W + R)/O$ (see equation (5.17)), so that $b_1 + b_3 = 1$. The relationship between dP/P and dm/m then depends on a_2. If $a_2 = 1$, $dP/P = dm/m$, and the increase in prices is equal to the devaluation. If $a_2 < 1$, prices rise less than the devaluation; and if $a_2 > 1$, inflation is possibly explosive. In Goldstein's empirically estimated model for the period 1954–71 using quarterly data the estimates for the post-devaluation period are $b_3 = 0.19$, $b_1 = 0.76$, and $a_2 = 0.56$. Substituting these values into equation (5.28) gives the result that prices rise by only 33 per cent of the rise in import prices, and by a lesser percentage of the devaluation if import prices do not rise by the full amount of the devaluation. These estimates appear to be very much on the low side owing to the low estimate of a_2. In recent years, at least, a_2 has been close to unity.

Harrod (1967b) has described devaluation as the most potent known instrument of domestic price inflation which has such sorry effects on human misery; and it has long been recognised that the inflationary effects of exchange-rate depreciation may counteract any relative price advantage conferred. Meade (1951) in his early pioneering work recognised that 'it would be useless to turn to the mechanism of variable exchange rates [to rectify imbalance] unless there were sufficient flexibility of real wage rates'; in other words devaluation will be ineffective if wages chase prices upwards. Henderson (1949) also expressed fears that all devaluation might do would be to promote internal inflation. Even Friedman (1953), a leading advocate of floating exchange rates, has conceded that the inflationary repercussions of exchange depreciation may be an objection to floating exchange rates in a particular country at a particular time.

The international monetarist school of economists in the United Kingdom, based originally at the London Business School, is also sceptical of exchange-rate adjustment. It argues that exchange depreciation is irrelevant to balance-of-payments adjustment not only because balance-of-payments deficits and policies must necessarily be transient, as in the monetary approach to the balance of payments (see Chapter 7), but also because domestic prices will ultimately rise by the extent of the devaluation. Ball, Burns and Laury (1977) of the London Business School develop three models, each of which predicts that, with free collective bargaining, wages and prices are likely to rise eventually by the full extent of the devaluation. They are wholly sceptical of the elasticity approach, at least as far as imports are concerned. The authors say:

we have been unable for a number of years to establish any significant relationship between relative prices and the demand for imported goods in the UK. Any effect on the import of goods resulting from changes in the exchange rate affect the level of imports only through their expenditure reducing effects – there are no substitution effects.

Their first model is the same as the model empirically tested by Goldstein using equations (5.26) and (5.27). Their second model is structurally the same as the first model, except that the GDP deflator rather than consumer prices enters the wage equation with a co-efficient of unity, and the GDP deflator is a weighted average of changes in unit labour costs and world prices. Their third model is often referred to as the 'Scandinavian' model of inflation where the price of traded goods adjusts to the level of world prices, and wages in both the traded- and non-traded-goods sectors adjust to the traded-goods price level, so that any change in exchange rates will ultimately increase the domestic price level by an equivalent amount. The model is as follows. First, let

$$\frac{dP}{P} = \lambda_1 \frac{dP_T}{P_T} + (1 - \lambda_1) \frac{dP_{NT}}{P_{NT}} \tag{5.29}$$

where P_T is the price of traded goods, P_{NT} is the price of non-traded goods, and λ_1 is the share of traded output in total output. Second

$$\frac{dP_T}{P_T} = \frac{dP_w/P_w}{k} \tag{5.30}$$

where P_w is the world price level, and k is the exchange rate (i.e. the home currency price of foreign currencies). Third

$$\frac{dP_{NT}}{P_{NT}} = \frac{dw_{NT}}{w_{NT}} - \frac{dQ_{NT}}{Q_{NT}} \tag{5.31}$$

where w_{NT} is wages in the non-traded-goods sector, and Q_{NT} is productivity in the non-traded-goods sector. Assume

$$\frac{dw_{NT}}{w_{NT}} = \frac{dw_T}{w_T} = \frac{dP_T}{P_T} + \frac{dQ_T}{Q_T} \tag{5.32}$$

Substituting (5.32) into (5.31) and the result into (5.29) gives:

$$\frac{\mathrm{d}P}{P} = \lambda_1 \frac{\mathrm{d}P_T}{P_T} + (1-\lambda_1)\left[\frac{\mathrm{d}P_T}{P_T} + \left\{\frac{\mathrm{d}Q_T}{Q_T} - \frac{\mathrm{d}Q_{NT}}{Q_{NT}}\right\}\right] \text{(5.33)}$$

Remembering that $\mathrm{d}P_T/P_T = (\mathrm{d}P_w/P_w)k$, the model says that the rate of price increase will be equal to the rate of increase in the world price index measured in local currency plus a proportion $(1 - \lambda_1)$ of the gap between productivity growth in the traded- and non-traded-goods sectors. The influence of world prices is dominant and any fall in the exchange rate will ultimately increase the domestic price level by an equal amount (unless productivity growth in the non-traded-goods sector is markedly higher than in the traded-goods sector).

Payments Imbalances in the World Economy

A combination of *J*-curve effects and domestic inflation induced by currency depreciation is probably one of the major explanations why payments imbalances have continued to persist in the world economy despite the massive nominal exchange rate realignments that have taken place since fixed exchanges rates were abandoned in 1972. For the early years 1972 to 1977, both Triffin (1978) and Kaldor (1978) have shown how countries' balance-of-payments surpluses and deficits remained largely impervious to exchange rate changes, and even moved perversely. Table 5.1 gives evidence for 10 industrialised countries. The five surplus countries of Japan, Switzerland, Germany, the Netherlands and Belgium and Luxembourg increased their joint surplus by $8 billion from 1972 to 1977 while their exchange rates appreciated on average against the dollar and other currencies by approximately 50 per cent. In the five deficit countries of the US, Canada, UK, Italy and France, their joint deficits increased by $16.7 billion, while their exchange rates depreciated on average by approximately 25 per cent. Japan's surplus nearly doubled with an effective appreciation of 28 per cent, and the German surplus rose sevenfold with an effective appreciation of 43 per cent. The US deficit doubled with an effective depreciation of 13 per cent.

The experience since 1977 has been little different, and is shown in Table 5.2. The German and Japanese surpluses have continued to grow, despite, in the latter case, a substantial appreciation of the Japanese yen. The US deficit has continued to grow by alarming proportions, and the UK has moved into substantial deficit. In these

TABLE 5.1

The unchanging pattern of major OECD countries' surpluses and deficits on current account, 1972–8 (in billions of dollars)

	Exchange-rate changes*		Surpluses and deficits				
	Vis-à-vis the $	Effective rates	1972	1973	1974–6 Average	1977	1978 Forecast
Surplus							
countries			10.2	8.0	9.8	18.2	28.8
Japan	+35	+28	6.6	−0.1	−0.6	11.0	17.5
Switzerland	+83	+62	0.2	0.3	2.1	3.7	4.8
Germany	+58	+43	0.8	4.3	5.8	3.8	5.0
Netherlands	+48	+22	1.3	2.4	2.2	0.2	1.5
Belgium-							
Luxembourg	+40	+12	1.4	1.2	0.3	−0.5	0
Deficit countries			−8.0	−5.9	−12.7	−24.7	−24.3
United States	—	−13	−9.9	−0.4	−2.6	−20.2	−25.0
Canada	+ 1	− 2	−0.7	0	−3.3	−3.9	−3.5
United							
Kingdom	−27	−37	0.3	−2.2	−4.4	0.3	1.8
Italy	−29	−41	2.0	−2.7	−3.5	2.3	3.3
France	+13	− 1	0.3	−0.7	−4.1	−3.2	−0.8

Sources: Exchange rates: *International Financial Statistics*, lines ah x and am x of country tables. Surpluses or deficits on current account: OECD, *Economic Prospects*, July 1978.
* Percentage appreciation (+) or depreciation (−) of dollar rates and of effective multilateral exchange rates from May 1970 to 1977.

Source: R. Triffin, *Gold and Dollar Crisis: Yesterday and Tomorrow*, Essays in International Finance No. 132, Princeton University, December, 1978.

TABLE 5.2

The current balance of payments and changes in nominal exchange rates in major industrial countries

	Current balance $ billion		Changes in exchange rates 1978–89	
	1978	1989	Against $	Effective rates
US	− 15	− 106		+ 8%
Japan	+ 17	+ 57	+ 68%	+ 20%
France	+ 7	− 4	− 35%	− 10%
Germany	+ 9	+ 56	0	+ 9%
Italy	+ 2	− 11	− 40%	+ 10%
UK	+ 1	− 34	− 22%	+ 23%

cases, there has been some appreciation of the effective exchange rate, although in the UK case there has also been a substantial depreciation against the dollar. France's position worsened despite substantial currency depreciation. It remains an open question, of course, whether the 'perverse' movements would have been even larger in the absence of exchange rate changes.

Even if demand elasticities sum to greater than unity, currency depreciation may still not be effective, even if a nominal depreciation brings about a real depreciation. Outside the confines of the partial equilibrium framework adopted by the elasticities approach, supply elasticities matter both in themselves (see earlier in the chapter) and as determinants of the terms of trade (see below). What happens to expenditure (or absorption) as the terms of trade change also matters. For example, if the terms of trade decline, and if expenditure does not fall by as much as real income, the balance of payments will worsen. Whether real income is allowed to fall or not as currency depreciation takes place is also of importance. We have already shown (see equation (5.11)) that if money expenditure is increased to keep the level of real income the same (and money expenditure is reduced in the appreciating countries to keep real income unchanged) the elasticity condition for depreciation to be successful becomes $1 + m_1 + m_2$, where m_1 is the marginal propensity to import of the depreciating country and m_2 is the marginal propensity to import of the other countries. Taking a depreciation against the world as a whole, the sum of m_1 and m_2 could be quite large – of the order of 0.6. This makes the Marshall–Lerner condition much more stringent, if a successful devaluation is interpreted as one that improves the balance of payments without real income being reduced.

DEVALUATION AND THE TERMS OF TRADE

The elasticity approach to balance-of-payments adjustment has also traditionally been concerned with the effects of devaluation on the barter terms of trade.[6] The effect that devaluation has on the terms of trade is also important for other theoretical approaches to balance-of-payments adjustment, particularly the absorption approach. The matter can be considered quite briefly because no *a priori* prediction can be given as to whether the terms of trade will deteriorate or improve. It was originally assumed that the terms of trade would change in the same direction and to the same extent as the devaluation. But this argument ignores the income, and hence expenditure, effects of devaluation, which will be partly a function of the price elasticities of demand. It can be shown (e.g. Stern, 1973) that the barter terms of trade will worsen or improve with a devaluation depending on whether the product of the elasticities of supply of exports and imports $(S_x S_m)$ is greater or less than the product of the elasticity of demand for exports and imports $(E_x E_m)$. If $S_x S_m > E_x E_m$ the terms of trade will worsen and if $S_x S_m < E_x E_m$ the terms of trade will improve. It was originally argued that because a country is more specialised in exports than imports, and given conditions of unemployment in which the elasticity of supply of exports is likely to be high, the terms of trade are likely to deteriorate. In practice the relevant elasticities will vary from country to country, and from circumstance to circumstance, and no generalisation can be made.

It is also relevant to mention that if the interest is in how devaluation affects real income through a terms-of-trade effect, it is not the barter terms of trade which are important but the single factoral terms of trade. This is equal to the net barter terms of trade adjusted for changes in the productivity of resources employed in the export sector in order to measure the total change in import-buying power. This question is considered more fully in the next chapter on the absorption approach to the balance of payments.

THE DIFFICULTIES OF MEASURING PRICE ELASTICITIES

No discussion of the elasticity approach to devaluation would be complete without mentioning the practical difficulties of measuring the price elasticity of demand for exports and imports on which the Marshall-Lerner condition depends so heavily. The difficulties are numerous. Orcutt (1950) has enumerated systematically the sources of bias that can creep into the estimation of price elasticities of demand. Orcutt orientated his argument towards those factors that may bias empirical estimates of demand elasticities downwards, mainly in an attempt to counter the elasticity pessimism prevalent at the time. Some of the points he makes are valid econometric ones. In the case of some of the factors the bias could go either way. In other cases subsequent analysis and research suggest that the point may not be an important one. Some other factors not mentioned by Orcutt may bias the measurement of price elasticities upwards.

Orcutt lists five factors biasing downwards empirically estimated price elasticities of demand for internationally traded goods: simul-

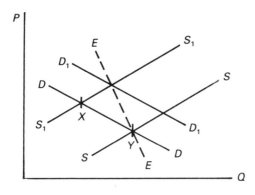

FIGURE 5.5

taneous-equation bias; aggregation bias; bias due to random observation errors in the price indices; short-run elasticities less than long-run elasticities; and elasticities lower for small price changes than for large ones. Let us consider these factors in turn.

The possibility of simultaneous-equation bias arises, as in all supply and demand analysis, because demand depends on price and price depends on quantity demanded if supply curves are less than perfectly elastic. Consider Figure 5.5. If the demand and supply curves shift together, the observed PQ points will lie on the dashed line EE, which, if interpreted as a demand curve, would in this example give a much lower price elasticity of demand than that given by the shape of the true demand curve DD. The problem referred to here would not arise if the price of imports (or exports) could be regarded as predetermined rather than endogenous. This could be assumed for a small country, which would then be a price-taker in world markets, or if the supply is perfectly elastic, in which case a shift in demand could not influence price and there would be no simultaneous-equation bias. Another approach which enables price to be treated as predetermined is to assume that the system is recursive so that cause and effect are assumed not to occur simultaneously. If price cannot be considered predetermined, the problem of simultaneous-equation bias can be minimised by making sure in the estimation procedure that it is the demand curve that is being estimated, and that no supply response to price is being picked up through shifts in demand. The way to do this is to consider explicitly all possible factors affecting demand so that the demand curve can be considered fixed. Then if there have been shifts in supply caused by factors other than those that shift demand, it can be assumed that the estimated *PQ* relationship is a demand relationship. In Figure 5.5, if *DD* is held constant, the shift in supply from *SS* to S_1S_1, which causes price to rise from *Y* to *X*, will trace out the true demand curve. Simultaneous-equation estimation techniques can also be used to minimise bias. When these are used the estimated elasticities are not significantly higher than those obtained by cruder estimation procedures. It is now generally conceded that downward simultaneous-equation bias is much less than first suspected, probably because no country is so big relative to world demand for world price to be affected by its demand.

Aggregation bias refers to the fact that there tends to be a correlation in practice between the price elasticity of goods and the observed range of price variation. This means that those goods which are elastic have a smaller impact on the aggregate price index than the importance of the imports warrants, and the elasticity estimates using aggregate data will be unduly influenced by goods with a low price elasticity. The aggregate estimate will tend to be biased downwards. A 'true' aggregate price elasticity incorporating all the disaggregated information, and which when multiplied by the aggregate price change gives an estimate of the total quantity change free of aggregation bias, is (see Magee, 1974)

$$e_p = \sum_i e_{pi} \ (m_i/M) \ \frac{\mathrm{d}P_i/P_i}{\mathrm{d}P/P} \tag{5.34}$$

where e_p is the aggregate price elasticity, e_{pi} is the individual product price elasticity, m_i/M is the share of product demand in total demand, *P* is the aggregate price level, and P_i is the individual product price.

Equation (5.34) can be derived in the following way. Take the case of imports. From a typical aggregate import demand function we can write:

$$\frac{\mathrm{d}M}{M} = e_y \frac{\mathrm{d}Y}{Y} + e_p \frac{\mathrm{d}P}{P} \tag{5.35}$$

where *M* is aggregate imports, *Y* is aggregate income, and e_y is the income elasticity of demand for imports. From the disaggregated import demand functions we have:

$$\frac{dM}{M} = \sum_i \frac{dm_i}{m_i} = \sum_i e_{yi} \left(\frac{dy_i}{y_i} \right) \left(\frac{m_i}{M} \right) + \sum_i e_{pi} \left(\frac{dP_i}{P_i} \right) \left(\frac{m_i}{M} \right) \quad (5.36)$$

For equation (5.35) to be compatible with equation (5.36) we must have:

$$e_y \left(\frac{dY}{Y} \right) = \sum_i e_{yi} \left(\frac{dy_i}{y_i} \right) \left(\frac{m_i}{M} \right) \quad (5.37)$$

and

$$e_p \left(\frac{dP}{P} \right) = \sum e_{pi} \left(\frac{dP_i}{P_i} \right) \left(\frac{m_i}{M} \right) \quad (5.38)$$

From equation (5.38) the aggregate price elasticity consistent with the disaggregated data is

$$e_p = \sum_i e_{pi} \ (m_i/M) \ \frac{dP_i/P_i}{dP/P} \quad (5.39)$$

which is equation (5.34). e_p is the weighted sum of the individual price elasticities only if $(dP_i/P_i)/(dP/P) = 1$ for all i, or if e_{pi} and $(dP_i/P_i)/(dP/P)$ are not correlated. If they are negatively correlated, as Orcutt suggests, the aggregate elasticity estimate will be biased downwards. Opinions differ as to the likely strength of this correlation. The problem can, of course, be avoided by analysing the elasticity of individual commodities separately and taking a weighted average. The difference between this result and the aggregate result would be one test of bias. Prais (1962) disaggregated US imports into five major commodity groups and estimated the appropriate parameters. The weighted average of the separately estimated elasticities was 1.6, exactly equal to the estimate using aggregate price and quantity data, suggesting no aggregation bias. Ball and Marwah (1962), in their study of US imports, also concluded the same. On the other hand, Barker (1970b) finds for the United Kingdom that relative price effects measured in an aggregate import demand function are both much smaller and less significant than those measured using disaggregated data. For the period 1955 to 1966 the directly estimated aggregate price elasticity of demand for imports is approximately -0.1. The aggregate estimate derived from a weighted average of disaggregated (five groupings) data is close to -0.7. Barker also makes the point that in analysing the effects of devaluation, pre-devaluation estimates of elasticities from aggregate data cannot be relied upon to hold in the post-devaluation periods because devaluation will alter the values of $(dP_i/P_i)/(dP/P)$. Import shares (m_i/M) may also alter.

On the question of observation errors as a source of bias, it is true that observation errors in the price series will bias the price elasticity towards zero, but only if the errors in the quantity variable are uncorrelated with the price (and income) variables. If the errors in the quantity variable are negatively correlated with the price variable (which they might be if the quantity variable has been obtained by dividing a value series by the price series subject to random errors), the estimated demand elasticity will exceed the actual elasticity in absolute value if the estimate is less than unity.

Short-run elasticity estimates may be lower than long-run elasticities, but this is hardly a 'source of bias'. Long-run estimates can be made.

Elasticity estimates for small price changes may be lower than for large price changes because there are economic and psychological costs in commodity substitution, and because the perception of price changes is more apparent in the case of large changes. However, evidence gathered by Goldstein and Kahn (1976) for twelve countries over the period 1955–73 does not support the hypothesis.

In response to Orcutt's five points, therefore, it can be concluded that while biases may exist in the aggregate price-elasticity estimates, they may go either way depending on the data used and on the equation specification. There is also an additional important factor which may give an upward bias, and that is the operation of non-price factors. If markets are cleared, as many are, by non-price factors which are correlated with prices, but these other variables are not included in the estimating equations, the price variable will pick up these effects and make the elasticity of demand with respect to price look greater than it is.

Finally, we make the point (stressed in Chapter 1) that the elasticity of demand for imports that have domestic substitutes is a weighted average of the domestic demand and supply elasticities of the commodity in question. If the domestic supply elasticity of the commodity varies, so will the elasticity of demand for imports. This is really the starting-point of the absorption approach to the balance of payments which argues that the response of the balance of payments to price changes depends on supply as well as on demand, and more broadly on the functioning of the total economy.

6
The Absorption Approach to the Balance of Payments

The weaknesses of the elasticity approach to balance-of-payments adjustment can be summed up by saying that it is partial-equilibrium analysis; it ignores supply conditions and cost changes as a result of devaluation; and it tends to neglect the income and expenditure effects of exchange-rate changes. At the very least the elasticities used by the approach ought to be total elasticities, not partial elasticities. But taking the total elasticities of exports and imports is tantamount to examining the relation between the balance of payments and the functioning of the economy as a whole. This insight is the starting-point of the absorption approach to the balance of payments which was originally developed by Alexander (1952) and subsequently elaborated on by Johnson (1958), though, arguably, with misleading conclusions.[1]

The absorption approach consists of regarding the balance of payments not simply as the excess of residents' receipts from foreigners over residents' payments to foreigners but rather as the excess of residents' *total* receipts over *total* payments. Formally

$$B = R_F - P_F \qquad (6.1)$$

where R_F is receipts by residents from foreigners, and P_F is payments by residents to foreigners. Since, however, all payments by residents to residents (P_R) are simultaneously receipts by residents from residents (R_R), B can be written as

$$B = R_F + R_R - P_F - P_R \qquad (6.2)$$

Hence

$$B = R - P \tag{6.3}$$

where R is total receipts by residents, and P is total payments by residents.

The absorption approach can either be applied to the balance of payments as a whole or to the balance of payments on current account. In the latter case the balance of payments is the difference between national income and national expenditure. Taking the national income equation $Y = C + I + X - M$, and labelling total expenditure A (for absorption), we have

$$B = X - M = Y - A \tag{6.4}$$

The balance of payments on current account is the difference between national output (income) and national expenditure. Within this framework any policy for balance-of-payments correction can be evaluated in terms of whether it raises Y relative to A, because this is the condition for balance-of-payments improvement. Since from the income equation, $Y - C$ equals saving (S), the balance of payments can also be expressed as

$$B = X - M = S - I \tag{6.5}$$

and any balance-of-payments correction policy can also be evaluated in terms of whether it raises saving relative to investment.

Policies to raise Y are termed *expenditure-switching* policies and must not be accompanied by an equal rise in A if the balance of payments is to improve. Devaluation, tariffs, quotas on imports, subsidies to exports, and price and quantity adjustments of all kinds to increase exports and reduce imports are all examples of expenditure-switching policies. At full employment, when Y cannot increase, expenditure-switching must be accompanied by reductions in A if the balance of payments is to improve.[2] Otherwise there would be no resources to devote to meeting the increased demand for exports and import substitutes. Reducing A by itself, of course, would cause unemployment. Policies to reduce A are called *expenditure-reducing* and must not be accompanied by an equivalent fall in Y if the balance of payments is to improve. Expenditure-reducing policies accompanying expenditure-switching policies at full employment must reduce expenditure on traded goods, otherwise expenditure-switching will not be successful. All the factors on which the success of a devaluation depends can be analysed within the framework of the absorption approach without the need for elasticity estimates and *ceteris paribus* assumptions.

Let us now consider in greater detail the effect of a devaluation within the framework of the absorption approach. Since $B = Y - A$, $\Delta B = \Delta Y - \Delta A$. First, devaluation will have a direct effect on income (ΔY_D). It will also have a direct effect on absorption (ΔA_D) plus an indirect effect through the change in income (i.e. $\alpha \Delta Y_D$, where α is the propensity to absorb).[3] Thus

$$\Delta B = \Delta Y_D - \Delta A_D - \alpha \Delta Y_d \tag{6.6}$$

$$= \Delta Y_D (1 - \alpha) - \Delta A_D \tag{6.7}$$

The condition for devaluation to improve the balance of payments is

$$\Delta Y_D (1 - \alpha) > \Delta A_D \tag{6.8}$$

There are thus two relations to consider: first, the direct effect of devaluation on income and the value of α; and second, the direct effect of devaluation on absorption.

THE DIRECT EFFECT OF DEVALUATION ON INCOME

There are at least three important direct effects of devaluation on income: an idle resource effect; a terms-of-trade effect; and a resource-reallocation effect. If there are idle resources, the effect of devaluation will be to increase real income as demand is switched to home-produced goods. How much income increases will depend on the degree of import substitution, the propensity of other countries to import, and the value of the foreign-trade multiplier. The idle resource effect on income will improve the balance of payments, however, only if $\alpha < 1$. If the propensity to absorb is greater than unity, the balance of payments will worsen. The propensity to absorb comprises mainly the sum of the propensities to consume and to invest as income changes. If the propensity to consume is high, a positive propensity to invest could cause α to exceed unity. Alexander seemed to be of this view.

The effect of devaluation on the terms of trade can go either way. As we saw in Chapter 5, the terms of trade will improve or deteriorate in the devaluing country according to whether the product of the elasticity of supply of exports and imports is less than or greater than the product of the two elasticities of demand. If the terms of trade improve, the effect on income and the balance of payments will depend on the same factors as a positive idle resource effect. If the terms of trade deteriorate, real income will fall and the balance of payments will worsen if $\alpha < 1$, but improve if $\alpha > 1$. It is clearly fallacious to argue, as under the elasticity approach, that a decline in the terms of trade will necessarily improve the balance of payments if the Marshall-Lerner condition is satisfied, since income may fall by more than absorption. The real-income change is not confined to the change in the buying power of exports over imports. What happens to productivity in the export sector is also important. This is the notion of the single factoral terms of trade. The net barter terms of trade may deteriorate, but real income may rise because of an increase in productivity in the export sector.

Machlup (1956) also points out that there are substitution effects as well as income effects as the terms of trade alter. These are price-induced changes in absorption which are not included in α. They must be considered alongside other factors which affect absorption directly as devaluation takes place.

Finally, there may be a resource-reallocation effect favourable to income if the exchange rate has been previously overvalued and if trade restrictions are removed at the same time. Overvaluation of a currency in effect subsidises the production of non-traded goods relative to traded goods. If productivity is lower in the non-traded-goods sector, devaluation of the exchange rate will shift resources from the lower- to the higher-productivity sector. This means that a reduction in absorption at full employment may not be necessary for the trade balance to improve.

THE DIRECT EFFECT OF DEVALUATION ON ABSORPTION

If there is full employment and income cannot increase, or if $\alpha \geq 1$ so that induced absorption increases by as much as or more than the increase in income, then any favourable impact on the balance of payments from devaluation must come from a direct reduction in absorption. The primary direct effect of devaluation on absorption may be expected to be the dampening effect of rising prices on consumption which may come about through a variety of mechanisms such as a real-balance effect, income redistribution, and money illusion. In addition interest rates must be expected to rise. The real-balance effect refers to the desire of people to hold a constant proportion of their real income in the form of real-money balances. If the value of real-money balances is eroded by rising prices, people will attempt to accumulate more nominal balances, which they do by reducing expenditure out of real income. Hence the operation of a real-balance effect will tend to reduce absorption directly. Rising prices will also tend to redistribute income towards groups with higher marginal propensities to save and this will also cause a fall in consumption. Income will tend to be redistributed (i) from weak groups who are generally poorer to strong (richer) groups who can defend themselves against rising prices; (ii) from wages to profits, particularly if devaluation makes the export sector more profitable and wages do not adjust fully to price increases; and (iii) from taxpayers to governments, which will increase saving if the marginal propensity to save of governments is higher than that of taxpayers. Money illusion, which may exist in the short run, will cause real expenditure to fall as people continue to spend the same amount in money terms even though prices have risen, or as they fail to increase their money expenditure in *proportion* to the rise in prices, which is perhaps more likely.[4] Interest rates will tend to rise with inflation because of a reduction in the real value of money supply and increased uncertainty affecting the demand for money. Rising interest rates might be expected to reduce consumption and investment expenditure.

Real absorption in the economy will also be affected directly by the change in the home price of imports. If the elasticity of demand for imports is less than unity, there will be more spending in domestic currency on imports, and real expenditure on domestic goods will fall. A contemporary example of this type of effect was the oil price increase of 1973–4 which threw the developed countries of the world into prolonged recession. The cutback in imports, however, was not in general sufficient to compensate for the fourfold increase in the price of oil or to compensate for lost exports resulting from the slow-down of world trade. While absorption fell, income fell by more. It is possible for devaluation to be deflationary if the increased expenditure on imports in *domestic currency* (if imports are inelastic in demand) exceeds the increased domestic currency value of exports.

There are other forces which may increase absorption and worsen the balance of payments. Expectations about future price rises may increase absorption. Wages may rise faster than prices, and the velocity of circulation of money may rise, thus adding to aggregate monetary demand.

THE INTERACTION BETWEEN CHANGES IN INCOME AND CHANGES IN ABSORPTION[5]

We have considered the direct effect of devaluation on income and absorption and also the indirect effect of changes in income on absorption via the marginal propensity to absorb (α). Changes in absorption, however, will also affect income. Equation (6.7) omits this consideration, and it is a weakness of Alexander's original analysis. A model is required which incorporates both the effect of changes in income on absorption, and the effect of changes in absorption on income. When the latter effect is incorporated into equation (6.7) the condition for the balance of payments to improve as a result of devaluation can be interpreted in the same way as before, but the magnitude of the change in the balance of payments will be different. To complete the model by incorporating the income effects of changes in absorption, let the total change in income be the sum of the direct effect of devaluation on income (ΔY_D) and the indirect effect (ΔY_I) brought about by the change in absorption:

$$\Delta Y = \Delta Y_D + \Delta Y_I \tag{6.9}$$

and let

$$\Delta Y_I = \beta \Delta A \tag{6.10}$$

where β is the proportion of the change in absorption that falls on domestic goods ($0 < \beta \leq 1$). Similarly, let the total change in absorption be the sum of the direct effect of devaluation on absorption (ΔA_D) and the indirect effect (ΔA_I) brought about by the change in income:

$$\Delta A = \Delta A_D + \Delta A_I \tag{6.11}$$

where, as before,

$$\Delta A_I = \alpha\Delta Y \; (\alpha > 0) \tag{6.12}$$

Substituting (6.10) into (6.9) and (6.12) into (6.11) gives

$$\Delta Y = \Delta Y_D + \beta\Delta A \tag{6.13}$$

and

$$\Delta A = \Delta A_D + \alpha\Delta Y \tag{6.14}$$

and solving (6.14) and (6.13) simultaneously we have

$$\Delta Y = \frac{\Delta Y_D + \beta\Delta A_D}{1 - \beta\alpha} \tag{6.15}$$

and

$$\Delta A = \frac{\Delta A_D + \alpha\Delta Y_D}{1 - \beta\alpha} \tag{6.16}$$

The change in the balance of payments resulting from devaluation is thus:[6]

$$\Delta B = \Delta Y - \Delta A = \frac{\Delta Y_D(1 - \alpha) - \Delta A_D (1-\beta)}{1 - \beta\alpha} \tag{6.17}$$

and the balance of payments will improve if

$$\frac{\Delta Y_D (1 - \alpha)}{1 - \beta\alpha} > \frac{\Delta A_D (1 - \beta)}{1 - \beta\alpha} \tag{6.18}$$

Comparing equation (6.17) with equation (6.7), if devaluation increases income directly, the balance of payments will again only improve if $\alpha < 1$. The magnitude of the improvement now depends, however, on $\beta\alpha$. If $0 < \beta\alpha < 1$, the magnitude of the improvement will be greater than in the simple model. If $\beta\alpha > 1$, however, the system will be unstable. On the absorption side, if devaluation decreases absorption directly, this will improve the balance of payments provided $\beta < 1$. This condition will be met as long as the fall in absorption is not wholly on domestic output. The magnitude of the improvement depends on the value of $(1 - \beta)/(1 - \beta\alpha)$. If this is less than unity, the impact of a reduction in absorption on the balance of payments will be less than in the simple model. Again if $\beta\alpha > 1$, the model is unstable.

STRENGTHS AND DANGERS OF THE ABSORPTION APPROACH

While the absorption approach to the analysis of balance-of-payments adjustment may be analytically superior to the elasticity approach, it is clearly not the case that elasticities and relative price changes are unimportant, or that the information needed to evaluate whether devaluation will be successful in rectifying balance-of-payments disequilibrium is any easier to come by. The conventional supply and demand elasticities, and what happens to the relative price of traded and non-traded goods, affect both income and absorption, but by how much and in what direction depends on many unknowns. What is the extent of the idle resource effect, and the terms-of-trade effect, on income? What is the value of the propensity to absorb? By how much does a rise in the internal price level dampen absorption, if at all? What is the value of β? In using the absorption approach to the analysis of devaluation, answers to all these questions, and many more, must be known.

Perhaps the major contribution of the absorption approach to balance-of-payments correction has been to highlight more clearly the policy prerequisites for balance-of-payments adjustment. In particular, it stresses the fact, in a way that the elasticity approach does not do (at least explicitly), that at full employment devaluation must be accompanied by expenditure-reducing policies if devaluation is to be successful. Otherwise there are no available resources to supply more exports and import substitutes unless productivity is raised. It is not a coincidence that whereas the elasticity approach was developed, and found favour, in conditions of unemployment prior to the Second World War, the absorption approach has been developed in the full-employment conditions of the post-war era.

Many attempts have been made to synthesise the elasticity and absorption approaches to the balance of payments, notably by Alexander (1959), Michaely (1960) and Tsiang (1961), but the synthesis is not necessary if it is recognised that elasticities and relative price changes affect income and absorption. The absorption approach embraces the elasticity approach. It must do so since it works with the identity $B = Y - A$. It is certainly misleading to attempt a synthesis by modifying the elasticity formula to accommodate income effects, because the two effects cannot strictly be dichotomised. Relative price changes, combined with elasticities, affect income, and income changes affect relative prices and elasticities. In the last resort both the absorption and elasticity approaches depend on relative price movements, so that the two approaches, as Michaely (1960) has argued, are not in conflict:

> an increase in the ratio of international to domestic prices, which is essential for a decrease in the import surplus according to the relative prices approach, can take place if and only if there is a decrease in absorption, and a decrease in absorption can occur only if there is an increase in the general price level. Hence the two approaches to the analysis of devaluation must lead to the same conclusions.

The major danger in employing the absorption approach to the balance of payments is that the cause of balance-of-payments disequilibrium may be misinterpreted, leading to the incorrect policy prescriptions if the goals of economic policy are to be achieved simultaneously. Since the equation $B = Y - A$ is an identity derived from the national income accounts, it is incorrect to infer, as many have done,[7] that balance-of-payments deficits are necessarily *caused* by plans to spend in excess of plans to produce. *Ex ante* Y and A may be in balance but the balance of payments may move into deficit because of a deterioration in competitiveness or because of sectoral difficulties, with some sectors experiencing excess supply and unable to export. *Ex post* both these problems would show up in the national accounts as $Y < A$. The reason would not be, however, that plans to spend had exceeded income, but that income had fallen. In addition a government wishing to maintain full employment may have expanded demand to accommodate the balance-of-payments deficit. The implied excess of payments by residents over receipts by residents has unfortunately led followers of the absorption approach to view balance-of-payments deficits necessarily as a monetary phenomenon in a causal sense. But it is clear from what has just been stated that this is not necessarily so. The test of whether excess monetary expansion is the cause of a balance-of-payments deficit is to observe what happens to unemployment when monetary expenditure is reduced. If the deficit is eliminated without causing unemployment, this is *prima facie* evidence that the deficit is caused by excess monetary demand. If unemployment rises, the origin of the deficit must lie elsewhere. It is, of course, a golden rule in economics that causation can never be inferred from identities without adequate theorising and without due regard to the facts of any particular case.

THE MONETARY ASPECTS OF BALANCE-OF-PAYMENTS DEFICITS

All this is not to deny that balance-of-payments disequilibrium may have monetary origins, or will have monetary repercussions. The other major contribution of the absorption approach to the balance of payments has been to highlight the monetary aspects of balance-of-payments deficits, neglected by the elasticity approach. Indeed, the absorption approach is the forerunner of the monetary approach to the balance of payments. As we saw earlier, a deficit must mean an excess of payments by residents to foreigners over receipts by residents from foreigners. This means that there must be a net purchase of foreign exchange from the foreign-exchange authority or a run-down of foreign assets. This must imply in turn that the stock of privately held money must be decreasing, that the cash balances of residents are being run down, and domestic money is being transferred to the foreign-exchange authority. If the monetary authorities do not increase the supply of money, there exists what Johnson (1958) has called a *stock deficit*, which should ultimately be self-correcting as interest rates rise, credit tightens, and aggregate expenditure falls. There may, however, be a severe loss of reserves before the deficit is corrected, and more unemployment if the deficit is not *caused* by an excess supply of money in the first place. Stock deficits are supposed to be temporary, yet in a growing economy it is possible to conceive of a continuous stock deficit caused by the desire of residents to purchase foreign assets on a continuous basis as their resources increase through time.

If the monetary authorities respond to the depletion of cash balances by creating credit, the stock deficit will not be self-correcting and the balance-of-payments deficit will persist. This is called a *flow deficit*. Flow deficits need correcting by expenditure-reducing policies if the cause of the deficit is excess monetary demand, or by expenditure-switching and structural policies if the credit creation is designed to preserve full employment in the face of an 'autonomous' deterioration in the balance of payments.

In the monetary theory of the balance of payments, which is examined and evaluated more fully in the next chapter, the bond market and the capital account of the balance of payments are introduced. Now if there is excess demand in the goods market, there must be excess supply in the money and bond markets combined.[8] If the bond market is in equilibrium, then we have the situation discussed above in which there is an excess supply of money which leads to a loss of foreign-exchange reserves. If the money market is in equilibrium, however, the excess demand for goods must mean an excess supply of bonds, leading to a surplus on the capital account of the balance of payments. A current-account deficit on the balance of payments thus only leads to balance-of-payments disequilibrium in the total currency flow (or balance for official financing) sense if there is an excess supply of money, in which case reserves are lost. If there is an excess supply of bonds, the current account is financed by a capital inflow. The neatness of the approach, and the apparent policy implications, should not be allowed to obscure the fact, however, that the practical difficulty of diagnosing the cause of the balance-of-payments deficit still remains. An excess supply of money is not necessarily the cause of the deficit, and, if it is not, the deficit can only be controlled or rectified by monetary policy at the expense of domestic employment. In many instances an excess supply of money may merely be a symptom of a much more fundamental source of balance-of-payments difficulty, such as domestic supply constraints or an autonomous loss of domestic and export markets.

DOMESTIC CREDIT EXPANSION

Changes in a country's domestic money supply are made up of changes in the level of foreign-exchange reserves and the level of domestic credit expansion (DCE). If the economy is running a balance-of-payments deficit, the loss of reserves reduces any increase in the domestic money stock that is taking place and understates the way in which domestic monetary policy is affecting the economy and the balance of payments. In the late 1960s DCE targets were imposed in the United Kingdom in an attempt to make monetary policy more rigorous. Setting a DCE target means that the money supply must vary positively with changes in the reserves; expand when the balance of payments is in surplus, and contract when the balance of payments is in deficit – very much as under the old gold standard. When a country's currency is weak the policy has some merit as a quasi-automatic adjustment device, though it could lead to excessive deflation. Similarly, when a currency is strong DCE targets may lead to an excessive increase in the money supply, and consequent inflationary pressure. In 1977, in the United Kingdom, when the sterling exchange rate strengthened, DCE targets were relegated to the background in favour of targets for the broad-based definition of money, M3. A strong assumption of the monetary approach to the balance of payments, examined in the next chapter, is that the money supply varies positively with the level of foreign-exchange reserves, and that the effect of reserve changes on the money supply cannot be sterilised by the monetary authorities using open-market operations.

7
The Monetary Approach to the Balance of Payments

As we said in the introductory remarks in Chapter 4, the focus of the monetary approach to the balance of payments is on the balance of payments as a whole (the current and the capital account) so that a balance-of-payments disequilibrium is equivalent to a change in the level of international reserves. The essence of the argument is that balance-of-payments disequilibrium must be considered as the outcome of stock disequilibrium between the supply of and demand for money. Balance-of-payments difficulties are a monetary phenomenon which can be corrected by monetary adjustment. Traditional balance-of-payments adjustment policies can only be successful to the extent that they eliminate the stock disequilibrium between the supply of and demand for money. Let us develop a formal model of the monetary approach, and outline its assumptions, as a prelude to evaluating its usefulness in contributing to an understanding of balance-of-payments problems and their solution. The model outlined here draws on the presentation by Hahn (1977) in his review of the Frenkel and Johnson (1976) volume on *The Monetary Approach to the Balance of Payments*. The monetary approach assumes that exchange rates are pegged, that the economy is in long-run full-employment equilibrium, that the demand for money is a stable function of income, that changes in the money supply do not affect real variables, that in the long run a country's price level and interest rate converge on the world level because of the high elasticity of substitution between goods in international trade and highly mobile capital, and that the changes in the money supply brought about by changes in the level of foreign-exchange reserves are not sterilised by the monetary authorities. The assumptions are strong by any standards and their significance will be considered later.

From the national accounts, aggregate demand equals aggregate supply, i.e. there is zero excess demand, so that:

$$X_g = (Y - A) + (M - X) = 0, \tag{7.1}$$

where X_g, is the excess demand for goods, Y is income, A is domestic expenditure, M is imports and X is exports. Total demand is $A + X$, and total supply is $Y + M$. Rearranging (7.1) gives:

$$B = (X - M) = (Y - A), \tag{7.2}$$

where B is the balance of payments. Now consider in the first instance the case of an economy where the only asset is money. In a two-asset model of money and goods, by Walras's Law the excess supply in one market must equal the excess demand in the other. Hence:

$$(Y - A) = (M_D - M_s), \tag{7.3}$$

which from (7.2) implies:

$$B = (M_D - M_s) = X_m \tag{7.4}$$

where M_D is the demand for money, M_s is the supply of money and X_m is the excess demand for money. That is, a balance-of-payments surplus implies an excess demand for money and a balance of payments deficit implies an excess supply of money.[1]

The excess demand for (or supply of) money is the difference between the demand for money, assumed to be a stable function of income, and the supply of money of domestic origin, both defined in a stock sense. Thus:

$$X_m = k(Y) - \bar{M} \tag{7.5}$$

where $\bar{M}$ is the domestically determined component of the money supply controlled by the domestic monetary authorities. An excess demand for money, associated with a balance-of-payments surplus, leads to an increase in the supply of money through the accumulation of international reserves, assuming that the effect of an increase in reserves on the domestic money supply is not sterilised by the monetary authorities using open-market operations and selling bonds. As the supply of money increases, the excess demand for money is eliminated and the balance-of-payments surplus tends to zero. Conversely, an excess supply of money associated with a balance-of-payments deficit leads to a decrease in the money supply through the loss of international reserves, again assuming no sterilisation of the reserve loss by open-market operations, and the balance-of-payments deficit tends to zero. Thus, if changes in the reserves are not sterilised, it is a fundamental proposition of the monetary approach that a balance-of-payments disequilibrium is a temporary phenomenon representing a stock disequilibrium in the money market which will ultimately be self-correcting. That this is the main feature of the monetary approach is clear from Johnson (1972), who contends that the basic assumption of traditional balance-of-payments theory is that the monetary consequences of deficits or surpluses are sterilised so that a deficit or surplus is treated as a flow equilibrium. By contrast, he says, the new monetary approach assumes (asserts!) that the monetary inflows and outflows associated with surpluses or deficits are not sterilised, or cannot be within the period relevant to policy analysis – but instead influence the domestic money supply. Since the demand for money is a stock demand, not a flow demand, variations in the supply of money relative to demand must work towards an equilibrium between the demand for and supply of money with a corresponding equilibration of the balance of payments. Deficits and surpluses represent phases of stock adjustment in the money market, and not equilibrium flows. Movements in the terms of trade, the level of income and other real factors are unimportant as causal explanations of payments disequilibrium, or as methods of adjustment, unless they affect the balance between the supply of and demand for money. Balance-of-payments deficits are a monetary phenomenon associated with an excess supply of money. In the framework of the monetary approach the level of reserves is the only variable than an excess supply of money can affect because long-run equilibrium in the goods market is assumed, the interest rate is given and the demand for money is stable.[2]

Extending the model to more than one asset, the fundamental equations of the monetary approach are easily modified. For example, introducing bonds into equation (7.4) would give

$$B = X_m + X_b \tag{7.6}$$

where X_b is the excess demand for bonds. If $X_m = 0$, then $B = X_b$;

that is, a balance-of-payments surplus implies an excess demand for bonds, and a deficit implies an excess supply of bonds.[3] In this case a surplus will be 'financed' by capital outflows and there will be no accumulation of reserves, and a deficit will be financed by capital inflows and there will be no loss of international reserves. In both cases adjustment takes place without a change in money balances.

Having briefly stated the essence of the monetary approach in formal terms, let us now evaluate the approach. From the fundamental equations which form the basis of the monetary approach, it is clear that balance-of-payments disequilibrium cannot be interpreted solely as a monetary phenomenon in the *causal* sense of an excess supply of or demand for money in the money market. Consider equation (7.1). As we said in considering the absorption approach to the balance of payments, it is quite possible for expenditure (absorption) and income to be in balance *ex ante* and yet for the balance of payments to be in deficit because for one reason or another domestic producers cannot sell what they have left over after satisfying home buyers. Thus it is possible that $X_g - B = A - Y = 0$, with $B < 0$. If this is so, balance-of-payments disequilibrium is consistent with *ex ante* equilibrium in the money market. It might be argued that a small country in a large world economy can sell all the goods it wants at the ruling world price, but this is not necessarily the case. The law of one price in competitive export markets does not mean that demand is unlimited. *Ex post*, of course, income would fall, so that $A > Y$, which would show up in equation (7.4) as $X_m < 0$, or an excess supply of money. The excess supply of money, however, would be a symptom of the payments deficit, not the cause.

In the two (or many) asset model a monetary explanation of balance-of-payments disequilibrium would need even closer scrutiny. As equation (7.6) shows, the balance-of-payments disequilibrium may reflect disequilibrium in the market for capital assets and be wholly consistent with *ex ante* equilibrium in the money market. The selling of bonds may lead to a deficit which is then financed by capital inflows as interest rates rise. In fact the attempt to spend in excess of income could result from the selling of a whole range of assets – bonds, shares, land, buildings, etc. – and have nothing to do with excess expansion of the money supply or dishoarding.

Let us turn now to some of the assumptions of the monetary approach. A basic assumption is that the demand for money is stable. If it is not stable, the balance of payments cannot be predicted from changes in the money supply alone. Increases in the money supply may induce increases in the demand for money, and decreases in the money supply may induce dishoarding. Most of the factors that may cause the demand for money to change as the supply changes, such as income and interest rates, are ruled out by assumption, but these are matters to be proved rather than assumed for the everyday conduct of balance-of-payments policy. To understand what is happening to the balance of payments, and whether disequilibrium may be self-correcting or not, the long-run characteristics of steady-state equilibrium are hardly relevant. In practice, over long periods relevant to analysis and policy, the level of income and interest rates may vary significantly with variations in the quantity of money, making it impossible to predict movements in the balance of payments from changes in the money supply alone. There is not a one-to-one relation between changes in the domestic money supply and the level of reserves. Whitman (1975) concludes her survey of 'global monetarism' by saying that most of the more revolutionary policy implications of the monetary approach to the balance of payments miss the boat for applicability to current problems. To assume that real output – even in the long run – is determined exogenously, and that money does not affect real variables in an economy, is nonsense. There is far too much emphasis, she argues, on the long-run static equilibrium state which is never reached, while ignoring the short and medium term, which are important for forecasting and for normative policy prescription. The concentration on the long run assumes away all the problems that make the balance of payments a 'problem'.

Tsiang (1977) also raises the important question of the specification of the demand for money function. In the basic monetary approach the demand for money appears to be specified primarily as a function of the transactions demand for money, being made a stable function of income. Yet an increase in the transactions demand for money cannot imply a withholding of money from spending because by definition it is meant to be spent. Therefore, an increase in the demand for money for transactions purposes cannot lead to a balance-of-payments surplus; nor can a reduced demand for money for transactions purposes lead to a deficit if the money is not to be spent. Tsiang argues that only the demand for money for asset purposes should be included in the demand for money function, for only variations in the asset demand will affect the spending on goods.

A serious question mark must also be raised over the basic assumption of the monetary approach that the effect of changes in international reserves on the domestic money supply cannot be sterilised, so that balance-of-payments deficits must represent phases of stock disequilibrium which will ultimately be self-correcting. The monetary authorities can and do indulge in open-market operations to neutralise the effect of changes in international reserves on the domestic money supply, so that a balance-of-payments deficit associated with an excess supply of money is not necessarily rectified by a loss of reserves and a reduction in the money supply. Reserves will fall, but the excess supply of money will remain.

On the question of policy we have the proposition that balance-of-payments adjustment policies cannot be successful in rectifying payments disequilibrium except to the extent that they equilibrate the money market. Thus tariffs, devaluation and expenditure-reducing policies can only rectify a deficit if they reduce the supply of money relative to the demand, or raise the demand for money relative to the supply. Moreover, the success of expenditure-switching policies such as devaluation can only be temporary. A number of explanations can be invoked in support of this view. First, devaluation cannot change the relative price of traded goods because domestic prices rise by the extent of the devaluation. Second, because of the high substitutability between traded goods, all countries are price-takers and each country's price level is determined by the level of world prices. Hence devaluation cannot affect relative prices measured in a common currency. Note, however, that even accepting the 'law of one price' there could still be devaluation effects on trade arising from shifts between the non-traded and traded-goods sectors of the economy, unless it is assumed that the price of non-traded goods changes in line with traded goods. Third, and most in keeping with the spirit of the 'domestic' monetary approach (as opposed to the 'international' monetary approach to balance-of-payments problems), it is argued that, starting from stock equilibrium, devaluation cannot improve the balance of payments permanently because any increase in the demand for money as a result of devaluation (see below) will be matched by an equal rise in the supply of money through an accumulation of reserves. Prices and the stock of money rise in proportion, leaving the balance of payments unchanged.

The scepticism of the monetary approach concerning the effectiveness of traditional balance-of-payments adjustment policies may be shared by those who do not accept the outlook and assumptions of the monetary approach to balance-of-payments analysis. While few would agree that balance-of-payments disequilibrium is necessarily a transient phenomenon, many would share the view, though not necessarily for the same reasons, that tariffs, devaluation and other expenditure-switching policies can only have transient effects, and that the main mechanism through which they work is a real-balance effect. This was originally stressed by the absorption approach to the balance of payments in contrast to the elasticity approach with its stress on the substitution of home for foreign goods.

So far the monetary approach to the balance of payments has been discussed on the assumption of pegged exchange rates. If exchange rates are allowed to float, the assumptions are that the balance of payments looks after itself, there is no movement in the reserves, and the money supply is entirely under the control of the domestic monetary authorities. Because there are no reserve movements, and consequent changes in the money supply, countries are insulated from disturbances in other countries. In practice, of course, countries are not indifferent to the exchange rate, and exchange rates are not allowed to fluctuate freely to produce balance-of-payments equilibrium in the total currency flow sense. Thus even under floating, if it is managed floating, reserve movements will take place. Even if they did not, however, one country is not necessarily insulated from monetary disturbances in another country because in a world of capital mobility interest-rate changes will cause capital to move from one country to another, thus affecting the conditions for equilibrium in the money market.

We can end this chapter by saying that the monetary approach to the balance of payments is useful in stressing that balance-of-payments disequilibria have monetary consequences, and in helping to understand the process of balance-of-payments adjustment, but it is not very useful, and may be misleading, for the understanding of the causes of balance-of-payments difficulties. A balance-of-payments deficit may have nothing to do with an excess supply of money in a causal sense, and its treatment as a monetary phenomenon may therefore be totally misplaced. As we saw earlier, the money market may be in equilibrium and yet a deficit may emerge on the balance of payments owing to real exogenous changes at home and abroad. Such a deficit could not be relied on to correct itself, and monetary correction would not be the appropriate policy instrument. Likewise, in an economy with assets other than money, disequilibrium in the balance of payments may arise through disequilibrium in the markets for capital, and monetary correction would not be appropriate unless the authorities are indifferent to the state of the current account.

Johnson (1958) once argued that the fundamental contribution of the absorption approach to the balance of payments was to point to the need to combine expenditure-reducing policies with expenditure-switching policies at full employment. The question might now be asked, how should we think differently of balance-of-payments policy in the light of the monetary approach? We think not very differently. The absorption approach first introduced the notion of a self-correcting stock deficit and inferred that balance-of-payments difficulties may be due to an excess supply of money. Also within the absorption approach, the real-balance effect assumes importance as the main mechanism of balance-of-payments adjustment resulting from expenditure-switching policies. The absorption approach does not stress quite so strongly as the monetary approach the transient nature of balance-of-payments adjustment policies, but this simply means that adherents of the monetary approach must be less sanguine about the possibility of achieving simultaneous internal and external balance with the traditional mix of policy instruments. The main contribution of the monetary approach is undoubtedly to stress that surpluses and deficits will induce changes in the money stock, at least in the short run, and that this will affect economic behaviour. But to argue that by these changes the balance of payments will tend to zero is to assert what needs to be proved theoretically and empirically. In neither the absorption approach nor the monetary approach can the authorities afford to regard balance-of-payments deficits as transient whether the deficits have monetary or real causes. If the deficits are monetary in origin, there is not necessarily a one-to-one relationship between changes in reserves and changes in the money supply; and changes in the money supply cannot be guaranteed to eliminate the disequilibrium in the money market if the demand for money is unstable. If the deficit is real in origin, monetary correction, if it did occur, would be at the expense of full employment. The underlying disequilibrium would remain. The monetary approach is right to warn, of course, that the monetary authorities should not exacerbate or perpetuate a deficit by excessive monetary expansion, but that is common sense which does not need a new theoretical approach for its understanding.

8
Simultaneous Internal and External Balance

The achievement of simultaneous internal and external balance is the prime task of macroeconomic policy in most countries. In some countries there may not be a conflict between the achievement of internal balance and balance-of-payments equilibrium. Circumstances may be such that the goals of full employment and a satisfactory growth rate can be achieved without a balance-of-payments deficit emerging. In many countries, however, the potential conflict between internal and external balance, which was discussed in Chapter 4, materialises frequently. In the United Kingdom the conflict between balance-of-payments equilibrium and faster growth has been acute since the Second World War, and in recent years the achievement of full employment has also become problematical.

From the standpoint of theory there are three environments that need to be considered. The first is the case where external balance is defined excluding the capital account, with the possibility of exchange-rate flexibility. The second is the case where external balance includes the capital account and the exchange rate is fixed. The third is the case where external balance includes the capital account and the exchange rate is flexible. A fourth possible case was the situation described in Chapter 4 where balance-of-payments equilibrium is defined in terms of the current account and the exchange rate is fixed. This case presents a severe dilemma for policy-makers because in this situation there would seem to be only the one instrument of monetary and fiscal policy to achieve the two independent objectives of internal and external balance. Meade's (1951) pioneering work considered the first case outlined of the reconciliation of internal and external balance under flexible exchange rates with external balance defined in terms of the current account. Meade showed that the conflict between internal and external balance could be reconciled if monetary and fiscal policy were used for internal balance and the exchange rate used for external balance. But suppose there are limitations on the use of the exchange rate as a policy weapon, as there seemed to be in the 1950s and 1960s. According to Meade's analysis this would leave monetary and fiscal policy to reconcile the two objectives. It was this problem that Mundell (1962, 1963) attempted to explore, investigating the possibility of using monetary and fiscal policy as separate instruments by redefining balance-of-payments equilibrium to include the capital account. Since the capital account of the balance of payments is sensitive to interest-rate differentials between countries, Mundell was able to show that the conflict between internal and external balance could be reconciled by using monetary policy to achieve external balance and fiscal policy to achieve internal balance. Following the earlier argument in Chapter 1, however, about how balance-of-payments equilibrium ought to be defined for the conduct of economic policy, there is a clear difference between the approaches of Meade and Mundell. Meade's analysis is concerned with *adjusting* the balance of payments to conditions prevailing in the real economy. By contrast, the use of monetary policy to improve the capital account is essentially a policy of *financing* balance-of-payments disequilibrium which postpones the necessary adjustment and possibly stores up difficulties for the future. The models of Meade and Mundell will be considered below together with a third category of model in which the definition of external balance includes the capital account, and the exchange rate is also variable. The fundamental question in each of the models is which policy to assign to which objective. This is called *the assignment problem*. As we shall see, the appropriate allocation of policy instruments to objectives becomes very much an empirical matter depending on the relative sensitivity of targets to instruments, or on what Mundell has called *the principle of effective market classification*. Assume two objectives or targets (Y_1 and Y_2) and two policies or instruments (X_1 and X_2) and that each target is responsive to both instruments. There are thus two structural relationships:

$$Y_1 = a_{11} X_1 + a_{12} X_2$$

and

$$Y_2 = a_{21} X_1 + a_{22} X_2$$

The principle of effective market classification says assign instrument X_1 or X_2 to Y_1 according to whether $a_{11}/a_{21} \gtrless a_{12}/a_{22}$. The instrument not assigned to Y_1 is then assigned to Y_2. Alternatively, we could say, instrument X_1 should be assigned to Y_1 or Y_2 according to whether $a_{11}/a_{21} \gtrless a_{12}/a_{22}$, the remaining instrument being assigned to the policy not paired with X_1.

In the models outlined below we shall be dealing with a single country with no foreign repercussions.

INTERNAL AND EXTERNAL BALANCE UNDER FLEXIBLE EXCHANGE RATES WITH NO CAPITAL MOVEMENTS

Consider Figure 8.1. On the vertical axis internal balance is measured (arbitrarily) in terms of the state of employment, and on the horizontal axis external balance is measured by the current account of the balance of payments. Drawing a vertical line to represent external balance, and a horizontal line to represent internal balance, gives four quadrants or zones indicating combinations of internal and external circumstances from which the appropriate combinations of policies to reconcile internal and external balance can be deduced. Simultaneous internal and external balance is achieved at P. In zones II and IV internal and external balance are not in conflict. In zone II the expansion of demand will both reduce unemployment and the balance-of-payments surplus. In zone IV a reduction in demand will both reduce 'overheating' in the economy and the balance-of-payments deficit. The two objectives of internal and external balance are not independent and therefore one policy instrument will suffice in both cases. In practice, of course, it is highly unlikely that expansion in zone II or deflation in zone IV will move an economy smoothly and directly to the point of simultaneous balance at P. The probability is that the one policy or the other will move the economy into zone I or III before P is reached, in which case the problem of conflict will arise.

The conditions prevailing in zone I would be unusual. It would be a very 'competitive' economy that combined a balance-of-payments surplus with the fullest possible employment. If this situation did prevail, however, the natural thing to do would seem to be to use monetary and fiscal policy to deflate the economy to achieve internal balance and to appreciate the currency to achieve external balance. To expand demand in order to reduce the surplus would overheat the

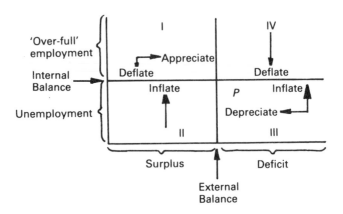

FIGURE 8.1

economy even more. If currency appreciation is successful in reducing the surplus, however, this in itself will be deflationary, and deflation by monetary and fiscal policy may not be needed. Which combination and sequence of policies is pursued depends, therefore, on the exact nature of the internal and external inbalance.

To be in zone III is a much more common occurrence. In this case the natural thing to do would seem to be to use demand expansion to produce full employment and to depreciate the currency to rectify the deficit. To deflate in order to rectify the deficit would simply cause more unemployment. If currency depreciation is successful in reducing the deficit, however, this in itself will be expansionary, and further expansion using monetary and fiscal policy may cause 'overheating'. As in zone I, therefore, which combination and sequence of policies is pursued depends on the nature of the disequilibrium.

To appreciate the problem more clearly we use in Figure 8.2 the famous Swan (1963) diagram which measures the ratio of international prices to home prices on the vertical axis and real expenditure on the horizontal axis. The *AA* curves represent internal-balance schedules which are combinations of relative prices and real expenditure that can sustain a given level of employment. Suppose A_2A_2 represents internal balance defined as full employment. According to Figure 8.2 this can be achieved either with a relatively low level of domestic expenditure and a high ratio of international to home prices (with exports relatively cheap and imports relatively dear), or with a higher level of expenditure and a lower ratio of international to home prices. Curves above and to the right of A_2A_2 represent given states of

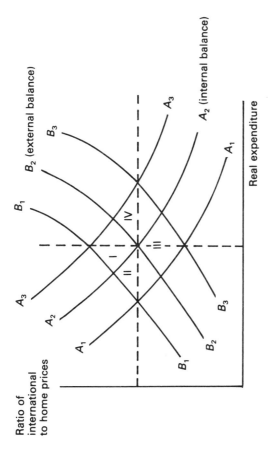

FIGURE 8.2

'overfull' employment, and curves below and to the left of A_2A_2 represent given states of unemployment. The *BB* curves show combinations of real expenditure and relative prices that can sustain a given balance of payments. Let B_2B_2 represent external balance. The upward slope of B_2B_2 shows that this can be achieved either with a relatively low level of expenditure and a low ratio of international to home prices, or a higher level of expenditure combined with a higher ratio of international to home prices. *BB* curves above and to the left of B_2B_2 represent surplus and *BB* curves below and to the right of B_2B_2 represent deficit. Only where A_2A_2 and B_2B_2 cross is there simultaneous internal and external equilibrium. As before, four zones of economic conditions are defined lying between the two curves. In zone I there is overfull employment and balance-of-payments surplus; in zone II unemployment and balance-of-payments surplus; in zone III unemployment and balance-of-payments deficit; and in zone IV overfull employment and balance-of-payments deficit. Note, however,that while the zone indicates the state of employment and the balance of payments that a country is experiencing, this information is not enough for deciding the *direction* of policy. What *quadrant* (given by the intersection of the two dashed lines) the country is in must also be known because the causes of disequilibrium differ between the two halves of each zone. For example, in zone III, which represents balance-of-payments deficit and unemployment, the nature of the conflict differs between the left and right side of the vertical dashed line. To the left a slight increase in expenditure, and then a rise in the ratio of international to home prices brought about by currency depreciation, are required to bring about simultaneous internal and external balance. To the right an increase in expenditure would be inappropriate. What is required is a reduction in expenditure so that depreciation to rectify the deficit does not lead to excessive demand expansion. Similar arguments would apply in other zones.

Care must also be taken in formulating policy to ascertain whether the observed situation is permanent or temporary. For example, productivity improvement will shift all *AA* curves upwards and all *BB* curves downwards, but if the productivity improvement is only temporary a country may act as if it is in zone IV when its long run position is really in zone II. Policies appropriate to zone IV would be inappropriate in relation to the underlying long-term condition of the economy.

INTERNAL AND EXTERNAL BALANCE UNDER FIXED EXCHANGE
RATES WITH CAPITAL MOVEMENTS

According to the model presented above, if exchange rates are fixed,
there is no solution to the conflict between internal and external
balance. If external balance is redefined to include the capital account, however, Mundell (1962) has shown that internal and external
balance is possible under fixed exchange rates, using interest-rate
(monetary) policy for external balance and fiscal policy for internal
balance. We first present the basic Mundell model, and then consider
simultaneous internal and external balance within the standard
macroeconomic framework of *IS-LM* curve analysis. Consider Figure
8.3. *BB* is the external-balance schedule which traces the locus of
combinations of the rate of interest and the budget surplus (at full
employment) along which the balance of payments (including the
capital account) is in equilibrium. The schedule has a negative slope
because rising interest rates will attract capital inflows, and for the
balance of payments to stay in equilibrium the budget surplus must
fall. Any point above and to the right of *BB* represents a balance-of-

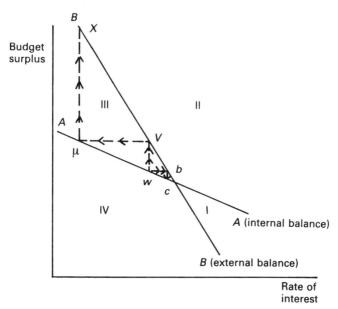

FIGURE 8.3

payments surplus, and any point below and to the left of BB represents a balance-of-payments deficit.

AA is the internal-balance schedule which traces the locus of combinations of the rate of interest and the budget surplus along which there is full employment. This schedule must also have a negative slope because tighter (laxer) monetary policy must be offset by laxer (tighter) fiscal policy to stay on the schedule. Any point below and to the left of AA represents overfull employment, and any point above and to the right of AA represents unemployment. Internal and external balance will be achieved simultaneously where the two curves cross, with the appropriate rate of interest and budget surplus. Again, four zones can be distinguished between the two curves: I = overfull employment and surplus; II = unemployment and surplus; III = unemployment and deficit; and IV = overfull employment and deficit. The relative steepness of the two curves is crucial to the question of the assignment of policies to the two objectives of internal and external balance. It can be shown that if BB is steeper than AA, monetary policy must be assigned to external balance and fiscal policy to internal balance for the achievement of both objectives.[1] Let us first consider the slopes of the curves. It can be demonstrated that BB must be steeper than AA as long as capital inflows are sensitive to variations in the interest rate, and that the difference in the steepness of the curves depends on the degree of responsiveness of capital flows to the rate of interest and on the marginal propensity to import. The proof is as follows. The absolute slope of AA is the ratio between the responsiveness of domestic expenditure to the rate of interest and the responsiveness of domestic expenditure to the budget surplus. Now if capital flows are constant, the balance of payments depends only on expenditure (via the propensity to import), and hence the BB schedule also measures the ratio between the responsiveness of domestic expenditure to changes in the rate of interest and to changes in the budget surplus. If, however, net capital inflows are positively related to the rate of interest, the budget surplus must be changed by more than in their absence if balance-of-payments equilibrium is to be maintained. Thus BB must be steeper than AA.

It remains to show that if BB is steeper than AA, the system will only be stable if monetary policy is used for external balance and fiscal policy is used for internal balance. In zones II and IV there is no assignment problem because there is no clash of objectives, and monetary and fiscal policy can work in the same direction. However, suppose in Figure 8.3 the economy is at *w*, with internal balance combined with a balance-of-payments deficit, and consider what would happen if fiscal policy is used to achieve external balance and monetary policy is used to achieve internal balance. To correct the balance-of-payments deficit by fiscal policy requires moving to *V*, but this will upset internal balance, causing unemployment. To use monetary policy to cure the recession requires moving to *u*, which would cause the balance of payments to go into deficit again. Fiscal policy to remedy the deficit would require moving to *X*, but this causes even more unemployment. The system is unstable. Suppose instead, however, that monetary policy is used to correct the balance-of-payments deficit and fiscal policy to maintain full employment. The economy would then move from *w* to *b* to *c*, towards simultaneous equilibrium, and the system would be stable. The same argument applies in zone I, where a conflict of objectives also exists, but not such a compelling one for the authorities to reconcile.

The assignment rule is based (as stated above) on what Mundell calls the principle of effective market classification, which says that policies should be paired with the objectives on which they have the most influence. The principle is an extension of the Tinbergen rule that there must be as many policy instruments as there are independent objectives (targets), except that in the latter case the rule does not say which instrument should be paired with which objective. Pursuing Mundell's rule, the use of monetary policy for external balance and the use of fiscal policy for internal balance accords with the principle of effective market classification because the ratio of the effect of monetary policy on external balance to its effect on internal balance is greater than the ratio of the effect of fiscal policy on the balance of payments to its effect on internal stability.[2]

Before going on to consider the simultaneous achievement of internal and external balance in the more familiar macroeconomic framework of *IS-LM* curve analysis, there are certain limitations and criticisms of Mundell's model that must be mentioned. We leave until last the assumption of fixed exchange rates. The first point to make is that, strictly speaking, it is not only the interest rate of the country concerned that is relevant to the analysis but the interest rate relative to that of other countries. The analysis must implicitly assume that interest rates elsewhere remain fixed. If they do not remain unchanged, internal and external balance may be impossible to achieve. Either international co-operation would have to be sought, or internal balance would have to be sacrificed for external balance –

monetary policy having been rendered ineffective. The same limitation applies, of course, to the Meade-Swan model, where exchange
depreciation in one country may be thwarted by competitive exchange depreciation in other countries. Second, Mundell's model is
sometimes criticised on the grounds that it assumes that international
capital movements are flows, whereas they represent stock adjustments to internal stock disequilibrium between the demand for and
supply of money. If capital movements do reflect stock adjustments,
an ever-increasing interest rate (or interest-rate differential) would
be required to secure external balance. This criticism is not a strong
one, however. In a growing economy capital movements have two
components: a stock-adjustment component and a flow component.
A flow component exists because, as wealth increases, it has to be
distributed among competing assets. Thus a policy of maintaining a
constant interest-rate differential between itself and the rest of the
world may be sufficient for a country to achieve external balance by
attracting the flow component from additions to wealth. A third
criticism of Mundell is that the assignment of monetary policy to
external balance will produce resource misallocation because it distorts the allocation of resources between consumption and investment at home, and because the balance between home and foreign
investment is decided on the basis of the health of the balance of
payments, not on productivity criteria. All policies of balance-of-
payments correction, however, have resource-allocation effects.
Demand-contraction policies would be wasteful of resources;
exchange-rate depreciation may have unfavourable internal repercussions which then lead to policies such as wage and price control
which distort the allocation of resources. The question is not which
balance-of-payments policy has no resource-allocation effects but
which has the least unfavourable. A fourth criticism is that it is
assumed that policy-makers have full knowledge of the slopes of the
curves and that policy adjustment takes place in a smooth and
co-ordinated way. If there is not full knowledge, and policy changes
are not smooth and co-ordinated, the assignment of policies could
lead to divergence from the path towards simultaneous internal and
external equilibrium and to over-shooting. A fifth criticism, and the
most serious, is that using interest rates for external balance is not a
balance-of-payments *adjustment* policy but a method of *financing*
balance-of-payments disequilibrium. The state of the balance of
payments in relation to the functioning of the real economy will

either remain the same or probably worsen, and there is a limit to the extent to which interest rates can be raised to attract capital to compensate for this 'real' disequilibrium. Mundell's policy prescription for simultaneous balance gives temporary respite but no more. Williamson (1971) has argued that there are no circumstances in which it would be desirable to pursue Mundell's strategy rather than adjust the current account because the interest burden will grow through time, reducing investment, further worsening the current account, and so on.

Finally, Mundell's model only gives rules for assignment under fixed exchange rates. Under flexible exchange rates the assignment problem is much more complex because interest-rate policy may now have relatively stronger effects on internal balance than fiscal policy. For example, a policy of monetary contraction and high interest rates, by inducing capital inflows, would tend to cause the exchange rate to appreciate, leading to a further reduction in demand in the economy greater than the reduction in demand brought about by an equivalent fiscal contraction which would tend to reduce interest rates, depreciate the currency, and counter the contraction. Likewise, a policy of monetary expansion, leading to a lowering of interest rates and capital outflows, would tend to depreciate the currency, leading to a further expansion of demand greater than the expansion of demand brought about by an equivalent fiscal expansion which would tend to raise interest rates, appreciate the currency by inducing capital inflows, and counter the expansion. Fleming (1962) was one of the first to show that the effect of a given change in the money supply will always be greater under flexible exchange rates than under fixed rates, and that the effect of a change in the money supply will be greater than a budgetary change of the same amount under flexible exchange rates. Thus it would seem that, according to the Mundell rule, monetary policy should be used for internal balance, with the achievement of external balance left to the exchange rate. But this may be a hasty judgement, because if the reserve effects of surpluses and deficits are not sterilised by the monetary authorities, a surplus due to monetary contraction will increase the money supply and a deficit due to monetary expansion will contract the money supply, and this will offset the effect of monetary policy on income. A lot would seem to depend on how quickly exchange rates equilibrate the balance of payments and whether reserve movements are sterilised.[3]

INTERNAL AND EXTERNAL BALANCE IN AN *IS-LM* CURVE
FRAMEWORK

The traditional macroeconomic framework for considering internal equilibrium, and which has useful pedagogic virtues, is *IS-LM* curve analysis, which shows the conditions for simultaneous equilibrium in the money market and the goods market. This model can be extended to the open economy, where the slope of the *IS* curve is affected by the level of imports, and the position of the curve is partly dependent on the exchange rate. An external-balance schedule can then be superimposed, and policies examined for internal and external equilibrium under fixed and flexible exchange rates. The model has the advantage over Mundell's in that the goods and money markets are integrated so that fiscal policy now has explicit interest-rate effects. Using this model fiscal policy is defined as shifts in the *IS* curve and monetary policy as shifts in the *LM* curve.

On a diagram (see Figure 8.4) which measures the interest rate on the vertical axis and the income level on the horizontal axis, the *IS* curve is the locus of points at which savings equals investment at different levels of income given the rate of interest. It slopes downwards from left to right, giving a higher level of income as the interest rate falls. Since imports will rise as income rises, the *IS* curve will be steeper in an open economy than in a closed economy since the multiplier effect from a given fall in the interest rate will be less. Any autonomous increase in demand, including government fiscal policy, will shift the curve up and to the right. The curve is defined for any given price level, p. The *LM* curve is the locus of points at which the supply of money equals the demand for money at different levels of the rate of interest, given the level of income. It slopes upwards from left to right showing the interest rate rising as the level of income rises, which results from an increased transactions demand for money with the supply of money fixed. In practice the *LM* curve will be horizontal over part of its range because there exists a floor to the rate of interest, and it will become vertical at high levels of income if there is a limit to the velocity of circulation of money (i.e. a limit to the extent to which income can be financed with a fixed supply of money). For exposition, however, the curve is drawn linear in Figure 8.4, in keeping with the linear structural models that generate these relations.[4] Increases in the supply of money will shift the curve outwards to the right, and decreases in the money supply will shift it inwards to the left. There will be a different *LM* curve for each price

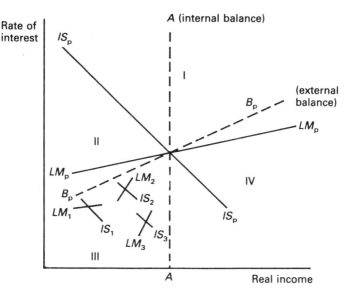

FIGURE 8.4

level *p*. Where the *IS* and *LM* curves cross, the money market and the goods market are both in equilibrium. For the sake of argument, let us suppose that this point of intersection also corresponds to full employment so that it can be used to locate the internal-balance schedule *AA*. Points to the left of *AA* represent unemployment and points to the right of *AA* represent overheating of the economy.

An external-balance schedule (inclusive of the capital account) can now be superimposed on the diagram, drawn through the locus of the combinations of the interest rate and the level of income which would maintain external balance. The curve (*BB*) must slope upwards from left to right in the interest-rate-income plane because as income rises, increasing the level of imports, the interest rate must rise to attract compensating capital flows to maintain balance.[5] Points above *BB* represent a balance-of-payments surplus and points below *BB* represent a balance-of-payments deficit. The crossing of the *AA* and *BB* schedules again defines four zones: I = overfull employment and surplus; II = unemployment and surplus; III = unemployment and deficit; and IV = overfull employment and deficit. Zones I and III are the conflict zones, with zone III the most typical and problematical. Since all the curves are drawn on the assumption of a given exchange rate, we can consider in this framework both policies for internal and external balance under fixed exchange rates (as in Mundell's model) and also policies under flexible exchange rates which will shift the position of all three curves. A depreciation of the exchange rate will shift the BB curve downwards because external balance will now be achieved (if the conditions for a successful devaluation are met) at a lower rate of interest, given the level of income, or at a higher level of income, given the rate of interest. The IS curve will shift upwards to the right if depreciation is expansionary, and the LM curve will shift upwards to the left because as prices rise the real value of the money supply will decline. For comparative static equilibrium analysis the BB curve needs to be drawn steeper than the LM curve, otherwise a devaluation cannot be shown to produce a new equilibrium at a higher level of income. Out of equilibrium there is no reason why the BB curve should not be flatter than the LM curve.

THE USE OF MONETARY AND FISCAL POLICY UNDER ALTERNATIVE EXCHANGE-RATE REGIMES

We can consider again the Mundell assignment problem. It was originally argued that because the ratio of the effect of monetary policy on external balance to its effect on internal balance is greater than the ratio of the effect of fiscal policy on the balance of payments to its effect on internal stability, monetary policy ought to be assigned the task of external balance and fiscal policy the task of internal balance. We now show in more detail how the question of which policies to pursue, and thus the mix, depends on the initial conditions, the slopes of the curves, and the exchange-rate regime in operation. Under fixed exchange rates, suppose an economy is in zone III, where the crossing of the IS and LM curves gives recession and a balance-of-payments deficit. If the BB curve is steeper than the LM curve (case 1 in Figure 8.4), the Mundell rule holds whatever the initial conditions within the zone because expansionary fiscal policy would lead to an even greater balance-of-payments deficit. If the BB curve is flatter than the LM curve (cases 2 and 3 in Figure 8.4), it does not matter which policy is pursued for external balance because expansionary fiscal policy improves the balance of payments.[6] In case 3, however, monetary policy would have to be contractionary to maintain internal balance, while in case 2 both monetary and fiscal policy must be expansionary for internal and external balance. If the *BB* curve is negatively sloped because capital movements are income-sensitive, there would be a strong case for using monetary policy for internal balance and fiscal policy for external balance.

Under flexible exchange rates the situation is even more complex. If the economy is not on the *BB* curve, the exchange rate will alter and shift all the curves simultaneously. Both internal and external equilibrium will be affected, and simultaneous internal and external balance will not be achieved until all curves intersect at the point of intersection of *AA* with *BB*. As suggested earlier, if under flexible exchange rates monetary policy is relatively more powerful than fiscal policy in its impact on the domestic economy, monetary policy must be assigned the task of internal equilibrium. Again, everything depends on the initial starting-point, the slopes of the curves and how much each curve shifts as a result of exchange-rate changes.

THE ASSIGNMENT OF POLICIES IN THE UNITED KINGDOM

Fausten (1975) has made a bold attempt to assess the theoretical validity of the Mundell decision rule for the assignment of economic policies under fixed exchange rates and to examine the consistency of policies in the UK context. Fausten concludes, like others, that the assignment rule of monetary policy for external balance and fiscal policy for internal balance is not logically valid as a universal proposition, and that the policy-mix approach, and particular rules, were unsuitable for UK requirements in the 1960s. Fausten argues his case on three main grounds. First, the policy-mix approach is inadequate because it is a short-term approach and disregards the causes of balance-of-payments disequilibrium. It contains no adjustment mechanism to reduce the need for further capital inflows. On the contrary, continual financing of external deficits is required, probably at higher and higher interest rates if the mobility of international capital represents stock adjustments rather than flows. Second, the approach assumes that only the current account is affected by income changes (i.e. capital flows are insensitive to income) and that only the capital account is affected by changes in the rate of interest. Further, it is assumed that increases in income always affect the balance of payments adversely, while increases in the rate of interest affect it favourably. In practice a wide range of behavioural responses is possible. Fausten shows that if capital flows are income-sensitive and exports are interest-sensitive, it is not possible to specify a unique assignment rule. Everything depends on the relative parameter values. Third, using estimated relationships for the UK economy, Fausten questions the appropriateness of assigning monetary policy to the external-balance target. To the extent that the authorities pursued the assignment rule, he contends that they went astray. In fact, however, he finds a discrepancy between the actual and intended thrust of monetary policy. The restrictiveness of monetary policy for external reasons was invariably weakened through the generous extension of finance to the public sector and the desire for a stable gilt-edged market.

9
A History of the UK Balance of Payments

Although the primary purpose of this chapter is to describe the balance-of-payments experience of the United Kingdom since 1950, it will be helpful as an introduction to place the experience in historical perspective, relying heavily on the statistical tables compiled by Mitchell and Deane (1962). Starting from 1854, data will be given on imports, exports, the balance of trade, the over-all balance on current account, indices of the volume of imports and exports, and the terms of trade. Throughout the chapter emphasis will be given to discussion of the statistics rather than to events and policies, and the focus will be on the real sector of the balance-of-payments accounts rather than on international monetary developments. The chapter contains an appendix written by one of us just after the collapse of the Bretton Woods system, expressing scepticism that Britain's balance-of-payments problems (and slow growth) would be permanently solved by allowing the exchange rate to float. It makes interesting reading now that Britain has locked itself into the Exchange Rate Mechanism of the European Monetary System.

1854 TO 1939

Table 9.1 provides data for the items referred to above for the period 1854 to 1939. The statistics largely speak for themselves, but certain points may be noted. The trade balance over the period was always in deficit (in contrast to post-1950, when in six years it was in surplus). Up to the First World War the average trade deficit was just over £100 million per annum, with a slight trend deterioration through time. The current-account balance was in surplus, however, by

TABLE 9.1
Balance-of-payments statistics (£m)

	Imports c.i.f.	Exports (including re-exports) f.o.b.	Merchandise trade balance	Balance of overseas investment earnings	Balance of all other invisible trade	Bullion and specie	Balance on current account	Index of import volume (1880 = 100)	Index of export volume (1880 = 100)	Terms of trade (1880 = 100)
	(1)	(2)	(3)	(4)	(5)	(6)	(7)	(8)	(9)	(10)
1854	152.4	115.8	−36.6	+12.6	+33.4	−3.6	+5.8	33	40	94.6
1855	143.5	116.7	−25.9	+12.9	+34.7	−7.8	+13.9	31	40	89.4
1856	172.5	139.2	−32.1	+14.9	+40.9	−1.9	+21.8	36	48	91.6
1857	187.8	146.2	−40.4	+16.2	+44.8	+6.5	+27.1	36	49	87.1
1858	164.6	139.8	−23.8	+15.9	+40.2	−9.9	+22.4	37	48	98.0
1859	179.2	155.7	−22.6	+16.9	+43.2	−1.4	+36.1	39	52	98.2
1860	210.5	164.5	−45.5	+18.7	+48.0	+2.5	+23.7	45	55	94.9
1861	217.5	159.6	−57.6	+19.9	+50.0	+2.1	+14.4	47	51	98.1
1862	225.7	166.2	−58.8	+20.7	+51.9	−2.3	+11.5	48	48	105.8
1863	248.9	196.9	−51.4	+21.3	+60.1	−3.5	+26.5	49	51	107.2
1864	275.0	212.6	−61.5	+22.9	+66.0	−4.6	+22.8	49	51	104.7
1865	271.1	218.8	−51.2	+24.1	+68.4	−6.4	+34.9	52	55	107.0
1866	295.3	238.9	−55.2	+26.4	+74.5	−12.7	+33.0	56	61	110.0
1867	275.2	225.8	−48.6	+28.2	+72.1	−9.5	+42.2	56	62	107.8
1868	294.7	227.8	−65.5	+31.1	+75.5	−4.6	+36.5	60	66	100.3
1869	295.5	237.1	−57.5	+31.1	+75.2	−4.1	+46.7	62	70	103.1
1870	303.3	244.1	−57.5	+35.3	+76.8	−10.5	+44.1	65	76	102.3

TABLE 9.1 (cont)
Balance-of-payments statistics (£m)

	Imports c.i.f.	Exports (including re-exports) f.o.b.	Merchandise trade balance	Balance of overseas investment earnings	Balance of all other invisible trade	Bullion and specie	Balance on current account	Index of import volume (1880 = 100)	Index of export volume (1880 = 100)	Terms of trade (1880 = 100)
	(1)	(2)	(3)	(4)	(5)	(6)	(7)	(8)	(9)	(10)
1871	331.0*	283.6*	−46.0	+39.5	+82.4	−4.4	+71.3	75	85	109.4
1872	354.7	314.6	−36.8	+44.3	+89.8	+0.7	+98.0	75	88	113.0
1873	371.3	311.0	−56.3	+51.7	+90.6	−4.7	+81.3	78	85	117.2
1874	370.1	297.7	−69.1	+56.6	+90.9	−7.5	+70.9	80	84	113.2
1875	373.9	281.6	−90.5	+57.8	+89.6	−5.6	+51.3	85	84	111.6
1876	375.2	256.7	−117.8	+57.5	+91.1	−7.6	+23.3	87	81	105.4
1877	394.4	252.4	−141.5	+55.5	+96.5	+2.6	+13.1	90	84	98.5
1878	368.8	245.5	−121.8	+55.1	+89.1	−5.7	+16.9	90	84	102.4
1879	363.0	248.8	−111.8	+55.9	+88.0	+4.4	+35.5	93	89	101.7
1880	411.2	286.5	−121.1	+57.7	+96.4	+2.6	+35.6	100	100	100.0
1881	397.0	297.1	−94.5	+59.5	+95.0	+5.6	+65.7	98	110	96.7
1882	413.0	306.7	−100.0	+62.8	+97.5	−2.6	+58.7	103	111	99.6
1883	426.9	305.4	−116.9	+64.4	+102.1	−0.8	+48.8	109	114	98.5
1884	390.0	295.9	−91.1	+66.8	+95.0	+1.6	+72.3	105	115	99.9
1885	371.0	271.5	−98.5	+70.3	+90.7	−0.2	+62.3	106	109	102.5
1886	349.9	268.9	−79.5	+74.0	+83.8	+0.6	+78.9	107	114	104.4
1887	362.2	281.2	−78.5	+79.5	+87.3	−0.6	+87.7	112	119	106.4
1888	387.6	298.5	−85.9	+84.5	+92.7	+0.6	+91.9	118	127	102.3

TABLE 9.1 (cont)
Balance-of-payments statistics (£m)

	Imports c.i.f.	Exports (including re-exports) f.o.b.	Merchandise trade balance	Balance of overseas investment earnings	Balance of all other invisible trade	Bullion and specie	Balance on current account	Index of import volume (1880 = 100)	Index of export volume (1880 = 100)	Terms of trade (1880 = 100)
	(1)	(2)	(3)	(4)	(5)	(6)	(7)	(8)	(9)	(10)
1889	427.6	315.6	−105.0	+88.5	+99.1	−2.0	+80.9	128	132	103.0
1890	420.7	328.2	−86.3	+94.0	+99.6	−8.8	+98.5	127	134	109.1
1891	435.4	309.1	−122.1	+94.3	+99.6	−2.4	+69.4	131	127	107.4
1892	423.8	291.6	−128.9	+94.7	+96.7	−3.4	+59.1	133	122	107.0
1893	404.7	277.2	−124.6	+94.7	+85.6	−3.7	+53.0	130	117	109.3
1894	408.3	273.8	−131.5	+92.6	+88.4	−10.8	+38.7	140	122	114.4
1895	416.7	285.8	−126.5	+93.6	+87.8	−14.9	+40.0	148	133	110.8
1896	441.8	296.3	−137.9	+96.0	+92.3	+6.4	+56.8	155	140	110.8
1897	451.0	294.2	−153.9	+97.0	+94.7	+0.8	+41.6	159	138	110.0
1898	470.5	294.1	−168.9	+101.2	+96.8	−6.2	+22.9	164	137	109.3
1899	485.0	329.5†	−153.7	+103.2	+102.7	−9.8	+42.4	166	146	112.2
1900	523.1	354.4	−167.0	+103.6	+109.1	−7.5	+37.9	166	140	120.0
1901	522.0	347.8	−173.1	+106.5	+106.7	−6.2	+33.9	171	141	118.1
1902	528.4	349.2	−178.4	+109.1	+107.9	−5.3	+33.3	175	150	114.1
1903	542.6	360.4	−181.3	+112.2	+113.6	+0.3	+44.8	177	154	112.4
1904	551.0	371.0	−179.1	+113.4	+115.5	+0.7	+51.7	179	157	113.3
1905	565.0	407.6	−155.9	+123.5	+120.1	−6.2	+81.5	182	173	112.6
1906	607.9	460.7	−146.0	+134.3	+131.0	−1.8	+117.5	187	186	114.4

1907	645.8	517.9	−126.8	+143.8	+142.4	−5.3	+154.1	190	201	114.9
1908	593.0	456.7	−135.6	+151.0	+132.5	+6.8	+154.7	182	185	114.7
1909	624.7	469.5	−154.2	+158.0	+138.3	−6.5	+135.6	189	193	109.4
1910	678.3	534.2	−142.7	+170.0	+146.7	−6.7	+167.3	193	210	107.9
1911	680.2	556.9	−121.2	+177.3	+146.8	−6.0	+196.9	199	218	112.6
1912	744.6	598.9	−143.8	+186.9	+158.6	−4.6	+197.1	214	230	112.5
1913	768.7	634.8	−131.6	+199.6	+168.2	−11.9	+224.3	220	239	116.2
1914	696.6	526.2	−	−	−	−	−	−	−	−
1915	851.9	484.0	−	−	−	−	−	−	−	−
1916	948.5	603.9	−	−	−	−	−	−	−	−
1917	1064.2	596.8	−	−	−	−	−	−	−	−
1918	1316.2	532.3	−	−	−	−	−	−	−	−
1919	1626.2	963.3	−	−	−	−	−	195	170	92
1920	1932.6	1557.3	−386	+200	+395	+43	+252	−	−	−
1921	1085.5	810.3	−	−	−	−	−	187	164	89
1922	1003.1	723.2	−183	+175	+150	+13	+155	205	178	91
1923	1096.2‡	885.8‡	−210	+200	+148	+16	+153	228	182	94
1924	1277.4	940.0	−337	+220	+190	+12	+86	236	179	97
1925	1320.7	927.4	−393	+250	+188	+10	+54	244	161	95
1926	1241.4	778.5	−463	+250	+199	−12	−26	252	184	96
1927	1218.4	832.1	−386	+250	+219	−3	+79	244	188	99
1928	1195.6	843.9	−352	+250	+225	−7	+117	257	193	98
1929	1220.8	839.0	−382	+250	+233	+16	+117	249	157	91
1930	1044.0	657.6	−386	+220	+194	−5	+25	254	120	82
1931	861.3	454.5	−407	+170	+134	+33	−70	224	120	82
1932	701.7	416.0	−286	+150	+86	−17	−67	224	121	80
1933	675.0	417.0	−258	+160	+103	−201	−196	234	129	82
1934	731.4	447.2	−284	+170	+117	−142	−139	237	139	83
1935	756.0	481.1	−275	+185	+108	−56	−38			

TABLE 9.1 (cont)
Balance-of-payments statistics (£m)

	Imports c.i.f.	Exports (including re-exports) f.o.b.	Merchandise trade balance	Balance of overseas investment earnings	Balance of all other invisible trade	Bullion and specie	Balance on current account	Index of import volume (1880 = 100)	Index of export volume (1880 = 100)	Terms of trade (1880 = 100)
	(1)	(2)	(3)	(4)	(5)	(6)	(7)	(8)	(9)	(10)
1936	847.8	501.4	−346	+200	+127	−227	−246	252	142	85
1937	1027.8	596.5	−431	+210	+176	−99	−144	267	154	90
1938	919.5	532.3	−388	+200	+122	+74	+8	254	136	82
1939	885.5	485.6	–	–	–	–	−250	–	–	–

* Denotes that up to 1870 the values of imports and re-exports were computed by the Board of Trade. All other values were declared by shippers.

‡ Denotes that the value of new ships abroad was included in exports for the first time in 1899, when it came to £9.2 million.

† Southern Ireland was treated as foreign from 1 April 1923.

Sources: Columns 1 and 2 are from Imlah (1958). Column 3 is from Mitchell and Deane (1962, pp. 283–4). Column 3 is from Mitchell and Deane (1962, pp. 333–5). Up to 1913 the data are based on Imlah (1958) and from 1920 are taken from the Board of Trade Journal. (Note that because of the different sources of data, col. 3 does not agree precisely with the difference between col. 2 and col. 1. It is col. 3, however, which is used to derive the over-all balance on current account in col. 7.) Columns 4 to 7 are from Mitchell and Deane (1962, pp. 333–5). Columns 8 and 9 are from Mitchell and Deane (1962, pp. 328–9). The indices to 1913 are from Imlah (1958), and from 1920 were provided by the London and Cambridge Economic Service. The present authors put the latter indices on the same basis as the Imlah indices using base 1880 = 100. Column 10 is from Mitchell and Deane (1962, pp. 331–2). The index to 1913 is from Imlah (1958), and from 1920 from the Board of Trade Journal (4 August 1951). The present authors put both series on the same basis using base 1880 = 100.

approximately £70 million per annum, owing to a healthy surplus on overseas investment earnings and other invisible trade. Between the First and Second World Wars the average trade deficit was £340 million per annum; and although the surplus on overseas investment earnings and other invisible trade increased, the improvement was not enough to offset the trade deficit. Over the whole period there was a small annual average deficit on current account, with the deficit years occurring in the 1930s.

Up to 1914 the balance of payments was helped by a slight trend improvement in the terms of trade, the terms-of-trade index rising by some 20 per cent over the sixty-year period from 1854. By contrast there was a marked deterioration in the terms of trade after 1913, the index falling from 116 in 1913 to 82 in 1938 (1880 = 100).

The growth in the volume of imports over the period 1854 to 1914 was slightly faster than the growth in the volume of exports, offsetting the improvement in the terms of trade. The import-volume index rose 5.6 times, from 33 in 1854 to 220 in 1913, while the export volume index rose fivefold, from 40 in 1854 to 239 in 1913. There was a noticeable surge in the growth of exports immediately preceding the First World War. In the interwar period the deterioration in the trade balance and current account was not only a function of the worsening terms of trade. More significant was the absolute fall in the volume of exports while the volume of imports continued to grow. By 1938 export volume was 20 per cent below the level of 1920 and 43 per cent below the level of 1913.

1940 TO 1950

For obvious reasons the balance of payments during the war period went into serious deficit, as shown in Table 9.2. The combined deficit on current and long-term capital accounts averaged £750 million per annum.

In the immediate post-war years, the balance of payments made a dramatic recovery, while there was a slight deterioration in the terms of trade. Export volume increased by 75 per cent between 1946 and 1950, while import volume increased much more slowly by only 25 per cent, largely because of import controls. The merchandise trade balance improved in successive years, which, combined with a surplus on invisible account, turned the balance of payments on current account from deficit into surplus over the three years 1948 to 1950.

TABLE 9.2
Balance-of-payments statistics 1940–50 (£m)

	Imports c.i.f. (1)	Exports (including re-exports) f.o.b. (2)	Merchandise trade balance (3)	Invisible balance (4)	Balance on current account (5)	Balance of current and long-term capital (6)	Index of import volume (1958=100) (7)	Index of export volume (1958=100) (8)	Net barter term of trade (1958=100) (9)
1940	1082	393				−804	78	37	91
1941	986	324				−816	64	26	95
1942	997	271				−663	60	19	102
1943	1234	234				−680	64	15	94
1944	1309	266				−659	69	16	102
1945	1104	339				−875	56	24	99
	(f.o.b.)								
1946	1063	960	−103	−127	−230	+18	62	52	99
1947	1541	1180	−361	−20	−381	−84	70	57	92
1948	1790	1639	−151	+177	+26	+305	72	72	89
1949	2000	1863	−137	+136	−1	−48	78	80	91
1950	2312	2261	−51	+358	+307	+363	78	91	90

Sources: Columns 1 and 2, data for 1940 to 1945 from London and Cambridge Economic Service, *Key Statistics 1900–1966*, table K, p. 14; data for 1946 to 1950 from Mitchell and Deane (1962, p. 142). Columns 3 to 6, data from Mitchell and Deane (1962, p. 142). (The figure in column 6 for the period 1946 to 1950 include the *balancing item* and are therefore not comparable with later years.) Columns 7 to 9, data from London and Cambridge Economic Service, *Key Statistics 1900–1966*, table K, p. 14.

Despite the improvement, the pound was devalued from $4.03 to $2.80 in 1949.

As argued by Cairncross (in Cairncross and Eichengreen, 1983), however, the decision to devalue was not related primarily to the state of the overall balance of payments, but to the trade and payments deficit with the dollar area, and to the decline in reserves in 1949. British trade with the dollar area was in deficit by £252m in 1948 and £296m in 1949, while the gold and dollar deficit in total was £406m in 1948 and £348m in 1949. Total reserves were falling at the rate of £20m a month in 1949 from a level of £400m. There was a very real prospect that, without action to stem speculation, the reserves would become exhausted. The impact of devaluation appears to have been mixed, and difficult to judge precisely, because so much else happened in the aftermath including the Korean war in 1951 which affected prices considerably and distorted trade patterns. Cairncross argues that there can be no doubt that the reserve loss was stemmed and that the dollar shortage was eased in the short run. The total balance of payments with the dollar area (including capital transactions) registered a surplus of £306m in 1950, while the trade deficit alone fell to only £88m. Large deficits were to emerge again in 1951, however. But Cairncross detects a longer run reorientation of exports to the dollar area, which he attributes to devaluation, with the ratio of exports to the United States to exports to the sterling area rising from 20 per cent in 1947/49 to 28 per cent in 1952/54. The ratio of imports from the two sets of countries in turn, fell from 60 per cent to 47 per cent.

In an earlier study Flanders (1963) concluded:

> the weakening of Britain's competitive position *vis-à-vis* other devaluing countries indicates that exchange rate adjustment was not a sufficient condition for improving her foreign trade position, though it may have been necessary and it is at least probable that the position would have deteriorated more if there had been no devaluation.

Flanders examines the value share of UK exports in the four commodity groups of iron and steel, power-generating machinery, textiles and vehicles over the period 1949 to 1955 in relation to (i) world exports, (ii) exports of other devaluing countries, and (iii) exports of non-devaluing countries. Except for exports of iron and steel and power-generating machinery to non-devaluing countries, the share of

UK exports in all other markets continued to fall. While the results by themselves would suggest a perverse elasticity of substitution for UK exports in most markets, Flanders believes it is more likely that other adverse factors were to blame, offsetting a normal negative elasticity of substitution – factors such as: the Korean war; the recovery of the Japanese and West German economies; relaxation of trade controls and regulations; and inelasticity of UK export supply. What is really relevant, however, is not what happens to export shares as a result of a devaluation but whether devaluation raises permanently the trend rate of growth of exports relative to imports. The United Kingdom's share of world exports was declining before the war and has declined since. So, for that matter, has the United Kingdom's share of world production and imports. These facts, however, need not necessarily prevent a country enjoying a balance-of-payments surplus, as the United Kingdom was later to do in the 1950s. In fact there is no evidence to suggest that the devaluation of 1949 did raise the rate of growth of exports, or lower the rate of growth of imports, permanently. Indeed, economic theory would suggest that the best that devaluation can do is to exert a once-and-for-all impact on the *levels* of exports and imports, leaving the growth rates unchanged (see Chapters 11, 12 and 13).

The question might also be raised of whether devaluation would have been resorted to had the balance-of-payments statistics at the time been accurate. When the decision to devalue was taken it was thought that the aggregate balance-of-payments deficit for the years 1946 to 1948 was over £1000 million. It is now known that it was much less as Table 9.2 shows; and in 1948 there was actually a surplus on the current account and on the basic balance. Other instances will be mentioned later of possibly precipitate action being taken on the balance of payments on the basis of figures which have exaggerated the deficit.

1951 TO 1959

Although the emphasis here is on describing the performance of the balance of payments on current account, the history of the balance of payments and of balance-of-payments policy cannot be understood without brief mention of the United Kingdom's role as an international banker, and sterling's role as a reserve currency, which have made the gold and foreign-currency reserve position of the United Kingdom an element of such vital importance. Because of the large holdings of sterling by foreigners and the persistent threat of their removal from London, the exchange rate was also continually under threat in the 1950s and 1960s, notwithstanding surpluses earned on the current account. It was eventually weakness on capital account (both short and long term), unrelated to any *serious* weakening on the current account, that precipitated devaluation in 1967, and which led sterling to depreciate so dramatically from 1972 to 1978. For reference purposes Table 9.3 gives the value of official reserves and liabilities of the United Kingdom since 1950. It can be seen that throughout the 1950s and 1960s the value of external liabilities, as a claim on the reserves, was four to five times higher than the value of reserves. The ratio has generally improved since then (except 1974–76) through a combination of reasons: the revaluation of gold; the accumulation of reserves to hold the exchange rate down, and the use of means, other than reserves, to finance balance of payments deficits.

The balance-of-payments statistics for the period 1951 to 1959, as well as up to the present, are contained in Table 9.4. The improvement in the balance of payments that was apparent in the immediate post-war years continued into the 1950s. The large trade deficit in 1951 is attributable to the Korean war and the sharp rise in commodity prices, but from 1952 there is a gradual improvement punctuated only by deterioration in periods of excessive overheating of the economy. The improvement in the merchandise balance compared with the inter-war period and before was against a background of a commitment to full employment which was largely achieved, which makes the balance-of-payments record even more remarkable. In 1956 and 1958 there were actually slight surpluses recorded on the trade balance, a phenomenon achieved on only three previous occasions since 1800 – in 1816, 1821 and 1822. The performance of the trade balance, combined with a surplus on invisible account (albeit deteriorating), produced a surplus on current account in seven out of the nine years between 1951 and 1959, the exceptions being 1951 and 1955. Excluding the abnormal (war) year, 1951, the average surplus on current account was £154 million per annum. Apparently the Treasury's target surplus was £450 million in order to allow room for net overseas investment and to build up reserves. It is not clear, however, whether this is the criterion by which the performance of the balance of payments ought to be judged. Overseas investment and reserve accumulation are not macroeconomic goals that directly affect the living standards of people (except to reduce them in the short run), and the figure itself is entirely arbitrary. The only real standard by which the balance of payments may be judged unsatisfac-

TABLE 9.3

U.K. official reserves and external liabilities of the public sector since 1950

	Gold and convertible currency reserves (£m.)	External liabilities of the public sector (£m.)
1950	1178	4060
1951	834	4143
1952	659	3786
1953	899	4004
1954	986	4179
1955	757	4045
1956	799	4091
1957	812	3918
1958	1096	3976
1959	977	4212
1960	1154	4432
1961	1185	4504
1962	1002	4106
1963	949	3737
1964	827	3861
1965	1073	4273
1966	1107	4844
1967	1123	5145
1968	1109	5428
1969	1053	5842
1970	1178	5419
1971	2526	5646
1972	2405	5799
1973	2795	6615
1974	2955	8998
1975	2700	10633
1976	2485	14625
1977	10975	18092
1978	10380	15593
1979	13220	15185
1980	13275	14901
1981	11960	14394
1982	12939	17272
1983	12805	18383
1984	13219	20999
1985	13201	20.3b
1986	17424	23.9b
1987	27008	27.6b
1988	28711	29.1b
1989	26281	27.4b

Sources: London and Cambridge Economic Service, *Key Statistics 1900–1966*; and the *United Kingdom Balance of Payments: 1990 Edition* (London, HMSO). b stands for billion.

tory in this period is the low rate of growth of output compared with other industrialised countries. A higher growth rate, assuming that would have been physically possible, would undoubtedly have raised the rate of growth of imports, which would have worsened the balance of payments without a corresponding increase in the rate of growth of exports. If there was a balance-of-payments problem in the 1950s, it was the inability of the rate of growth of exports to finance a higher rate of growth of real output. It was the attempt to achieve faster growth by simply expanding demand, without first an expansion of exports, which produced such difficulties for the UK economy in the early 1960s and early 1970s, and from 1985. In Chapters 12 and 13 attention will be devoted to the balance-of-payments constraint as a source of international growth-rate differences and to the importance of export-led growth in an open economy.

Over the period 1951 to 1959 there was a slight tendency for the volume of imports to grow faster than the volume of exports, but nothing to suggest the emergence of a fundamental disequilibrium in the balance of payments at the prevailing full-employment growth rate. Import volume grew 23 per cent between 1951 and 1959 while export volume grew 17 per cent, but as far as the balance of payments is concerned this adverse tendency was offset by a 25 per cent improvement in the terms of trade.

The two major so-called balance-of-payments crises in the 1950s which invoked domestic deflation were in 1955 when the economy was clearly overheated and there was also rumour of full sterling convertibility, and the speculative attack on sterling in 1957 when Bank Rate was raised to the record high level of 7 per cent to protect the capital account of the balance of payments. The Radcliffe Committee (1959) remarked (and interestingly, in the light of the history of the 1960s and the belief of many that the UK balance of payments has been in fundamental disequilibrium since the Second World War) that 'the repeated exchange crises have not been due . . . to any failure on the part of the UK to pay her way but to the volatility of various elements in the balance of payments and to the lack of reserves adequate to withstand the resulting pressure on them'.

1960 TO 1969

There seems to be a general consensus that while the balance of payments was reasonably healthy before 1959, from that date it

TABLE 9.4

Balance-of-payments statistics since 1951 (£m)

	Imports f.o.b.	Exports (including re-exports) f.o.b.	Merchandise trade balance	Invisible balance	Balance on current account	Balance of current and long-term capital account (basic balance)	Balance for official financing*	Index of import volume (1970=100)	Index of export volume (1970=100)	Terms of trade (1970=100)
	(1)	(2)	(3)	(4)	(5)	(6)	(7)	(8)	(9)	(10)
1951	3424	2735	−689	+320	−369	n.a.	−334	48	53	72
1952	3048	2769	−279	+442	+163	+29	−175	44	50	77
1953	2927	2683	−244	+389	+145	−49	+296	48	51	82
1954	2989	2785	−204	+321	+117	−74	+126	49	53	82
1955	3386	3073	−313	+158	−155	−277	−229	55	57	81
1956	3324	3377	+53	+155	+208	+21	−159	55	59	83
1957	3538	3509	−29	+262	+233	+127	+13	56	60	85
1958	3377	3406	+29	+317	+346	+148	+290	57	58	91
1959	3642	3527	−115	+287	+172	−112	+18	61	61	91
1960	4138	3737	−401	+173	−228	−457	+325	68	63	92
1961	4043	3903	−140	+187	+47	+64	−339	67	65	95
1962	4103	4003	−100	+255	+155	+14	+192	69	67	97
1963	4450	4331	−119	+244	+125	−35	−58	72	70	96
1964	5111	4568	−543	+185	−358	−749	−695	75	72	94
1965	5173	4913	−260	+230	−30	−274	−353	76	77	97
1966	5384	5276	−108	+238	+130	−63	−547	78	79	98
1967	5840	5441	−599	+330	−269	−451	−671	84	82	100
1968	7145	6433	−712	+468	−244	−422	−1410	93	84	97

Year	1	2	3	4	5	6	7	8	9	10
1969	7478	7269	−209	+691	+482	+385	+687	94	97	96
1970	8142	8128	−14	+835	+821	—	+1287	100	100	100
1971	8820	9030	+210	+904	+1141	—	+3146	104	107	101
1972	10154	9412	−742	+945	+203	—	−1265	117	107	101
1973	14449	11881	−2568	+1570	−998	—	−771	134	122	90
1974	21513	16282	−5233	+2047	−3184	—	−1646	136	132	75
1975	22440	19185	−3257	+1731	−1524	—	−1465	126	126	81
1976	29041	25080	−3961	+3189	−772	—	−3629	134	137	80
1977	34005	31683	−2322	+2375	+53	—	+7361	142	148	82
1978	36573	34981	−1592	+2715	+1123	—	−1126	149	152	87
1979	43814	40471	−3342	+2890	−453	—	+1905	166	158	87
1980	45792	47149	+1357	+1487	+2843	—	+1372	157	161	85
1981	47416	50668	+3251	+3496	+6748	—	−687	151	110	85
1982	53421	55331	+1911	+2741	+4649	—	−1284	159	164	84
1983	62237	60700	−1537	+5325	+3787	—	−820	172	167	83
1984	75601	70265	−5336	+7168	+1832	—	−1361	191	181	83
1985	81336	77991	−3345	+6095	+2750	—		197	191	83
1986	82141	72656	−9485	+9462	−24	—		212	199	79
1987	90669	79446	−11223	+7042	−4182	—		228	210	80
1988	101854	80776	−21078	+5927	−15151	—		259	219	81
1989	116632	92792	−23840	+4714	−19126	—		279	230	82

*Figures from 1978 refer to *total official financing* (see note 2 to Chapter 1).

Sources: Columns 1 to 5, data for 1951–5 are taken from Mitchell and Deane (1962, p. 142), from 1956 the data are from *U.K. Balance of Payments*, various editions, HMSO. Column 6, data from *Bank of England Historical Abstract*, no. 1, 1970. Column 7, ibid. for years 1951–5, and for later years *U.K. Balance of Payments*, various editions. (*Balance for official financing is synonymous with total currency flow*). Columns 8 to 10, data for 1951 to 1966 are taken from London and Cambridge Economic Service, *Key Statistics 1900–1966*, p. 14, and for later years from *National Institute Economic Review*, and *U.K. Balance of Payments, 1990 Edition*.

moved into a state of underlying disequilibrium, in the sense of an inability of the economy to achieve the full employment of resources without a payments deficit emerging. The emergence of such a classic conflict was the cue for many economists, though by no means all, to advocate either devaluation, or the abandonment of fixed exchange rates, as the solution to the dilemma. The advocacy of exchange-rate adjustment was rarely accompanied, however, by any detailed analysis of the nature of the difficulties in the early years of the 1960s, or a thorough consideration of the consequences that a fall in the exchange rate would have on the domestic economy. A consensus on a matter, moreover, does not mean that the view is necessarily correct. But if a disequilibrium in the balance of payments did emerge in the sense defined above, exchange-rate adjustment is only appropriate if the cause of the disequilibrium is a loss of price competitiveness, or possibly to give breathing space to tackle the true causes, and then only if the deleterious inflationary repercussions on the internal economy can be avoided.

The emergence of a deficit in 1960 from a surplus in 1959 cannot be attributed to a sudden deterioration in price competitiveness. In fact the current-account deficit in 1960, against which restrictive domestic action was taken in 1961, turned out to be exaggerated. Instead of an assumed deficit of £344 million, and the forecast of another substantial deficit, in 1961, the true deficit for 1960 turned out to be £228 million, and there was a surplus of £47 million in 1961. There was a larger deficit on the basic balance in 1960 caused by an adverse movement in the long-term capital account, but this cannot be attributed to adverse relative price movements either. In 1962 and 1963 the current balance moved further into surplus, with if anything the level of exports above trend, which is hardly evidence of a strongly deteriorating competitive position. The fact of the matter is that international price competitiveness, measured by relative export prices or relative unit labour costs, did not deteriorate over this crucial period leading up to the balance-of-payments crisis of 1964. Ray (1966) shows that over the period 1958 to 1964 total wage costs per unit of output in the United Kingdom rose 11 per cent compared with 12 per cent in Japan, 12 per cent in Italy, 22 per cent in West Germany, 6 per cent in France, and −5 per cent in the United States. MacGeehan (1968), in her survey of competitiveness, confirms that between 1960 and 1965 unit labour costs in the United Kingdom grew more slowly than in Europe. (For a discussion of measures of competitiveness, see Chapter 11.) Import volume grew by 20 per cent between 1959 and 1963 and export volume by 15 per cent – a ratio no different from that of the 1950s.

Despite the facts Coppock (1965) argues that the poor performance of the current-account balance of payments in the early 1960s merely reflects the general uncompetitiveness of the UK economy in world trade in manufactures, and that all the evidence adds up to a convincing case for the existence of fundamental disequilibrium for which the appropriate remedy is devaluation. He says:

> the persistence of [balance-of-payments] crises in conjunction with the underlying trends in the U.K. foreign trade and the balance of payments may be held to justify the view that there has been a cumulative tendency towards fundamental disequilibrium and that devaluation may be an appropriate or even an essential part of a package deal to restore equilibrium.

It is true that he qualifies his judgement by saying:

> devaluation cannot be expected to remove the deep-seated deficiencies of British business in productivity growth and export promotion or the institutional bias towards inflation which are generally accepted as the causes of our troubles. A permanent solution to the British problem requires the correction of these deficiencies [but, he goes on] . . . the immediate situation calls for short term relief to improve the balance of payments position and to enable us to recover lost ground.

In presenting his case he includes the year 1964 in calculating the average annual balance of payments on current account for the early years of the 1960s, but surely it cannot be claimed that the deficit that emerged in 1964 was the result of relative price deterioration. The worsening of the trade deficit from £119 million in 1963 to £543 million in 1964 is attributable entirely to the massive upsurge in the value of imports from £4450 million to £5111 million resulting from the very rapid rate of expansion of demand. The worsening of the trade deficit caused the current account to move into deficit from a surplus in 1963; and an even larger deficit emerged on the long-term capital account to give a basic balance-of-payments deficit of £749 million, the largest (until then) in peace-time history. The difficulties of 1964 were cyclical and were on the capital account; they were not the result of forces to be rectified by exchange-rate depreciation.

The Labour government opposed devaluation in 1964. According to Stewart (1977) the opposition was on three main grounds: first, the fear that the Labour Party would be branded as the Party of devaluation; second, because (to quote Harold Wilson, the Prime Minister) it may well have started off an orgy of competitive beggar-my-neighbour currency devaluations which would have plunged the world into monetary anarchy; and third, a deep-seated distrust of the price mechanism. It would be misleading to give the impression, however, that there was an academic consensus in favour of devaluation opposed only by obstinate politicians on the left. In the early 1960s Sir Roy Harrod and Thomas Balogh (who became personal adviser to the Prime Minister, Harold Wilson, in 1964) came out strongly against devaluation, and in the second half of 1966 three more eminent economists of very different political persuasions all expressed doubts. Professor Hicks (1966) remarked: 'It is widely supposed that the only reason why we do not devalue is the obstinacy of Mr Wilson. But economists may be grateful for the obstinacy of Mr Wilson and for the good advice on this matter we may be sure he is receiving . . . There is really no alternative while our position is so weak but to cling to the existing parity.' Professor Joan Robinson (1966) expressed scepticism about the wisdom of devaluation in conditions of full employment:

In a situation where there is some unemployment and unused capacity in many lines, a devaluation increases activity and improves the balance of trade at one stroke. But when there is near full-employment already[1] it is liable merely to increase the pressure of demand for labour, while the rise in price of imports increases the pressure for higher money wage rates, so that before long the competitive advantage of lower home costs is completely lost.

Then Lord Robbins declared in the House of Lords on 28 July 1966: 'I welcome greatly the declaration . . . expressing the firm decision of the government not to resort to this expedient [i.e. devaluation]. I do not think indeed that in present circumstances this view that we should have devalued has much practical applicability.' Later, in April 1967, Professor Ball (1967) expressed strong opposition to devaluation on the grounds of elasticity pessimism and noted that the advocation of devaluation seemed to be based more on despair than on any positive merits. When devaluation eventually took place in November 1967, several economists opposed it, and there was wide disagreement on the measures necessary to make devaluation effective (see Hutchison, 1977). Harrod (1968a, 1968b) continued to attack its appropriateness and wisdom, and Hawtrey (1969a, 1969b) continued to argue, as he had for many years, that the source of the United Kingdom's difficulties was not an overvalued pound, but an undervalued pound causing excess demand at home.

The response to the 1964 balance-of-payments deficit was the traditional one of demand deflation, coupled with the imposition in October 1964 of a 15 per cent import surcharge on all imports except food and some raw materials. The surcharge was reduced to 10 per cent in April 1965 and removed entirely in November 1966. There have been several different approaches to the estimation of the effects of the surcharge. One has been to use import demand equations (see Chapter 11) to forecast imports over the surcharge period and to attribute to the surcharge the difference between actual and forecast imports. Johnston and Henderson (1967) adopted this approach using quarterly data and estimated a reduction in imports due to the surcharge of between £115 million and £165 million at current prices. Using this method Black, Kidgell and Ray (1967) of the National Institute of Economic and Social Research estimated a surcharge effect of £200 million. The weakness of this approach is that it makes no allowance for residual errors which occur in the normal course of forecasting, which in the case of imports could be as high as plus or minus £100 million. This difficulty can be overcome by incorporating the surcharge into the import equations as an independent variable and estimating the effect directly. Black, Kidgell and Ray (1967) also adopted this approach and estimated a reduction in imports due to the surcharge of £380 million at current prices. A third method of approach used by Barker (1970b) is to include the surcharge as part of the price paid by the importer, using this price to explain the behaviour of imports, and then to recalculate import prices excluding the surcharge and use the equations to estimate imports in the absence of the surcharge. The effect of the surcharge is calculated to be a reduction in imports of £462 million.[2] Barker suggests that perhaps this estimate is closer to the true figure than the lower estimates given, particularly in view of the large unanticipated rise in manufactured imports in 1967 after the surcharge was removed. Between 1966 and 1967 there was a 13 per cent rise in the volume of manufactured and semi-manufactured good imports, and in 1968 imports exceeded forecasts following devaluation in November 1967.

From the balance-of-payments statistics post-1964, it is fairly clear that the balance of payments responded to the deflationary (and other) measures taken. Import growth fell in 1965 and 1966, while export volume grew at close to 7 per cent per annum. The visible deficit shrunk, and the balance on current account moved into surplus in 1966.[3] The basic balance was in deficit by less than £100 million, though the balance for official financing was much larger, at over £500 million. The question is, why did the situation deteriorate so markedly in 1967 as to make devaluation unavoidable, when the pressure of demand was falling, and early in the year both the Bank of England and the National Institute of Economic and Social Research were forecasting an over-all surplus? The initial source of difficulty was the slow-down in the growth of world trade which reduced the volume of exports, while imports grew at an annual rate of 7 per cent. Even so, the balance of payments was still in surplus in the middle of the year and there was little pressure on sterling in the foreign-exchange markets. The steady decline in fortunes started with the Middle-East crisis in June and the subsequent closure of the Suez Canal, which prompted the heavy selling of sterling. Short-term interest rates in the United States and in the Euro-dollar market began to rise, and this also exacerbated the pressure on sterling. The June trade figures announced in July were disappointing, and discussion of devaluation began to appear in the press, all of which added further to the strain in the foreign-exchange market. In the third quarter of 1967 a balance-of-payments deficit was registered, and a general lack of confidence caused further losses of foreign exchange. By September shipments of exports began to be affected by strikes in the Liverpool and London docks. This was the final straw which confirmed in the minds of foreigners the apparent precariousness of the UK position. The consensus that measures would have to be taken to protect the balance of payments and the reserves, which might include devaluation, itself made worse the outflow of funds. The speculative pressure against sterling became so intense that what was predicted occurred: the pound was devalued from $2.80 to $2.40 on 18 November. The devaluation was forced by a speculative crisis, rather than by any crisis on trading account. The bad trade figures in the third quarter of 1967 were largely the result of seasonal factors; and abstracting from the slow-down in the growth of world trade, the accounts even reveal some underlying improvement (see Thirlwall, 1970). It is also now known that because of a mistake in the recording of exports there was only a small over-all cumulative deficit on the current account of the balance of payments between 1964 and devaluation day, contrary to what was thought at the time. i.e. that the current account was chronically unhealthy. One might add that had the expansion of demand in 1964 not been so irresponsible, the current account over the period would have recorded a substantial surplus, and the country may have comfortably ridden the crisis of confidence in 1967 precipitated largely by external events.

According to the second volume of the Crossman diaries (1976) most members of the Cabinet were in favour of the pound floating in 1967, as opposed to either devaluation or import controls. Only Harold Wilson and James Callaghan were against. Crossman records a dinner on 1 November 1967 attended by himself, Mrs Barbara Castle, Thomas Balogh, Mr Peter Shore and Mr Tony Benn: 'There is no disagreement among us . . . we all know that we should float the pound and not devalue to a fixed point. We all agree that import controls will be quite ineffective.' Crossman also describes how in the Steering Committee on Economic Policy, on 8 November, Wilson isolated Callaghan as the only anti-depreciationist. After Callaghan had described devaluation as a catastrophe, Wilson is supposed to have replied: 'I am politically open on the subject. I am prepared to think there could be some merit in a free decision, and in that case we must of course decide whether we float or devalue by a certain amount. My mind is not closed.' Crossman's account of the lead up to devaluation is rather different from Wilson's own account (1971). Wilson says:

> though a contingency plan for devaluation of sterling had long been in the Treasury files . . . change in parity was not in contemplation. The Governor [of the Bank of England] met with the Chancellor and me at no. 10 [late October 1967]. I asked him specifically whether a recommendation to devalue was in his mind. He said flatly that it was not . . . As we entered November sterling was still under pressure, but unlike July 1966, there was hardly a serious commentator pressing for devaluation.

DEVALUATION, 1967

In this section the effects of devaluation are considered. The devaluation of the pound sterling from £2.80 to £2.40 reduced the dollar price of pounds by 14.3 per cent and raised the sterling price of dollars by

16.7 per cent. Other things remaining the same this would allow UK exporters to reduce prices in foreign currency in foreign markets by 14.3 per cent, and we should expect the sterling price of imports to rise by 16.7 per cent. Other things do not always remain the same, however. Exporters may alter the sterling price of exports and foreigners may alter the foreign price of domestic imports. What happens to sterling export prices depends on the pricing policies of manufacturers and the degree of inflation induced by rising import prices. The foreign price of imports depends on the elasticity of supply and the pricing policies of suppliers (see Chapter 5). The evidence is that export prices measured in sterling rose by about 8 per cent, and fell by about 6 per cent measured in foreign currency. Exporters apparently reaped the benefits of devaluation through a combination of expanding sales and a higher rate of profit per unit of sales. Import prices measured in sterling rose by 12 per cent in 1967–8 and by 5 per cent in 1968–9. Assuming no change in foreign prices, this would mean that the effect of devaluation on import prices was spread over a minimum of two years.

We shall consider here four major studies of the effect of the 1967 devaluation on the UK trade balance. Worswick (1971) examines the effect on exports and imports separately. On the export side he compares actual exports with predicted exports on the basis of pre-1967 behaviour. The United Kingdom's share of world trade in manufactures declined by 0.7 per cent per annum prior to 1967. Applying this figure to 1968 and 1969, Worswick calculates that exports should have been 14 per cent higher in 1969 than in 1967 in the absence of devaluation. In fact actual exports were 25 per cent higher. He attributes the 11 per cent difference to devaluation. With an 8 per cent increase in sterling export prices and an 11 per cent increase in the volume of exports, the effect of devaluation on the sterling value of exports is calculated to have been £1240 million. On the import side the volume of imports rose in 1968 and 1969, above the level predicted on the basis of past experience, apparently indicating a *perverse* price elasticity of demand for imports. Making the less extreme assumption, however, that devaluation had no effect on the volume of imports, Worswick calculates that the rise in the sterling price of imports raised the sterling import bill by £1060 million. The net effect on the trade balance is therefore estimated to have been +£180 million over two years. The effect of devaluation on the invisible account is estimated at +£330 million, giving a total positive contribution to the current account of £510 million over two years. In a later paper the staff of the National Institute of Economic and Social Research (1972) extend the analysis to 1970 and revise the estimates downwards, calculating that by 1970 the improvement in the trade balance was only £130 million, and in the current balance £425 million.

A study by Artus (1975) for the IMF puts the estimate of the beneficial effect of devaluation on the trade balance much higher than do Worswick and the National Institute. This is for two reasons. First, higher imports due to the higher pressure of demand induced by devaluation are subtracted.[4] Second, Artus assumes a cumulative relative price effect on the volume of imports of −3.5 per cent, whereas Worswick's study assumes no import-volume response. Artus's study gives an eventual improvement in the trade balance of £940 million by the end of 1971.

An interesting study by Masera (1974), who takes broadly the same approach as Worswick, is also concerned with lags in the response of import and export volumes to relative price changes as well as with the ultimate quantitative effect of devaluation on the trade balance. Masera estimates a *J*-curve effect (see Chapter 5) lasting until the third quarter of 1968, after which the trade balance shows a positive improvement compared with what it would otherwise have been. He estimates, however, that it took another three or four quarters for the initial losses to be made good, but ultimately there was a net improvement in the trade balance of £520 million up to the end of 1969. His estimate is higher than Worswick's because he argues that in 1967[5] there was a shift in the import propensity, which led to an underprediction of imports based on past trends and therefore to an underestimation of the import response to devaluation.

Figures of the order of magnitude cited above may suggest that devaluation was successful in relation to the level of the prevailing deficit. Such a judgement needs to be tempered with caution. First, the positive benefits last only so long as the competitive advantage gained by devaluation is not eroded by competition in world markets and/or domestic price inflation. Second, even if the competitive advantage is maintained, the positive balance-of-payments response does not put the economy on a higher growth path. The conflict between faster growth and balance-of-payments equilibrium remains, unless there is continual devaluation. Third, it is not clear that any of the studies takes adequate account of the rapid growth of world trade in 1968 which expanded in volume by 12 per cent compared with 1967. Some of the assumed devaluation effect on exports may have been due to this dramatic rise. Care must also be exercised in assuming that what may have been a successful exercise in the past can be repeated in the future. The 1967 devaluation was assisted by two important factors, in addition to the rapid expansion of world trade. First, there was still in 1967 widespread money illusion in the economy. Price inflation had been mild up to then, and productivity growth and an improving terms of trade combined to raise real living standards by close to 3 per cent per annum. When the devaluation came, wages were slow to respond to the price increases, and the competitive advantage of devaluation was slow to be eroded by domestic price inflation. Inflation did accelerate, however; money illusion disappeared, and it is no coincidence that from that date the celebrated Phillips curve, found to be stable and negatively sloped over a long period of history, started to go awry. Devaluation, or currency depreciation, in the absence of money illusion in the labour market (or controls to produce the same result), cannot be successful.

The second factor which greatly assisted devaluation in 1967 was the contraction of domestic demand. By 1969 virtually the whole of economic policy was orientated towards the balance of payments. Tight monetary and fiscal controls were imposed in November 1968 and in the budget of 1969, giving a total fiscal contraction of over £1000 million, and in its Letter of Intent to the IMF on 22 May 1969, the government committed itself for the first time to a target for Domestic Credit Expansion:[6] 'The government's objectives and policies imply a domestic credit expansion for the private and public sectors in the year ending 31st March 1970 of not more than £400 million.' At the same time the government declared that it 'attaches the greatest importance to monetary policy, which provides an essential support to fiscal policies'. An import deposit scheme was also introduced to restrict imports and reduce liquidity simultaneously. Importers of manufactured goods were required to deposit 50 per cent of the value of imports with the government before the goods could be cleared from Customs and Excise. The required figure was reduced to 40 per cent in November 1969 and to 30 per cent in April 1970, and the scheme was finally ended in December 1970. With no interest payable on deposits, and deposits not repayable for 180 days, the scheme was equivalent to an import surcharge of about 2.5 per cent.

The outcome of this formidable array of policies to improve the balance of payments was that the current account moved into surplus in 1969 and reached a record level in 1971 of over £1000 million. The trade balance was still in deficit in 1969 and 1970, but so it had been since 1822 except for two years in the 1950s. So severe were the deflationary measures, however, and so rapid the growth of export volume (largely as a result of the rapid expansion of world trade), that the trade balance itself also moved into surplus in 1971, the surplus of £190 million being the largest in recorded history (until then). The 'full' employment trade balance would no doubt have been in deficit, but the current account would still have shown a surplus.

The declared aim of the Treasury in the 1950s and 1960s was to run a current-account surplus of £450 million to permit long-term overseas investment and to build up foreign-exchange reserves. By the end of the 1960s the objective had been achieved, though at some cost to employment. A policy of 'steady as she goes' would probably have consolidated the surplus and allowed the country to retain some of the benefits of devaluation for longer. As it was the surplus was frittered away by an irresponsible expansion of internal demand, reminiscent of what happened in 1964 and which led to the troubles and stagnation of the 1960s.

1970 TO 1979

The history of the balance of payments in the first years of the 1970s, before the pound was floated in June 1972, is told in Appendix 9.1 to this chapter. Before considering the balance of payments since the par value for sterling was abandoned, a reminder will be useful of the international events surrounding the UK decision. In August 1971, following a concerted speculative attack against the dollar, the convertibility of the dollar into gold at $35 per ounce was suspended and the world's major currencies began to float against each other for the first time since the Bretton Woods agreement of 1944.

The expectation was, however, that a new set of parities would be established with the dollar devalued against other major currencies, and this was duly accomplished by the Smithsonian agreement of December 1971. The dollar was devalued by 8 per cent by raising the price of gold from $35 to $38 per ounce, and the exchange margins allowed around the new parities were widened from 1 per cent to 2.25 per cent. The new parities could not be maintained for long, with large volumes of capital switching from one financial centre to another, and they finally broke down. The first currency to break was sterling in June 1972, though the current account of the balance of payments was still in good surplus. Switzerland followed in January 1973, and Italy later. Belgium, Denmark, West Germany, France and the Netherlands operated a joint float against the dollar for some time, keeping their own currencies within a 2.25 per cent margin of each other. In June 1973, however, West Germany was 'forced' to let the mark appreciate, and in January 1974 France left the joint float and allowed the franc to float freely.

The expectations held out for floating exchange rates were that they would lend stability to exchange rates, free domestic economic policy from external payments constraints, economise on the use of international reserves, and make management of the international monetary system easier. Alas, the reality has been far removed from the expectations. First, exchange-rate fluctuations have been quite violent by any standard, and possibly more disruptive than the periodic devaluations under the Bretton Woods system. Some evidence for the early years is presented by Hirsch and Higham (1974) who conclude that the sizeable fluctuations experienced cannot be attributed to destabilising official intervention, as some proponents of free floating tried to argue. If floating had been completely free, and not managed, the fluctuations would have been even greater. The exchange rate movements since 1974 have been even more turbulent rather than diminishing as the markets gained experience. Williamson (1983) has calculated the coefficient of variation (as a measure of volatility) of daily nominal exchange rates against the dollar around a six-month moving average (expressed as a percentage) for four major currencies pre- and post-1972. The results are shown in Table 9.5.

In the pre-1972 Bretton Woods era, the figures for the Deutschmark and French franc in 1969 are affected by par value changes (also the pound sterling in 1968 in the wake of devaluation in 1967). Where there were no par value changes, the measure of volatility was, on average, 0.2. Under floating after 1972, the degree of volatility is shown to be as high, if not higher, than in the earlier years when there were par value changes, and higher by a factor of between 5 and 10 than in years when there were no par value changes. Over a longer span of time, the sterling-dollar rate moved from $2.50 at the end of 1980 to $1.05 at the beginning of 1985 – a drop of nearly 60 per cent, – and up to $1.90 again in 1990, a rise of 90 per cent.

Second, domestic policy has not been freed from considerations of the balance of payments because floating has not lessened speculative pressure, and has failed to reduce trade imbalances (see Chapter 5, p. 176). Currency depreciation has led to speculative outflows and often

TABLE 9.5

Exchange rate volatility under pegged and floating exchange rates

	1968	1969	1975	1982
Deutschmark	0.3	1.2	1.7	1.6
French Franc	0.1	2.3	1.6	2.2
Japanese Yen	n.a.	n.a.	0.7	2.5
Pound Sterling	0.7	0.2	1.0	1.1

worsened payments imbalance, while currency appreciation has led to speculative inflows and mounting payments surpluses. Floating exchange rates have tended to weaken the weak and strengthen the strong out of all proportion to differences in the real economic performance of countries, and this has necessitated internal policies as draconian as under fixed exchange rates (even in conditions of unemployment). Interest-rate policy has continued to be dominated by consideration of the balance of payments, and in deficit countries such as the US there has been a growing demand for trade restrictions. There could be no stronger indictment of the inadequacy of exchange depreciation to rectify payments imbalance than the call for protectionism to become respectable. The UK Treasury itself has become more and more sceptical through time that a downward floating pound provides the answer to improving the country's balance of payments and removing the balance-of-payments constraint on faster growth. Work at the Treasury by Odling-Smee and Hartley (1978), using the Treasury macroeconomic model, suggests that over 50 per cent of the competitive advantage of exchange-rate changes is eroded within two years even on the weak assumption that it takes three years for wages to fully compensate for price increases. Since wages, in the absence of controls, tend in practice to adjust much more quickly, little competitive advantage from exchange depreciation can be expected at all. Odling-Smee and Hartley conclude that a *permanent* gain in competitiveness would require continual depreciation in excess of the resulting cost inflation, and could thus be achieved only at the cost of accelerating inflation. It should also be explicitly recognised that even if a competitive advantage could be maintained, this is not sufficient to allow the growth rate to be raised permanently. This would require a *continually growing* competitive advantage.

Because speculation has exacerbated exchange-rate instability, and failed to eliminate imbalances, there has been an even greater need, not less, for international reserves to 'ride out' crises, and an even greater need for international co-operation to compensate for the lack of international reserves and to manage the international monetary system.

In the United Kingdom the immediate effect of floating was for the exchange rate to depreciate and for the balance of payments to worsen. By the end of 1972 sterling had depreciated against the dollar, and against a trade-weighted average of twenty-one currencies (including the dollar), by 10 per cent. The trade-weighted average of these currencies is called the *effective exchange rate*.[7] By the end of 1973 the depreciation against the dollar was 11.2 per cent, and the depreciation of the effective exchange rate was 17.4 per cent, compared with the Smithsonian parities of December 1971. The exchange rate for the dollar, mark, the SDR, and the index of the effective exchange rate since 1971 are shown in Figure 9.1

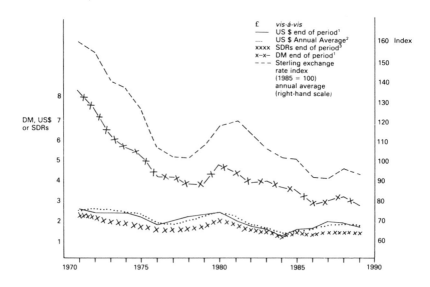

FIGURE 9.1 *Exchange rate movements since 1971*

1. Middle market telegraph transfer rates as recorded in London by the Bank of England during the late afternoon. End period relates to the last working day.
2. Average of trading day rates described above.
3. As calculated by the IMF.

DATA FOR FIGURE 9.1
Exchange rate movements since 1971

	US dollars	per £	SDRs per £	Deutschmarks per £	Sterling exchange rate index (Average 1985=100)
	End of period[1]	Annual average[2]	End of period[3]	End of period[1]	Annual average
1971	2.5522	2.4440	2.3510	8.3395	
1972	2.3481	2.5020	2.1627	7.5150	
1973	2.3235	2.4526	1.9258	6.2788	
1974	2.3495	2.3402	1.9181	5.6537	
1975	2.0231	2.2198	1.7285	5.2978	124.8
1976	1.7021	1.8046	1.4653	4.0165	107.0
1977	1.9185	1.7455	1.5691	4.0145	101.2
1978	2.0410	1.9197	1.5617	3.7146	101.0
1979	2.2250	2.1225	1.6883	3.8403	107.0
1980	2.3920	2.3281	1.8700	4.6931	117.7
1981	1.9110	2.0254	1.6392	4.2896	119.0
1982	1.6175	1.7489	1.4636	3.8505	113.7
1983	1.4520	1.5158	1.3855	3.9516	105.3
1984	1.1580	1.3364	1.1798	3.6535	100.6
1985	1.4455	1.2976	1.3151	3.5299	100.0
1986	1.4837	1.4672	1.2055	2.8524	91.5
1987	1.8870	1.6392	1.3193	2.9607	90.1
1988	1.8080	1.7796	1.3447	3.2047	95.5
1989	1.6125	1.6383	1.2217	2.7275	92.6

1. Middle market telegraph transfer rates as recorded in London by the Bank of England during the late afternoon. End period relates to the last working day.
2. Average of trading day rates described above.
3. As calculated by the IMF.
Source: Central Statistical Office: *The Pink Book 1990: United Kingdom Balance of Payments*, (London: HMSO, 1990).

The rapid depreciation of sterling in 1972 and 1973 raised the sterling payments for imports by much more than the increase in the sterling receipts from exports, and this helped to produce a merchandise trade deficit of over £2000 million in 1973, the largest in recorded history. The other major contributor to the enormous deficit was the steep rise in commodity prices. The import bill between 1971 and 1973 grew by nearly £6000 million. The balance on current account moved from a small surplus in 1972 to a deficit of nearly £1000 million in 1973.

None of these adverse trends had anything to do with the rise in the price of oil, which did not take place until December 1973. The quadrupling of oil prices led to severe difficulties in 1974, however. Not only did the UK oil bill rise by approximately £2500 million but exports also suffered as the world was plunged into recession through the inability of the OPEC countries to spend their surpluses. In 1974 the trade deficit rose to over £5000 million and the current-account deficit to over £3000 million. Against the background of a worsening payments imbalance, and the country working a three-day week as a result of the miners' dispute, with rumours also of a General Election, sterling came under increasing speculative attack in the early part of 1974. There was some recovery of sterling in the middle of the year, but the strong downward pressure continued at the end of the year, and at least $500 million was used from the reserves in December alone to support the exchange rate. There was heavy selling of sterling by the Arabian American Oil Company (Aramco), the world's largest oil consortium, after a request from Saudi Arabia that future oil royalties should be paid exclusively in dollars. Earlier in the year, to attract Arab oil revenue and to induce other sterling holders to maintain their balances in London, the Treasury announced a new exchange-rate guarantee scheme for official overseas sterling funds. The new guarantee was expressed in terms of the effective exhange rate instead of the dollar (which had been used for previous guarantee schemes). In return for the exchange-rate guarantee overseas holders of sterling were required to maintain between 60 and 70 per cent of their national reserves in London. On April Fools day 1974 it was announced that the Bank of England would publish, like some medieval ritual, the effective exchange rate daily at noon.

By the beginning of 1975 the effective exchange rate had depreciated by 22 per cent against the Smithsonian parities and the dollar price of the pound was down to $2.38. The Bank of England intervened to halt the slide of the exchange rate throughout most of 1975, but the downward trend continued. The internal domestic recession brought a virtual halt to the growth of imports, and both the trade deficit and the current-account deficit were cut by some £2000 million compared with 1974. The payments imbalance remained huge, however, despite depreciation.

The year 1976 was one of crisis. On 5 March (Black Friday) the pound fell below the $2 level, heralding in the 50p dollar. Once the psychological barrier had been broken, there were visions of the pound falling to $1.50, and even to a dollar a pound. The immediate cause of sterling's demise was the rumour that Nigeria might with-draw its sterling funds from London following a diplomatic row with the United Kingdom in which the High Commissioner in Lagos was expelled because of his unacceptability to the Nigerian authorities. The depreciation of the effective exchange rate for sterling reached 32 per cent. In May the pound fell below \$1.80 and the effective rate of exchange had fallen by nearly 40 per cent since 1971. The de-preciation from January to May alone was 12.5 per cent despite moderating inflation and an improving balance of payments on current account. The Bank of England was forced to raise the Minimum Lending Rate to a record high of 11.5 per cent. In a BBC interview, Mr Healey, the Chancellor of the Exchequer, declared that 'the value of the pound had gone down further than was justified by underlying economic trends and would soon bounce back again'. It might well be asked by what objective standards did the comparative industrial and commercial performance of the United Kingdom deteriorate by 40 per cent in relation to other countries during the previous three years. The truth is, of course, that there was no justification based on real factors for such a depreciation. The volatility of floating ex-change rates in general, and the demise of sterling in particular, is to be explained by the whims and sentiment of speculators, and by the political activities of creditors. This is the price that a country pays for short-term borrowing and for a central role in international economic affairs. The price for the UK people after 1972 was high and pro-tracted, and probably higher than if there had been a quick real adjustment to the rise in commodity prices in 1973 and 1974 with the exchange rate stabilised – by, if necessary, strict controls on capital movements. The pound continued its relentless slide into June. The City called for public expenditure cuts, government backbenchers called for an inquiry into the fall, and the Opposition in Parliament called for a halt to the slide. The Chancellor declared that the United Kingdom must keep its nerve and not panic, but against a back-ground of rumours and speculations the slide continued. On 7 June a \$5300 million loan was announced from the Group of Ten nations, available for six months. The pound rallied slightly and was also helped by the miners' vote in favour of the government's second stage of pay policy. On 28 September the foreign exchanges experi-enced their worst day since June 1972. The Chancellor, who was on his way to Hong Kong for a meeting of finance ministers, returned to London because of the heavy selling of sterling, which caused the rate to fall by over 4 cents during the day, closing at \$1.637. The

effective exchange rate fell to 44 per cent below the Smithsonian
parities. The Bank of England had, in fact, stopped supporting the
pound out of the reserves from 9 September. So much for free
floating avoiding the panic and disruption of fixed rates! Then, 25
October claimed the record as the worst day on the foreign exchanges
since June 1972. The pound plunged 5 cents in the day to $1.595, with
dealers blaming the fall on a report in the *Sunday Times* that an
agreement had been reached to let sterling fall to $1.50 as a condition
for an IMF stand-by credit. The depreciation of the effective exchange rate reached 47.6 per cent. The year ended with a smaller
current-account deficit than in 1975 but a much larger balance for
official financing because of the heavy outflow of short-term capital.

In 1977 pressure in the exchange market was reversed and the
Bank of England had difficulty in preventing the exchange rate from
rising. It is estimated that, during 1977, £10,000 million was sold to
buy up foreign currency to keep the pound from rising in value. By
the end of October the reserves had risen to $20,000 million, com-
pared with $4000 million at the end of 1976, giving the third largest
reserves in the world next to West Germany and Saudi Arabia. A
wiser policy would have been to let the exchange rate rise immediately. This would have reduced the import bill, probably raised
export receipts, and contributed to the battle against inflation which
might further have improved the balance of payments. On 31 October the Bank of England did end its policy of holding down the
exchange rate for fear that the excessive accumulation of reserves
would jeopardise control of the money supply. By the end of 1977 the
pound had risen to over $1.90 and the depreciation of the effective
exchange rate stood at 35 per cent.

In December measures were taken to ease exchange controls over
direct investment into the European Economic Community; and the
requirement applicable to all overseas portfolio investment that 25
per cent of the sales proceeds must be surrendered at the official
exchange rate (the so-called 'surrender rule') was abolished.

In 1978 the current account moved into substantial surplus from a
slight deficit in 1977. Throughout the year the American dollar came
under considerable pressure and the pound continued to rise against
the dollar, going above $2 on 20 October for the first time since
March 1976. The effective rate of exchange against European currencies depreciated slightly, however, ending the year at 62 per cent
of its 1971 level. In July there was the Bremen initiative to achieve
greater stability of European currencies, but the United Kingdom's

endorsement of the plans was lukewarm. There was a considerable increase in the outflow of private investment during the year, and this was reflected in a loss of foreign-exchange reserves despite the current-account surplus.

In 1979 the Conservative Party came to power and altered the course of economic policy in a strongly monetarist direction. The exchange rate continued to climb, and by the end of July had risen against the $US by 21 per cent in a year to $2.32, the highest level for four years. The effective rate of exchange also appreciated, standing at 73 per cent of its 1971 level. The rise was attributable partly to continued weakness of the American dollar and partly to relatively high UK short-term interest rates. The rise in the exchange rate was regarded with equanimity by the government in the international monetarist belief that a strong pound would mean a lower rate of domestic inflation. There began in 1979 the final dismantling of all exchange controls after forty years of restrictions. They were first eased in the Budget and then were substantially relaxed from 19 July. Currency became available without limit at the official exchange rate for all outward direct investment. UK residents became free to invest at the official exchange rate in most securities denominated and payable in the currencies of other EEC countries. Similar relaxation applied to foreign currency securities issued by international organisations of which the United Kingdom was a member. The final remaining controls were removed from 25 October. The level of capital outflows continued to increase in 1979. Total UK private investment overseas rose from £2.3 billion in 1977 to £6.5 billion in 1979. There was also a considerable inflow of both long- and short-term capital, giving a net surplus on capital account of over £2 billion, half of which was added to the reserves. The year 1979 also witnessed the biggest rise in the price of oil since 1973, which helped to worsen the visible trade deficit to over £3 billion – more than twice the visible deficit for 1978. There was also a 12 per cent rise in import volume compared with a much smaller rise in export volume of 4.5 per cent.

SINCE 1980

The early years of the 1980s witnessed a severe economic recession in the United Kingdom, against a background of world recession, an international debt crisis, the growing strength of the US dollar and turmoil in the foreign exchange markets. Between 1979 and 1983 gross domestic product was virtually stagnant, having actually fallen by 3.7 per cent between 1979 and 1981. Manufacturing output fell by 12 per cent and manufacturing employment by 24 per cent. Total private investment fell by 2 per cent and manufacturing investment fell by a colossal 38 per cent. The major part of the recession was indigenously induced by the restrictive monetary and fiscal stance of the government, which apart from its direct deflationary impact also contributed to an excessive appreciation of the exchange rate in 1979 and 1980. The severe economic recession, in combination with growing exports of oil, produced a surplus on the current account of the balance of payments in every year between 1980 and 1986. Very worrying from the point of view of the real economy, however, and its future prospects was the fact that in 1982/83 the country recorded a trade deficit in manufactured goods for the first time in its economic history which has got progressively worse.[8] Oil, and a surplus on the invisible account, now alone pay for essential raw materials and food and the country's appetite for foreign manufactured goods. As the production and export of oil level off and decline, this adverse trend will not be sustainable. The United Kingdom will have to export more manufactures or 'die'! Exchange rates continued to be volatile against a background of the growing strength of the dollar from 1981 on. In 1980, however, the pound was still strong. Amidst gold fever which pushed the price of gold close to $1000 per ounce, the pound continued to appreciate on the foreign exchange market. High interest rates in London and the strengthening of the current account of the balance of payments were important contributory factors. No doubt the United Kingdom's position as an oil producer also played a psychological part in giving confidence to overseas investors in sterling. In strictly economic terms, however, there is no reason why one part of the balance of payments should be singled out as contributing to the strength of a currency. The large current-account surplus of £3 billion came about largely through economic recession at home and the compression of imports. If the full employment of resources had been maintained, the current account would have been in substantial deficit, and then what would the price of sterling have been, notwithstanding Britain being an oil producer? By the end of October sterling had reached its highest level for seven years of $2.45. Despite the high exchange rate, export volume rose. The visible account was in surplus for only the seventh year in recorded history. Again there was a huge outflow of private investment overseas of close to £7 billion, but this was more than matched by inflows of short-and-long term capital, giving a net increase in the reserves during the year, pushing them to a record level of over £13 billion. Superficially, the balance of payments looked healthy, but not viewed against a background of deepening recession, growing import penetration, and an underlying deterioration in the non-oil account of the balance of payments.

Sterling reached its peak against the dollar at the end of 1980 ending over four years of virtually continual appreciation from the low of $1.55 during the exchange crisis of 1976. The next four years witnessed a remorseless decline ending in a low of near parity in February/March 1985. Throughout the period, the authorities appeared largely indifferent to the exchange rate. They appeared happy as it rose as a weapon against inflation and stoical as it fell in the conviction that market forces must prevail. Sterling began its long slide at the end of 1980 when interest rates fell. Later, sterling confonted the growing strength of the dollar, and weakened with the uncertainty over oil prices in a very depressed market. By the end of 1981, the rate stood at $1.80. During 1981, there was a massive current account surplus of £6.5 billion, one of the largest in the world and quite inexcusable. There is nothing virtuous in a balance-of-payments surplus while the real economy languishes. The surplus was wholly offset by a continuing high outflow of portfolio investment and other long-term capital flows amounting to over £8 billion. There was a record deficit on capital account of nearly £7 billion.

The exchange rate continued to fall in 1982, and ended the year at $1.55. The threat of lower oil prices as a result of the world recession became a particularly significant factor towards the end of the year. The current account remained in surplus at £4.6 billion helped by record oil exports running at £1 billion a month. The year will be remembered, however, as the first time in British economic history when more manufactured goods were imported than exported (measured on an overseas trade statistics basis). Total private investment overseas also continued to grow reaching £10.5 billion, of which over half was portfolio investment.

At the beginning of 1983, sterling was badly hit by falling oil prices. At an emergency meeting in January, OPEC failed to agree on a new price structure and production targets for oil, and by March the exchange rate had fallen to $1.40, well below its previous low of $1.55 in 1976. Sterling's effective exchange rate against all major currencies also reached a record low of 79. The rate steadied during the year, however, and ended at $1.43 against the dollar and at an index of 82.5 against all major currencies. The overall surplus on the current account of the balance of payments dwindled to £3 billion, as the economy showed signs of recovery, and overseas investment continued its upward trend reaching over £11 billion.

During 1984 sterling was overwhelmed by the strength of the dollar and had fallen to $1.15 by the end of the year. The dollar's strength puzzled many observers given the massive US current account deficit of over $100 billion, and the prospect of the US becoming the world's largest debtor. On the other hand, US real interest rates were at least four percentage points higher than in the UK, and the real economy showed exceptional strength compared with the still depressed economies of Europe. For a combination of reasons, therefore, the US was able to continue to attract massive net capital inflows. The UK authorities continued to remain indifferent to the exchange rate. The Chancellor of the Exchequer, Nigel Lawson, and the Bank of England continued to state publicly that there was no need to defend sterling by raising interest rates. Foreign exchange dealers interpreted the attitude as 'malign neglect' and reacted accordingly. The current balance of payments recorded a small surplus of £1.8 billion, while private investment overseas reached a colossal £15.9 billion. Between the 1970s and 1984, annual portfolio investment overseas rose by approximately £8 billion, compared with inward portfolio investment of only £1 billion. The trade deficit in manufactures continued to deteriorate and approached £4 billion on a balance of payments basis.

At the beginning of 1985, sterling remained very weak against the dollar and other currencies. There was the very real prospect of the rate breaking the 'psychological' barrier of one dollar to the pound, and this was the prediction of most foreign exchange dealers. The UK authorities, while continuing to deny that they had any particular target rate of exchange in mind, nonetheless acted and on 11 January interest rates were raised from 9.5 per cent to 10.5 per cent. The rise had no impact and on 14 January the banks' base rate rose to 12 per cent as the Bank of England introduced a minimum lending rate for the first time since 1981. The pound remained weak at $1.11, with sterling's effective rate at 70.6, both record lows. On 28 January, base rate was further raised to 14 per cent, led this time by the market rather than the Bank of England. The City labelled the day 'Black Monday'. The Chancellor of the Exchequer did his best to defend the rise in interest rates declaring that 'anxieties over sterling have been greatly overdone'! Uncertainty over oil prices and the mighty dollar continued to keep sterling weak, however, and by the end of February the official rate was $1.03, with trading at parity in hotels. But tides turn quickly in exchange markets and fears about the health of the American economy, the sustainability of the budget deficit and the deficit on the balance of payments, caused the dollar to gradually weaken. In addition, in September, the Group of Five countries of the US, Japan, West Germany, Britain and France announced concerted action to lower the value of the dollar.

The so-called 'Plaza Agreement' to push the dollar down heralded the first major attempt at international co-operation among industrial nations to achieve an agreed framework of exchange rates to reduce global payments imbalances. The US in 1985 was heading for a current deficit of $150 billion, and protectionist sentiment against Japan was growing. The very agreement precipitated the selling of the dollar, and by the end of the year, sterling had risen to $1.50. The second attempt at international policy co-ordination and exchange rate management was the 'Paris Accord' (or Louvre Agreement) of February 1987 which expressed a general preference for exchange rate stability and took action to strengthen the dollar.

The second half of the 1980s witnessed very rapid economic growth and recovery, following the deep recession of the early 1980s, leading to the claims of an 'economic miracle'. The growth of national income between 1985 and 1988 averaged 4 per cent per annum (more than double the rate of the 1970s), and the level of unemployment fell from 11 per cent in 1985 to 6.6 per cent in 1989. The cost was a rise in inflation from a low of 3.4 per cent in 1986 to nearly 10 per cent in 1990, and a massive deterioration in the current account of the balance of payments from a surplus of £3 billion in 1985 to a deficit of nearly £20 billion in 1989. Policy discussion came to be dominated by the question of whether the UK should join the exchange rate mechanism (ERM) of the European Monetary System (EMS) which effectively had become a deutschmark bloc owing to the emergence of the D-mark as the strongest European currency. The D-mark–sterling exchange rate started to become the focus of attention. At a meeting of the National Economic Development Council at the beginning of 1987, the Chancellor of the Exchequer, Nigel Lawson, declared that he was aiming to keep the pound at around DM2.90. This would be achieved by a mixture of interest rate policy and intervention in the foreign exchange market. Shadowing the D-mark became a deliberate act of policy, and in May 1987 interest rates were reduced explicitly to stop the pound from rising. There were already signs, however, of excessive monetary expansion. Financial liberalisation was proceeding apace; broad money targets (M3) were formally abandoned; the personal saving ratio was falling, and there was an enormous expansion of personal credit (from £90 billion in 1980 to £280 billion in 1987). Following the stock market crash of October 1987, monetary policy was further relaxed and interest rates fell below 8 per cent in order to allay an expected recession. The current account deficit in 1987 was over £3 billion, with a worsening deficit on manufactured trade and a dwindling surplus on oil from a peak of £8 billion in 1985 to £4 billion in 1987. It is interesting to recall that when the pound was high in the early 1980s, supposedly as a result of its petrocurrency status, which did so much harm to manufacturing industry, free market economists promised a natural exchange rate adjustment as the oil surplus dwindled leading to a spontaneous revival of manufacturing industry and trade. In practice, the exchange rate has been kept relatively strong by high interest rates in the attempt to curb inflation, and the manufacturing trade deficit continued to grow to over £17 billion in 1989.

In 1988, monetary expansion was fuelled by an April budget which gave away £6 billion in tax cuts. City of London analysts began to express concern at the severely worsening trade statistics. Their early forecasts of a current deficit of £10–12 billion proved too optimistic, since the deficit ended up at close to £14 billion. In an infamous newspaper interview, Chancellor Lawson castigated what he referred to as 'teenage scribblers in the City who jump up and down in an effort to get press attention'. Britain's trade deficit was a 'problem of success', it was argued, reflecting an investment boom as part of the 'economic miracle', and easily financeable by other countries' savings. In July, Mr Lawson announced in the House of Commons that the economy was as sound and as strong as it had been for fifty years; and in a by-election speech declared 'there is no reason why the trade deficit should bring to an end the success story of low inflation, sustained growth and falling unemployment'. Throughout 1988, Mr Lawson referred to the deficit as 'benign and self correcting' on the grounds that it reflected the outcome of the decisions of private individuals with regard to investment and saving, and was not the result of public profligacy since the government budget was in substantial surplus. A close look at the balance-of-payments accounts reveals, however, that the emerging deficit was not simply, or even mainly, the result of an investment boom in the economy. The growing deficit was spread right across manufacturing, particularly in vehicles and other consumer goods. Moreover, the deficit was being financed largely by 'hot' money, i.e. inflows via the banking system not by net long-term inflows. The long-term capital account of the balance of payments consisting of direct private investment and portfolio investment, was also in substantial deficit. On 25 November 1988, the City experienced its worst day of chaos since the 1987 stock market crash in the wake of the record monthly trade deficit for October of £2.43 billion. The pound fell, and interest rates were raised to 13 per cent – the ninth rise since June. The pound strengthened to $1.84 and DM 3.16.

By shadowing the D-mark in 1987, the Chancellor had indicated a preference to give up monetary targets in favour of greater exchange rate stability, to prepare sterling for entry into the ERM. Just before the budget of 1988, however, Mrs Thatcher insisted that exchange market intervention should stop, and blamed rising inflation on the Chancellor's attempt to shadow the D-mark. Open warfare developed between the Prime Minister and the Chancellor over exchange rate policy and the desirability of Britain joining the ERM, which began to make the conduct of economic policy extremely difficult, not least because of the uncertainty created in financial markets about whether the pound would be supported or not. Mrs Thatcher, advised by Sir Alan Walters, believed that exchange rates should be allowed to find their market level ('you can't buck the market') and that Britain could not contemplate membership of the ERM while inflation was rising and while other EC countries still imposed capital controls. Walters had described the ERM as 'half-baked' and was predicting, in any case, that the ERM would collapse with the complete liberalisation of capital flows. In 1989, with the pound under pressure, inflation and interest rates rising, and the economy out of control, Mr Lawson felt his role as Chancellor of the Exchequer, and steward of the nation's economy, being increasingly undermined. The final straw came in October 1989 with an article by Walters in the obscure American journal (the *American Economist*) which further attacked the ERM and received wide publicity in the British press. Lawson found his position untenable and resigned on the 26 October, writing to Mrs Thatcher as follows:

> the successful conduct of economic policy is possible only if there is, and is seen to be, full agreement between the Prime Minister and the Chancellor of the Exchequer. Recent events have confirmed that this essential requirement cannot be satisfied as long as Alan Walters remains your personal economic adviser.

Mrs Thatcher preferred to see Mr Lawson go rather than dismiss Alan Walters, but in the end she lost both, since Walters then also decided to step aside. John Major was appointed the new Chancellor, pronouncing himself in favour of a firm exchange rate. The pound had plummeted after Lawson's resignation and in November reached $1.57 – its lowest level since 1986. Interest rates had already been raised to 15 per cent in early October, before Lawson's resignation – their highest level since 1981. Meanwhile the current balance of payments continued to worsen, ending the year at nearly £20 billion. The visible deficit was £23.8 billion and the deficit on manufactured trade was £17.3 billion.

Into the 1990s interest rates remained at 15 per cent and the economy moved into recession. The payments deficit narrowed but not by much. Undoubtedly the most significant event was that on the 8 October 1990 the UK finally entered the ERM with margins of 6 per cent around the central parities – with the parity against the Deutschmark at DM2.95 to £1. Mrs Thatcher's capitulation became necessary in order to reduce interest rates from 15 to 14 per cent before the impending Conservative Party Conference. Disputes over Britain's attitude to Europe forced Mrs Thatcher's resignation as Prime Minister on 28 November and she was succeeded by John Major, with Mr Norman Lamont as Chancellor.

Britain's chronic balance-of-payments problem is not only the result of poor performance within the tradeable goods sector but also a function of the gross structural imbalance that has been allowed to develop over the years between the tradeable and non-tradeable goods sectors of the economy. This imbalance corresponds broadly to the imbalance between manufacturing and services since all manufactured goods are potentially tradeable whereas only about 20 per cent of service output is tradeable. Through the neglect of manufacturing industry, production has shifted towards non-tradeable goods, while the demand for tradeables is met from abroad. This situation is clearly not sustainable, and we shall have more to say on this in Chapters 14 and 15.

APPENDIX: A POLEMIC ON FLOATING THE POUND, 1972[9]

When the United Kingdom maintained a fixed rate of exchange for the pound, a more flexible system allowing the exchange rate to fluctuate more freely was, according to some, the only solution to the continual problems of balance-of-payments disequilibrium and slow growth. Greater exchange-rate flexibility, it was argued, would free the domestic economy from the constraints imposed by the necessity to maintain a balance on international trading account and would reduce the need for international reserves and foreign borrowing to defend the foreign-exchange value of sterling. A fluctuating pound would see the end of 'stop-go' policies and allow the economy to be run at any desired pressure of demand.

In June 1972, faced with a massive speculative attack on sterling, the decision was taken to abandon pegged exchange rates in favour of a system of managed floating – just one of many forms that greater exchange-rate flexibility may take. By the end of 1973 the pound had depreciated 20 per cent against a weighted average of other major currencies. Meanwhile the economic situation deteriorated rapidly. The years 1972 and 1973 witnessed unprecedented rates of inflation, and the 1973 balance-of-payments deficit was the largest in recorded history till then. Since the rise in oil prices did not take effect until the very end of the year, the origin of the difficulties clearly lay elsewhere. The question may well be asked whether exchange depreciation itself contributed to the growing economic difficulties, and whether exchange-rate flexibility is beneficial if it leads to a currency depreciating so much in such a short space of time.

The purpose here is to argue three points. First, the advocacy of greater exchange-rate flexibility should not be extended with approval to a system which permits such excessive depreciation so quickly. Second, the drastic sterling depreciation that was allowed to occur exacerbated the United Kingdom's economic difficulties. Third, while greater exchange-rate flexibility may be desirable, exchange depreciation itself is largely irrelevant as a policy weapon for tackling the long-run UK payments problem, which has its origin not so much in growing price uncompetitiveness as in a much higher UK income elasticity of demand for imports that the 'world' income elasticity of demand for UK exports. For this type of problem, common to less-developed countries, exchange depreciation can at best provide a temporary palliative. Indeed, it may make the ultimate cure more difficult.

The Case for Exchange-rate Flexibility

The general case of exchange-rate flexibility is well known and need be touched on only briefly here. Exchange-rate flexibility gives a central bank greater room for manoeuvre and avoids the necessity for a country to hold large reserves or to borrow abroad to maintain the exchange value of its currency if there is speculation against it. Indeed, the theoretical expectation is that, in a system in which the exchange rate is free to vary, speculation will on balance stabilise the currency, as any initial depreciation will induce the private speculator to move funds from the appreciating to the depreciating currency. This mechanism should serve to limit speculation against a currency, to arrest the depreciation, and to finance the deficit on the balance of payments caused by the relative price changes, until the quantities of imports and exports have had time to adjust to the change in the exchange rate. The more speculators are willing to support a currency which has depreciated, the more reserves are saved.

For speculation to be stabilising, there must be a consensus in the market about what a particular exchange rate should be and whether the existing rate is 'too high' or 'too low'. Since this condition may not be fulfilled, however, because it is often difficult to know what the correct rate is, floating rates may lead to a great deal of instability. The instability in currency markets in recent months is a good example. Because of uncertainty, exchange rates have tended to move hectically and erratically from one over-reaction to the next in a generally destabilising way. As far as sterling is concerned, there is still a great deal of uncertainty as to what the correct rate is, due in no small measure to the failure of the balance of payments to respond to the initial exchange rate depreciation in the way expected from economic theory.

A second main argument for exchange-rate flexibility is that it would avoid the necessity of domestic demand deflation – and unemployment – to correct a balance-of-payments deficit. To be sure, if exchange rate depreciation occurs in conditions of full employment, demand contraction is required in order to avoid excess demand. However, provided resources can be switched easily and quickly from the domestic to the export sector, there is no reason why this transition should lead to higher unemployment. Flexible exchange rates may therefore be a device for achieving simultaneous internal and external equilibrium if combined with the appropriate domestic policy. In July 1972 *The Economist* went so far as to argue that depreciation of the pound (plus wage restraint) would mean that 'Britain would probably break through to something like an economic miracle'!

Problems Stemming from Exchange-rate Flexibility

Managed floating, which the United Kingdom adopted in June 1972, is only one of many forms of exchange-rate flexibility. There was nothing in the discarded parity system to prevent exchange rates from being adjusted. Many would still hold the view that the old adjustable peg system would have been perfectly workable if only governments had been willing to make use of the provisions for adjustment. Other forms of exchange-rate flexibility widely canvassed consist of fixed parities with wider bands, sliding parities with and without wide bands, and completely free floating. Although greater exchange-rate flexibility may be desirable, it does not follow that a system of freely floating exchange rates is best. There are many considerations, which the proponents of floating exchange rates tend to ignore, which make one sceptical of floating as a means of achieving simultaneous internal and external equilibrium.

The first major consideration frequently ignored is the adverse repercussions that exchange-rate depreciation has initially on the balance of payments. These may be so severe and so prolonged as to cause destabilising speculation. A second is the risk that the impact of exchange depreciation on the domestic price of imports may severely affect, both directly and indirectly, the rate of domestic inflation in an open economy. In a popular article Professor H. G. Johnson once argued that 'the basic argument for floating exchange rates is so simple that most people have considerable difficulty in understanding it', and because a floating exchange rate keeps the foreign-exchange market cleared 'a floating rate would save a country from having to reverse its full-employment policies because they lead to inflation and deficit' (*The Times*, 9 December 1968). But there is no mention that exchange rate depreciation may generate further domestic inflation and widen the deficit. Full employment is not the only goal of economic policy and exchange rate depreciation will not necessarily remedy a balance-of-payments deficit.

Nature of the Balance of Payments

In discussing the effects of floating exchange rates, it is of crucial importance to draw a distinction between balance in the foreign-exchange market (the 'market' balance of payments) and the balance of payments as traditionally defined (i.e. the balance of expenditures and receipts on current and long-term capital account, or what is sometimes called the 'basic' balance of payments). Since an exchange rate is the price of one currency relative to another, it is obvious that a freely floating exchange rate will give balance in the foreign-exchange market, in the sense that, assuming no market intervention by central banks, the amounts bought and sold by other operators in the market must be the same. But the price of a currency which results in a balance in the foreign-exchange market does not guarantee a balance between expenditure and receipts on the current and long-term capital account of the balance of payments. A fall in the exchange rate will produce a market balance and basic balance only if the resulting change in relative prices between domestic and foreign goods is not offset by domestic price changes, and if export and import volumes respond by the correct amounts. If the volumes of exports and imports are reasonably responsive to changes in relative prices, then according to economic theory there will be an exchange rate which gives balance in both senses. However, the time lag between the exchange rate initially falling and the rate reaching a level which guarantees balance in both senses may be long; and what may happen to the domestic economy in the meantime may be extremely serious. Indeed, most of the economic theory of exchange-rate movements has been concerned with comparing two different equilibrium situations. It does not predict the path between these equilibria. Other dynamic theories, in which the economy would never reach the second equilibrium situation because the response of the economy to the initial change in the exchange rate is perverse, could be formulated. For example, one could postulate a scenario in which an initial depreciation of an exchange rate led to increased domestic inflation, which in turn reduced domestic confidence, which led to a fall in investment, and so on.

The UK Situation

The UK experience over the last two years makes a cautionary tale. A weak balance of payments, in the sense of severe speculation against the currency, caused the exchange rate to fall. Because imports and exports were relatively price inelastic in the short run, the balance of payments deteriorated, speculators were uncertain, and the exchange rate continued to fall. Sterling import prices rose, pushing up home costs and prices, and this stimulated the demand for higher wages. The competitive gains from currency depreciation were eroded and a spiral of domestic inflation and currency depreciation was set in motion, forcing the authorities to intervene, necessitating the use of reserves and foreign borrowing as under the old system of fixed exchange rates.

Let us consider in more detail the relationship between the depreciation of the pound and the United Kingdom's worsening economic difficulties up to the end of 1973. The severe depreciation of the pound may be said to have aggravated the United Kingdom's domestic economic difficulties in three main ways. First, it exacerbated the rate of domestic inflation. Second, it diverted attention from the essential need to maintain the domestic economy in balance. Third, it caused such deterioration in the balance of payments as to necessitate the use of restrictive demand-management policies at a time when the economy was slowing down. It is surely ironical that an exchange-rate policy designed to free the economy from the constraint of the balance of payments should have been followed eighteen months later, when there were still unemployed resources in the economy, by the biggest ever reduction in government expenditure, namely the cuts of £1200 million announced in the mini-budget of December 1973. Had the exchange rate been given more support to maintain some par value, we should almost certainly have been forced to restrain demand earlier but less drastically. This seems to be yet another example of an inability to conduct economic affairs with gradualism and moderation.

The sinking pound, by raising the sterling price of imports by more than would otherwise have been the case, exacerbated inflation directly and indirectly. The direct effect arises from the fact that over 20 per cent of total expenditure in the United Kingdom is on imports, so that for every 10 per cent rise in the sterling price of imports the price index may be expected to rise by at least 2 per cent. During 1973 the retail price index rose by approximately 10 per cent. Since the import price index rose by 27 per cent, of which 20 per cent was the direct result of sterling depreciation, we can say that the total contribution of import price increases to the domestic inflation was 5.4 per cent, of which 4 per cent can be attributed to the depreciation of sterling. Indirectly, exchange depreciation influences domestic inflation by its effect on the price of finished products, especially food, and hence on wage claims. Wage claims are extremely sensitive to the price of food, and the United Kingdom imports roughly 50 per cent of her food requirements. A fall in the exchange rate of 20 per cent, therefore, would be likely to raise the food price index by at least 10 per cent. In fact food prices in the United Kingdom in 1973 rose on average by 20 per cent, so that roughly half of that rise was the result of the effective depreciation of sterling, and was *within* the control of UK economic policy; the remaining half was the result of a rise in world food prices outside of UK control. Some may concur with Professor Viner (1964), who once remarked that 'the fixed exchange rate – cult, myth, rigidity, illogicality though it may be – is in many countries the sole surviving barrier to almost unrestrained inflation'. Even Professor Friedman (1953), a leading advocate of floating exchange rates, has conceded that the inflationary repercussions of exchange depreciation may be an objection to floating exchange rates in a particular country at a particular time. Could that country and time have been the United Kingdom in 1972, when world commodity prices were already rising and domestic inflation accelerating?

A second way in which the floating exchange rate aggravated the United Kingdom's difficulties was by relieving pressure on the foreign-exchange market, and thus giving a false sense of security with regard to the state of the economy. Whereas under a system of pegged exchange rates the necessity to control the domestic economy would have been apparent from the necessity to support the par value of sterling, with the pound floating it took an oil crisis, bottlenecks in particular sectors of the economy, inflation of over 10 per cent per annum, and a balance-of-payments deficit running at an annual rate of over £1000 million, for action to be taken to control the rate of expansion of the economy. It has been a perpetual failing of post-war governments to expand the economy too fast in the belief that an expansion of demand by itself can raise the long-run rate of growth of real supply. It happened in 1964, under fixed exchange rates, and it happened again under floating exchange rates, which the government of the day apparently believed would allow the country to expand while the balance of payments looked after itself.

As noted already, the balance of payments did *not* look after itself; it worsened dramatically, and this further aggravated the United Kingdom's economic difficulties. The increase in sterling payments for imports as a result of depreciation seems to have far exceeded the increase in sterling receipts from exports. From a surplus of £1061 million in 1971, the current account moved to a deficit in 1973 to the tune of £1470 million – a turn-round of approximately £2500 million. The possibility of a sharp deterioration in the current balance is of course recognised by the advocates of floating exchange rates, but the deterioration is supposed to be only short-lived until the quantities of imports and exports have had time to adjust to relative price changes. How long the deterioration lasts will, however, depend on many factors which need careful consideration before a policy of exchange-rate depreciation is embarked upon. It depends, first, on the domestic demand for imports and the foreign demand for exports being sensitive to relative prices. Second, there must be the possibility of increasing the supply of exports. Third, there must be some means of managing the exchange market pending the response of imports and exports. If speculators are not willing to finance the initial deficits that arise from exchange depreciation, the consequences of floating, as far as foreign indebtedness and reserve losses are concerned, can be as severe for a country as the consequences of having to defend the par value of a currency. In 1972 the United Kingdom suffered a reserve loss, and had to undertake net official borrowing of over £1000 million to finance a deficit on the current and long-term capital accounts (plus a large negative balancing item). In 1973, despite the size of the current-account deficit, the situation was eased by large inflows of long-term private investment and by public-sector borrowing on the Euro-dollar market. There was no official borrowing in 1973 and no net loss of reserves. Policy for 1974, when the current-account deficit is predicted to be double that of 1973, largely as a result of the rise in oil prices, is not yet clear. We know already, however, from the budget speeches, that foreign borrowing commitments of nearly $4.0 billion have already been entered into, to avoid, in Mr Healey's words, 'massive deflation'.

Over all, there can be no escape from the conclusion that floating the pound has been debilitating for the balance of payments, and for the economy at large. It is certainly questionable whether the consequences of maintaining fixed parities would have been any worse than the consequences of floating. A different mode of exchange-rate flexibility, or a 'dirtier' float, would almost certainly have been wiser.

Past Policy Towards the Exchange Rate

During the period of the last but one Labour government many economists[10] defended, on a variety of grounds, the government's attempt to preserve the par value of sterling between 1964 and 1967. Sir Roy Harrod (1967a) was strongly opposed to the 1967 devaluation and has described devaluation as 'the most potent known instrument of domestic price inflation which has such sorry effects on human misery'. Professor Ball (1967) also expressed doubts about the wisdom of devaluation and, in particular, scepticism over the role of prices in determining export performance:

> I believe that the non-price factors and the approach to marketing as a whole, together with the capacity problem, lie at the heart of the long-term trend, and that the problem of price is by no means the most significant factor that enters into the balance-of-payments equation. . . . Even if the once-for-all effect of a single change did provide a surplus on current account rapidly and of the right order of magnitude, we have done nothing to ensure that when long-run growth and expansion is resumed our position will not be further eroded. The result could be the need for yet another devaluation.

The defence of one of the present authors (Thirlwall, 1970), partly based on econometric evidence, was that the 1964 balance-of-payments deficit had little to do with the price uncompetitiveness of UK goods, and that the consequences of exchange-rate depreciation at that time would have been worse than the consequences of maintaining exchange stability.

Some may feel that they have been vindicated by subsequent events. The domestic cost inflation of the period 1967–74 almost certainly stems from the devaluation of the pound in 1967; and the subsequent floating of the pound merely perpetuated cost inflation without noticeably aiding the underlying balance of payments.

The circumstances in which the decision to float the pound was taken in 1972 bear an uncanny resemblance to the events preceding the devaluation in 1967. In 1967 the straw that broke the camel's back was unquestionably the Liverpool and London dock strikes in September. Speculation finally breached sterling's defences when a Labour back-bencher, Mr Robert Sheldon, asked a question in the House of Commons about the size of a loan agreement negotiated with foreign banks. At the time devaluation took place, however, the trade deficit was improving. The recorded deficit on current account was only £330 million in 1967 – within the margin of accounting error. Indeed, there was an error. In 1969 it was discovered by Board of Trade statisticians that owing to a change in regulations governing export registration exports had been systematically under-recorded since 1964 and that there was no overall deficit on current account between 1964 and 1967. Incidentally this is not the first time that concern with the balance of payments has been based on faulty statistics. When the pound was devalued in 1949 it was thought that the aggregate balance-of-payments deficit for the years 1946–8 was more than £1000 million. We now know from revised figures that it was only £737 million and that there had in fact been a slight surplus in 1948. Would the pound have been devalued by so much in 1949 had the correct figures been known? Would devaluation have been forced upon us in 1967 if the figures had been correct and the dockers had not gone on strike?

It was the prospect of a national dock strike, arising this time from a complex dispute over containerisation, which again prompted speculation against sterling in 1972. Further selling of sterling was precipitated by Mr Healey, then Shadow Chancellor, who announced in the House of Commons that he expected the pound to be devalued in July or August. In the three days prior to the pound being floated, over £1000 million of support for sterling was required. The balance of payments was still in surplus, however, and the reserves stood at $7100 million. Mr Barber, the Chancellor of the Exchequer, remarked in his budget speech that 'there was nothing in the objective facts of our balance-of-payments position or the level of reserves to justify these [speculative] movements. The trade balance has deteriorated in recent months but this was from an exceptionally and unusually favourable position.' The main motive for abandoning the pegged rate was clearly to avoid borrowing to support it. The question remains, however, whether it was necessary to allow the pound to depreciate by 20 per cent within a year, with the attendant inflationary repercussions – or could the same end have been achieved with a more orderly system of automatic exchange-rate flexibility which would have contained the amount of depreciation within any one year – as provided, for example, by a system of sliding parities?

Disappointing Results of Floating

The floating pound has not lived up to its expectations – at least to the expectation that it would give the government more freedom to pursue domestic goals while the balance of payments would look after itself. It could be argued, of course, that the floating pound has not been allowed to work, because the float was 'dirty', and because the economy was so over-extended that the resources were not available to satisfy export markets. The former argument is not convincing, since free floating would have led to even greater depreciation of the exchange rate. If the latter argument is accepted, the point is conceded that floating exchange rates by themselves are an inadequate weapon of economic policy, for what would seem to be implied is that if a country wishes to expand total demand faster than the rate of growth of productive potential, it will suffer an ever-deteriorating exchange rate, or at least deterioration for a long period of time, the consequenses of which for the domestic economy could be very serious. On the other hand, if a country does not wish to expand demand in excess of productive potential, there is little need for a floating exchange rate, and the uncertainties it breeds, when a more orderly system of exchange-rate flexibility could be adopted. The same argument can be applied to floating exchange rates as Professor Paish (1969) used to apply to incomes policy, namely that in conditions of domestic stability they are not necessary and in conditions of excess demand they are unworkable (or at least lead to consequences worse than the disease to be cured). A counter-argument would be that floating exchange rates are necessary to accommodate cost inflation. But this argument begs two questions: Is it desirable for countries to pursue policies which allow for cost inflation and which make cost inflation a permanent feature of economic life with no apparent benefit to the community at large? And is it the case that cost inflation has been in the past, and is likely to be in the future, a major source of balance-of-payments disequilibrium? The evidence up to 1967, when exchange-rate adjustment itself initiated a serious cost inflation, is that there was very little deterioration in the balance of payments attributable to growing price uncompetitiveness; and almost the lowest rate of increase in labour costs per unit of output in the Western world in 1973 did not prevent the United Kingdom from experiencing its largest deficit in recorded history.

Causes of Poor UK Export Performance

There were two major sources of the United Kingdom's payments troubles over the twenty-five years up to 1974: the periodic attempts to expand demand faster than the rate of growth of productive potential; and the long-term tendency for imports to grow faster than exports because the UK income elasticity of demand for imports exceeded the 'world' income elasticity of demand for UK exports. Floating the exchange rate was not the appropriate solution to either problem. The solution to the first (self-imposed) source of trouble is to keep domestic demand in line with productive potential and to desist from rushes for growth which in the past have involved expansions of monetary demand of up to 20 per cent in one year. The remedy for the second source of trouble is more complex, but since the origin of the problem lies not in price differences between countries but in the characteristics of the goods produced and sold, it would be surprising if the solution lay in exchange depreciation. On the contrary, there are good grounds for supposing that exchange depreciation may aggravate such a structural problem by ossifying the industrial structure which is the source of the trouble.

From an important and authoritative study by Houthakker and Magee (1969), which allows for the effects of relative price changes, it appears that the 'world' income elasticity of demand for UK exports is only 0.9 compared with a UK income elasticity of demand for imports of 1.7. This means that for a growth rate of world income of, say, 5 per cent, our exports may be expected to grow at $5.0 \times 0.9 = 4.5$ per cent per annum, while the full-employment rate of growth of imports would be $3.0 \times 1.7 = 5.1$ per cent per annum (assuming the UK rate of growth of capacity to be 3.0 per cent per annum). The fact that the United Kingdom's full-employment rate is less than that of other countries already provides a partial adjustment mechanism, but it is clear from the figures that if the rate of growth of imports is to be kept in line with the rate of growth of exports, the UK growth rate would have to be slowed to 2.6 per cent.[11] But the United Kingdom's major problem does not appear to be on the side of imports. The import elasticity is not so different from that of other countries. It is the export elasticity which is low compared with other countries. The UK export elasticity of 0.9 compares, for example, with 3.5 for Japan, 3.0 for Italy, and 2.4 for West Germany. Only the United States, with an elasticity of 1.0, appears to be in a comparatively weak position.

The basic payments problem therefore lies in the character of the goods produced and the markets in which they are sold. A favourable change in relative prices only makes the United Kingdom more competitive in the wrong range of goods. This type of problem is not untypical of the developing countries which produce and export mainly primary commodities the income elasticity of demand for which is low, and which import goods the income elasticity of demand for which is high. These countries have recognised that the correct approach to their difficulties is through structural change, and in particular by the encouragement, through protection and subsidisation, of the production of goods with high income elasticities of demand in world markets. A change in relative prices, if successful, can only affect the level of exports and imports; it will not necessarily raise the rate of growth of exports and lower the rate of growth of imports permanently, unless of course the change in relative prices is continuous, i.e. unless there is continual exchange rate depreciation. This is not feasible or desirable, for the reasons already discussed.

The major task of economic policy, if the United Kingdom is to tackle the balance-of-payments problem at its root, is not to look to exchange rate depreciation as the panacea, but to take measures at the micro level to encourage the production and export of goods which have a high income elasticity of demand in world markets (and which at the same time reduce the sensitivity of imports to increases in domestic income). Exchange rate depreciation merely gives indiscriminate benefit to all exporters, whereas the aim must be to boost exports in a discriminating way by the encouragement of certain types of activity. If it is accepted that the long-run average annual rate of growth of imports in relation to full-employment income is just over 5 per cent, and the 'world' growth rate is approximately 5 per cent, the elasticity of demand for UK exports needs to be increased only from 0.9 to just over 1.0 for balance-of-payments equilibrium to be achieved. One solution may lie in Kaldor's suggestion (*New Statesman*, 1 March 1974) of a general subsidy to manufacturing industry which would shift the balance of resources towards the manufacturing sector where the income elasticity of demand for goods may be expected to be higher. A subsidy would also be advantageous if it encouraged a revaluation of the pound. This would contribute to price stability at home; and sterling payments for imports would fall.

Need for Flexibility with Safeguards

Nothing that has been said above detracts from the case for a more automatic system of exchange-rate flexibility. The argument has been concerned with the wisdom of allowing the pound to depreciate so markedly in such a short space of time, and with questioning the relevance of exchange-rate depreciation as a solution to the United Kingdom's underlying payments problem. There is still the need for a flexible system of exchange-rate adjustment, with safeguards against speculation. What is required is a system which strikes a balance between minimising the degree of anti-social speculation and protecting the economy against imported inflation. A system of sliding parities, with bands around the parities, might achieve this. The flexibility of the slide and the band would remove the one-way option for speculators, and if the slide of the parity were confined to, say, 2 per cent per annum, exchange depreciation would be limited. But the causes of the underlying payments disequilibrium would still need to be tackled if the currency were not to depreciate continually.

Whatever long-term policies are pursued, an essential precondition for internal and external stability is that the exchange rate be stabilised, and preferably upvalued. Furthermore, let us banish the idea once and for all that floating exchange rates are a painless recipe for the achievement of simultaneous internal and external equilibrium. The only equilibrium that floating exchange rates guarantees is in the foreign-exchange market. But equilibrium in the foreign-exchange market is not only consistent with, but may also lead to, severe disequilibrium in the internal economy and in the basic balance of payments.

10
Import Functions

Economic theory would suggest three major factors determining a country's demand for imports. First, the capacity of the country to produce and supply the goods itself. Some imports are not competitive with domestic goods because the country does not have the physical capacity to produce them; others will be competitive, and the demand for them will partly depend on the ability of domestic producers to supply the substitutes. Second, the price of imports relative to the price of domestic substitutes will affect import demand. Third, the level of expenditure will affect the demand for imports. The composition of expenditure will also be important to the extent that the import content of different components of expenditure differs. For simplicity, however, and for the purposes of later chapters, it is assumed here that the import content of different items of expenditure is the same, so that income can be used as a proxy for expenditure in the import demand function. We stress again, however, that for income-determination analysis it is very important to recognise that there may be different import coefficients attached to different components of expenditure, and to relate imports to expenditure in deriving the foreign-trade multiplier (see Chapter 4). In addition to these three main factors, stock-building will also affect the demand for imports, as well as a host of non-quantifiable factors. If the non-quantifiable factors are correlated in any way with the quantifiable factors, they will affect the parameter estimates of the estimated import demand function. Changing tastes, and factors associated with tastes, as income changes, for example, may influence considerably the relationship between import demand and income.

The form of the import demand function may be assumed to be

multiplicative (linear in the logarithms), implying a constant elasticity of demand for imports with respect to the independent variables specified in the function. Thus let

$$M_t = aC_t^\lambda \left(\frac{P_f}{P_d} \right)_t^\psi Y_t^\pi \qquad (10.1)$$

where M is the quantity of imports, C is a measure of capacity utilisation in the importing country, P_f/P_d is the price of imports relative to the price of domestic goods measured in a common currency, Y is real income, λ is the elasticity of demand for imports with respect to capacity, ψ is the price elasticity of demand for imports, and π is the income elasticity of demand for imports.

If the function is not homogeneous of degree zero in money income and prices (i.e. there is money illusion), the import function is

$$M_t = aC_t^\lambda P_{ft}^\psi P_{dt}^\sigma Y_{mt}^\pi \qquad (10.2)$$

where Y_m is money income, and it is also recognised that the own price elasticity of demand for imports may differ from the cross elasticity of demand, i.e. $\psi \neq \sigma$.

It has also been suggested (Leamer and Stern, 1970) that if the import price deflator is unreliable, it may be better to specify imports in money terms. There is no one correct *a priori* specification of the import demand function. Investigators must proceed on a trial-and-error basis according to the data available, their reliability and the purpose of the study.

In some import studies investigators use a stock-adjustment model on the hypothesis that it takes time for importers to adjust imports to the desired level. From this model short- and long-run elasticities of demand for imports can then be derived. Consider the following model, which is a logarithmic transformation of equation (10.1):

$$\log M^*_t = \log a + \lambda \log (C_t) + \psi \log\left(\frac{P_f}{P_d} \right)_t + \pi \log(Y_t) \qquad (10.3)$$

where M^* is the desired level of imports. Now assume that it takes time for imports to adjust to the desired level, an equilibrium having been disturbed. The change in import demand between two periods

will equal some fraction of the difference between the desired level
and the level of imports in the previous period.

$$\log M_t - \log M_{t-1} = \delta(\log M_t^* - \log M_{t-1}), \text{ where } 0 < \delta < 1 \quad (10.4)$$

$$\text{or} \qquad \log M_t = \delta \log M_t^* + (1 - \delta) \log M_{t-1} \qquad (10.5)$$

Substituting equation (10.3) into (10.5) gives:

$$\log M_t = \delta \log a + \delta \lambda \log (C_t) + \delta \psi \log\left(\frac{P_f}{P_d}\right)_t + \delta \pi \log (Y_t)$$

$$+ (1 - \delta)\log M_{t-1} \qquad (10.6)$$

The short-run elasticities are $\delta\lambda$, $\delta\psi$ and $\delta\pi$. The long-run elasticities,
derived by setting $\log M_t = \log M_{t-1}$ (which is the long-run equilib-
rium condition), are:

$$\frac{\delta\lambda}{1 - (1-\delta)} = \lambda, \frac{\delta\psi}{1 - (1-\delta)} = \psi, \quad \text{and} \quad \frac{\delta\pi}{1 - (1-\delta)} = \pi$$

If $0 < \delta < 1$, the short-run elasticities will be lower than the long-run
elasticities. If adjustment to the desired level of imports is instan-
taneous, then of course $\delta = 1$, and there is no difference between the
short- and long-run elasticities.[1]

IMPORTS AND CAPACITY

Strictly speaking, a capacity or supply variable belongs to the import
demand function, in addition to a relative price variable, only if
excess demand at home is not eliminated by a change in the domestic
price level. Prices may not change for a number of reasons: first, the
demand curve for domestic goods may be very elastic, so that a
shortage of supply does not lead to a rise in price; second, for a
variety of reasons, manufacturers may resist raising prices; and third,
the supply of imports may be so elastic that no price change is
observed for domestic goods.

The above points can be illustrated diagrammatically. Assume import demand to be the difference between domestic demand and supply at the ruling market price (see also Chapter 1, p. 24). Suppose in Figure 10.1 that there is an equilibrium at price P_d, and then the supply curve shifts to S_1S_1, creating excess demand M_1M. If demand is less than perfectly elastic with respect to price, the domestic price in a free market should rise from P_d to P_{d1}, and there should be no change in import demand to explain in terms of supply deficiency, only in terms of a change in the relative price of domestic and imported goods. If prices do not change, however, the excess domestic demand will be filled by imports, which will have to be explained by some pressure of demand or capacity-utilisation variable. The explicit inclusion of a capacity variable as an independent argument in the import equation is to recognise that price may not act as a balance between supply and demand in the domestic market.

It is important to separate out the two influences of demand and supply on imports because if the latter exists, a given increase in income or expenditure will produce a larger increase in imports, the shorter the period over which the increase occurs. Import equations which ignore the supply or capacity effects will then tend to give exaggerated estimates of the income or expenditure elasticity of demand for imports. In some studies discussed below this point is met by distinguishing between the secular and the cyclical income elasticity of demand for imports, with the expectation that if supply effects are important the latter elasticity will be higher than the

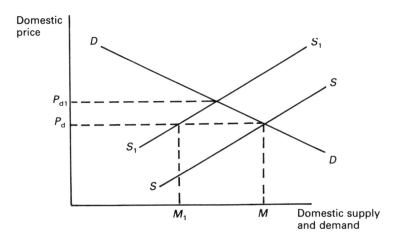

FIGURE 10.1

former. In an early study for the United Kingdom by Rees and Layard (1971) a distinct capacity variable is introduced and is measured by the proportion of manufacturers reported to be working at capacity. The variable is found to be highly significant for semi-finished capital goods and for consumer goods but not important in explaining imports of basic materials. The estimated capacity elasticities, holding expenditure constant, are 2.1 for semi-manufactured capital goods, 2.6 for finished capital goods, and 2.0 for consumer goods.

If a measure of capacity utilisation is not taken, capacity and income effects may be distinguished by making a distinction between the cyclical and trend income elasticities of demand for imports. These elasticities can be measured in the following way. Let

$$\log M_t^* = B_0 + B_1 \log \left(\frac{P_f}{P_d}\right)_t + B_2 \log Y_t^* \qquad (10.7)$$

where M^* and Y^* are the trend levels of M and Y, respectively. And let

$$(\log M_t - \log M_t^*) = \gamma(\log Y_t - \log Y_t^*) \qquad (10.8)$$

where $\log M_t - \log M_t^*$ and $\log Y_t - \log Y_t^*$ represent proportionate deviations of imports and income, respectively, from their trend levels. Substituting (10.7) into (10.8) gives:

$$\log M_t = B_0 + B_1 \log \left(\frac{P_f}{P_d}\right)_t + \gamma \log Y_t + (B_2 - \gamma) \log Y_t^* \qquad (10.9)$$

where γ is a measure of the cyclical elasticity and $(B_2 - \gamma)$ is a measure of the trend (or secular) elasticity. When Khan and Ross (1975) followed this procedure for a number of countries they obtained estimates for the UK economy of 0.936 for the cyclical elasticity and 0.889 for the trend elasticity. Marston (1971), in a similar but disaggregated study of UK imports, found a cyclical (capacity effect) elasticity of 3.63 for semi-manufactures and 2.15 for finished manufactures.

Attempts to expand the UK economy, even from a position of less than full employment, have typically led to large upsurges in imports greatly in excess of the normal incremental increase in demand for imports that one would expect as income and output expand. This rapid expansion of imports has partly represented stock-building, partly bottlenecks in particular sectors, but mainly the inability of domestic producers to meet the output demands made upon them in a short space of time. The faster the rate of expansion of demand, the greater the upsurge in imports has been. Moreover, there has been a tendency for imports to remain at a relatively high level once the rate of expansion has subsided and output has returned to its trend level – the so-called 'ratchet' effect.

The greater the speed of expansion, the greater the importance that capacity effects will assume. Brechling and Wolfe (1965) noticed that in the three booms of 1955, 1960 and 1964 the trade gap was wider in 1964 than in 1960, and wider in 1960 than in 1955, while the minimum unemployment rate had risen. They explain the phenomenon by the relative speed of expansion in successive booms and the difficulty of firms adjusting output to demand. They also show a ratchet effect operating, worsening the 'full' employment balance of payments through time. The ratio of imports to GDP rises in the booms but does not fall back to the pre-boom level when income returns to normal. Eltis (1967) also points to the fact that successive deficits on the balance of payments became larger in successive booms, and the surpluses smaller in successive slumps. His explanation, however, is the steady growth of net government invisible imports from under £100 million in 1953 to nearly £500 million in 1966. Eltis is clear, however, that the main factor accounting for the growth of imports in periods of expansion has been a lack of capacity and supply response. Paish (1968) makes the same point as Eltis, i.e. that the trend deterioration in the current account was mainly due, at least up to 1961, to a deterioration in the invisible account, not in the trade account. On the other hand, over the cycle 1962–6 the worsening of the trade balance, owing to the speed of expansion, was more serious than on invisible account. This was also the case during the 'Barber boom', 1971–3, and the 'Lawson boom', 1987–9. We have already noted in Chapter 4, the progressively worsening trade-off between the level of activity (as measured by unemployment) and the current account of the balance of payments, which may be partly the result of adverse capacity and 'ratchet' effects.

The effect of capacity constraints on imports is frequently discussed in official government reports, White Papers and the financial press. The National Economic Development Council Report on *Imported Manufactures* (1965) endorsed the widely held view that a shortage of capacity had caused sharp increases in imports, particularly in boom periods. Having talked with firms in the chemical, paper and board, textile and clothing, and iron and steel industries, the Report concluded:

> The largest annual increases in imports have occurred in years in which there has been a sharp upsurge of production and of stock-building, coupled with shortages of domestic productive capacity. . . . These increases have generally not been reversed in subsequent years. It may therefore be that the general upward trend of imports has been accentuated by the effects of temporary shortages of capacity, giving overseas producers an easy entry to the British market which they manage to retain and develop.

The government White Paper on *Industrial Strategy* (resulting from the Chequers agreement of November 1975) talks in a similar vein: 'Our manufacturing industry has not done as well as its competitors. In particular it has not responded adequately to changes in the pattern of world trade and suffers from structural rigidities which show themselves particularly in bottlenecks both of manpower and components in the early stages of economic upturns.' It was reported in *The Times* (17 January 1975), for example, that iron and steel imports in 1974 reached £700 million owing to the inability of domestic producers to meet booming demand.

IMPORTS AND LABOUR-MARKET BOTTLENECKS

Not one of the studies which have focused on the effect of capacity on imports is very specific about the nature of the capacity constraint. Both economic theory and casual empiricism would suggest that one of the most formidable constraints on the ability of domestic manufacturers to increase production is the availability of labour. A shortage of capital stock can be partly overcome by working capital more intensively – up to twenty-four hours a day if labour is available to work shift systems. A shortage of raw-material inputs can be met by importing. A shortage of labour, however, cannot be overcome so easily. There can be poaching by individual industries but at full employment this will cause shortages elsewhere. Hours worked can be increased but not to the same extent as for capital. There can also be a certain amount of substitution by other factors of production, but in the short run the supply of labour will be the binding constraint on output. When domestic output is limited by the availability of labour supply, and the domestic demand for output exceeds the supply, imports will be sucked in. Imports will be increasingly sensitive to the pressure of demand in the labour market until in the limit all additional increases in demand for output will be met by imports. It is possible to quantify the extent to which structural disequilibrium in the labour market, with shortages in some sectors and excess supply in others, has raised the annual UK import bill at the level of demand prevailing and at a hypothetical full-employment level. (The discussion and results draw heavily on work by Hughes and Thirlwall (1979) which uses data on imports, vacancies and unemployment classified by 113 Minimum List Headings (MLHs) of the Standard Industrial Classification (SIC) since 1963.)

The first question is to decide on a measure of labour-market bottlenecks. There is no one ideal measure. Given the labour-market data that are available on an industry basis, the vacancy–unemployment ratio is taken as the best measure of labour-market tightness. Unfortunately it is not possible to distinguish between the demand for and supply of skilled and unskilled labour. Having obtained a time-series measure of the strength of demand in the labour market industry by industry, the second question is how to measure the effect on aggregate imports of bottlenecks in particular sectors. There are two main approaches to this question, and these are outlined in Hughes and Thirlwall (1979). The first is to identify the industries in which a labour-market bottleneck effect has existed in the past and then to calculate how much less imports would have been in these industries had the pressure of demand in them been no greater than the national average. The hypothetical amount of imports saved industry by industry can be summed to obtain an aggregate figure. The second approach is the same as that which has been used in considering whether the dispersion of demand between markets worsens the conflict between price stability and full employment. A variable representing the dispersion of labour demand across industries is included in an import equation and from this it is possible to calculate what the level of imports would have been if there had been no dispersion of demand – that is, if there had been no bottlenecks in some sectors while excess supply existed in others. Both approaches are very fruitful and yield similar results.

Of the 113 industries examined, 54 show a significant relationship between imports and the pressure of demand in the labour market over the period 1963 to 1973, holding income and certain other variables constant, and they account for 61 per cent of total imports.

It would be wrong, of course, to conclude firmly from this evidence that it is definitely labour-market constraints that are the source of the problem without knowing the correlation between the pressure of demand in the labour market in these industries and other capacity constraints. But the evidence is suggestive, especially as in 41 of the 54 industries the vacancy-unemployment (v/u) ratio was higher than the national average of 0.42. If v/u in these 41 industries had been no higher than the national average, it is estimated that total imports would have been on average £326 million per annum lower (at 1970 prices).

Using the second approach gives a range of estimates depending on the specification of the import equation and the measure of dispersion used. The central estimates, however, come out at between £368/£422 million per annum, holding the average level of income and the average pressure of demand constant. These estimates are somewhat higher than that given by the first approach but are close enough to suggest that there is a bottleneck effect at work, the severity of which has increased the magnitude of the import bill by an average of between £300 and £500 million per annum over the period 1963 to 1973. At full employment, when sectoral bottlenecks are most acute, the cost of bottlenecks to the balance of payments is estimated to be £700 million. In the light of the balance-of-payments deficits in the 1970s, these figures may seem trivial for an individual year, but aggregated over a ten-year period it is a considerable bill to finance by exports and/or foreign borrowing. It must also be remembered that in the 1960s a deficit of £400 million would have been regarded as a severe balance-of-payments problem. The pound was devalued on a lesser figure in 1967.

As far as the over-all results for all 113 industries are concerned, the industries in which imports seem to be the most sensitive to the pressure of demand in the labour market belong to the engineering, electrical and metal groups, while the least sensitive belong to the food, drink and tobacco, mining, vehicles, and paper groups. In other broad industrial groupings the results are mixed, no doubt reflecting either the absence of capacity constraints or the difference in behaviour between competitive and non-competitive imports. The results have obvious policy implications for industrial strategy in particular, and for active manpower policy in general. A substantial proportion of manufacturing industry regularly reports to the CBI that their output is constrained by shortages of skilled labour, particularly in the engineering field.

IMPORTS AND INCOME (ESTIMATES OF INCOME ELASTICITIES)

A second important determinant of imports is expenditure, to be proxied here by income. A central estimate of the UK income elasticity of demand for aggregate imports in the 1950s and 1960s would be 1.5 (see Houthakker and Magee, 1969). In the 1970s and 1980s it was probably closer to 2: that is, for every 1 per cent rise in national income, imports into the UK rose by 2 per cent. An international comparison of income elasticities of demand for imports from various studies is given in Table 10.1.

An elasticity above unity will increase the ratio of imports to the measure of income through time.

Disaggregated studies show income elasticities much higher than the aggregate figure for some groups of commodities, particularly finished manufactured goods. If one looks at the history of manufactured imports in the UK, they started to increase rapidly in the 1950s, but not until 1960 did the share of manufactures in total imports reach its pre-war peak of 31 per cent. Thus, part of the post-war growth of manufactured imports can be considered as a catching-up

TABLE 10.1
Long-run income elasticities of demand for total imports

Country	Houthakker–Magee (1969)	Taplin (1973)	Goldstein–Khan (1976)	Samuelson et al. (1973)	Adams (1969)	Bairam (1988)	Wilson–Takacs (1979)
Austria	n.a.	1.04	n.a.	1.08	n.a.	2.24	n.a.
Belgium	1.94	1.27	1.75	1.38	1.21	2.64	n.a.
Canada	1.20	1.18	n.a.	0.95	0.90	1.77	1.87
Denmark	1.31	1.08	0.84	1.38	n.a.	–	n.a.
France	1.66	1.30	1.28	1.45	1.32	2.42	1.07
Germany	1.85	1.35	1.52	1.17	1.34	1.92	1.46
Italy	2.19	1.26	1.83	1.86	1.35	2.83	n.a.
Japan	1.23	1.12	1.30	1.26	0.93	–	1.69
Netherlands	1.89	1.27	2.04	1.56	1.35	2.0	n.a.
Norway	1.40	0.90	1.01	1.63	n.a.	1.43	n.a.
Sweden	1.42	1.02	1.33	1.13	n.a.	2.53	n.a.
Switzerland	2.05	1.25	n.a.	1.46	1.07	–	n.a.
United Kingdom	1.45	1.24	1.78	1.46	1.07	2.14	2.57
United States	1.68	1.81	1.84	1.89	0.76	2.22	4.03

Sources: M. Goldstein and M. S. Khan, 'Income ad Price Effects in Foreign Trade', in R. W. Jones and P. B. Kenen (eds), *Handbook of International Economics*, Vol II (Amsterdam: North-Holland, 1985); E. Bairam, 'Balance of Payments, the Harrod Foreign Trade Multiplier and Economic Growth: the European and North American Experience, 1970–85', *Applied Economics*, December, 1988.

process following pre-war, wartime and post-war trade controls. Since 1960, however, the growth has been even faster.[2] Panić (1968) finds it difficult to blame increases in the relative price of domestic goods for the upsurge of imports because from 1958 to 1967 the ratio of wholesale prices of domestic products to the unit value index of imports remained unchanged. He also believes that capacity constraints cannot be the whole story either because imports have continued to rise inexorably even in years of spare capacity. This has been even more true of the 1970s and 1980s than of the 1960s. Panić's list of possible explanations include: the poor quality, design and technological performance of domestic products; the slow growth of the economy and low investment, which has affected adversely the speed of process and product innovation; poor marketing techniques compared with foreign competitors; the growth of subsidiaries of foreign companies; and investment grants, which may have increased the quantity of imported capital goods.

In an international comparison of OECD countries, Taplin (1973) finds that the United Kingdom had the highest income elasticity of demand for total manufactured-good imports over the period 1953–4 to 1969–70. His estimates are as follows: the United Kingdom 2.61; Japan 1.77; West Germany 1.5; Italy 1.66; the Netherlands 1.25; Canada 1.42; and France 1.89.

In a comparative study of the United Kingdom, West Germany and France, taking the five main commodity groupings distinguished by the Standard Industrial Classification, Panić (1975) estimates the income elasticities of demand for imports shown in Table 10.2. Panić draws attention to the large discrepancy in the income elasticity of

TABLE 10.2

International estimates of income elasticities of demand for imports

	United Kingdom	West Germany	France
Food, beverages and tobacco	0.35	0.86	0.84
Basic materials	0.66	1.22	0.70
Fuels	2.47	2.66	1.26
Manufactured goods	3.09	2.14	2.19
Semi-finished	2.37	2.06	n.a.
Finished	4.30	3.52	n.a.
Total imports	1.82	1.31	1.63

Source: M. Panić, 'Why the U.K.'s Propensity to Import is High', *Lloyds Bank Review*, January, 1975.

demand for manufactured goods between the United Kingdom on the one hand and West Germany and France on the other. He attempts to explain the difference in terms of shifts in demand away from types of goods and services traditionally produced and the sluggishness of UK producers in adjusting supply to changes in demand. The United Kingdom's incapacity to grow quickly must have a bearing, he thinks, on the ability to adjust because of the link between growth, investment and the speed of technical change. It will be argued in Chapters 12 and 13 that the major constraint on growth in open economies is the balance of payments and that the slow growth rate of the United Kingdom is primarily a function of the slow rate of growth of exports, attributable no doubt to factors which also make the income elasticity of demand for imports relatively high. The syndrome of slow growth and a high income elasticity of demand for imports is part of a vicious circle.

Another comparative study by Humphrey (1976) gives similar results to those of Panić, with an estimated income elasticity of demand for imports of total manufactures of over 3, and for finished manufactures alone of over 4. Both estimates are significantly higher than those for West Germany and France. Humphrey attributes the high UK income elasticity of demand for imports to the fact that 'UK manufacturers are simply less able to satisfy marginal demand for finished manufacturers than is the case in other countries'. He supports his case by pointing to the low world income elasticity of demand for UK exports (to be discussed in the next chapter), and presumably believes that both phenomena are the result of a common cause, namely supply deficiencies in a capacity or quality sense.

The most recent estimate of the demand elasticity of total manufactures (Cuthbertson, 1985, Anderton and Desai, 1988), is approximately 2.7 with a composite marginal propensity to import of about 0.3.

With the publication of import (and export) data classified by Minimum List Headings of the Standard Industrial Classification (referred to earlier) it has become possible to estimate income elasticities of demand for imports at a highly disaggregated level.[3] Table 10.3 presents estimates for 30 industries with an income elasticity of demand for imports greater than 2 (Thirlwall, 1978). The estimates are made using the money values of imports and income because of the unavailability of import price deflators at such a disaggregated level. It can be said that if import prices have risen relative to domestic prices, the elasticity estimates will be underestimates of the real income

TABLE 10.3

Industries with a money income elasticity of demand for imports greater than 2

1958 MLH		UK income elasticity of demand for imports
381	Motor vehicles	3.7
492	Linoleum, leather cloth, etc.	3.5
442	Men's and boy's tailored outerwear	3.2
364	Radio and other electronic apparatus	2.9
395	Cans and metal boxes	2.8
382	Motor cycles	2.7
496	Plastics moulding and fabricating	2.6
365	Domestic electric appliances	2.6
362	Insulated wires and cables	2.6
313	Iron castings etc.	2.6
472	Furniture and upholstery	2.5
240	Tobacco	2.5
473	Bedding, etc.	2.4
444	Overalls and men's shirts, underwear, etc.	2.4
429	Other textile industries	2.4
272	Pharmaceutical and toilet preparations	2.3
443	Women's and girl's tailored outerwear	2.3
441	Weatherproof outerwear	2.3
499	Miscellaneous manufacturing industries	2.3
399	Metal industries not elsewhere specified	2.2
482	Cardboard boxes, etc.	2.2
445	Dresses, lingerie, infants' wear, etc.	2.2
363	Telegraph and telephone apparatus	2.2
411	Production of man-made fibres	2.1
339	Other drink industries	2.1
463	Glass	2.1
394	Wire and wire manufactures	2.1
495	Miscellaneous stationer's goods	2.1
213	Biscuits	2.1
369	Other electrical goods	2.1

elasticities if the demand for imports is price elastic, and overestimates if the demand for imports is price inelastic. If import prices have fallen relative to domestic prices, the converse of the above will be true.

IMPORTS AND RELATIVE PRICES (ESTIMATES OF PRICE
ELASTICITIES)

In estimating the influence of relative prices on import demand the relative price index should not be measured taking all domestic prices relative to import prices because many goods that enter the aggregate price index are not traded or substitutable for imports. The domestic wholesale price index would be better, or, ideally, a special index should be constructed. There is a discussion of measures of price competitiveness in international trade in the next chapter. Whatever measure is taken, however, there does not appear to have been any deterioration in relative prices over the crucial period when the UK balance of payments started to become noticeably weaker. According to Panić (1968), there was no deterioration from 1958 to 1967 in the UK wholesale price index relative to the unit value import index, and Morgan and Martin (1975), who constructed a special index of domestic prices comparable with import prices, find that the ratio of the two indices was remarkably static until the 1967 devaluation. Indices of relative producer prices and relative unit labour costs show a trend improvement in competitiveness up to 1976–7, but then a deterioration associated with the massive appreciation of sterling from 1979–81 (see Figure 11.3, p. 30).

The evidence on the importance of relative prices in determining imports is very mixed. Some studies for the United Kingdom find imports insensitive to price, other studies find some sensitivity. The Treasury model of the UK economy estimates the price elasticity of demand for imported goods to be of the order of 0.65, and for services 0.2. Rees and Layard (1971) estimate a long-run price elasticity for finished manufactures of 0.8 for the period 1959–69; Whitley (1979) estimates an equivalent price elasticity of 0.5 for the period 1963–76 and Anderton and Desai (1988) give a figure of 0.42 for the period 1968–86. At a disaggregated level work by Barker (1970a) gives the following estimates: food, drink and tobacco, 0.767; basic materials, 0.288 (perverse sign); fuels, 0.692; semi-manufactures, 1.427, and finished manufactures, 1.101. Another disaggre-

Balance-of-Payments Theory and UK Experience

gated study of consumer-good imports, capital goods and semi-manufactures by Hibberd and Wren-Lewis (1978) gives significant elasticities between 0.5 and 2.0.

Several surveys of the international evidence have been conducted, one of the most comprehensive being by Goldstein and Khan (1985). A selection of the long-run aggregate estimates for various countries from different studies is given in Table 10.4.

The elasticities are sometimes perverse but in general they are of the right sign and lie between zero and unity. The sensitivity of imports to relative prices seems to be the lowest of all in the United Kingdom taking an average of the estimates.

IMPORT PENETRATION

An income (or expenditure) elasticity of demand for imports in excess of unity leads to the increasing penetration of imports into the domestic market. Import penetration will also occur through upward shifts in the whole import function through trade liberalisation and increased international specialisation. For some products the penetration of imports into the United Kingdom has now reached alarming proportions, particularly in manufacturing industry. The Department of Trade and Industry publishes two measures of import penetration in manufacturing industry which are shown in Table 10.5. The ratio of imports to home demand measures the ratio of imports (M) to manufacturers' sales (S) plus imports (M) minus exports (X). It attempts to measure the penetration of the domestic market by imports relative to production for domestic use. In manufacturing as a whole the ratio has risen from 25.1 per cent in 1977 to 35.2 per cent in 1988, an increase of 40 per cent in eleven years. In some industries the ratio has nearly doubled during the same period. The ratio has risen particularly markedly in electrical and electronic engineering goods; motor vehicles; textiles; leather, and rubber and plastics. One weakness of this ratio, however, is that it may appear to rise unfavourably due to exports rising faster than imports. The second measure abstracts from this problem by showing the ratio of imports to manufacturers' sales plus imports. A third possible measure of import penetration is to take directly the ratio of imports to domestic output measured by the Census of Production. Hughes and Thirlwall (1977) adopted this approach in an early disaggregated study up to 1974 showing the same adverse trends. There was a

TABLE 10.4

Long-run price elasticities of the demand for total imports

Country	Houthakker-Magee (1969)	Adams *et al.* (1969)	Taplin (1973)	Goldstein-Khan (1980)	Beenstock-Minford (1976)	Samuelson (1973)	Gylfason (1978)	Stern *et al.* (1976)	Armington (1970)	Bairam (1988)
Austria	n.a.	n.a.	n.a.	-0.82	n.a.	-1.42	-1.21	-1.32	-1.37	...
Belgium	-1.02	-0.61	-0.65	-0.48	-2.90	...	-2.57	-0.83	-1.11	...
Canada	-1.46	-0.62	-1.59	-0.20	-2.50	-1.29	...	-1.30	-1.30	...
Denmark	-1.66	n.a.	-0.85	-0.42	n.a.	-0.23	n.a.	-1.05	-1.26	...
France	...	-0.81	-0.39	n.a.	-1.31	-0.79	-0.46	-1.80	-1.53	...
Germany	-0.24	-0.85	-0.61	-0.25	-0.74	-0.92	-1.36	-0.88	-1.48	...
Italy	-0.13	...	-1.03	-0.45	-0.88	-1.01	-0.32	-1.03	-1.42	-0.32
Japan	-0.72	...	-0.81	n.a.	-1.21	...	...	-0.78	-1.47	n.a.
Netherlands	...	-0.24	-0.02	n.a.	...	...	-1.65	-0.68	-1.13	...
Norway	...	n.a.	-1.20	n.a.	n.a.	...	n.a.	-1.19	-1.19	...
Sweden	-0.79	n.a.	-0.76	-0.84	n.a.	-0.80	n.a.	-0.79	-1.30	...
Switzerland	-0.84	n.a.	-1.10	n.a.	n.a.	...	n.a.	-1.22	-1.35	n.a.
United Kingdom	-0.21	...	-0.22	...	...	...	...	-0.65	-1.38	-0.33
United States	-1.03	-1.16	-1.05	-1.12	-1.04	...	-1.12	-1.66	-1.73	...

... indicates zero or wrong-signed coefficient on relative prices.

Source: M. Goldstein and M. S. Khan, 'Income and Price Effects in Foreign Trade', in R. W. Jones and P. B. Kenen (eds), *Handbook of International Economics*, Vol II (Amsterdam: North-Holland, 1985).

TABLE 10.5
Import penetration ratios for products of manufacturing industry

	1980 SIC Class	1977	1978	1979	1980	1981	1982	1983	1984	1985	1986	1987	1988[1]
Ratio 1 imports/ home demand													
Div 2–4 Manufacturing industries	21–49	25.1	26.0	26.9	26.2	27.8	29.0	31.1	33.4	34.3	34.3	35.2	35.2
Class:													
Metals	21–22	32	31	32	33	30	33	36	43	45	:	:	:
Other minerals and mineral products	23–24	12	12	13	12	12	12	13	15	15	15	18	18
Chemicals and man-made fibres	25–26	27	28	30	29	31	34	36	39	41	41	43	42
Metal goods n.e.s.	31	9	10	10	11	11	12	13	14	16	16	18	19
Mechanical engineering	32	30	32	29	29	32	32	32	34	36	37	38	40
Office machinery and data processing equipment	33	84	92	92	96	96	105	106	105	100	100	93	91
Electrical and electronic engineering	34	30	31	31	31	36	39	42	44	47	47	49	48
Motor vehicles and their parts	35	35	35	41	39	42	47	52	51	50	51	48	48
Other transport equipment	36	45	41	38	38	41	39	42	51	45	45	42	:
Instrument engineering	37	51	52	53	52	58	56	55	57	57	56	58	:
Food, drink and tobacco	41–42	17	18	18	16	16	16	17	18	18	18	18	:
Textile industry	43	27	31	33	34	39	39	41	44	44	45	47	48
Leather and leather goods	44	32	34	40	40	42	42	44	44	49	46	49	49
Clothing and footwear	45	25	26	29	29	33	33	33	36	35	36	39	39
Timber and wooden furniture	46	28	27	29	27	29	29	32	32	30	31	31	30
Paper, printing and publishing	47	21	19	19	19	20	19	20	21	21	21	22	22
Rubber and plastics processing	48	17	18	18	18	21	22	24	25	26	27	28	26
Other manufacturing industries	49	34	35	36	41	48	38	38	39	38	39	46	44

Ratio 2 imports/home demand and exports

Div 2–4 Manufacturing industries	Class	19.9	20.6	21.6	20.7	21.8	22.9	24.9	26.4	26.7	26.9	27.5	27.8
Div 2–4 Manufacturing industries	21–49	27	26	27	29	26	27	30	34	35	..	..	..
Class:													
Metals	21–22	10	10	11	10	10	11	12	13	13	13	15	16
Other minerals and mineral products	23–24												
Chemicals and man-made fibres	25–26	19	20	21	20	22	23	25	26	26	27	28	28
Metal goods n.e.s.	31	8	9	9	10	10	11	12	13	14	14	16	17
Mechanical engineering	32	19	21	19	19	20	20	22	24	24	25	26	28
Office machinery and data processing equipment	33	51	54	53	52	57	61	63	60	54	56	52	52
Electrical and electronic engineering	34	21	22	23	23	27	29	31	32	33	33	35	35
Motor vehicles and their parts	35	23	25	31	28	30	35	40	39	39	41	38	40
Other transport equipment	36	30	27	26	26	25	24	25	28	27	26	24	..
Instrument engineering	37	34	35	35	33	36	35	38	39	40	40	40	..
Food, drink and tobacco	41–42	16	16	16	14	15	15	15	17	17	17	17	..
Textile industry	43	21	25	26	26	30	31	33	35	35	36	38	38
Leather and leather goods	44	25	27	32	31	34	33	34	34	37	36	37	38
Clothing and footwear	45	21	22	25	25	28	29	29	32	31	31	33	34
Timber and wooden furniture	46	26	26	27	26	27	28	31	31	29	30	30	29
Paper, printing and publishing	47	19	17	18	17	18	18	18	20	19	19	20	20
Rubber and plastics processing	48	14	14	15	14	17	18	20	21	22	22	23	22
Other manufacturing industries	49	25	25	27	31	36	31	31	32	31	31	36	35

[1] Provisional.

Source: *Annual Abstract of Statistics 1990*

positive trend in the penetration ratio in 15 of the 17 Orders of the Standard Industrial Classification and in 106 of the 120 Minimum List Heading industries. Particularly adverse trends were found in clothing and footwear; leather; textiles; electrical engineering, and instrument engineering. Moreover, there was evidence of an accelerating trend.

If the rising trend which comes from upward shifts in the import function is not compensated by an autonomous improvement in export performance relative to output,[4] growing import penetration poses a severe threat to employment and the manufacturing base. For an industry in which imports grow relative to output at a rate of 10 per cent per annum, the import penetration ratio would double in roughly seven years, which could pose a serious threat to the industry's survival. In a world of increasing specialisation it is almost inevitable that the level of import penetration will continue to rise. What is important is that it should not rise faster than in other countries, or faster than the performance of exports relative to the *full-employment* rate of growth of output.

11
Export Functions

THE DETERMINANTS OF EXPORTS

The factors affecting the quantity of goods exported by a country will be the same as those affecting a country's demand for imports, though they may be expected to differ in relative importance. First, there is the ability and willingness of domestic producers to supply, which depends partly on capacity and partly on the domestic pressure of demand, which may divert goods away from foreign markets to the home market. Second, the price of exports compared with prices charged by foreign competitors in different export markets may be expected to exert some influence. Third, the level of income and expenditure in foreign markets will affect the quantity of exports sold. In addition, a host of non-price factors may be expected to affect the demand for exports – such as the quality, design and reliability of goods, and the time it takes for their delivery. Some of these factors, more difficult to quantify, are discussed in Chapter 14.

Like the import function, the export function is assumed for convenience to be multiplicative, implying a constant elasticity of exports with respect to each of the explanatory variables specified in the export function. Hence the export function may be written:

$$X_t = aC_t^{\gamma} \left(\frac{P_d}{P_f} \right)_t^{\eta} Z_t^{\varepsilon} \tag{11.1}$$

where X_t is the quantity of exports, C is a measure of capacity utilisation in the home country, P_d/P_f is the price of exports relative to competitors' prices in export markets measured in a common currency, Z is the level of 'world' income, γ is the elasticity of exports with respect to changes in capacity utilisation (or pressure of demand), η is the price elasticity of demand for exports, and ε is the world income elasticity of demand for exports.

If the function is not homogeneous of degree zero in money income and prices (i.e. there is money illusion), the function may be written:

$$X_t = aC_t^\gamma P_{dt}^\eta \, P_{ft}^\delta \, Z_{mt}^\varepsilon \qquad (11.2)$$

where Z_m is world income measured in money terms, and it is also recognised that the 'own' price elasticity of demand for exports may differ from the cross elasticity (i.e. $\eta \neq \delta$).

If equations (11.1) and (11.2) are thought of as demand equations, the capacity variable, strictly speaking, does not belong except to the extent that prices do not adjust as the supply of exports varies. In periods of excess supply, prices will not fall if the demand for exports is perfectly elastic in world markets; similarly, the price of exports may not be raised as a rationing device when domestic demand pressure is diverting exports to the home market. If export behaviour is to be explained in these circumstances, a supply variable must be included in the export function as an independent argument. Let us consider each of the factors mentioned above, and examine the empirical evidence relating to the United Kingdom.

EXPORTS AND CAPACITY

When the United Kingdom enjoyed relatively full employment in the 1950s and 1960s, it used to be claimed that a part of the reason for her relatively poor export performance was that the internal pressure of demand was excessive, leaving insufficient capacity to supply exports that would be readily absorbed by the world at the ruling market price. Export performance was thought to be negatively related to the internal pressure of demand and the level of domestic capacity utilisation. What is the theoretical prediction, and what is the evidence? The theoretical prediction about the division of output between home and foreign sales depends on the assumptions made about firm behaviour, and on the shape of the demand curve facing firms in foreign markets.[1] For example, assume a single-product profit-maximising firm which is a price-maker in the home market and a price-taker in foreign markets, so that the demand curve facing the firm is downward-sloping at home and horizontal abroad. The allocation of the firm's output between the two markets is shown in Figure 11.1 H stands for the home market and F for the foreign market.

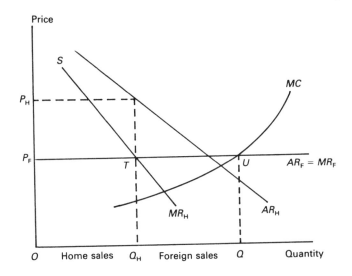

FIGURE 11.1

The total output of the firm is Q, where the producer maximises profits by equating marginal cost (MC) with marginal revenue in both markets (MR_H and MR_F). Total output is divided between OQ_H for the home market and Q_{HQ} for the foreign market, giving a price in the domestic market of P_H and a price in the foreign market of P_F. Now the total marginal revenue curve is the horizontal sum of the marginal revenue curves in each market, which equals STU in Figure 11.1. If the MC curve cuts the total MR curve to the right of T, the equilibrium level of output does not change with an increase or decrease in the domestic demand for output. Thus in this particular model it can be said that if the domestic demand for output increases, the quantity available for export will fall; and if domestic demand falls, the quantity available for export increases. The quantity of exports will vary inversely with the internal pressure of demand.

Now suppose the firm is a price-maker in world markets so that the demand curve facing the firm slopes downwards in both markets. The total marginal revenue curve will now no longer have a kink in it. Thus when demand in the home market changes, the equilibrium level of output will also change. What happens to the quantity of output available for export depends on whether output increases or decreases more or less than the increase or decrease in domestic demand. This in turn will depend on the shape of the MC curve. If

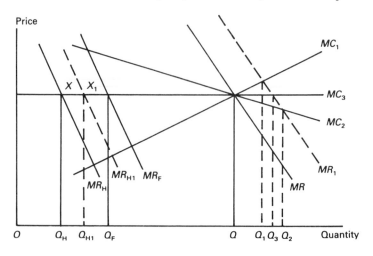

FIGURE 11.2

MC is increasing, an increase in home demand will cut exports because total output will increase by less than domestic demand. If MC is decreasing, an increase in domestic demand will increase exports because total output will increase by more than domestic demand. If MC is constant, the quantity of exports will remain unaffected. These propositions are illustrated in Figure 11.2.

The total marginal revenue curve (MR) in Figure 11.2 is the sum of MR_H and MR_F. The equilibrium level of output is Q, divided between OQ_H for the home market and OQ_F for export. Now suppose there is an increase in domestic demand which shifts MR_H to MR_{H1}, and which at the same time shifts MR to MR_1 by the same amount. The new equilibrium level of home sales is at Q_{H1}, and whether this affects the availability of output for exports depends on the response of total output. If MC is increasing (MC_1), it is clear that output rises less than the increase in domestic demand, to Q_1, and export volume will fall. If MC is decreasing (MC_2), output rises to Q_2, which is more than the increase in domestic demand, and the supply available for export increases. Finally, if MC is constant (MC_3), output rises to Q_3, which exactly equals the increase in domestic demand, and exports remain the same.

Needless to say, if the firm is not a profit-maximiser and there is a disturbance of domestic demand, it is difficult to know, and impossible to predict *a priori*, what the relation will be between changes in the internal pressure of demand and export performance.

In the formal theoretical models outlined above, an increase in the pressure of domestic demand makes production for the home-market relatively more profitable than exporting in very competitive markets, and this is presumably part of the mechanism which produces an inverse relation between domestic demand pressure and export performance. Some models of export behaviour (see Winters, 1974) take explicit account of changes in the profitability of exporting, hypothesising that for any given degree of demand pressure on capacity the extent to which exports are cut back will be directly related to the profitability of home sales relative to exports. Winters allows for this by specifying the model:

$$X_t = A_t + \beta_0 C_t + \beta_1 (\pi_t C_t) \qquad (11.3)$$

where π_t is the relative profitability of exports measured by the ratio of the domestic price index for manufactures to the export unit value index for manufactures. (We later discuss different measures of competitiveness and profitability.) Winters finds that profitability affects export performance, in addition to the level of capacity utilisation itself, though not necessarily independently of it.

Before turning to the empirical evidence of the relationship between export performance and the internal pressure of demand, a distinction needs to be made between models which are designed to explain the *level* of exports and models which are designed to explain export performance relative to other countries, i.e. a country's *share* of total world exports. While the level of export performance depends on capacity, competitiveness and the level of 'world' income, export performance relative to other countries depends on capacity, competitiveness and the *geographic and commodity composition of trade*. The level of 'world' income becomes largely irrelevant in explaining shares, since the variable is more or less common to all but very large countries. It is now the 'direction' of trade that is important. The slower the growth in demand for the commodities that a country exports, and the slower the growth of the markets to which it exports, the more unfavourable a country's share of total exports will become, other things remaining the same. Some studies of export performance examine both the level of exports and variations in the export share in relation to the internal pressure of demand, and where this is so both findings will be reported. (For a detailed analysis of the apparent unimportance of the direction of trade as an explanation of the United Kingdom's declining share of total world exports, see later in the chapter.)

One of the earliest studies of UK export performance and the internal pressure of demand is that by Ball, Eaton and Steuer (1966) for the period 1954 to 1964. Working first with a model to explain the level of exports, only world demand emerged as an important explanatory variable. At a time when most economists still believed in the importance of relative prices, however, the authors were moved to remark that 'such an interpretation is open to strong *a priori* and statistical objections. It is difficult to believe that price and non-price competition have not played an important role in determining the downward trend in the UK share [of total exports] over the period studied.' They seem to attribute their poor and unexpected results to multicollinearity between variables. This leads them to divide the level of UK exports by the level of world trade and to work with the UK share of total exports as the dependent variable in the analysis. When this is done their relative price variable becomes statistically significant, but the internal pressure of demand variable as measured by an index of the ratio of industrial output to its trend level remains insignificant. The authors then include in their estimating equation the UK share of world output as a measure of non-price factors affecting the United Kingdom's declining share of world trade. When this is done the internal pressure of demand variable becomes significant. The authors also include a time trend in the analysis, which is another way of picking up the effect of non-quantifiable adverse influences. Again they find the internal pressure of demand variable statistically significant. Ball, Eaton and Steuer conclude over all that if the average pressure of demand in the United Kingdom over the period had been lower at 2.5 per cent unemployment (instead of approximately 1.5 per cent), the level of exports would have been some £80 million to £180 million per annum higher (at 1960s prices), depending on the precise year taken.

Henry (1970) undertakes a similar study to the one above, but at a disaggregated industry level, taking different countries. He examines five UK industries over the period 1953 to 1965, and in addition thirteen Belgian and eight US industries, testing the basic hypothesis that domestic sales are preferred, and exports discriminated against, when the domestic pressure of demand is high. Demand pressure is measured by the ratio of the actual value of the industrial production index to its trend value, and the effect of periods of high and low pressure of demand are distinguished using dummy variables. There seem to be a number of industries where at a high pressure of demand exports are sensitive to domestic demand and not to world demand, and where at a low pressure of demand exports are sensitive to world demand but not to domestic demand. His evidence supports the capacity hypothesis, but there appears to be no particular industry or industry characteristic associated with the phenomenon. The adverse impact of demand pressure on exports appears to be quite pervasive.

Smyth (1968) examines the pressure-of-demand hypothesis but relates the UK share of total exports to the rate of change of demand rather than to the absolute level of demand pressure. He also tests for a ratchet effect to see whether the export share falls more when the rate of change of demand is positive than it rises when the rate of change of demand is negative. The idea that a ratchet mechanism may operate originates from the work of Brechling and Wolfe (1965), mentioned in the last chapter, who observed successive deteriorations in the trade balance in successive booms. Smyth finds that comparing the end-boom years 1955, 1960 and 1964, the percentage decline in the share of exports was greater in 1964 than in 1960 and greater in 1960 than in 1955, while the average pressure of demand was lower in 1964 than in 1960 and lower in 1960 than in 1955. This is casual empirical support for the Brechling-Wolfe hypothesis applied to exports alone, and is supported by statistical regression analysis. Smyth finds no support for the Oppenheimer (1965) assertion, made in response to Brechling and Wolfe, that the United Kingdom's poor export performance can be attributed to a lack of competitiveness. Changes in relative prices in Smyth's study seem to have no impact on the UK share of total exports.

One manifestation of a high internal pressure of demand is that if the market is not cleared through price adjustment, the waiting-time for export orders to be dispatched may lengthen. If the waiting-time for existing orders lengthens, this may affect the quantity of new export orders and hence the quantity of future deliveries. Steuer, Ball and Eaton (1966) have examined the relationship between waiting-time and export orders for machine-tools using quarterly data for the United Kingdom, the United States and West Germany over the period 1956 to 1962. The authors find that the flow of foreign orders received by the UK machine-tool industry was influenced more by long delivery delays than by relative prices. West German waiting-time (though not US waiting-time) also affected orders for UK machine-tools. West Germany and the United Kingdom are apparently stronger competitors than the United States and the United Kingdom. In quantitative terms, a one-month rise in UK waiting-time reduces orders by about 10 per cent, and a one-month fall in West German waiting-time reduces UK orders by about 20 per cent.

In a similar study Artus (1973) investigates the export production behaviour of machinery industries (including machine-tools) in the United Kingdom, the United States and West Germany, using quarterly data from 1956 to 1971. A 10 per cent increase in demand resulted ultimately in an increase in export delivery time of twenty days for UK machinery (an increase of 6.7 per cent), five days for US machinery (4.7 per cent), and eighteen days for West German machinery (4.5 per cent). For machine-tools, the lengthening of the delivery time was eight days for the United Kingdom (2.6 per cent) and ten days for the United States (4.6 per cent). Using the work of Steuer *et al.*, Artus calculates that a 10 per cent increase in UK demand will ultimately reduce the United Kingdom's export of machine-tools by 3 per cent. To our knowledge, there have been no more recent studies of the relation between capacity and UK export performance.

A word of warning is in order in interpreting an inverse relation between a country's share of total world exports and the internal pressure of demand. If the elasticity of demand for a country's exports with respect to the growth of world trade is less than unity, the country's share of exports is bound to fall as world trade grows and to rise as world trade slumps. If cycles of expansion and contraction within the domestic economy broadly coincide with cycles in world trade, the finding of an inverse relation between export share and the internal pressure of demand may be a reflection not simply of capacity constraints but of many factors, including the characteristics of goods, causing the elasticity of demand for exports with respect to world trade to be less than unity. Most models of the UK economy (see Anderton and Dunnett, 1987) give an estimate for this elasticity of approximately 0.6. The elasticity of exports with respect to world trade is less than with respect to world income since world trade grows faster than world income.

EXPORTS AND WORLD INCOME (ESTIMATES OF INCOME
ELASTICITIES)

All the evidence we have indicates that it is the growth of world income and world trade that is the major determinant of the growth of a country's exports, with the United Kingdom being no exception. In all export demand functions the variable standing for world

TABLE 11.1

Long-run activity elasticities of demand for total exports

Country	Houthakker–Magee (1969)	Basevi (1973)	Goldstein–Khan (1978)	Deppler–Ripley (1978)* †	Wilson–Takacs (1979)	Bairam (1988)
Austria	n.a.	n.a.	n.a.	1.08	n.a.	1.37
Belgium	1.87	1.29	1.68	1.03	n.a.	1.92
Canada	1.41	1.15	n.a.	0.69	1.97	2.04
Denmark	1.69	n.a.	n.a.	1.08	n.a.	1.04
France	1.53	n.a.	1.69	0.70	2.14	2.16
Germany	0.91	1.33	1.80	1.11	1.59	–
Italy	2.68	1.18	1.96	1.12	n.a.	1.58
Japan	3.55	1.62	4.22	1.45	n.a.	–
Netherlands	1.88	0.85	1.91	0.65	n.a.	1.08
Norway	1.59	n.a.	n.a.	0.75	n.a.	1.48
Sweden	1.75	1.22	n.a.	1.14	n.a.	1.81
Switzerland	1.47	n.a.	n.a.	0.82	n.a.	–
United Kingdom	1.00	0.61	0.92	0.90	1.75	1.31
United States	0.99	0.92	1.01	1.32	2.15	1.83

* Refers to manufactured exports only.
† Refers to cyclical changes in real income.

Source: M. Goldstein and M. S. Khan, 'Income and Price Effects in Foreign Trade', in R. W. Jones and P. B. Kenen (eds), *Handbook of International Economics*, Vol II (Amsterdam: North-Holland, 1985).

income or world trade is always significant, and in many cases is the only variable that appears to matter. The United Kingdom's problem, which we shall elaborate upon in Chapters 12, 13 and 14, is that the world income elasticity of demand for her exports seems to be much lower than for other industrialised countries, which makes the rate of growth of UK exports relatively low.

An international comparison of income elasticities of demand for exports from different researchers is shown in Table 11.1.

The average estimate for the UK is the lowest of all the countries, and one third of the estimate for Japan. Recent research by Landesmann and Snell (1989) suggests that the elasticity has risen in the 1980s but not much above unity.

EXPORTS AND RELATIVE PRICES (ESTIMATES OF PRICE ELASTICITIES)

There are a number of factors which affect a country's price competitiveness in world markets: the domestic rate of inflation; production costs per unit of output; and changes in the exchange rate. This makes it difficult to define one unique measure of price competitiveness. Rather, there are a number of complementary measures, each with certain advantages and disadvantages.[2] The appropriateness of the various measures will depend partly on the nature of the market being analysed. In very competitive markets, for example, where a virtually identical good is being sold, relative prices can hardly change and an index of relative prices is unlikely, therefore, to be a good predictor of sales. In this case some measure of profitability, or relative costs would be more useful.

One measure of export price competitiveness used in some studies is the ratio of export prices to a weighted average of the export prices of major competitors expressed in a common currency. The measure suffers from a number of limitations, however. First, as mentioned above, it is not appropriate for use if the market is very competitive. Second, the index is based on unit values which may not make proper allowance for changes in the composition of exports. Third, the index measures competitiveness only in relation to the exports of competitors and leaves out of account competitiveness in relation to domestic producers in the various export markets. This weakness could in principle be overcome by calculating the ratio of export prices to some weighted combination of competitors' export prices and domestic producers' wholesale prices in the export markets. A fourth limitation is that the index measures only delivery prices and not quotations, and therefore only reflects trade that actually takes place rather than underlying competitive conditions. Strictly speaking, any price at which business is actually transacted is by definition competitive. Moreover, as Posner and Steer (1979) have noted, if costs rise in a marginally competitive export industry, forcing the industry's product out of the export market, the aggregate index may register an improvement in competitiveness! The basic problem is that the index may not give a good indication of the ability of the export sector to produce as efficiently as foreign competitors, or the willingness of exporters to supply (which depends on profitability). Efficiency and cost changes will be reflected in profitability in competitive markets where the export price is determined by world prices. To measure the relative profitability of exports, the ratio of export prices to wholesale prices may be taken, as in Figure 11.3.

Another measure of competitiveness which is used by the IMF, and which best explains export trends in the work of Enoch (1978) at the Bank of England is relative unit labour costs normalised for

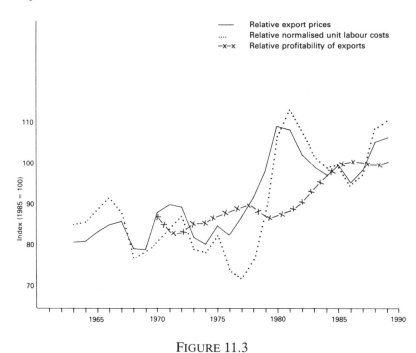

FIGURE 11.3

DATA FOR FIGURE 11.3

Measures of competitiveness of UK manufactured goods (1985=100)

	Relative export prices	Relative normalised unit labour costs	Relative profitability of exports
1963	81.2	85.2	
1964	81.3	86.0	
1965	83.5	89.2	
1966	85.3	92.1	
1967	86.2	88.3	
1968	79.7	77.1	
1969	79.2	78.9	
1970	88.3	81.0	87.3
1971	90.2	84.6	83.5
1972	89.8	87.2	83.2
1973	82.2	79.3	85.6
1974	80.7	78.7	85.6

continued on p. 302

DATA FOR FIGURE 11.3 *continued*

	Relative export prices	Relative normalised unit labour costs	Relative profitability of exports
1975	85.1	82.8	87.5
1976	82.9	74.3	88.5
1977	87.2	72.2	89.8
1978	92.0	77.3	90.0
1979	98.6	88.9	83.7
1980	109.2	106.6	87.6
1981	108.4	113.3	88.7
1982	102.2	108.4	90.6
1983	99.5	102.1	94.2
1984	97.5	99.3	97.5
1985	100.0	100.0	100.0
1986	95.7	95.2	100.7
1987	98.9	97.2	100.5
1988	105.8	108.8	99.7
1989	106.5	110.7	100.1

Source: *Economic Trends*, Annual Supplement 1990 Edition (HMSO).

cyclical variations in output so that labour costs are related to potential output rather than to actual output. This measure is claimed to have several advantages. First, it covers potential as well as actual exporters. Second, it measures, in effect, a combination of both price competitiveness and profitability. Third, it overcomes in principle the problem of the export price index incorporating only successful export quotations. The problems with the index are that labour costs are not the only costs of production, and that producers in one country may work on a lower profit margin than in others. Which index to use, however, is essentially an empirical question.

The different measures of competitiveness discussed above are shown in Figure 11.3 for the United Kingdom over the period 1970 to 1989. There is no presumption, of course, that in the base year UK producers were necessarily competitive in any absolute sense. Lower values for the first two indices, and a higher value for the relative profitability of exports, represent a more competitive position.

Sometimes the indices move in the same direction, at other times not. Some interesting features are apparent, however. Over the long run, the indices of relative export prices and normalised unit labour costs show a trend deterioration in competitiveness, while the index of relative profitability of exports shows a trend improvement. Periods of currency depreciation have improved competitiveness in the short run, but then the advantage has been lost. Improvements in competitiveness have not, in general, arrested the decline in the UK's share of world exports. How much different export performance would have been had there not been changes in competitiveness, however, is an open question, depending on one's judgement of the export price elasticity, which we now consider.

The empirical evidence available for the United Kingdom shows that export volume is responsive to a change in price competitiveness, though the response lag for the price elasticity of demand to exceed unity may exceed two years. Some studies conclude that the price elasticity never exceeds unity. Some representative estimates of the price elasticity of demand for UK exports, using different measures of competitiveness and different sample data, are as follows: Hutton and Minford (1975), 1.5; Duffy and Renton (1970), 2.5; Houthakker and Magee (1969), 1.24; Junz and Rhomberg (1965), 1.86 (short run), 2.27 (long run); and Batchelor and Bowe (1974), 1.13 to 2.80. Posner and Steer (1979) have summarised the estimates of export price elasticities implied by the major UK macroeconomic models (see Table 11.2).

TABLE 11.2

Empirical estimates of export price elasticities for the United Kingdom

	One year	Two years	Long run	Period of estimation
London Business School	0.37	0.39	0.99	1951–76
Cambridge Economic Policy Group	0.35	1.23	2.36	1960–76
National Institute of Economic and Social Research	0.46	1.13	1.61	1967–75
Treasury	0.26	0.65	1.30	1966–76

Some of the UK macro-models now use different measures of competitiveness (see Anderton and Dunnett, 1987). The National Institute of Economic and Social Research continues to use relative export prices, and estimates a long-run price elasticity (after 12 quarters) of 0.6–0.7. The London Business School uses labour costs relative to a weighted sum of the world price of manufactured exports and producer input prices, and estimates an elasticity of approximately 0.3. The Treasury, on the other hand, measures short-run competitiveness by profitability and long-run competitiveness by UK total costs relative to world total costs.

An international comparison of long-run price elasticities of demand for exports is given in Table 11.3.

These estimates put the price elasticity between 1 and 2 for most countries. In other words, in the long run, the Marshall-Lerner condition for a successful devaluation would be fulfilled *if all the other necessary conditions are met*. We repeat, however, that there is no guarantee that an induced change in competitiveness through exchange depreciation can be retained for any length of time, so that any balance-of-payments gain is temporary. Second, an improvement in competitiveness may not be enough to counter other adverse factors affecting export performance. Third, as we shall see in the next chapter, a once-for-all change in competitiveness cannot raise the balance-of-payments equilibrium growth rate permanently. A continual improvement in competitiveness would be required.

Studies which relate a country's export share to relative prices are estimating the elasticity of substitution of one country's exports for another. Thus the estimates are a combination of the 'own' price elasticity and the cross elasticity of demand in both sets of countries. Special assumptions would have to be made to deduce the 'own' price elasticity of demand for exports for any one of the countries. Junz and Rhomberg (1965, 1973) find a relation between relative price changes and market shares, but only after a lag of three years, with the full effect coming after five years. The share elasticity for the United Kingdom is estimated to be approximately 1.7 in their 1973 study and 3 in their 1965 study.

EXPORT PERFORMANCE IN MANUFACTURING

It was pointed out in Chapter 9 that in 1982 the balance of trade in manufactures (on an overseas trade statistics basis) turned negative

TABLE 11.3

Long-run price elasticities of the demand for total exports

Country	Houthakker–Magee (1969)	Goldstein–Khan (1978)	Hickman–Lau (1973)	Beenstock–Minford (1976)	Basevi (1973)	Samuelson (1973)	Adams et al. (1969)	Gylfason (1978)	Stern et al. (1976)
Austria	n.a.	n.a.	-0.93	n.a.	n.a.	-1.21	n.a.	...	-0.93
Belgium	...	-1.57	-1.02	-0.84	n.a.	-1.14	...	...	-1.02
Canada	-0.59	n.a.	-0.84	-1.00	-0.59	-1.10	-0.23	...	-0.79
Denmark	-0.56	n.a.	-1.28	n.a.	n.a.	-1.06	n.a.	n.a.	-1.28
France	-2.27	-1.33	-1.09	-1.59	n.a.	-1.28	-1.06	...	-1.31
Germany	-1.25	-0.83	-1.04	-1.90	-1.68	-1.12	-0.65	-0.38	-1.11
Italy	-1.12	-3.29	-0.93	-1.91	-0.72	-1.29	-0.25	-1.91	-0.93
Japan	-0.80	...	-0.50	-3.00	-2.38	-1.04	-0.71	-2.13	-1.25
Netherlands	...	-2.72	-0.95	-2.10	-2.39	-1.07	-0.59	-0.88	-0.95
Norway	...	n.a.	-0.80	n.a.	n.a.	-1.16	n.a.	n.a.	-0.81
Sweden	-0.47	n.a.	-1.99	n.a.	-1.92	n.a.	n.a.	n.a.	-1.96
Switzerland	-0.58	n.a.	-1.01	n.a.	n.a.	-1.51	n.a.	n.a.	-1.01
United Kingdom	-1.24	-1.32	-1.27	-1.47	-0.71	-1.28	-0.48	-0.32	-0.48
United States	-1.51	-2.32	-1.38	n.a.	-1.44	-1.13	-0.60	-0.62	-1.41

... indicates zero or wrong-sign on coefficient.

Source: M. Goldstein and M. S. Khan, 'Income and Price Effects in Foreign Trade', in R. W. Jones and P. B. Kenen (eds), *Handbook of International Economics*, Vol II (Amsterdam: North-Holland, 1985).

for the first time in British history. The adverse trend has continued. It is of some interest, therefore, to examine the export orientation and performance of the major sectors of British manufacturing industry. Table 11.4 shows the ratio of exports to manufacturers' sales for 17 major sectors. The export orientation of the Office Machinery and Data Processing Equipment industry is clearly the highest. In most industries the ratio is less than 50 per cent with an average for manufacturing as a whole of 29 per cent. Table 11.5 shows the balance between exports and imports by sector at a more disaggregated level, and where the deterioration in trade performance has taken place. In 1973, the balance of trade in manufactures as a whole was a healthy surplus of £1.37 billion. Fifteen sectors had a deficit but none larger than in the paper industry of £273 million. In 1983, 18 sectors had developed a deficit, and a massive one in some cases. In 1988, 23 sectors had a deficit with deficits of over £1 billion in paper, textiles, telecommunications, electrical machinery, and clothing. But the major sector accounting for the overall deficit of over £17 billion was vehicles with a deficit of £6.2 billion compared with a surplus fifteen years previously. Without foreign exchange from North Sea oil, such a huge deficit on manufactured trade would not be sustainable since there is also a deficit in food and raw materials, and a surplus on invisible account sufficient to cover three deficits of the order of magnitude required is simply not feasible. The big question mark facing the United Kingdom in the future is what happens when the UK becomes once again a net importer of oil.

THE UNITED KINGDOM'S DECLINING SHARE OF WORLD EXPORTS

The UK share of world exports has fallen from over 20 per cent in 1950 to approximately 7 per cent in 1989. This decline has been common to both manufactured goods and services. The UK's share of world trade in manufactures is now just over 6 per cent, and its share of world trade in services is just over 7 per cent. Service exports constitute approximately one-quarter of total exports. Some observers have taken this decline as a measure of the weakness of the UK balance of payments. It is difficult to subscribe to this view without some qualification. Indeed, Harrod (1967a) once described the view as 'surely the most absurd ever perpetrated in a diagnosis', adding that 'the British share of world exports has declined, is declining and will continue to decline, hopefully at an accelerated

TABLE 11.4
Export sales ratios for products of manufacturing industry

	1980 SIC Class	1977	1978	1979	1980	1981	1982	1983	1984	1985	1986	1987	1988*
Ratio exports/ manufacturers' sales													
Div 2–4 Manufacturing industries	21–49	25.7	26.1	25.1	26.5	27.3	27.2	26.6	28.4	30.2	29.4	30.3	28.9
Class:													
Metals	21–22	22	22	23	21	23	23	25	32	35	..	..	..
Other minerals and mineral products	23–24	17	16	15	16	15	14	14	14	15	15	16	16
Chemicals and man-made fibres	25–26	35	36	36	38	39	41	42	45	48	48	47	46
Metal goods n.e.s.	31	14	13	12	14	14	14	12	13	14	13	13	13
Mechanical engineering	32	44	44	42	45	47	45	40	42	43	42	42	40
Office machinery and data processing equipment	33	80	90	90	96	94	108	110	107	100	100	91	90
Electrical and electronic engineering	34	37	37	33	34	36	38	37	39	43	43	43	41
Motor vehicles and their parts	35	42	38	36	38	41	38	37	37	37	34	34	30
Other transport equipment	36	47	45	43	42	50	53	55	63	55	59	57	..
Instrument engineering	37	50	51	53	55	59	57	51	52	50	48	52	..
Food, drink and tobacco	41–42	9	11	10	10	10	11	10	10	11	11	12	..
Textile industry	43	27	27	27	30	30	29	28	30	31	30	32	32
Leather and leather goods	44	27	26	29	32	30	33	33	35	38	36	40	38
Clothing and footwear	45	19	18	18	19	20	18	18	18	19	18	21	19
Timber and wooden furniture	46	7	7	6	7	6	6	6	6	6	5	5	5
Paper, printing and publishing	47	11	11	10	10	10	10	10	10	11	11	11	10
Rubber and plastics processing	48	22	21	20	23	24	22	22	22	22	21	22	20
Other manufacturing industries	49	37	38	36	36	38	28	28	28	28	28	34	31

* Provisional.

Source: *Annual Abstract of Statistics 1990.*

TABLE 11.5
Trade performance in manufacturing (SITC classification)
£ million

	Balance between exports and imports		
	1973	1983	1988
5. Chemical and related products			
51. Organic chemicals	+10.8	+471.0	+785
52. Inorganic chemicals	+11.4	+138.5	+195
53. Dyeing, tanning and colouring materials	+80.2	+333.6	+395
54. Medicinal and pharmaceutical products	+154.2	+604.1	+859
55. Essential oils and perfume materials: toilet, polishing and cleansing materials	+45.3	+269.0	+328
56. Fertilisers, manufactured	−20.3	−102.8	−114
57. Explosives and pyrotechnic products	+7.8	+26.0	−821
58. Artificial resins and plastic materials and cellulose esters and ethers	+18.6	−343.3	−295
59. Chemical materials and products, not elsewhere specified	+87.0	+413.7	+686
6. Manufactured goods classified chiefly by material			
61. Leather, leather manufactures, nes, and dressed furskins	+16.4	+48.9	+66
62. Rubber manufactures, nes	+64.1	+32.2	−83
63. Cork and wood manufactures (excluding furniture)	−228.8	−493.6	−882
64. Paper, paperboard, and articles of paper pulp, of paper or of paperboard	−273.1	−1363.2	−2529
65. Textile yarn, fabrics, made-up articles nes, and related products	+106.3	−1035.5	−1701
66. Non-metallic mineral manufactures, nes	−63.0	−90.5	−330
67. Iron and steel	+59.9	+70.2	+24
68. Non-ferrous metals	−123.4	−361.8	−856
69. Manufactures of metal, nes	+130.2	+215.1	−587
7. Machinery and transport equipment			
71. Power generating machinery and equipment	+348.9	+903.3	+838
72. Machinery specialised for particular industries	+413.2	+604.5	−188
73. Metalworking machinery	+41.6	+73.8	−21
74. General industrial machinery and equipment, nes, and machine parts, nes	+200.4	+487.6	+33
75. Office machines and automatic data processing equipment	−21.0	−970.7	−982
76. Telecommunications and sound recording and reproducing apparatus and equipment	−118.2	−924.7	−1418
77. Electrical machinery, apparatus and appliances, nes, and electrical parts thereof (including non-	−9.6	−517.8	−1470

electrical counterparts, nes, of electrical
household type equipment)

78. Road vehicles (including air cushion vehicles)	+500.6	−2669.6	−6256
79. Other transport equipment	+123.2	+1096.7	+1307

8. Miscellaneous manufactured articles

81. Sanitary, plumbing, heating and lighting fixtures and fittings, nes	+3.3	−18.4	−137
82. Furniture and parts thereof	−18.7	−232.7	−611
83. Travel goods, handbags and similar containers	−10.3	−111.8	−207
84. Articles of apparel and clothing accessories	−153.9	−736.1	−1694
85. Footwear	−48.7	−418.6	−697
87. Professional, scientific and controlling instruments and apparatus, nes	+59.3	+168.7	+507
88. Photographic apparatus, equipment and supplies and optical goods, nes watches and clocks	−18.5	−288.7	−461
89. Miscellaneous manufactured articles, nes	−5.4	−263.2	−1014
Total manufactured goods	**+1369.6**	**−4985.9**	**−17,328**

Source: *Annual Abstract of Statistics, 1989.*

pace'. Without wishing to concur with the last sentiment, Harrod is right that the decline should occasion no surprise, and there is nothing incompatible between a declining share of total world exports and a healthy balance of payments at a satisfactory growth rate. The health of the balance of payments depends on the relation between the absolute level of exports and imports associated with a given growth rate, not on the growth of exports relative to the growth of total world exports. While the UK export share has fallen, the UK share of world imports has also fallen. The decline in both shares has a common explanation, namely that the UK share of the world's manufacturing population and output has declined as resources have shifted from agricultural to industrial activities throughout the world. The United Kingdom's legitimate worry is that some of her European neighbours, even in the face of these changing world conditions, have managed to retain their share of world exports. It is not without interest, therefore, to analyse this declining share. Is it that the United Kingdom is exporting commodities the demand for which is growing slower than for all commodities? Is it that the United Kingdom is exporting commodities to markets where demand is rising more slowly than in other markets? Or is the United Kingdom losing its share in all commodity and geographic markets regardless of whether they are fast- or slow-growing? A classificatory device is available to help answer these questions which divides a country's changing share of world trade between any two periods into three components: (i) that part due to the commodity composition of trade, which may be called the *differential product growth effect*; (ii) that part due to the destination of trade, which may be called the *differential market growth effect*; and (iii) that part due to the decreasing share of all individual commodity and geographic markets because of growing price uncompetitiveness, non-price factors, supply constraints, low income elasticities of demand, and so on. This third component is obtained as a residual and is sometimes called a 'competitiveness' effect. As we shall see from the studies that have been done, the United Kingdom's declining share of world exports cannot be accounted for by the commodity composition or destination of trade and must therefore be the result of an over-all declining share of every market. The classificatory device to be outlined is taken from Magee (1974), but the methodology is a standard one widely used in regional analysis for analysing interregional differences (see Dixon and Thirlwall, 1975b).

An individual country is denoted by the subscript k, the world by subscript w, the base year by o, and the terminal year by t. A country's base-year share of world exports can therefore be expressed as X_{ok}/X_{ow}, and its terminal-year share as X_{tk}/X_{tw}. The relationship between the two ratios is given by $(1 + g_k)/(1 + g_w) = R$, where g stands for the rate of growth of exports and R can be called the relative growth factor. Thus:

$$\frac{X_{tk}}{X_{tw}} = \left\{ \frac{1 + g_k}{1 + g_w} \right\} \frac{X_{ok}}{X_{ow}} = R \left(\frac{X_{ok}}{X_{ow}} \right) \qquad (11.4)$$

Another way of writing R is:

$$R = \sum_i \left\{ \frac{1 + g_k^i}{1 + g_w} \right\} \frac{X_{ok}^i}{X_{ok}} \qquad (11.5)$$

where the is stand for individual commodities. Although the terms in the denominator contain no i superscripts they are kept to the right of the summation sign for reasons which will become clear shortly.

The numerator of (11.5) can be expanded to:

$$\sum_i (1 + g_k^i) X_{ok}^i = \sum_i \sum_j (1 + g_k^{ij}) X_{ok}^{ij} \qquad (11.6)$$

where the *j*s refer to individual markets (destinations). Equation (11.5) can thus be written:

$$R = \sum_i \frac{1}{(1 + g_w)X_{0k}} \sum_j (1 + g_k^{ij})X_{0k}^{ij} \qquad (11.7)$$

Multiplying top and bottom of equation (11.7) by $(1 + g_w^i)X_{0k}^i$ gives:

$$R = \sum_i \frac{(1 + g_w^i)X_{0k}^i}{(1 + g_w)X_{0k}} \sum_j \frac{(1 + g_k^{ij})X_{0k}^{ij}}{(1 + g_w^i)X_{0k}^i} \qquad (11.8)$$

Multiplying top and bottom of equation (11.8) by $(1 + g_w^{ij})$ gives:

$$R = \sum_i \frac{(1 + g_w^i)X_{0k}^i}{(1 + g_w)X_{0k}} \sum_j \frac{(1 + g_k^{ij})(1 + g_w^{ij})X_{0k}^{ij}}{(1 + g_w^{ij})(1 + g_w^i)X_{0k}^i} \qquad (11.9)$$

$$\text{(a)} \quad \text{(b)} \qquad \text{(c)} \qquad \text{(d)} \quad \text{(e)}$$

We now have the relationship between a country's share of exports in the base and terminal year as the product of three factors:[3]

(i) (a) × (b): that is, a country's export share may change because the country specialises in commodities which grow relatively faster/slower than the average for all commodities. This is the *differential product growth* effect.

(ii) (d) × (e): that is, a country's export share may change because the country concentrates its products in markets which grow relatively faster/slower than the average for all markets. This is the *differential market growth* effect.

(iii) (c): that is, a country's export share may change because the country's share in every market is increasing/decreasing due to a host of factors connected with competitiveness and the characteristics of the products exported.

It is obvious that even if a country maintains its share of every product in every market ((c) = 1), its share of total exports may still go down because its exports are orientated towards relatively slowly growing products or slowly growing markets.

To estimate the actual magnitude by which exports have suffered as a result of a declining share of world trade due to the three 'explanations' above, the same methodology can be applied but in a slightly different way. First, define the difference between actual exports and what they would have been had they grown at the world rate, thereby maintaining the share constant:

$$X_{tk} - (1 + g_w)X_{0k} \qquad (11.10)$$

The effect of product composition difference is:

$$\sum_i (1 + g_w^i)X_{0k}^i - (1 + g_w)X_{0k} \qquad (11.11)$$

The differential market growth effect is:

$$\sum_j \sum_i (1 + g_w^{ij})X_{0k}^{ij} - \sum_i (1 + g_w^i)X_{0k}^i \qquad (11.12)$$

Thus

$$X_{tk} - (1 + g_w)X_{0k} = (11.11) + (11.12) + \text{a residual}$$

where the residual

$$= X_{tk} - \sum_j \sum_i (1 + g_w^{ij})X_{0k}^{ij}$$

Studies which have applied the methodology for analysing changes in the UK share of world exports largely refer to trade in manufactures, *e.g.* Major (1968), National Economic Development Council (1963), and Panić and Seward (1966). Major (1968) and Kreinin (1967) attempt to estimate the change in the absolute magnitude of exports resulting from changing shares. Panić and Rajan (1979) have investigated the distribution of exports between fast- and slow-growing product categories in world trade in the United Kingdom, France, West Germany and Japan. The broad commodity and geographic composition of UK exports (and imports) since 1979 is given in Tables 11.6 and 11.7 in the appendix to the chapter.

Major (1968) takes nine areas and seven commodities (63 'markets' in all) over the period 1954 to 1966, during which the UK share of world exports of manufactures fell from 20.9 per cent to 13.1 per cent. He finds that only 9 per cent (or 2 percentage points) of the fall in share can be accounted for by the area/commodity composition of trade. The major part of the declining share is attributed to a falling share in every market. In fact, of the 63 markets, in only eleven did the share not fall. The cumulative value of lost exports (compared with the maintenance of a constant share) is estimated at $31.7 billion. Since biases in trade towards slowly expanding commodities and markets cannot account for the major part of the United Kingdom's declining share of total manufacturing exports. Major concludes that the loss must therefore be due to 'declining competitiveness in the broadest sense'. The National Economic Development Council (1963) reaches the same conclusions for the period 1954 to 1960, and gives the following reasons for the declining share: the ending of discrimination in favour of the United Kingdom in sterling area countries; the relatively slow rate of expansion of output and productivity in the United Kingdom; the faster increase in costs and prices in the United Kingdom compared with other countries; and poor design, quality, delivery and salesmanship.

Panić and Seward (1966) examine the period 1959 to 1964, during which the decline in the UK share of total exports was from 16.7 per cent to 13.3 per cent. They examine three hypotheses: declining competitiveness; unfavourable commodity structure; and unfavourable market structure. They contend that the price argument is not convincing because, at least over the period 1959 to 1964, export prices rose no faster than in other countries. They also dismiss the unfavourable commodity structure argument on the grounds that the UK share of total exports in expanding and declining commodities in world trade is similar to other countries. The unfavourable market structure argument is dismissed as well since they note that the area pattern of trade has shifted towards the EC countries, which is one of the most rapidly expanding markets. Panić and Seward favour a supply-side explanation of the United Kingdom's declining share of world trade. This could either mean capacity difficulties in a supply sense, or the production of goods with unfavourable characteristics giving them a lower world income elasticity of demand than similar goods of other countries.

Panić and Rajan (1979), in their international comparison of the structure of trade according to the growth performance of industries over the period 1955 to 1973, find that the United Kingdom's disadvantage (compared with France, West Germany and Japan) lies not in the broad product structure of her exports but in the poor relative performance in all markets.

One of the most recent comprehensive studies of export shares is by Fagerberg (1988) who examines trends in 15 major industrialised countries over the period 1960 to 1983. The growth of export shares is made a function of the rate of change of relative unit labour costs, the growth of world trade, the investment–output ratio, and the growth and level of technology measured by R & D expenditure and patent applications. For the UK, and most other countries, the impact of changing relative unit labour costs is negligible. Fagerberg concludes that the main factor behind the losses in market shares seems to be the slow growth in productive capacity caused by the low share of national resources devoted to investment. This, in turn, however, could be due to the low elasticity of exports to world trade growth and world income growth, caused by the unfavourable non-price characteristics of goods: a vicious circle that we will elaborate on in Chapter 13.

The upshot of the extensive research on the United Kingdom's share of world exports is that the decline is not the result of a heavy weighting of goods towards slow-growing markets or slow-growing products; rather, that in the same markets and in the same goods (broadly defined) as other countries, UK products sell less well. In other words, the problem lies with the supply and characteristics of the goods themselves, not the markets in which they are sold or the range of goods produced. It could be, of course, that *within* the broad categories of goods defined, the United Kingdom is producing a product the market for which is growing relatively slowly, and that a more disaggregated analysis would show the commodity bias of trade to be an important explanation of the United Kingdom's declining share of world exports. Barna (1963) addressed himself to this question by examining forty fast- and slow-growing products within the industries of machinery, transport equipment and chemicals. He found that the UK share of fast-growing industries in world trade, even at a disaggregated level, is only marginally below the average for other major countries studied. Having earlier expressed doubts about the conclusions of more aggregative studies (*The Times*, April 1963), Barna supports their conclusions by finding that the United Kingdom's slow export growth has been the result of a slower increase in the sales of both fast- and slow-growing products. The initial bias in trade is apparently not important.

Accepting this fundamental point, on which all the studies seem to agree, the deeper question is still why UK products of a similar type to those of other countries are treated as inferior. The explanation would seem to lie with the view expressed by Panić and Seward (1966), and those who have advanced a neo-technology theory of trade (e.g. Kravis, 1956), that the slow growth of the UK economy and its lack of investment and technical progressiveness have made the country weak in the production of the most recently developed and technically advanced products. It is the newness and technical sophistication of products, together with their marketing, which make them income elastic in world markets, ensuring that shares rise in every market. The importance of the income elasticity of demand for exports in world markets, in relation to the domestic income elasticity of demand for imports, in determining a country's growth rate is discussed in the next chapter. The virtuous circle that may be set up between higher export growth and higher output growth is discussed in Chapter 13, and some of the non-price factors that determine the growth of exports are discussed in Chapter 14. The view taken here is that while the slow growth of exports may well be a reflection of the slow growth of the economy, the growth of exports itself must be raised before the rate of growth of the economy can be improved, unless the income elasticity of demand for imports can be drastically reduced. Otherwise there will be an intolerable balance-of-payments strain in the transition from expanding demand to raise the growth rate and the benefits from this feeding through to export performance. To raise the rate of growth of exports requires raising the income elasticity of demand for exports in world markets. Exchange rate depreciation is not the answer, and any improvement in internal price competitiveness would have to be on a continuous basis to raise the rate of growth of exports permanently.

NORTH SEA OIL AND THE BALANCE OF PAYMENTS

North Sea oil started to save and earn foreign exchange immediately it came on stream in 1973, and in 1980 the United Kingdom became a net exporter of oil. The production of oil, and the oil trade balance, are shown in Figure 11.4. The trade balance in oil is now just over £1 billion. In addition, the various taxes and royalties that the government collects gives it around 70 per cent of the earnings from North Sea oil which at their peak amounted to over £10 billion per annum. These earnings of foreign exchange and tax revenue provided the country with a golden opportunity to embark on a programme of economic rejuvenation. Instead, there was economic retrenchment and the early 1980s witnessed the worst recession since the Great Depression of the 1930s. Over the period 1979 to 1983, national output was virtually stagnant, and actually fell by 3.7 per cent between 1979 and 1981; unemployment rose by over two million; investment contracted, and the demise of manufacturing industry accelerated. It appears that the tax revenue from North Sea oil was largely used to finance growing levels of unemployment and to reduce the size of the Public Sector Borrowing Requirement (i.e. saved), and that the foreign exchange was used to purchase ever

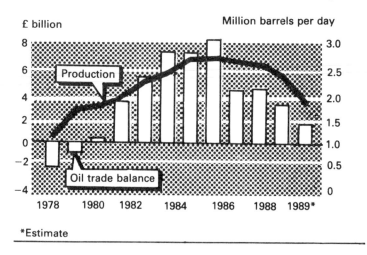

FIGURE 11.4   *UK oil trade and production*
Source: Royal Bank of Scotland.

increasing quantities of foreign manufactured goods largely for consumption purposes, and for investment abroad. In short, there appears to be little, if anything, to show for the bounty of North Sea oil.
What should have been a blessing seems to have turned out to be a
curse. Economic historians will look back with incredulity at this
period in British economic history when the country was one of the
major oil producers in the world, yet suffered so chronically.

It has been argued by some (e.g. Kay and Forsyth, 1980) that the
production and export of a natural resource like oil must inevitably
lead to a contraction of the manufacturing sector of an economy
because oil can only be exchanged for tradeable goods, of which
manufactures are prime examples. The mechanism through which
this contraction is supposed to take place is through an appreciation
of the exchange rate. This indeed will occur in a static economy at full
employment where there is no increase in output, on condition, also,
that the foreign exchange earnings are neither accumulated at home
nor invested abroad. On these assumptions, the exchange rate will
rise by the full amount justified by the foreign exchange gains from
oil. On the demand side, exchange rate appreciation reduces the
demand for domestic tradeables and increases the demand for foreign
tradeables. On the supply side, the profitability of producing domestic tradeables falls relative to the profitability of non-tradeables.

Both mechanisms cause the domestic production of tradeable (manufactured) goods to fall. If the balance of payments must balance, the foreign exchange gain from a natural resource must have its counterpart in a net foreign exchange loss elsewhere in the accounts. The adverse trade balance in manufactures in the United Kingdom, apparent since 1983, is sometimes rationalised in these terms. This impact of a natural resource discovery on the tradeable goods sector of an economy is sometimes referred to as the Dutch disease, following observation of the contraction of the manufacturing sector in Holland after the discovery of natural gas.

To a certain extent, the Dutch disease mechanism appeared to operate in the years 1979 and 1980 when the exchange rate was allowed to rise by some 35 per cent (see Figure 9.1), which must have contributed substantially to the growth of import penetration during this period and added to the loss of jobs in manufacturing industry. It cannot be stressed too forcefully, however, that there is nothing inevitable about the Dutch disease. There are plenty of antidotes. There are so many ways in which the foreign exchange earnings from a natural resource can be dissipated that there is no necessity for the exchange rate to rise or for domestic tradeable goods' production to fall. Let us consider some of the options. First, a foreign exchange surplus can be used for investment abroad. If investment abroad increases by as much as the foreign exchange gain from the natural resource, the exchange rate will remain unchanged. This option appeals to some because it provides a country with an income in the future when the foreign exchange earnings from the natural resource may decline. To a certain extent, this has happened in the United Kingdom, facilitated by the abandonment of exchange controls. Interest rate policy can also be used to discourage foreign capital inflows which will also hold down the exchange rate. Secondly, a foreign exchange surplus can be used to add to foreign exchange reserves. This is an attractive option for countries that have traditionally suffered from a shortage of reserves. The United Kingdom has added substantially to its reserves in recent years and this has been partly made possible by revenue from North Sea oil. Thirdly, starting from less than full employment, an economy can be expanded and this will use foreign exchange and stimulate domestic production at the same time. There are two broad types of expansion from internal sources – consumption led and investment led. A foreign exchange surplus could be used to bring about an immediate increase in real living standards by supporting an increase in consumption. This, however, is a dangerous policy for a country with traditionally slow growth and structural weaknesses in its balance of payments if the foreign exchange gain is temporary and consumption standards are hard to curtail. The most sensible policy, in an economically weak country like the United Kingdom, would be to use a surplus to mount a programme of investment to re-equip and revitalise major sectors of industry in order to rectify structural weaknesses particularly in other sectors of the balance-of-payments account. This is the only type of expansionary policy that can bring lasting benefit to an economy from a short-term 'windfall' gain. This is what could and should have happened in the United Kingdom with revenue from the North Sea. Unfortunately the fruits of the North Sea coincided with the implementation of a programme of 'monetarism' (a euphemism for deflation), and the foreign exchange gains and tax revenue were largely wasted in maintaining unemployed resources and immediate consumption. To attribute the decline in industrial output and employment in the United Kingdom from 1979 to North Sea oil would be highly misleading and disingenuous, although as we mentioned above the appreciation of the exchange rate played a part in the early years. The point to be made again, however, is that the appreciation was not inevitable. It could have been avoided by a combination of the policy options discussed above. Now that the production and export of oil are levelling off, the prospects for the balance of payments and the real economy are bleak indeed if other adverse trends continue.

APPENDIX: COMMODITY AND GEOGRAPHIC COMPOSITION OF UK EXPORTS AND IMPORTS

TABLE 11.6

Commodity composition of visible trade (£m)

	1979	1980	1981	1982	1983	1984	1985	1986	1987	1988	1989
Exports											
Food, beverages and tobacco	2 908	3 233	3 615	3 940	4 230	4 677	4 937	5 450	5 537	5 482	6 503
Basic materials	1 320	1 495	1 351	1 387	1 653	2 069	2 199	2 112	2 251	2 134	2 360
Oil	4 143	6 118	9 092	10 671	12 486	14 834	16 115	8 189	8 445	6 018	5 907
Other mineral fuels and lubricants	166	296	508	551	602	457	662	464	303	242	256
Semi-manufactured goods	12 462	13 867	13 017	13 980	15 864	18 134	19 921	20 819	22 438	24 096	26 881
Finished manufactured goods	18 488	21 010	21 881	23 334	24 284	28 421	32 319	33 617	38 213	40 816	48 597
Commodities and transactions not classified according to kind	984	1 130	1 204	1 468	1 581	1 673	1 838	2 005	2 259	1 988	2 288
Total	40 471	47 149	50 668	55 331	60 700	70 265	77 991	72 656	79 446	80 776	92 792
Imports											
Food, beverages and tobacco	5 841	5 515	5 896	6 598	7 259	8 297	8 660	9 417	9 532	9 969	10 747
Basic materials	3 695	3 505	3 437	3 468	4 251	5 074	5 041	4 635	5 222	5 469	5 927
Oil	4 881	5 810	5 986	6 033	5 514	7 901	8 014	4 119	4 262	3 221	4 426
Other mineral fuels and lubricants	517	742	883	1 081	1 274	2 029	2 257	1 872	1 561	1 469	1 479

cont. on p. 320

TABLE 11.6 cont.

Semi-manufactured goods	11 836	12 532	11 679	13 143	16 003	18 696	20 338	21 753	24 321	28 034	31 033
Finished manufactured goods	16 404	16 917	18 722	22 077	26 878	32 386	35 667	38 808	44 442	51 978	61 267
Commodities and transactions not classified according to kind	640	771	813	1 021	1 058	1 218	1 359	1 537	1 329	1 714	1 753
Total	43 814	45 792	47 416	53 421	62 237	75 601	81 336	82 141	90 669	101 854	116 632

Visible balance

Food, beverages and tobacco	−2 933	−2 282	−2 281	−2 658	−3 029	−3 620	−3 723	−3 967	−3 995	−4 487	−4 244
Basic materials	−2 375	−2 010	−2 086	−2 081	−2 598	−3 005	−2 842	−2 523	−2 971	−3 335	−3 567
Oil	−738	308	3 106	4 638	6 972	6 933	8 101	4 070	4 183	2 797	1 481
Other mineral fuels and lubricants	−351	−446	−375	−530	−672	−1 572	−1 595	−1 408	−1 258	−1 227	−1 223
Semi-manufactured goods	626	1 335	1 338	837	−139	−562	−417	−934	−1 883	−3 938	−4 152
Finished manufactured goods	2 084	4 093	3 159	1 257	−2 594	−3 965	−3 348	−5 191	−6 229	−11 162	−12 670
Commodities and transactions not classified according to kind	344	359	391	447	523	455	479	468	930	274	535
Total	−3 342	1 357	3 251	1 911	−1 537	−5 336	−3 345	−9 485	−11 223	−21 078	−23 840

Source: Central Statistical Office, *The Pink Book 1990: United Kingdom Balance of Payments* (London: HMSO, 1990).

TABLE 11.7

Geographic composition of visible trade (£m)

	1979	1980	1981	1982	1983	1984	1985	1986	1987	1988	1989
Exports											
European Community*	18 084	21 467	21 938	24 267	27 956	32 962	37 898	34 739	39 026	40 904	47 296
Other Western Europe	4 766	5 581	5 054	5 282	6 021	7 072	7 548	7 154	7 791	7 457	8 159
North America	4 763	5 279	7 125	8 360	9 526	11 464	13 295	12 116	12 998	12 652	14 435
Other developed countries	2 472	2 656	2 922	3 245	3 153	3 704	3 800	3 643	4 088	4 524	5 516
Oil exporting countries	3 648	4 816	5 991	6 505	6 133	5 801	5 943	5 496	5 282	4 935	5 719
Rest of world	6 737	7 348	7 638	7 671	7 909	9 260	9 504	9 507	10 262	10 304	11 667
Total	40 471	47 149	50 668	55 331	60 700	70 265	77 991	72 656	79 446	80 776	92 792
Imports											
European Community*	20 767	20 709	21 899	25 590	30 645	36 426	40 456	43 562	48 502	54 455	62 266
Other Western Europe	5 880	5 805	6 145	6 653	8 434	10 802	11 616	11 418	12 462	13 458	14 896
North America	5 810	6 819	6 853	7 523	8 526	10 517	11 073	9 505	10 378	12 374	15 162
Other developed countries	2 752	2 844	3 089	3 957	4 589	5 210	6 013	6 447	6 960	8 037	8 630
Oil exporting countries	2 940	3 885	3 448	3 254	2 605	2 698	2 644	1 873	1 622	1 840	1 936
Rest of world	5 665	5 730	5 984	6 445	7 438	9 948	9 534	9 336	10 744	11 691	13 742
Total	43 814	45 792	47 416	53 421	62 237	75 601	81 336	82 141	90 669	101 854	116 632

cont. on p. 322

TABLE 11.7 cont.

Visible balance

European Community*	−2 683	758	39	−1 323	−2 687	−3 463	2 556	8 823	−9 476	−13 551	−14 970
Other Western Europe	−1 114	−224	−1 091	−1 371	−2 413	−3 730	−4 068	−4 264	−4 672	−6 001	−6 737
North America	−1 047	−1 540	272	837	1 000	947	2 222	2 611	2 619	278	−727
Other developed countries	−280	−188	−167	−712	−1 436	−1 506	−2 213	−2 804	−2 872	−3 513	−3 114
Oil exporting countries	708	931	2 543	3 251	3 528	3 103	3 299	3 624	3 659	3 096	3 783
Rest of world	1 072	1 618	1 654	1 226	471	−687	−30	172	−482	−1 386	−2 075
Total	−3 342	1 357	3 251	1 911	−1 537	−5 336	−3 345	−9 485	−11 223	−21 078	−23 840

* Figures for all years relate to the eleven countries.

Source: Central Statistical Office, *The Pink Book 1990*; *United Kingdom Balance of Payments* (London: HMSO, 1990).

12
The Balance-of-Payments Equilibrium Growth Rate

In the long run a country cannot grow faster than the rate of growth of output consistent with balance-of-payments equilibrium on current account.[1] We call this growth rate the balance-of-payments equilibrium growth rate (y_B). In this chapter the import and export functions specified in Chapters 10 and 11 are used to determine the balance-of-payments equilibrium growth rate and to highlight its major determinants. An attempt is then made to estimate the balance-of-payments equilibrium growth rate for a variety of countries, including the United Kingdom, using some simplifying, though not unrealistic, assumptions. It is shown how closely the actual growth experience of several advanced industrial countries approximates to the rate of growth of export volume divided by the income elasticity of demand for imports (i.e. x/π), which defines a country's balance-of-payments equilibrium growth rate on the assumption that relative prices in international trade are sticky. The findings of this chapter underline the importance of raising the *rate of growth* of exports to improve the balance of payments permanently, and lend support to export-led growth models (which are considered in the next chapter).

The importance of a healthy balance of payments for growth can be stated quite succinctly. If a country gets into balance-of-payments difficulties as it expands demand before the short-term capacity growth rate is reached, then demand must be curtailed, supply is never fully utilised, investment is discouraged, technological progress is slowed down, and a country's goods compared with foreign goods become less desirable, so worsening the balance of payments still further, and so on. A vicious circle is initiated. By contrast, if a country is able to expand demand up to the level of existing productive capacity, without balance-of-payments difficulties arising, the pressure of demand upon capacity may well raise the capacity growth rate. There are a number of possible mechanisms through which this may happen: the encouragement of investment, which would augment the capital stock and bring with it technological progress; the supply of labour may increase by the entry into the work-force of people previously outside or from abroad; the movement of factors of production from low-productivity to high-productivity sectors; and the ability to import more may increase capacity by making domestic resources more productive. It is this argument that lies behind the advocacy of export-led growth, because it is only through the expansion of exports that the growth rate can be raised without the balance of payments deteriorating at the same time. Believers in export-led growth are really postulating a balance-of-payments constraint theory of why growth rates differ. It should be stressed, however, that the same rate of export growth in different countries will not necessarily permit the same rate of growth of output because the import requirements associated with growth will differ between countries, and thus some countries will have to constrain demand sooner than others for balance-of-payments equilibrium. The relation between a country's growth rate and its rate of growth of imports is the income elasticity of demand for imports.

THE DETERMINATION OF THE BALANCE-OF-PAYMENTS
EQUILIBRIUM GROWTH RATE

Balance-of-payments equilibrium on current account measured in units of the home currency may be expressed as

$$P_{dt} X_t = P_{ft} M_t E_t \qquad (12.1)$$

where X is the quantity of exports, P_d is the price of exports in home currency, M is the quantity of imports, P_f is the price of imports in foreign currency, E is the exchange rate (i.e. the domestic price of foreign currency), and t is time. In a growing economy, starting from equilibrium, the condition for balance-of-payments equilibrium through time is that the rate of growth of the value of exports equals the rate of growth of the value of imports, i.e.

$$p_{dt} + x_t = p_{ft} + m_t + e_t \qquad (12.2)$$

where lower-case letters represent rates of change of the variables.

Following Chapter 10, but omitting capacity as a variable (for simplicity), the quantity of imports demanded may be specified as a multiplicative function of the relative price of imports and domestic substitutes (measured in a common currency so capturing the effect of exchange-rate changes) and of domestic income. Thus:

$$M_t = \left(\frac{P_{ft} E_t}{P_{dt}} \right)^{\psi} Y_t^{\pi} \tag{12.3}$$

where M_t is the quantity of imports, P_{ft} is the foreign price of imports, P_{dt} is the domestic price of import substitutes, Y is domestic income, ψ is the price elasticity of demand for imports ($\psi < 0$), and π is the income elasticity of demand for imports ($\pi > 0$). The rate of growth of imports may be written:

$$m_t = \psi \, (p_{ft} + e_t - p_{dt}) + \pi(y_t) \tag{12.4}$$

where lower-case letters again represent rates of change of the variables.

Following Chapter 11, again omitting the capacity variable (for simplicity), the quantity of exports demanded may also be expressed as a multiplicative function, in which the arguments in the demand function are the price of domestic goods relative to foreign goods (again measured in a common currency to capture the effect of exchange-rate changes) and the level of world income. Thus:

$$X_t = \left(\frac{P_{dt}}{E_t P_{ft}} \right)^{\eta} Z_t^{\varepsilon} \tag{12.5}$$

where X_t is the quantity of exports, P_{dt} is the domestic price of exports, P_{ft} is the foreign price of goods competitive with exports, Z_t is the level of world income, η is the price elasticity of demand for exports ($\eta < 0$), and ε is the world income elasticity of demand for exports ($\varepsilon > 0$).

The rate of growth of exports may be written:

$$x_t = \eta(p_{dt} - e_t - p_{ft}) + \varepsilon(z_t) \tag{12.6}$$

Substituting equations (12.4) and (12.6) into (12.2) we can solve for the rate of growth of domestic income consistent with balance-of-payments equilibrium (y_{Bt}):

$$y_{Bt} = \frac{(1 + \eta + \psi)(p_{dt} - p_{ft} - e_t) + \varepsilon(z_t)}{\pi}$$ (12.7)

Remembering the signs of the parameters ($\eta < 0$, $\psi < 0$, $\varepsilon > 0$, and $\pi > 0$), equation (12.7) expresses several fundamental economic propositions:

(i)   Domestic prices rising faster than foreign prices will worsen the balance-of-payments equilibrium growth rate if the sum of the price elasticities of demand for exports and imports is greater than unity in absolute value (i.e. if $|\eta + \psi| > 1$).

(ii) Devaluation or currency depreciation, i.e. a rise in the domestic price of foreign currency ($e_t > 0$) will improve the balance-of-payments equilibrium growth rate provided the sum of the price elasticities of demand for imports and exports exceeds unity in absolute value, which is the so-called Marshall-Lerner condition (i.e. if $|\eta + \psi| > 1$).[2] Notice, however, the important point that a once-for-all depreciation of the currency cannot raise the balance-of-payments equilibrium growth rate permanently. After the initial depreciation, $e_t = 0$, and the growth rate would revert to its former level. To raise the balance-of-payments equilibrium growth rate permanently would require continual depreciation, i.e. $e_t > 0$ in successive periods.

(iii) A faster growth of world income will raise the balance-of-payments equilibrium growth rate.

(iv) The higher the income elasticity of demand for imports (π), the lower the balance-of-payments equilibrium growth rate.

The interesting question is, how well does equation (12.7) predict the actual growth experience of countries, and can we derive any simple rule or 'law'? First of all, it must be noted that there may be an asymmetry in the system. While a country cannot grow faster than its balance-of-payments equilibrium growth rate for very long, unless it can finance an ever-growing deficit, there is little to stop a country growing slower and accumulating large surpluses. In particular this may occur where the balance-of-payments equilibrium growth rate is so high that a country simply does not have the physical capacity to grow at that rate. This typifies many oil-producing countries, and would also seem to typify the experience of Japan, as we shall see below.

To calculate the balance-of-payments equilibrium growth rate from equation (12.7) for a number of countries requires a substantial amount of data and estimates of parameters and variables which are not readily available. If the assumption is made, however, that there is no *long-run* change in relative prices measured in a common currency, i.e. $(p_{dt} - p_{ft} - e_t) = 0$, equation (12.7) reduces to:

$$y_{Bt} = \frac{\varepsilon(z_t)}{\pi} \qquad (12.8)^3$$

or, from equation (12.6) on the same assumption,

$$y_{Bt} = \frac{x_t}{\pi} \qquad (12.9)$$

Such a simple formula from a complicated expression certainly makes the empirical task easier. How realistic is the assumption used to derive the simple formula? Many models (see Ball, Burns and Laury, 1977; Wilson, 1976) suggest that over the long period there can be little movement in relative international prices measured in a common currency, either because of arbitrage, or because exchange rate changes lead to equiproportionate changes in domestic prices (see chapters 3 and 5). In the expression $(p_{dt} - p_{ft} - e_t)$ either domestic and international prices move together or changes in e_t cause p_{dt} to change by the same amount (or a combination of both) so that $p_{dt} - p_{ft} - e_t = 0$.

The result in equation (12.9) is a dynamic version of the static foreign trade multiplier first derived by Harrod in 1933, namely

$$\frac{\Delta Y}{\Delta X} = \frac{1}{m} \qquad (12.10)$$

where m is the marginal propensity to import $(\Delta M/\Delta Y)$. Harrod derived this result on exactly the same assumptions that we have used above namely that relative prices measured in a common currency (or the real terms of trade) remain unchanged, and that there is no other (net) autonomous expenditure other than exports so that trade balance is always preserved. On these assumptions we can multiply the left-hand side of (12.10) by X/Y and the right hand side by M/Y which gives:

$$\frac{\Delta Y}{\Delta X} \cdot \frac{X}{Y} = \frac{\Delta Y}{\Delta M} \cdot \frac{M}{Y} \qquad (12.11)$$

or

$$\frac{\Delta Y}{Y} = \frac{\Delta X/X}{\dfrac{\Delta M}{\Delta Y} \cdot \dfrac{Y}{M}} = \frac{x}{\pi} \qquad (12.12)$$

which is the result in (12.9). Harrod believed that an understanding of the foreign trade multiplier was indispensible to an understanding of the relative economic performance of industrial countries. McCombie (1985) has also shown that this basic result in equation (12.9) or (12.12) can be interpreted as a Hicks supermultiplier where export growth is the dominant component of autonomous demand to which other components of demand adapt. In other words, a faster growth of exports allows investment growth and consumption growth to be faster than otherwise would be the case without a country getting into balance-of-payments difficulties. Exports are unique in the sense that they are the only component of demand which pays for the import requirements for faster growth. Investment led growth does not necessarily earn foreign exchange to pay for import requirements, nor does consumption led growth.

How well does the dynamic Harrod trade multiplier (or Hicks supermultiplier) predict the growth performance of industrial countries?[4]

A FUNDAMENTAL LAW OF GROWTH

Applying equation (12.9) to international data gives a remarkable approximation to the growth experience of many countries in the post-war years. It might almost be stated as a fundamental law that, except where the balance-of-payments equilibrium growth rate exceeds the maximum feasible capacity growth rate, the rate of growth of a country will approximate to the ratio of its rate of growth of exports and its income elasticity of demand for imports. The approximation itself would seem to vindicate the assumptions used to arrive at the simple rule in equation (12.9). We report here two studies, one by Thirlwall (1979b), the other by Bairam (1988).

In the first study, the model is tested on two sets of data for the growth of output and exports: one for the period 1953 to 1976 (Kern, 1978), and the other from Cornwall (1977) for the period 1951 to 1973. On the income elasticity of demand for imports, Houthakker and Magee's (1969) estimates have been taken as applying to the whole of these periods even though they were only estimated for the period 1951 to 1966. They are the best consistently estimated international estimates available, but are probably now on the low side. The data, and the results of applying equation (12.9), are presented in Table 12.1. In this table there is a general tendency for the estimates of the balance-of-payments equilibrium growth rate to be higher than the actual growth rate, which, if true, would produce a balance-of-payments surplus. For countries which built up surpluses the estimates are consistent with the empirical evidence. Japan is a striking example of a country where the gap between its actual growth rate and its balance-of-payments equilibrium growth rate resulted in the build-up of a huge payments surplus. Presumably Japan could not grow faster than it did because of an ultimate capacity ceiling. But Japan still grew considerably faster than other countries because demand was unconstrained and induced its own supply of factors of production. For countries which moved into deficit over the period, the estimate of their balance-of-payments equilibrium growth rate must be too high. As suggested above, this may be because the assumed income elasticity of demand for imports is an underestimate for the period stretching into the late 1960s and 1970s. Also, relative price movements combined with various price elasticity conditions cannot be entirely ruled out as determinants of the balance of payments even though they may be of minor significance compared with income movements and income elasticities of demand for imports and exports.

In general, however, there is a very close association across countries between the actual growth experience and the growth rate predicted by the dynamic Harrod trade multiplier (balance-of-payments constrained growth) model. The rank correlation between the actual and predicted rates is 0.764 for the period 1951–73 and 0.891 for the period 1953–76. The estimate of the UK balance-of-payments constrained growth rate over the 1950s and 1960s and into the 1970s is approximately 2.7 to 2.9 per cent, the lowest of any

TABLE 12.1

Calculation of the growth rate consistent with balance-of-payments equilibrium, 1951–73, 1953–76

Country	%Δ in real GNP (y)		%Δ in export volume (x)		Income elasticity of demand for imports (π)	Predicted growth rate from applying equation (12.9)	
	1951–73	1953–76	1951–73	1953–76		1951–73	1953–76
USA	3.7	3.23	5.1	5.88	1.51	3.38	3.89
Canada	4.6	4.81	6.9	6.02	1.20	4.84	5.02
West Germany	5.7	4.96	10.8	9.99	1.89	5.71	5.29
Netherlands	5.0	4.99	10.1	9.38	1.82	5.55	5.15
Sweden	—	3.67	—	7.16	1.76	—	4.07
France	5.0	4.95	8.1	8.78	1.62	5.00	5.42
Denmark	4.2	3.58	6.1	6.77	1.31	4.65	5.17
Australia	—	4.95	—	6.98	0.90	—	7.76
Italy	5.1	4.96	11.7	12.09	2.25	5.20	5.37
Switzerland	—	3.56	—	7.20	1.90	—	3.79
Norway	4.2	4.18	7.2	7.70	1.40	5.14	5.50
Belgium	4.4	4.07	9.4	9.24	1.94	4.84	4.76
Japan	9.5	8.55	15.4	16.18	1.23	12.52	13.15
UK	2.7	2.71	4.1	4.46	1.51	2.71	2.95
South Africa	—	4.97	—	6.57	0.85	—	7.73

Sources: Data for 1951–73 from J. Cornwall, *Modern Capitalism: Its Growth and Transformation* (London: Martin Robertson, 1977). Data for 1953–76 from D. Kern, 'An International Comparison of Major Economic Trends 1953–76', National Westminster Bank Quarterly Review, May, 1978. Estimates of π from H. S. Houthakker and S. P. Magee, 'Income and Price Elasticities in World Trade', *Review of Economics and Statistics*, May, 1969.

of the countries in the sample. This is associated with the lowest rate of growth of export volume of any of the countries in the sample.

The study by Bairam (1988) extends the analysis into the 1980s taking as his sample period 1970–85. He estimates his own export and import demand functions to derive estimates of the income elasticities of demand for exports and imports. He applied both equations (12.8) and (12.9) to the data, with the results shown in Table 12.2. On the whole, the results of applying equation (12.8) are not so strong as equation (12.9) which Bairam ascribes to poor estimates of ε in many cases. The UK's balance-of-payments equilibrium growth rate of 2.2 per cent from equation (12.9) compares with the actual growth rate over the period of 1.9 per cent – again the lowest in the sample. Some

TABLE 12.2

Estimated export and import income elasticities (ε and π) and average values of the rates of growth exports (x), domestic income (y) and balance-of-payments constrained income (y_{Bi})

Region/ Country	Growth rates (% per annum):					
	ε	π	x	y	$y_{B1}=(ε/π)z$ (Equation (12.8))	$y_{B2}=(1/π)x$ (Equation (12.9))
Western Europe, large countries:						
1. France	2.16	2.42	6.3	3.5	2.3	2.6
2. West Germany	0.77*	1.92	5.0	2.4	1.0	2.6
3. Italy	1.58	2.83	5.2	2.6	1.5	1.8
4. UK	1.31	2.14	4.7	1.9	1.6	2.2
Western Europe, small countries:						
5. Austria	1.37	2.24	6.8	3.3	1.6	3.0
6. Belgium	1.92	2.64	5.0	2.7	1.9	1.9
7. Denmark	1.04	4.12*	4.6	2.2	0.6	1.1
8. Finland	1.59	1.94	5.9	3.4	2.1	3.0
9. Ireland	3.99*	2.63	13.8	3.7	3.9	5.2
10. Netherlands	1.08	2.00	4.3	2.4	1.4	2.2
11. Norway	1.48	1.43	4.4	3.9	2.7	3.1
12. Sweden	1.81	2.53	3.8	2.2	1.9	1.5
Southern Europe:						
13. Greece	2.97	2.13	8.7	3.8	3.6	4.1
14. Portugal	2.48	1.69	6.1	4.1	3.8	3.6
15. Spain	1.40	2.67	4.8	3.1	1.4	1.8
16. Turkey	3.75*	2.68	18.5	5.0	3.9	6.9
17. Yugoslavia	1.42	1.83	5.8	4.3	2.0	3.1
North America:						
18. Canada	2.04	1.77	5.0	3.4	3.0	2.8
19. USA	1.83	2.32	5.7	2.5	2.1	2.5

Average value of the rate of growth of world income (z) during the period under consideration was 2.8 per cent per annum. * indicates a coefficient not significantly different from zero at the 0.95 confidence level.

other countries have lower estimated balance-of-payments equilibrium growth rates than the UK and presumably were able to grow faster through favourable relative price effects and/or capital inflows.

As far as the predictive power of the model is concerned, there are two parametric tests that can be performed. The first is to run a regression of the actual growth rate on the predicted rate and test whether the coefficient differs significantly from unity or not. If not, then the predicted rate from the model will be a good predictor of the actual rate. When y is regressed on y_{B2} in Table 12.2, the result is $y = 0.99y_{B2}$, with a standard error of the regression coefficient of less than 0.1. The coefficient does not differ significantly from unity. One criticism of this test, however, is that π which is used to estimate y_{B2} is itself a stochastic variable which may bias the results. To overcome this problem, a second test of the model is to calculate $\pi(\pi^*)$ that would make $y = y_{B2}$, and compare the result with the actual estimate of $\pi(\hat{\pi})$ from the import demand function. If the hypothesis cannot be rejected that $\pi^* = \hat{\pi}$, then y_{B2} will be a good predictor of y. When this test is performed, the model is supported in the vast majority of cases. Bairam concludes: 'The results obtained . . . consistently suggest that the overall economic growth is determined by the Harrod foreign trade multiplier. This means that overall economic performance of a country depends upon the values of its income elasticities of exports and imports.'

THE MODEL WITH CAPITAL FLOWS

The model presented above can be extended to include capital flows, so relaxing the requirement that trade is balanced. Using equation (12.1) we now have:

$$P_{dt}X_t + C_t = P_{ft}M_tE_t \tag{12.13}$$

where C_t is capital flows measured in domestic currency ($C_t > 0 =$ inflow). Equation (12.13) is an identity. Capital flows must fill the difference between imports and exports; the balance of payments must balance (see Chapter 1). Taking rates of change of the variables, and using equations (12.4) and (12.6) for the growth of imports and exports, gives an expression for the growth of income consistent with overall balance of payments equilibrium of:

$$y^*_{Bt} = \frac{\left(1 + \psi + \dfrac{E}{R}\eta\right)(p_{dt} - p_{ft} - e_t) + \dfrac{E}{R}\varepsilon(z_t) + \dfrac{C}{R}(c_t - p_{dt})}{\pi} \tag{12.14}$$

where all the variables and parameters are the same as before and

E/R and C/R are the shares of export receipts and capital flows, respectively, in total receipts to finance the import bill.

If there are no capital flows, and relative prices measured in a common currency do not change, equation (12.14) reduces to the earlier result in equations (12.8) and (12.9). If relative prices remain unchanged, the model with capital flows will give a higher or lower growth rate than the rate predicted from the simple model without capital flows according to whether $(c_t - p_{dt}) \gtrless x_t$, i.e. whether the growth of real capital flows is greater or less than the rate of growth of export volume.

It is apparent that any country's growth rate associated with overall balance of payments equilibrium can be disaggregated into four component parts:

(i)   a pure term of trade effect: $(p_{dt} - p_{ft} - e_t)/\pi$

(ii) the effect of relative price changes working through import and export elasticities:

$$\left(\psi + \frac{E}{R}\, \eta \right) (p_{dt} - p_{ft} - e_t)/\pi$$

(iii) the effect of the exogenous growth of world income:

$$\frac{E}{R}\, \varepsilon\, (z_t)/\pi$$

(iv) the effect of real capital inflows/outflows:

$$\frac{C}{R}\, (c_t - p_{dt})/\pi$$

For an empirical application of this model to a selection of developing countries, see Thirlwall and Hussain (1982) and Bairam (1990).

Use of the Model for Forecasting and Simulation

Our basic expression for the balance-of-payments equilibrium growth rate is equation (12.7).

$$y_B = \frac{(1 + \eta + \psi)\,(p_d - p_f - e) + \varepsilon\,(z)}{\pi} \qquad (12.15)$$

This basic expression can be used for both policy analysis and for forecasting purposes, given estimates of the parameters of the model and forecasts of the exogenous variables. As far as policy analysis is concerned, it is possible to solve for any of the variables and parameters in the expression above consistent with a particular target rate of growth (y_B^*). One important variable under a government's control is the nominal exchange rate. In the equation above, e is the rate of change of the exchange rate measured as the domestic price of foreign currency. We can solve for e consistent with any target growth rate, y_B^*, i.e.

$$e = \frac{\varepsilon(z) - y_B^* \, \pi}{1 + \eta + \psi} \tag{12.16}$$

For example, suppose the target rate of growth is set at 3 per cent per annum (since all other countries are growing at 3 per cent per annum, $z = 0.03$), that $\varepsilon = 1.0$ and $\pi = 2.0$ (not dissimilar to the estimates for the UK), and that the sum of the price elasticities of demand for exports and imports ($\eta + \psi$) is -1.5, so that the Marshall-Lerner condition is satisfied. Substituting these values into equation (12.16) gives:

$$e = \frac{1.0(0.03) - (0.03)2}{1 - 1.5} = 0.06$$

In other words, to achieve a target rate of growth of 3 per cent per annum consistent with balance-of-payments equilibrium would require currency depreciation of 6 per cent per annum. This is necessary basically to offset the unfavourable discrepancy between the income elasticity of demand for exports and imports which otherwise would cause imports to grow faster than exports if the country grew at the same rate as the rest of the world.

The model presented above has been used by Turner (1988) of the Macroeconomic Modelling Bureau at the University of Warwick for forecasting UK growth prospects. Using forecasts of the growth of world income, Turner estimates a balance-of-payments equilibrium growth rate for the UK over the five years 1987 to 1992 of not more than 1 per cent per annum. On the assumption that the UK can sustain a current deficit of £5 billion per annum for five years, the maximum growth rate sustainable (without a fall in the exchange rate) rises to between 1 and 1.5 per cent per annum. For the growth rate to average 2 per cent per annum with an annual deficit of £5 billion, a fall in the exchange rate of 20–30 per cent would be required. The prospects look bleak.

If the exchange rate is ruled out as a policy instrument (as under systems of pegged exchange rates such as the ERM), and import controls are contemplated, the model can be solved for the income elasticity of demand for imports that would be required, namely:

$$\pi = \frac{(1 + \eta + \psi)(p_d - p_f - e) + \varepsilon(z)}{y_B^*} \qquad (12.17)$$

For example, suppose the exchange rate is fixed and domestic prices are rising by 8 per cent per annum while foreign prices are rising at only 4 per cent per annum. Given the previous values of $(\eta + \psi)$, ε and z gives:

$$\pi = \frac{(1 - 1.5)(0.04) + 1(0.03)}{0.03} = 0.3$$

This represents a very low income elasticity of demand for imports, but none the less would be the value required to sustain 3 per cent growth in the face of growing price uncompetitiveness and a low income elasticity of demand for exports.

An alternative longer-term strategy would be to raise the income elasticity of demand for exports (ε) through policies to improve the various aspects of non-price competition, to be discussed in Chapter 14. The required ε for 3 per cent growth, given the values of the variables and parameters assumed above, would be:

$$\varepsilon = \frac{y_B^* \pi - (1 + \eta + \psi)(p_d - p_f - e)}{z} \qquad (12.18)$$

Therefore:

$$\varepsilon = \frac{(0.03)2 - (1 - 1.5)(0.04)}{0.03} = 2.4$$

This is a relatively high income elasticity of demand for exports – at least by UK standards – although achieved by successful exporting countries such as Japan and South Korea.

CONCLUSION

The simple policy conclusion for most countries, including the United Kingdom, is that if they wish to grow faster they must first raise the balance-of-payments constraint on demand. To raise the rate of growth of productive capacity (by improving productivity, for example), without being able to raise the rate of growth of demand because of a balance-of-payments constraint, will merely lead to unemployment. If the balance-of-payments equilibrium growth rate can be raised, however, by making exports more attractive and by reducing the income elasticity of demand for imports, demand can be expanded without producing balance-of-payments difficulties; and, within limits, demand can generate its own supply by encouraging investment, absorbing under-employment, raising productivity growth, and so on. The explanation of growth-rate differences lies primarily in differences in the rate of growth of demand by activating and inducing the growth of supply, and the major constraint on the rate of growth of demand in most countries is the balance of payments. The model and the empirical evidence lend strong support to the advocates of export-led growth.

The deeper question lies in why the balance-of-payments equilibrium growth rate differs between countries and why it is so low in the United Kingdom. The answer must be primarily associated with the characteristics of goods produced, which determine the income elasticity of demand for a country's exports, and a country's propensity to import. For countries like the United Kingdom with a slow rate of growth of exports, combined with a relatively high income elasticity of demand for imports, the message is plain: the goods produced by the country are relatively unattractive at both home and abroad.

13
Export-led Growth

In the last chapter the importance of raising the rate of growth of exports was emphasised for the maintenance of balance-of-payments equilibrium at a permanently higher growth rate. If a continuous improvement in relative price competitiveness is ruled out as being unattainable, the major determinant of the growth of exports is the income elasticity of demand for exports, for any given growth of world income.

The export-led growth models to be found in the literature on applied growth theory, which will be elaborated on later, concentrate more on export-led growth setting up a virtuous circle of faster growth and faster exports than on simply relieving a country of the balance-of-payments constraint on demand. There is a problem with these models of the virtuous-circle type, however, which is that they do not contain a balance-of-payments equilibrium condition or constraint. The implicit assumption seems to be that provided it is export growth that is the engine of growth, as distinct from domestic autonomous demand, the balance of payments will look after itself. Indeed, it is assumed in some models that the initial export growth and trade surplus generates such favourable responses in the economy that the balance-of-payments surplus actually grows. No consideration is given to the possibility that the rate of growth of income determined by the structure of the model may generate a rate of growth of imports greater than the rate of growth of exports, thereby imposing a constraint on the export-led growth rate if balance-of-payments equilibrium is a requirement. The import side in export-led growth models seems to have been neglected. This, of course, is not to pour cold water on export-led growth models. If the balance of payments is constraining the actual growth rate before the capacity rate is reached, then growth led by export demand, as opposed to other elements of demand, will raise the constraint; and if the actual growth rate can reach the capacity rate, the capacity rate itself may be raised. But it cannot be taken for granted in export-led models that there is no constraint on growth at all. If balance-of-payments equilibrium is a requirement, the equilibrium growth rate in an export-led growth model must reflect this requirement, otherwise the model may be useless for predictive purposes.

Models of export-led growth are typically very unspecific about the precise relationship between the rate of growth of exports and income, and how much income growth might be associated with a given growth of exports. It is clear from historical and present-day evidence, however, that exports tend to grow faster than income, which must make one immediately suspicious of models, for predictive purposes at least, which set the rate of growth of income equal to the rate of growth of exports. There is no doubt a variety of explanations as to why the rate of growth of exports typically exceeds the rate of growth of income through time, but a balance-of-payments constraint, related to the characteristics of goods traded, is one powerful explanation. It is obvious that if the income elasticity of demand for imports is greater than unity, and there is no continual compensating improvement in competitiveness, an equality between the rate of growth of exports and income would generate a higher rate of growth of imports than exports, and income growth would sooner or later have to be curtailed. Thus, as long as the income elasticity of demand for imports is greater than unity, which it is for most countries, the ratio of export growth to income growth will almost certainly show an historical tendency to exceed unity. If the growth equation is specified as $y_t = \gamma (x_t)$, with $\gamma < 1$, we would predict from equations (12.6) and (12.7) in the previous chapter that if relative prices measured in a common currency do not change, $\gamma = 1/\pi$.

This weakness of traditional export-led growth models can be rectified by incorporating the balance-of-payments equilibrium condition specified in the previous chapter. Before doing so, however, it will be useful to do two things: first, to discuss further the relationship between the balance-of-payments constrained growth rate (y_B) and the actual and capacity rates of growth (y_A and y_C); second, to consider some of the early (unconstrained) models that have laid stress on export growth as the key determinant of a virtuous circle of growth. The possible relationships between y_B, y_A and y_C are now outlined:

(i) $y_B = y_A = y_C$ Balance-of-payments equilibrium and full employment

(ii) $y_B = y_A < y_C$ Balance-of-payments equilibrium and growing unemployment

(iii) $y_B < y_A = y_C$ Increasing balance-of-payments deficit and full employment

(iv) $y_B < y_A < y_C$ Increasing balance-of-payments deficit and growing unemployment

(v) $y_B > y_A = y_C$ Increasing balance-of-payments surplus and full employment

(vi) $y_B > y_A < y_C$ Increasing balance-of-payments surplus and growing unemployment

It is a fundamental proposition in economics that in the long run, when all resources are fully utilised, a country's actual growth rate cannot exceed its capacity rate determined by the rate of growth of the labour force and the productivity of labour – the Harrodian natural rate of growth.[1] The UK experience has been that the country has rarely had the opportunity to grow at its capacity rate because the balance-of-payments equilibrium growth rate has been below it. The United Kingdom has approximated to situation (iv) above. The lure of export-led growth lies in the possibility of moving from situation (iv) to at least (i), if not (v) (the Japanese case), where the balance-of-payments equilibrium growth rate lies above the capacity growth rate, allowing the actual growth rate to equal the capacity growth rate without balance-of-payments difficulties arising. Indeed, in this situation the export-led growth advocates argue that the buoyancy of demand at full employment will raise the capacity growth rate, for the reasons outlined in the previous chapter: the encouragement to investment and technical progress; the augmentation of other factors of production; the increased mobility of factors of production from low-productivity to high-productivity sectors; and the ability to import more may increase capacity by making domestic resources more productive. In this spirit Cornwall (1977) argues persuasively that the major explanation of growth-rate differences between countries is differences in the pressure of demand to which supply adjusts, though for reasons we shall consider later (and question) he does not believe that the balance of payments has been a constraint on demand in the United Kingdom. As far as the UK economy is concerned, it is difficult to know what a faster rate of growth of exports might do for the capacity growth rate because export performance in the past has never been good enough to escape a balance-of-payments constraint before the capacity growth rate has been reached. It is frequently argued, however, that if only the United Kingdom did not run into balance-of-payments difficulties before full employment is reached, demand would not have to be contracted, investment would remain high, and that these conditions in the long run would raise the capacity growth rate closer to that of other countries. While the argument is speculative, it would be surprising if the UK growth record relative to other countries since the Second World War did not have something to do with the characteristics of its trading position compared with other countries, particularly its low rate of growth of exports combined with a relatively high income elasticity of demand for imports. Certainly part of Japan's phenomenal success must be related to the fact that, as we showed in Chapter 12, its growth rate consistent with balance-of-payments equilibrium has exceeded by a considerable margin its actual growth rate, which has continually pressed on its capacity rate.

Kaldor (1974) has argued that the main cause of unemployment in the United Kingdom in the last hundred years, barring periods of acute depression, has not been oversaving but insufficient exports relative to the level of imports which would be required at full employment:

> despite commitment to full employment from 1944 it took a very long time – in fact until 1967[2] – before it was realised that the true effect of the new system [i.e. commitment to full employment] was simply to transmute the chronic pre-war unemployment problem into the chronic post-war balance of payments problem.

Kaldor goes on to say that what the United Kingdom has really suffered from has been the slow growth of exports, a historical fact which can be explained by the industrialisation of other regions of the world which constantly narrowed the markets for UK goods. Kaldor was a strong believer in export-led growth, maintaining that the common feature of all industrial economies is that their economic growth has been invariably led by a faster growth of exports which has given a higher rate of growth of industrial productivity. He claimed that the United Kingdom could have grown at 5 per cent per annum had it achieved export growth of 10 to 15 per cent per annum.

To sum up we can make two propositions. First, that up to the capacity growth rate a country's actual growth rate is fundamentally determined by its rate of growth of exports in relation to the growth of imports if it is to maintain balance-of-payments equilibrium. Second, it is probable that a country's capacity growth rate is also partly determined by its export performance because of the link between high demand and the response of factor supplies, and because faster growth itself generates faster productivity growth. This is the idea of a virtuous circle of growth led by exports, which we now develop.

MODELS OF EXPORT-LED GROWTH

In the European context, Lamfalussy (1963) was one of the first economists to propound an export-led growth theory to account for differences in the growth performance of Western European countries. In Lamfalussy's model export-led growth is important for three main reasons: (i) the rate of growth of exports, as a determinant of demand, is likely to be an important determinant of investment; (ii) growth requires imports, and if exports do not rise as fast as import requirements, growth will be constrained by the balance of payments; and (iii) the smaller the domestic market, the greater the importance of external demand in enabling economies to reap economies of scale in production to make enterprises viable that would not otherwise be so. Lamfalussy envisages a virtuous circle commencing with higher exports leading to more investment, which in turn leads to a higher rate of growth of productivity, lower export prices and thus higher exports. There is, however, no explicit balance-of-payments constraint in his model.

Beckerman (1962) sees a similar virtuous circle in export-led growth, but his model also lacks a balance-of-payments equilibrium condition: demand determines investment and growth; an important component of demand is exports (and it is only this component of demand that can help to balance the import requirements at a higher level of demand); a high level of demand and investment is favourable to growth, which contributes to greater competitiveness and further export demand. Beckerman claims that the growth of exports is closely related across countries to the growth of competitiveness, and that differences in competitiveness are mainly a function of differences in productivity growth. As Caves (1970) rightly noted, Beckerman's model in its original form lacks an equilibrium condition. Also, the export demand function is of a very *ad hoc* nature, making the *rate of growth* of exports a function of the *absolute* difference between domestic and foreign prices. Using the more conventional multiplicative export demand function, which makes the rate of growth of exports depend on the difference between the rate of growth of domestic and foreign prices, also gives the model an equilibrium condition. The Beckerman model, as here modified, runs as follows: export growth is a function of the difference in the rate of growth of domestic and foreign prices; faster export growth leads to faster productivity growth; faster productivity growth contributes to a lower rate of growth of wage costs per unit of output *if wages do not rise in line with productivity*; a lower rate of increase in wage costs per unit of output leads to a lower rate of domestic price increase; and a lower rate of domestic price increase leads to a faster rate of growth of exports. The virtuous circle is complete. If the model is formulated algebraically, using linear relations, with signs correctly specified in the model, we have:

$$x = a_0 - b_0 (p_d - p_f); \quad a_0 > 0, b_0 > 0 \qquad (13.1)$$

where x is the rate of growth of exports, p_d is the rate of growth of domestic prices, p_f is the rate of growth of foreign prices, and a_0 represents the rate of growth of exports determined by other factors (e.g. the growth of world income). Also:

$$r = a_1 + b_1 (x); \quad b_1 > 0 \qquad (13.2)$$

where r is the rate of growth of labour productivity. Also:

$$w = a_2 + b_2 (r); \quad 0 < b_2 < 1 \qquad (13.3)$$

where w is the rate of growth of wages. Finally:

$$p_d = w - r \qquad (13.4)$$

Substituting (13.3) into (13.4) gives:

$$p_d = a_2 + (b_2 - 1) r \qquad (13.5)$$

Substituting (13.2) into (13.5) gives:

$$p_d = a_2 + (b_2 - 1)(a_1 + b_1 x)$$
$$= (a_2 - a_1 + b_2 a_1) + (b_2 b_1 - b_1) x \qquad (13.6)$$

Substituting (13.6) into (13.1) gives:

$$x = a_0 - b_0 [(a_2 - a_1 + b_2 a_1) + (b_2 b_1 - b_1) x] + b_0 (p_f) \qquad (13.7)$$

Solving for the equilibrium growth rate of exports gives:

$$x = \frac{a_0 - b_0 (a_2 - a_1 + b_2 a_1) + b_0 (p_f)}{1 + b_0 b_1 (b_2 - 1)} \qquad (13.8)$$

Note that the virtuous circle of export-led growth depends crucially on the rate of increase in wages being less than the rate of increase in productivity (i.e. $b_2 < 1$). If $b_2 = 1$, there would be no 'circular' process: that is, no induced rate of growth of exports from the initial expansion of exports itself. Balassa (1963) has also argued that if wages respond to the level of employment, the virtuous circle may be choked. He is concerned that if $b_2 < 1$, Beckerman's model may lead to diverging country growth rates which are not observed in practice. The model is easily modified by relating changes in wages to the level of unemployment, using a Phillips curve relation. This makes for stability by causing wages and prices to rise faster in regions where export growth is high than in regions where export growth is sluggish and unemployment high. Divergence of growth rates may take place until full employment is reached, but then the virtuous circle would break down. Beckerman (1963) replies that wage-rate increases between countries bear little relation to unemployment-rate differences. This is clearly an empirical matter. A lot would seem to depend on the extent to which labour supply can adjust to demand across countries. The work of Cornwall (1977) suggests that labour is very flexible and that demand and growth have not been constrained in Europe in the post-war period by a lack of factor supplies. Beckerman stresses an economy obtaining its initial advantage in trade through a favourable movement in relative prices: that is, through some competitive shock such as devaluation. It has already been shown in Chapter 12, however, that a once-for-all competitive shock cannot raise the rate of growth of exports permanently. Continual devaluation (or depreciation) would be required. By contrast, we stress here the importance of countries obtaining their initial trading advantage in goods with a high income elasticity of demand in world markets, which affects the term a_0 in equation (13.1).

Before proceeding to develop our own model, incorporating a balance-of-payments equilibrium condition, a brief examination of Caves's (1970) comments on the empirical content of the individual functions making up the export-led growth models of Lamfalussy and Beckerman may be useful to clarify the argument. He makes two major points but neither is substantial enough to alter one's view on the importance of export growth for simultaneous balance-of-payments equilibrium and a high rate of growth of income. First, Caves asks, 'what is special about the growth of exports compared with the growth of any other component of aggregate demand of equal size?' Beckerman himself gives the answer when he argues that if other items of demand are expanded businessmen may fear that demand growth will not continue smoothly because of the balance-of-payments implications of the expansion of other types of demand. Caves seems to recognise this as the crucial point, but then says: 'but it does attribute to business enterprises an aversion to demand fluctuations induced by public authorities that defies easy credibility'. Caves appears to be questioning the influence of the level of demand on investment. But if investment is sensitive to the pressure of demand in relation to capacity output, the point made by the export-led growth school remains valid if export-led growth raises the rate of growth at which a balance-of-payments constraint becomes operative. Caves's second point concerns the relationship between higher export growth and a higher rate of productivity growth. He contends that there may be a link between export and output growth on the one hand and productivity growth on the other, but the direction of causation is anything but clear. This question relates to the controversy over the Verdoorn relationship.[3] Suffice it to say that while productivity growth is obviously a component of output growth, there are also good economic reasons why higher output growth should be a stimulus to productivity growth. The question is not whether there is a relationship but whether the estimate of the relationship is biased owing to its two-way nature.

Another recent critic of the idea that growth is constrained by the balance of payments is Cornwall (1977), who argues that the forces that lead to the rapid growth of output, such as technological change and entrepreneurial dynamism, also work to relieve a country of a balance-of-payments constraint. He rightly observes that the developed countries with recurring balance-of-payments difficulties have also been the slow growers, but he wants to argue from this that it is the slow growth that has caused the balance-of-payments difficulties – rather than the other way round. It is hard to accept this view. It is not the case that all of the forces that lead to rapid output growth in a country necessarily improve the balance of payments. Population growth is one obvious force. Another is rapid productivity growth if it comes about largely through economising on men rather than through the expansion of output. Technological change may be expected to improve productivity at home and also increase the desirability of a country's goods abroad, but this is only one of many factors behind the growth of output. In fact Cornwall's argument does not fit the UK experience, where, if anything, productivity growth and the capacity growth rate have risen, and yet the balance-of-payments constraint has not improved because the forces making for the rise in productivity have not improved the demand characteristics of the goods exported.

As we indicated earlier, Kaldor was a strong devotee of the export-led growth school and became one of its major protagonists. He presented many models in words, one of which (Kaldor, 1970) Dixon and Thirlwall (1975a) have attempted to formalise. We shall use this latter model to incorporate a balance-of-payments equilibrium condition. Kaldor's argument is essentially the Hicksian view that it is the growth of autonomous demand which governs the long-run rate of growth of output. In open economies export demand is the main component of autonomous demand, so that the rate of growth of exports governs the long-run rate of growth of output to which investment and consumption adjust. Kaldor is not explicit on the form of the export demand function but seems to be suggesting the conventional multiplicative function:

$$X_t = \left(\frac{P_{dt}}{E_t P_{ft}} \right)^{\eta} Z_t^{\varepsilon} \tag{13.9}$$

where the variables and parameters are defined as in equation (12.5) in Chapter 12. The rate of growth of exports may then be written:

$$x_t = \eta(p_{dt} - p_{ft} - e_t) + \varepsilon (z_t) \tag{13.10}$$

where lower-case letters represent rates of change of the variables. The rate of growth of income outside the economy (z_t), the rate of change of competitors' prices (p_f) and changes in the exchange rate (e_t) are taken as being exogenous. The rate of growth of domestic (export) prices (p_d) is assumed to be endogenous, however, and is derived from a mark-up pricing equation of the form:

$$P_{dt} = (W/R)_t (T)_t \tag{13.11}$$

where W is the level of money wages, R is the average product of labour, and T is $1 + \%$ mark-up on unit labour costs. Thus:

$$p_{dt} = w_t - r_t + \tau_t \tag{13.12}$$

where lower-case letters represent rates of change of the variables.

The third relation in Kaldor's model, which gives a virtuous circle of export-led growth, is the dependence of the growth of labour productivity on the growth of output, which is Verdoorn's law referred to earlier:

$$r_t = r_{at} + \lambda(y_t) \tag{13.13}$$

where r_{at} is the rate of autonomous productivity growth, and λ is the Verdoorn coefficient. Equation (13.13) makes the model 'circular' since the higher the rate of growth of output, the faster the rate of growth of productivity; the faster the rate of growth of productivity, the lower the rate of increase in prices; and the lower the rate of increase in prices, the faster the rate of growth of exports and hence output. It is also the Verdoorn relation which gives rise to the possibility that once an economy obtains a growth advantage it will keep it. Suppose, for example, that an economy obtains an advantage in the production of goods with a high income elasticity of demand in world markets, which raises its growth rate above that of other countries. Because of the Verdoorn effect, productivity growth will then be higher, and the economy will retain its competitive advantage in these goods, making it difficult for other countries to establish an advantage in the same commodities. The income elasticity of demand for exports is probably the most important determinant of comparative export performance; and the income elasticity of demand for imports must likewise assume key importance in an export-led growth model which incorporates a balance-of-payments equilibrium condition. The lower the income elasticity of demand for imports, the higher the growth rate consistent with balance-of-payments equilibrium, other things remaining the same. In models of cumulative causation in which some economies produce goods which are expanding quickly in demand while other economies produce goods which are sluggish in demand, it is the difference between the income elasticity characteristics of exports and imports which is the essence of the theory of divergence between 'centre' and 'periphery' and between industrial and agricultural economies. This is also the essence of Kaldor's view that the opening-up of trade between economies may create growth-rate differences which are sustained or even widened by the process of trade, for example the United Kingdom *vis-à-vis* the European Economic Community.

Combining equations (13.10), (13.12) and (13.13) gives an expression for the rate of growth of exports:

$$x_t = \eta \ (w_t - r_{at} - \lambda y_t + \tau_t - p_{ft} - e_t) + \varepsilon \ (z_t) \qquad (13.14)$$

AN EXPORT-LED GROWTH MODEL WITH A BALANCE-OF-PAYMENTS CONSTRAINT

Kaldor's model, formalised above, also lacks a balance-of-payments equilibrium condition, and could therefore overpredict the sustainable rate of growth depending on the assumed relation between y_t and x_t. Equation (13.14), however, can be combined with a balance-of-payments equilibrium condition to give an export-led growth model which expresses the idea that export growth may establish a virtuous circle of growth, but which also recognises explicitly that what is happening to imports is also a determinant of growth if balance-of-payments equilibrium must be maintained in the long run. The balance-of-payments equilibrium condition is (see equation (12.2) of Chapter 12):

$$p_{dt} + x_t = p_{ft} + m_t + e_t \qquad (13.15)$$

Substituting equation (12.4) for m_t and equation (13.14) for x_t gives the export-led growth rate consistent with balance-of-payments equilibrium:

$$y_t = \frac{(1 + \eta + \psi)[w_t - r_{at} - \lambda y_t + \tau_t - p_{ft} - e_t] + \varepsilon(z_t)}{\pi}$$

$$(13.16)$$

Therefore

$$y_{Bt} = \frac{(1 + \eta + \psi)[w_t - r_{at} + \tau_t - p_{ft} - e_t] + \varepsilon(z_t)}{\pi + \lambda(1 + \eta + \psi)} \quad (13.17)$$

This compares with the equilibrium growth rate derived from the Kaldor model without a balance-of-payments equilibrium condition, letting $y_t = \gamma(x_t)$, of:

$$y_t = \frac{\gamma[\eta(w_t - r_{at} + \tau_t - p_{ft} - e_t) + \varepsilon(z_t)]}{1 + \gamma \eta \lambda} \quad (13.18)$$

Note that if the price and income elasticities of demand for imports are both unity (i.e. $\psi = -1$ and $\pi = 1$) and $\gamma = 1$, equation (13.17) collapses to (13.18) because the balance of payments would always be in equilibrium whatever the rate of growth of income and foreign prices. In an export-led growth model without a balance-of-payments constraint, γ must take on that value which preserves balance-of-payments equilibrium as income and the price of imports change. Export-led growth incorporating the idea of a virtuous circle through the Verdoorn coefficient (λ) will raise the equilibrium growth rate above what it would otherwise be only if the Marshall-Lerner condition is satisfied, i.e. if $|\eta + \psi| > 1$. Comparing equations (12.7) and (13.17) it can be seen that the Verdoorn coefficient in the denominator of (13.17) will only raise the balance-of-payments equilibrium growth rate if the bracketed term is negative, which implies that the two (negative) elasticities must sum to greater than unity. There is no guarantee, of course, that a country at any point in time will grow at its export-led growth rate consistent with balance-of-payments equilibrium. If the country grows faster, however (assuming it has the capacity to do so), it will run into deficit; if it grows slower, it will accumulate surpluses; and in either case the actual growth rate may be less than the capacity rate, causing growing unemployment. Note again from equation (13.17) that the exchange rate would have to be depreciating continually ($e_t < 0$) for exchange depreciation to raise the balance-of-payments equilibrium growth rate permanently, and then only if the Marshall-Lerner condition is satisfied and wages do not rise.

As far as United Kingdom history is concerned, the export-led model incorporating an explicit balance-of-payments equilibrium condition is a far better predictor of the actual growth experience than the unconstrained model of equation (13.18). When the unconstrained model was applied to data for the period 1951 to 1966 (see Dixon and Thirlwall, 1975a) it predicted a growth rate of 4 per cent on the basis of the following parameter values: $\eta = -1.5$, $w_t + \tau_t = 0.06$, $r_{at} = 0.02$, $p_{ft} = 0.02$, $\varepsilon = 1.0$, $z_t = 0.04$, $\lambda = 0.5$, and $\gamma = 1$. Since the actual growth rate over the period was 2.8 per cent, it was mentioned at the time that the model may be overpredicting because of a balance-of-payments constraint – apart from any constraint on capacity. If 4 per cent were a permissible rate consistent with balance-of-payments equilibrium, the country should have enjoyed a growing surplus, but it did not. In order to apply the balance-of-payments equilibrium model (equation (13.17)) estimates are required of the additional parameters ψ and π. It is assumed that imports are insensitive to price, and we take Houthakker and Magee's (1969) estimate for π of 1.51. Using equation (13.17), with the exchange rate fixed (as it was over this period), we obtain an estimate of the growth rate consistent with balance-of-payments equilibrium of 2.4 per cent. This is closer to the actual growth rate of 2.8 per cent, and the discrepancy between the two rates is consistent with the balance of payments moving into deficit over the period.[4]

Applying the equations to the post-1966 period does not give such reasonable results, probably because the period has been one of general economic upheaval, and the model is very sensitive to small variations (errors) in the variables and in the assumed parameter values. When the constrained model (equation (13.17)) is applied to the data over the period 1967 to 1976 the estimated growth rate is 5.2 per cent, compared with the actual growth rate of 1.8 per cent per annum.[5] Since the country moved into substantial deficit, the model is clearly over-predicting. It could be that the UK income elasticity of demand for imports is much higher than the assumed value of 1.51, or that the price elasticity of demand for UK exports is less than the assumed 1.5. Assuming the lesser value of unity (so that with $\psi = 0$, the Marshall-Lerner condition is just satisfied) allows us to apply the simple growth rule enunciated in equation (12.8), which gives a balance-of-payments equilibrium growth rate of $0.03 \div 1.51 = 2$ per cent. This looks much more consistent with the facts, particularly if the income elasticity of demand for imports has risen. A figure for π of approximately 2 would give a balance-of-payments equilibrium growth rate of 1.5 per cent per annum over the period, and this would be entirely consistent with the actual growth experience and the balance of payments on current account moving into substantial deficit. Despite the effort of formulating a fairly sophisticated export-led growth model, incorporating the idea of a virtuous circle led by exports, the empirical evidence suggests that the simple growth rules set out in equations (12.8) and (12.9) of the previous chapter are better predictors of actual growth performance. This is not to disparage export-led growth models which incorporate a virtuous circle. It is rather to suggest that the link between exports and growth via the Verdoorn effect may not be very important either because relative prices do not change or because the price elasticities of demand for exports and imports are not high enough to matter. Again we conclude that everything would seem to hinge on the income elasticities of demand for exports and imports. It is in this sense that we refer to the balance of payments as a structural problem.

14
The Balance of Payments as a Structural Problem

The UK balance of payments has acted as a serious constraint on the attainment of other macroeconomic goals since the Second World War, particularly the achievement of faster, investment-led growth. As the economy has expanded towards its capacity level, bottlenecks in particular sectors of the economy have raised the aggregate level of imports in excess of the demand for exports, necessitating contraction of the economy. Likewise, attempts to grow faster in order to match the growth rates of other European countries have resulted in imports growing more rapidly than exports, and experiments of domestic demand-led growth have had to be abandoned. In the last two chapters the prime importance of the growth of exports, and the income elasticity of demand for imports, as determinants of domestic economic performance have been stressed. Nevertheless a strong body of opinion has traditionally argued that the fundamental problem of the UK balance of payments has been a lack of price competitiveness in world markets, because unit costs of production in the United Kingdom have risen faster than elsewhere, and that the most appropriate solution to this problem is to let the currency depreciate. Since 1972 the pound sterling has in fact depreciated substantially against the dollar and other major currencies, as shown in Figure 9.1, p. 246.

The argument that the UK balance-of-payments problem has been one of price uncompetitiveness, coupled with an inflexible exchange rate up to 1972, contains a number of explicit and implicit assumptions, some of which were questioned in Chapter 5 on the elasticity approach to balance-of-payments adjustment. It assumes that costs and prices have had an independent tendency to rise faster in the United Kingdom than elsewhere, that the demand for traded goods is determined primarily by relative prices, that if relative prices fall the demand for domestic goods is sufficiently elastic, that manufacturers make the appropriate pricing response to a change in the foreign value of the currency and reap the benefit, that the production capacity is available to meet increased export demand and the increased demand for import substitutes, that the effects of currency depreciation are not fully eroded by the domestic inflation which depreciation breeds, and so on. Many economists, formerly believers in the efficiency of exchange-rate changes, are now questioning these explicit and implicit assumptions and the relevance of relative price adjustment as a method of balance-of-payments adjustment and as a means of relieving the balance-of-payments constraint on full employment and faster growth in the United Kingdom. The reasons for scepticism are axiomatic. The balance of payments has been *increasingly* problematical since the pound was devalued in 1967 and then allowed to float in 1972. The promise of a new dawn held out by the currency depreciation school has not materialised. It is true that the balance of payments improved between 1968 and 1971, but that was mainly due to the sharp upturn in world trade and at the expense of domestic employment. When the economy was expanded during 1972–3 the record surpluses that had been built up on current account not only melted away but became record deficits. This was caused largely by a consumption-led boom, but the deteriorating balance-of-payments situation was also worsened by the currency depreciation itself which reduced the foreign-currency earnings from exports without noticeably decreasing the foreign-currency expenditure on imports. The commodity boom and oil price increase made matters even worse in 1973 and 1974, and the balance of payments only began to recover in 1977 after a prolonged stagnation of output and consumption and the increased flow of North Sea oil. The oscillations of the pound in the 1980s merely created uncertainty. It is difficult to detect any significant raising of the balance-of-payments equilibrium growth rate from currency depreciation itself. In the light of the experience of the last two decades the United Kingdom's weak balance of payments is increasingly seen as a structural problem related both to the *capacity* to produce and to the *characteristics* of goods produced and exported, both of which are *not directly* amenable to exchange-rate depreciation.

Textbooks dealing with the balance of payments also traditionally treat balance-of-payments disequilibrium as something that can be rectified by appropriate relative price adjustments. By contrast, one of the purposes of this book is to stress that many countries' balance-of-payments difficulties originate from the supply side and in non-price factors, for which price adjustment is not the appropriate response. Downward price adjustment, by manipulating exchange rates, merely makes countries more competitive in the short run in goods with a given set of characteristics which were the source of the balance-of-payments difficulty in the first place. In a growth context continual depreciation would be required to raise the balance-of-payments equilibrium growth rate permanently, and again the industrial structure would be ossified. Certainly it is difficult to see how the United Kingdom's long-run balance of payments could be improved at full employment by continual exchange depreciation. The more recent monetary approach to the balance of payments offers nothing by way of prescription either. If the balance-of-payments constraint on growth is to be alleviated, the concentration of policy must be on the supply side. More specifically, following the arguments in Chapters 12 and 13, policy must be directed to raising the rate of growth of exports by non-price means. Given the growth of world income, the growth of exports is primarily a function of the world income elasticity of demand for exports; and the income elasticity of demand for exports, in turn, is a function of the type of goods produced within the product range – their quality, reliability, marketing, and so on. The world income elasticity of demand for UK exports is very low by international standards, approximately unity, and the elasticity of demand for UK exports with respect to the growth of world trade is even lower.[1] The latter elasticity, which the Treasury estimates to be about 0.6, accounts for the United Kingdom's declining share of world trade. The former elasticity (particularly its low magnitude) lies at the root of the United Kingdom's long-run balance-of-payments difficulties. In this chapter, we emphasise the non-price factors affecting the balance of payments, and the importance of removing the balance-of-payments constraint on growth if an expanding industrial sector is to be preserved. Improving the non-price factors should regenerate the industrial sector without a loss of jobs and help to remove the balance-of-payments constraint on growth at the same time. Simply to revitalise industry by increasing productivity, without removing the balance-of-payments constraint on growth, will cause employment in the industrial sector to contract and unemployment to rise.

NON-PRICE FACTORS DETERMINING EXPORTS AND IMPORTS

The National Economic Development Office's Report on non-price factors in international trade, written by David Stout (1977), stresses two broad aspects of non-price competitiveness: first, the act of selling; second, aspects of the product including design, ease of maintenance, quality, reliability, delivery time and after-sales service. To quantify the importance of these factors is not easy, and the anecdotal evidence that these factors matter is perhaps stronger than the actual evidence, but from the work of the National Economic Development Office and other organisations, and the statements of industrialists and impartial observers, no one can doubt that they rank in importance with price, and in many cases may be the decisive influence in the decision of foreigners whether to buy British and in the decision of the British whether to buy foreign. Here we refer briefly to some representative work and statements of organisations and individuals under the general headings of *marketing*, and *quality, design and reliability*.

Mr David Orr (1978), ex-Chairman of Unilever, has defined marketing as

> the skill of providing the right product for delivery at the right time in the right place at the right price and with the right back-up service – for a profit. [He goes on] the most decisive factors today are concerned with design, styling, packaging, advertising; and for capital goods – credit terms, delivery dates, reliability, technical service and so on.

A six-month delivery delay on a large order, when the money or goods could have been invested profitably, more than offsets any price advantage over a competitor charging a higher price but who can deliver immediately. Mr Orr believes that marketing and selling need to be accorded much higher prestige in the hierarchy of business.

With regard to the act of selling, a study by the British Export Trade Research Organisation (1975) found that leading UK companies had either no one, or only one permanent export representative, in key foreign markets compared with an average of eleven for West German and Japanese companies. A recent survey of language competence in 1500 UK companies argued that the shortage of staff speaking a foreign language is costing Britain millions of pounds

every year in lost exports and could be disastrous for British industry's hopes in Europe after 1992.

The danger of currency depreciation is that it can lead manufacturers to slide progressively 'down market' in the quality of exports,
supplying the world with exports of goods with low unit values. This
danger of depreciation is particularly stressed in the work of the
National Economic Development Office (Stout, 1977), which makes
the distinction between eliminating a competitive disadvantage
through currency depreciation, which is a static process, and the need
for dynamic change in a growth context (if the balance of payments is
to be improved permanently), which the act of depreciation may
thwart because it perpetuates the production of the same commodities,
presumably of inferior design and style to those of other countries.
Certainly the profitability of exporting must be maintained but not at
the expense of neglecting what the market is demanding.

Brech and Stout (1981) present some evidence that a depreciation
in the UK's exchange rate may, indeed, have worsened the quality of
British exports. They construct an index of 'trading up' and 'down'
which is based on the changing composition of 40 categories of
exports in the machine tool sector as between high and low unit value
products. They found that over the period 1970–80, the index was
positively correlated with the change in the exchange rate indicating
that a depreciation was associated with 'down trading' or the substitution of low for high unit value goods. The authors conclude:

> For deep-seated structural and institutional reasons, economic
> agents in the UK adapt slowly and hesitantly to either market or
> technology changes. There is, therefore, a trend decline in UK
> non-price competitiveness. This decline is reflected in a relatively
> low income elasticity of demand for UK manufactures. There are
> usually strong social and political pressures to try to maintain
> growth at a rate relative to the rest of the world which is inconsist-
> ent with this trend towards product obsolescence. The trend
> decline is therefore partially compensated for, in its effect on the
> balance of payments, by episodes of nominal and (temporarily
> *real*) devaluation. However, the remedy is inappropriate, not just
> because, after a lag of a few quarters, domestic inflation liquidates
> most of the relative price advantage, but because recourse to
> devaluation has two effects. The greater ease with which older
> products, which tend also to be more price elastic, can be sold

provides some exporters with a soft short-run option to the painful, expensive and risky process of developing superior products. On top of this, those firms who have launched products early in their life-cycle alongside older products, find, following a devaluation, that the demand for the older products has risen more strongly. Those of them who behave passively, retain labour and expand investment for the production of the older products instead of moving more resources into the new. This type of outcome is consistent with the pricing behaviour to be expected at least in the less concentrated UK industries where some temporary rigidity in sterling prices can be expected following devaluation. On balance, given some short-sightedness among UK entrepreneurs, the devaluation that was a result, in part, of failures of NPC [non-price competition] in the past may therefore feed back and further reduce it, leading UK manufacturing even further down-market.

Over the years strong evidence has been emerging from the work of the National Economic Development Office that the United Kingdom tends to export relatively low-valued products within a given product range, and to import relatively high-valued products, compared with West Germany and France. The evidence for this comes from analysis of industries covered by NEDO's thirty-five Sector Working Parties and from the work of Connell (1979). If true, this would account for the low world income elasticity of demand for UK exports and the higher income elasticity of demand for imports. This would also account for the fact that while the United Kingdom exports goods which are expanding rapidly in demand, and to geographic markets which are also expanding, none the less the UK share of world trade has fallen more than in the case of other industrialised countries. The average unit values of West German exports were found to be higher than those of UK exports in 29 out of the 35 industry groups, and in 23 out of 34 in the case of the comparison with France. While part of the difference could be accounted for by the United Kingdom having lower prices for similar goods, probably the major factor lies in differences in the product mix and differences in product quality. It is this evidence which suggests that the United Kingdom is specialising in 'down-market' or inferior products. Connell's study, for example, reports the unit values of exports of non-electrical machinery for the years 1962 and 1975 for a number of advanced countries. Non-electrical machinery exports are generally complex and technically sophisticated products where differences in non-price competitiveness are likely to be of paramount importance (and account for about one fifth of total UK exports). Measured in dollars per tonne, the UK had the second smallest increase in unit value, superseded by Japan, France, the Netherlands, West Germany and Sweden by between 30 and 150 per cent.

The other side of the coin is the continued export success of countries where the currency has appreciated. Higher unit values for exports and lower unit values for imports than other countries may be the result, of course, of a country's costs and prices being too high, but not if its exports are growing fast and its share of world trade is rising. Despite a 30 per cent appreciation of the Deutschmark between 1973 and 1977, West German exports continued to expand rapidly. The former German Minister of Finance, Mr Hans Apel, explained thus: 'obviously the variety and the quality of German goods fit almost exactly what the customer wants. Also, customers can rely on the dates of delivery promised by German suppliers being met' (Artus and Sosa, 1978).

The National Economic Development Office Report on *Imported Manufactures* (1965) ascribed import penetration to, among other things: higher relative prices and costs, a shortage of capacity in boom periods coupled with a 'ratchet' effect, poor technical performance of the home product (particularly in mechanical engineering products, electronic capital goods and scientific instruments), and a slow marketing response by UK manufacturers.

The National Economic Development Council survey of *Investment in Machine Tools* (1965) asked UK machine-tool users why they bought foreign machines. Only 5 per cent said price was the main factor. The more important factors were (percentage of respondents listing the factor as the main one in parentheses): technical superiority of the foreign product (30 per cent); machine specifications not available in the United Kingdom (21 per cent); quick and reliable delivery (20 per cent); willingness of foreign producers to meet special requirements (8 per cent); and better after-sales service (5 per cent). Technical factors were cited by over one-half of the sample in the decision to buy foreign goods.

In other work by the National Economic Development Office, pertinent factors have emerged on an industry-by-industry basis. In machine-tools, for technologically advanced products, export success seems to depend primarily on delivery and reliability. The unit values of the exports of machine-tools appear to be lower than the unit values of imports, which suggests that the United Kingdom is not competing successfully in the most sophisticated machine-tool product groups. In pumps and valves the technical quality of UK products is good but the industry seems to lack the organisational support and resources necessary to match the marketing, delivery and after-sales service of competitors. In electric motors, the Sector Working Party concludes that UK industry is deficient in establishing overseas marketing and technical networks, and in delivery. In electronics, consumer goods suffer from a reputation of poor quality and apparently have not been designed in the past with the European market in mind. In clothing, it is concluded that designs and fashions are often out of line with continental preferences, and that quality and design are often sacrificed to keep price down. In construction equipment, reliability and after-sales service is of key importance.

The Central Policy Review Staff Report on the *Future of the British Car Industry* (1975) considered the competitive weakness of the industry to be due to: inadequate distribution networks; slow delivery; high costs, low productivity and under-investment; over-manning; poor labour relations; slow work-pace and line-speeds; and product unsuitability relative to market conditions and requirements.

Management cannot escape responsibility for poor quality, inferior design, lack of reliability, delivery delays and lack of interest in marketing abroad. Some would lay the blame squarely on management's shoulders, and lift it from the traditional scapegoats, the trade unions and the British worker: 'The root of Britain's export problems are outstandingly bad managers, lack of interest, and terrible communications' (letter to *The Times*, 5 December 1977). The writer of the letter concerned, who runs an importing business in France, refers to one UK company who received his order in January, promised delivery in April and then decided in August that it was no longer interested in exporting. Another two companies increased price without notice. Another company promised delivery which did not arrive, and letters requesting an explanation produced no response. Other evidence suggests that the experience of this one particular foreign buyer is not atypical.

Weak management is one of the key issues highlighted by the Director-General of NEDO in the most recent assessment of the UK trade performance in five industrial sectors showing the greatest trade deficit, namely motor-cars and parts; clothing and textiles; consumer electronics; building materials, and tourism (National Economic Development Council, 1990). We will quote the conclusions of this assessment in full as a fitting conclusion to this section of the chapter.

The analysis suggests that a lack of relative quality embodied in UK goods has had a bearing on their trade performance. The problem has not been one of a general retreat from high specification products but of an inadequate performance against customer requirements at both the high and the low end of the product and quality range.

In many specific areas past problems may well have been overcome but difficulties remain in areas such as design and build quality. The answer to this is through the promotion of the total quality approach to management pioneered in Japan which is gaining rapid acceptance throughout the industrialised world. Several Sector Groups have been active in promoting this and the Council may wish to endorse their approach.

The barriers to the adoption of total quality include weaknesses in the basic education of the work force and in its subsequent training, and deficiencies in the nation's technology base. Basic research in the universities, the provision of a sufficient quantity of technically skilled graduates and investment by companies in R&D, are all areas where there are comparative weaknesses in the UK. But the principal question that must be asked is why when the UK has very successful industries such as Pharmaceuticals, Aerospace and the provision of Financial Services which have to draw their labour from the same educational and training background, the performance of other industries like motor vehicles and clothing is in contrast so disappointing. It is tempting to infer that managements in these areas have too often been content to accept low quality standards and that they have set more mediocre objectives for their companies than the economy's more successful businesses. If that is the case managerial weaknesses and a willingness to acquiesce in low quality and performance standards has played a significant role in the underperformance of these industries.

THE 'NEW' TRADE THEORIES

Non-price competition lies at the heart of several new theories of trade that have been developed in recent years to replace the static, price-based theory of comparative cost, and to account for the growing phenomenon of intra-industry trade between countries. As countries get richer through time there tends to be a shift of emphasis within sectors towards product novelty, quality and reliability, and in general towards high value-added products where non-price factors are critically important. These new trade theories are sometimes referred to as neo-technology theories of trade because product quality, reliability, sophistication etc., depend in the main on technical progress and innovation, which in turn will depend to a large extent on research and development. The definition of scientific and technological innovation, now used by the OECD, the so-called Frascati definition, identifies six stages in the innovation process, namely, research and development, new product marketing, patent work, financial design engineering, tooling-industrial engineering and manufacturing start.

One of the pioneering theories was the technological gap model of Posner (1961) which argued that a country which first introduces a new product may export it, at least until imitators come into the market. Economies of scale enjoyed by the innovators will keep the country ahead as long as the imitation lag is longer than the demand lag. As imitation proceeds and novelty wears off, the theory of comparative costs will reassert itself.

A natural development of this theory of trade was the idea of the product-cycle developed by Vernon (1966) and Hirsch (1967). Trade in products will go through cycles where non-price characteristics are important in the early stages of a product's life, but as production gradually shifts from innovator to imitator, price competition becomes more important.

The growing phenomenon of intra-industry trade, first documented in detail by Grubel and Lloyd (1971), has lent strong support to these theories, and has been a major impetus behind their development. Differences in costs and prices cannot explain trade between countries in the 'same' product. The basis of intra-industry trade must lie in non-price competition or product differentiation. Following the characteristics approach to demand theory pioneered by Lancaster (1971), a differentiated product is one that offers a bundle of attributes or characteristics different from its competitors. Countries will export goods intensive in one set of characteristics and import goods intensive in another. Intra-industry trade will be more important the more similar countries are since there will not be specialisation according to cost differences. Davies (1976) has tested this hypothesis for UK trade with the EEC and USA. He looks at trade balances in 945 sectors with France, Germany, Italy, USA and Japan. A broad correspondence is found between the similarity of factor endowments and intra-industry trade.

Barker (1977) has put forward a similar 'variety hypothesis' of trade which argues that: 'as real income increases, purchasers tend to buy more varieties of a product, and since a greater number of these varieties is available from abroad rather than from home sources, the share of imports in demand tends to increase. For imports as a whole the quantity of imports tends to rise more than proportionately with real per capita income.' Both the Davies and Barker models predict that the greater intra-industry trade, the higher the income elasticity of demand for imports and exports because the greater the product differentiation and variety of products. This prediction has been tested by Barker who finds a high correlation between intra-industry trade and the income elasticities of demand for imports across fifteen countries from 1951 to 1966 (using the Houthakker and Magee estimates of income elasticities reported in Chapter 5, 10 and 12). Also the amount of imports supplied by different sources is found to rise as income rises. The enormous trade deficit that the UK now has with Germany undoubtedly has something to do with the similarity of industrial structures and the growth of trade based on product differentiation and variety.

STUDIES OF NON-PRICE COMPETITION

In practice, it is not easy to measure non-price competition. Proxies have to be taken such as R & D expenditure as a measure of input into the innovative process; the number of patents issued as a measure of the output of innovative activity, or the level of education and skill intensity employed in various industries. All the measures have their weaknesses. Patent statistics may not accurately reflect differences in innovative activity *between* firms, sectors or countries, while R & D and education statistics measure inputs not outputs. However, there is evidence that R & D and patent statistics are correlated. As reported in Pavitt and Soete (1980), a comparison among US industrial sectors shows a correlation between a sector's share of total R & D and its share of patents (excluding aerospace and motor vehicles from the sample). This correlation is also evident across OECD countries in 1975, taking patents registered by OECD countries in the US.

In empirically testing the importance of non-price factors in the determination of trade performance, it is also probably wise to make a distinction between capital goods, consumption goods, and the production of basic materials. In capital goods, technical effort is directed mainly to the design and development of new products which have superior technical characteristics. In this sphere, R & D expenditure will be extremely important. In consumption goods, such as food, textiles, furniture etc., advertising expenditure and design are likely to be more important than R & D. In basic materials, technical effort will be mainly directed to cost reductions through factor-saving innovation. This being so, price will matter more for consumer goods and basic materials than for capital goods with a high research intensity.

Many aggregate and industry studies have been undertaken which show a strong link between export performance and various measures of non-price competition, particularly in the capital goods sector. We report here some of the major studies, focusing mainly, although not exclusively, on studies of the UK.

Pavitt and Soete (1980) have examined export performance in 40 sectors across 22 OECD countries over the period from 1963 to 1977. Their measure of non-price competition is the number of patents registered in the US. The hypothesis is that the greater the resources devoted to innovation, and the more patents taken out, the more competitive a country will become with respect to products and processes. Exports in 1977 for each sector (per head of the population) are regressed on the cumulative number of patents per head over the period 1963 to 1976. The correlation coefficient is significant at the 98 per cent confidence level for 23 out of the 40 industries. The relation is strongest in the capital goods industries and also in chemicals and some transport equipment, and weakest in traditional products and consumption goods.

A study by Mayes, Buxton and Murfin (1988) for NEDO examines UK trade with France, Germany, Japan and the USA in 15 manufacturing industries over the period from 1970 to 1983. R & D expenditure is used as the main measure of non-price competition, and treated as a stock variable. In every industry, cumulative R & D expenditure is a highly significant determinant of trade performance.

Greenhalgh (1990) has tried to separate the role of price and non-price factors in determining UK trade performance in 39 sectors (including 23 manufacturing sectors) over the period from 1954 to 1981. Three hypotheses are tested: (i) that industries with high levels of innovation will be net exporters; (ii) successful innovators will face higher income elasticities of demand for their products and lower price elasticities, and (iii) innovative industries will use more highly qualified manpower and invest more in R & D. Product quality is measured by the number of innovations and patents. The number of innovations appears to be an important explanation of trade performance in about one half of the sectors covered, although, surprisingly, not in the two sectors of mechanical and electrical engineering where innovation has been most active. In only one third of the sectors was there a significant price effect. Greenhalgh concludes: 'price is not necessarily the most salient characteristic of complex manufactured products whose typical quality is changing rapidly through time'. Within manufacturing, the relation between *net* exports (exports minus imports) and the income variable is negative in two thirds of the cases, indicating that the income elasticity of demand for imports is greater than for exports. This in itself is a reflection of the UK's relative inferiority in the production of 'up-market' products.

RESEARCH AND DEVELOPMENT EFFORT

The UK has been losing market share for some time in almost every sector of the economy. The message of the foregoing analysis is that countries neglect non-price competition, and its determinants, at their peril. This is also the conclusion to emerge from the extensive research carried out by the Science Policy Research Unit at Sussex University (e.g. Pavitt (1980)): that Britain's performance in technical innovation has been unsatisfactory for a long time relative to competitors, and this is a major explanation of Britain's relative economic decline. R & D effort appears to have been particularly weak. For example, between 1967 and 1975, Britain was the only OECD country where industry financed R & D declined absolutely. The performance continues to be poor absolutely and relative to other countries. From 1969 to 1983, the real growth of total R & D expenditure averaged 1.8 per cent per annum, the lowest rate of all industrialised countries. The experience in the first half of the 1980s is shown in Figure 14.1. The absolute amount of expenditure is large, but the rate of growth of 1.6 per cent has been the lowest of all countries, and slower than the growth of GDP. Much of the expenditure is on defence and aircraft, which does not enhance the competitiveness of British industry directly.

Equally worrying is the finding by Dunning and Pearce (1985) that the UK tends to specialise in low research intensity activities.

Research intensity is defined in terms of R&D expenditure relative to sales.[2] Comparative specialisation is measured by a country's share

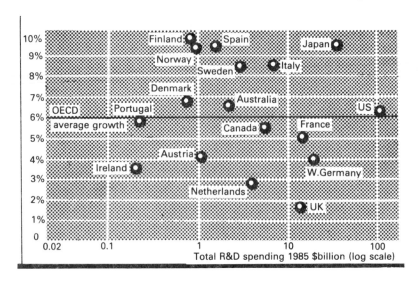

FIGURE 14.1   *R&D growth in OECD countries, 1981–85*
Source: OECD.

of sales in an industry relative to the country's total share of all sales. The figures are given in Table 14.1. Compared with its major competitors, the UK has a weak sales performance in high intensity research activities, and yet it is the sectors at the top of the research intensity range that have in the past recorded the fastest rate of growth (Smith, 1986). Explanations have to be sought for this weakness of British industry. Large firms have a role to play. According to Smith (1986), countries with the largest and fastest growing giant firms have been the most competitive in international markets.

The UK's largest industrial companies are smaller than those in the US, Japan and West Germany. In 1984 the turnover of the UK's twenty largest companies was only 26 per cent of the US level; 61 per cent of the Japanese level, and 73 per cent of the turnover of the twenty largest German companies. The Sussex Science Policy Research Unit stresses the generally poor academic and professional training of British managers and engineers. Successful technical innovation requires an integration of R & D, marketing and planning and this requires high level personnel.

The UK is particularly weak relative to Germany, which is responsible for a large part of the UK trade deficit. A study by Patel and Pavitt (1989) shows that Germany took out more patents in the

TABLE 14.1

Measures of comparative specialisation according to research intensity

	UK	US	Japan	Germany	France
High research intensive activities	0.6	1.1	1.4	1.5	1.2
Medium research intensive activities	1.2	0.7	1.4	1.5	1.2
Low research intensive activities	2.0	1.1	0.8	1.5	1.2

Source: J. H. Dunning and R. D. Pearce, *The World's Largest Industrial Enterprises 1982–1983* (London: Gower, 1985).

US than did the UK in all 33 industrial sectors examined. Moreover, there was a much greater concentration of technological activities in 22 out of the 33 sectors. Freeman (1979) has argued 'perhaps the biggest single long term contrast between British and German industry has been in the number and quality of engineers deployed in all managerial functions in manufacturing.'

A much earlier study by Freeman (1965) of the electronic capital goods industry has turned out to be very prescient in its conclusion, and we let Freeman have the final word which lends strong support to the central argument of this chapter. In discussing the government's role in R & D, he concluded 'the government should consider the prospective contribution to the balance of payments since an unsatisfactory balance of payments has been – *and is likely to be* [emphasis added] – the main obstacle to faster growth in Britain'.

15
Deindustrialisation and the Balance of Payments[1]

Over the last three decades, the United Kingdom has been experiencing a severe process of deindustrialisation measured by the relative and absolute loss of jobs in industry. A relative decline in the share of industrial employment in total employment has been a common occurrence in other advanced industrialised countries but the absolute loss of jobs in the UK started sooner, and has been more severe, than anywhere else in the world. Industrial employment peaked in 1966 and since then four million jobs have been lost in manufacturing and nearly five million in industry (which includes mining, construction and public utilities). In 1966, the level of industrial employment was 11.5 million, today it is 6.6 million; the level of manufacturing employment was 9.1 million, today it is 5.1 million. All industries have been affected and all regions of the country. By contrast, in countries such as Canada, the USA, Japan and Italy, manufacturing employment was increasing in the 1960s, 1970s and 1980s. Belgium, France, Germany and Holland have experienced job losses in industry, but not to the extent of the UK. A comparison of the experience of the OECD countries in recent years is shown in Table 15.1.

DOES DEINDUSTRIALISATION MATTER?

Most countries set themselves the macroeconomic goals of full employment, faster growth, balance-of-payments equilibrium (as an intermediate objective necessary for the achievement of other objectives), and stable prices. Deindustrialisation on the scale experienced by the UK is proving to be inconsistent with the achievement of these

TABLE 15.1
Manufacturing employment in OECD countries 1960–86* (000's)

	1960	1979	Change 1960–79 (%)	1986	Change 1960–86 (%)
Canada	1 406†	2 047	+45.6	1 985	+41.2
USA	16 796	21 040	+25.3	18 994	+13.1
Japan	7 990	11 070	+38.5	12 290	+53.8
Australia	1 111	1 177	+5.9	1 061	−4.5
Austria	858	(850)	−1.0	876	+2.1
Belgium	1 043	888	−14.9	741	−29.0
Denmark‡	741	793	+7.0	742	+0.1
Finland	431	582	+35.0	532	+23.4
France	6 322	5 291	−16.3	4 506	−28.7
Germany	(9 433)§	(8 370)	−11.3	7 723	−18.1
Greece‡	598	994	+66.2	1 012	+69.2
Iceland‡	24	38	+58.3	42‖	+75.0
Ireland	168†	(228)	+35.7	200	+19.1
Italy¶	3 735	4 716	+26.3	4 038	+8.1
Luxembourg¶	53	58	+9.4	52	−1.9
Netherlands	1 082	(1037)	−4.2	959	−11.4
Norway	331	370	+11.8	346	+4.5
Portugal	571	(865)	+51.5	919	+60.9
Spain	2 009	2 742	+36.5	2 166	+7.8
Sweden‡	1 499	1 359	+9.3	(1 287)	−14.1
Switzerland‡	1 227	1 229	+0.1	1 213	+1.1
Turkey	885	1 572	+77.6	1 904	+115.1
UK	**8 996**	**7 253**	**−19.3**	**5 243**	**−41.7**

Figures in brackets are not strictly comparable with previous years.
* Wage and salary earners in the manufacturing sector unless otherwise specified.
† 1961.
‡ Civilian employment in industry.
§ 1962.
‖ 1983.
¶ Wage and salary earners in industry.

Source: S. Bazen and A. P. Thirlwall, *Deindustrialisation* (London: Heinemann, 1989).

goals, and there is no evidence that other activities (e.g. services) can adequately compensate. All the major macroeconomic trade-offs are worse today than at any time since 1950. The inflation–unemployment trade-off is worse; the unemployment–balance-of-payments trade-off is worse (see Figure 4.2, Chapter 4), and the growth–balance of payments trade-off is worse.

As far as unemployment is concerned, deindustrialisation will lead to increased unemployment if the growth of employment elsewhere in the economy is insufficient to absorb the labour shed by the manufacturing sector (unless the size of the workforce declines). Since 1966, the process of deindustrialisation in the UK has led to higher unemployment in a purely statistical sense since the growth of employment in other activities has not compensated, as Table 15.2 indicates.

It can be seen that over the period under review, the total labour force continued to increase, while total employment fell and the numbers unemployed rose substantially. In the period 1966–79, total industrial employment fell by nearly three million, while service

TABLE 15.2
Changes in Employment 1966–87 (000's)

	1966–79*	1971–83†	1983–87
Change in labour force	+ 134	+ 241	+1600
Change in total employment‡	− 959	−2106	+ 750
Change in unemployment§	+1063	+1640	− 80
Change in employment in:			
Agriculture	− 110	− 30	− 29
Manufacturing	−2008	−1728	− 380
Other production industries	− 706	− 268	− 187
Services	+ 865	− 81	+1344
Changes in self-employment and			
armed forces	+ 90	+ 343	+ 637

* Based on SIC 1968 classification.
† Based on SIC 1980 classification.
‡ Excluding self-employed.
§ Excluding school-leavers.

Source: S. Bazen and A. P. Thirlwall, *Deindustrialisation* (London: Heinemann, 1989).

employment only rose by 800,000. During the recession years 1979–83, total industrial employment fell by another two million and service employment also fell. Only in the period 1983–7 did the increase in service employment (much of it part-time) rise to compensate for the fall in industrial employment, and contribute to a fall in unemployment. Overall, however, the economy has failed to provide enough new jobs to compensate for deindustrialisation. The result has been higher unemployment. The much publicised Report from the House of Lords Select Committee on Overseas Trade in 1985 predicted higher unemployment from the neglect of manufacturing industry, with little prospect of reduction, together with a stagnating economy with rising inflation, driven up by a falling exchange rate and an irreplaceable loss of gross domestic product. To quote directly from the Report:

> the Committee takes the view that, together, these prospects constitute a grave threat to the standard of living of the British people . . . failure to recognise these dangers now could have a devastating effect on the future economic and political stability of the nation . . . the situation in which we find ourselves is not self-correcting: things will not come right of their own accord. Urgent action is required, not only by government but by everyone.

Deindustrialisation has serious implications for the overall growth of GDP, and therefore for future living standards relative to other countries. The UK has already slipped from being the sixth richest country in the world in 1950 to seventeenth in the *per capita* income stakes, and the sustainable rate of growth seems to be decelerating. From 1950 to 1973 (with the first oil shock) the average rate of growth of GDP was 2.5 per cent per annum. From 1973 to 1979, growth averaged 1.7 per cent, and during the 'Thatcher decade' of the 1980s it averaged 2.2 per cent per annum. Manufacturing growth has often been described as the 'engine of growth', and with good reason. There is a strong association across countries between the importance of manufacturing in the total economy and the level of *per capita* income, and between the growth of manufacturing output and the growth of gross domestic product. The latter association is not simply due to the fact that manufacturing output constitutes a significant fraction of total output, giving a spurious correlation. In the first place the strength of the relationship is confirmed when the growth of non-manufacturing is related to the growth of manufacturing. Secondly, the major part of the growth of GDP comes from productivity growth, and we know from other empirical evidence (see Thirlwall, 1983a) that, in 'normal' (non-recessionary) times, there is a strong positive correlation between manufacturing output growth and manufacturing productivity growth on the one hand (Verdoorn's law), and between manufacturing output growth and productivity growth outside manufacturing on the other. Neither the growth of agriculture nor the growth of services appears to induce productivity growth to the same extent. Manufacturing seems to be the sector where major improvements in productivity are possible owing to both static and dynamic returns to scale, or increasing returns in the widest sense. Static returns relate to the size and scale of production units where in the process of doubling the linear dimensions of equipment, the surface increases by the square and the volume by the cube. Dynamic economies refer to increasing returns brought about by technical progress embodied in capital accumulation; learning by doing, and external economies in production resulting from the interaction between demand and supply in a cumulative expansionary process. This is the idea of increasing returns as a macroeconomic phenomenon in which the more demand is focused on commodities with a large supply response, and the larger the demand response (direct and indirect) induced by increases in production, the higher the growth rate and productivity growth are likely to be.

The link between manufacturing growth and productivity growth outside manufacturing arises because many non-manufacturing activities are characterised either by diminishing returns or by surplus labour or both (e.g. land-based activities and many labour intensive service industries). Thus whenever industrial output and employment expand, labour resources are drawn from these other sectors, which raises the average product in these sectors either because output is not affected at all or because the less productive marginal person is absorbed. In addition, the expansion of industry will automatically generate an increase in the stock of capital employed in industry. Thus, industrial expansion generates resources, while hardly diminishing the output of other sectors, in a way that other sectors, by their very nature, would find hard to emulate.

Taken together, these relationships between manufacturing growth and overall productivity growth mean that a country which obtains an initial advantage in productive activities that have favourable growth characteristics will tend to sustain that advantage by exploiting increasing returns to scale, both static and dynamic, leading to higher productivity and competitiveness. For example, a favourable shock which increases the rate of growth of output in manufacturing will lead to faster productivity growth, which in turn, by making goods more competitive, expands the demand for output, which again induces productivity growth, and so on. This is a virtuous circle model of growth of the type we discussed in Chapter 13. By contrast, if the growth of manufacturing languishes, the opposite occurs, creating a vicious circle of low economic growth, low productivity growth, deteriorating competitiveness and the shedding of labour from the manufacturing sector owing to a lack of domestic and foreign demand for the products. The balance of payments will also suffer.

The demise of British manufacturing industry is now posing severe consequences for the balance of payments. Traditionally, as we saw in Chapter 9 on the history of the UK balance of payments, Britain ran a deficit on visible trade financed by a surplus on the invisible account (i.e. earnings from insurance, shipping and other financial services provided by the City of London). Within the (negative) visible account, there was a surplus on manufactured trade which partially (but not entirely) helped to pay for a deficit in food and raw materials (including oil). In the last ten years or so, the situation has radically altered for the worse. The surplus on trade in manufactures has gradually dwindled. In 1983, there was a deficit for the first time in British economic history, and now the deficit is £10 billion or more. At the same time, the surplus on oil is diminishing (see Chapter 11), and may shortly disappear. This leaves the traditional surplus on invisible account to pay not only for the deficit in trade in food and raw materials, but also for Britain's insatiable appetite for foreign manufactured goods. The situation is clearly not sustainable, since there is no evidence that the service sector can generate the export earnings to finance such huge deficits. The House of Lords Committee on Overseas Trade estimated that only 20 per cent of service activities are tradeable, whereas virtually all manufactured goods are potentially tradeable. Moreover, international trade in service activities is hotting up. Already, Britain's share of world exports of services has fallen from 12 per cent in 1970 to 7 per cent today, and the decline looks like continuing. There is a very real danger that at some point on the ladder of industrial decline, a process of circular and cumulative causation will set in, with manufacturing decline affecting adversely exports and imports, while the deteriorating balance of payments itself, by imposing constraints on domestic demand, further worsens the prospects for manufacturing industry. The dependence of competitiveness on productivity growth, and of productivity *growth* on output growth, as outlined above, provide the linchpins of such a model of downward and cumulative causation.

THE CAUSES OF DEINDUSTRIALISATION

Several hypotheses can be advanced to explain the process of deindustrialisation in the UK. Five popular views are the pace of technical change; the pre-emption of resources by government for non-industrial uses; the impact of North Sea oil; the growing improvement in the balance of trade in non-manufactures, and the weak trade performance of the UK manufacturing sector, which can be considered both as a cause and a consequence of deindustrialisation. We shall argue that the last hypothesis is the most convincing explanation.

The technical change hypothesis does not stand up to either historical scrutiny or the test of international comparison. Technical progress itself is the progenitor of industrialisation and the growth of industrial employment. It is possible that at certain stages in history a sudden technological breakthrough may destroy in the short run more jobs than are generated, but over the long run there are three powerful reasons why technological progress is not the enemy of employment. The first is that technical progress is the main factor behind rising real incomes, and higher spending out of higher real incomes creates jobs throughout an economic system. When the demand for industrial products becomes saturated, it is possible that further technical progress may then lead to a loss of industrial jobs, but even developed economies are still far removed from this stage, let alone markets abroad. Secondly, technical progress not only opens up new and more productive ways of making existing products and satisfying existing needs, but creates new products and new demands. The washing machine, the vacuum cleaner, the refrigerator, the automobile and the aeroplane created many more jobs than they destroyed, and now pocket calculators, television games, video cassette recorders and home computers are doing the same. Thirdly, technical change requires investment for its embodiment, so that whether it is labour saving or labour using, it adds to aggregate demand in the system as a whole. Technical progress may thus lead to a decline in employment in specific industries, depending on the balance between job destruction in the industry and the extra employment generated by the increasing demand for the industry's product, but it is unlikely to lead to a loss of jobs in industry *as a whole* provided aggregate demand is maintained. It is to the demand side that we must look for explanations of declining industrial employment, not to the speed of technical progress. If technical progress was the explanation, we should expect countries experiencing the most rapid technical progress to show the largest declines in industrial employment. In practice, the contrary seems to be the case. Some of the most technologically progressive countries, such as Japan, have experienced the largest increases in industrial employment. It would be misleading, therefore, to attempt to explain the decline in industrial employment in the UK since 1966 in terms of technical change and its acceleration. On the contrary, it could be argued that it is because technical change has been *sluggish*, both in the field of new processes and in new products, that industrial decline has set in by encouraging the shift of demand from domestically produced to foreign produced goods which have become more price competitive through faster process innovation and more desirable through faster product innovation.

The idea that deindustrialisation has been associated with the pre-emption of resources by government is associated with the names of Bacon and Eltis (1976) who argue that over the years there has been a tendency in all developed countries for government expenditure on non-marketable output to increase, which has absorbed resources and manpower that would otherwise have been productively employed in manufacturing industry. Moreover, the public has not in general been willing to pay for increased non-marketable output by higher taxation and a reduction in the consumption of marketable output, so that investment and the balance of payments have suffered. The hypothesis clearly has little relevance to countries where industrial employment has actually *increased* through time, but in any case, what has to be shown is that the public sector *pulled* the manpower out of industry, and that industry otherwise would not have shed labour. This is an argument very hard to sustain in the context of the United Kingdom (see Thirlwall, 1978). There is little evidence of labour shortage over the period and that manufacturing industry was starved of labour by excessive demands of the public sector. What happens to employment in industry depends on the balance between the growth of demand for output and labour productivity growth. If output growth falls below productivity growth, employment will decline. How much industrial output grows depends on how fast demand in the total economy is allowed to grow. Over the period analysed by Bacon and Eltis, it was not possible for demand to be expanded to allow output growth to match industrial productivity growth, without the economy running into severe balance-of-payments difficulties. It is the slow growth of demand for industrial output which has been the main cause of industrial employment decline, and if services had not expanded, unemployment would have been much higher than it was. Moreover, most of the fall in industrial employment has been male, while most of the increase in employment outside industry has been (part-time) female. These facts also undermine the Bacon and Eltis thesis. In the 1980s, since advancing their thesis, industrial employment has continued to decline while the government has been cutting its expenditure on non-marketable output in real terms. The facts on deindustrialisation can only be satisfactorily explained by the slow growth of demand for industrial output relative to potential output.

As far as North Sea oil is concerned, the fact that the exchange rate was allowed to rise in 1979 undoubtedly contributed to the contraction of manufacturing industry; but, as we argued in Chapter 11, the rise in the exchange rate was not the *inevitable* consequence of North Sea oil. In any case, the process of deindustrialisation began in the 1960s, and therefore as a long-term trend it has nothing to do with the more recent exploitation of North Sea oil.

Similar to the theory of how North Sea oil contributed to deindustrialisation is the argument by Rowthorn and Wells (1987) that Britain's deteriorating balance of trade in manufactures and associated deindustrialisation has been the inevitable outcome of a growing improvement in the balance of trade in non-manufacturing, particularly in food and raw materials. Because the balance of payments on current account has to tend to zero in the long run, an improvement in one sector of the accounts must lead to deterioration elsewhere. The problem with the argument is that within the framework of a zero sum balance, each of the two sectors has its dual. Rowthorn and Wells lay all the stress on autonomous improvement in the non-manufacturing balance, leaving the manufacturing balance to adjust. But as we discussed in the last chapter there are all sorts of autonomous factors that have weakened UK manufacturing industry and independently worsened the manufacturing trade balance. Manufacturing cannot simply be treated as 'passive' or as an innocent victim of the system. Indeed, one question that immediately springs to mind is why did the emerging non-manufacturing sector not lead to a faster rate of economic growth if there was no serious (autonomous) industrial decline? Britain has had the lowest rate of economic growth, and of exports, of any industrialised country since 1950. This would indicate weakness right across the board. There are several autonomous forces that have been at work, associated with poor industrial performance, that have weakened the trade balance in manufacturing: for example, the inability to compete as tariffs have been removed; lack of innovation and technical dynamism resulting in import substitution; changes in tastes coupled with slow product development; switches in demand associated with superior foreign marketing, and so on. Furthermore, if the major cause of deindustrialisation was the autonomous improvement in non-manufacturing trade, one might expect the effect on the trade balance in manufactures to be fairly evenly spread across countries in relation to trade shares, but this is not so. The deficits are concentrated, particularly with Germany and Japan. This suggests (autonomous) industrial weakness relative to these two countries.

The most convincing explanation of progressive deindustrialisation in the UK is the overall weakening of the foreign trade sector, with a slow growth of exports relative to other countries, and in relation to the propensity to import (see also Singh, 1977). In the long run, no country can grow faster than at that rate consistent with balance-of-payments equilibrium on current account and, as we showed in Chapter 12, if the real terms of trade do not change significantly, this rate is determined by the rate of growth of export volume divided by the income elasticity of demand for imports. Attempts to grow faster than this rate mean that exports cannot pay for imports, and the economy comes up against a balance of payments constraint on demand, which affects the industrial sector's ability to grow as fast as labour productivity. A decline in employment is then inevitable.

The relation between the growth of manufacturing output (g_m) and the growth of total income (y) may be expressed as:

$$g_m = \mu\,(y) \tag{15.1}$$

where μ is the elasticity of manufacturing output with respect to total income, or a measure of the income elasticity of demand for manufactured goods. Given μ, and the growth of total income consistent with balance-of-payments equilibrium, the rate of growth of manufacturing output consistent with balance-of-payments equilibrium ($\bar{g}_m$) is also determined:

$$\bar{g}_m = \mu \, (y_B) \tag{15.2}$$

where y_B is the balance-of-payments equilibrium growth rate that we defined in Chapter 12. If y_B can be approximated by the rate of growth of exports (x) divided by the income elasticity of demand for imports (π), the maximum long-run rate of growth of manufacturing output is

$$\bar{g}_m = \frac{\mu x}{\pi} \tag{15.3}$$

The only ways to increase the long-run rate of growth of manufacturing output, given the over-all constraint of the balance of payments, are to raise μ by producing goods with a higher income elasticity of demand, to raise the rate of growth of total exports by making all goods more desirable abroad, and to lower π by making all foreign goods less desirable. If $\bar{g}_m$ is less than the rate of growth of labour productivity in manufacturing, less labour will be demanded. What are the facts? For the period 1951 to 1966 we estimate the balance-of-payments constrained growth rate to have been about 2.4 per cent. For the period since then our simple rule predicts an estimate of between 1.5 and 2.0 per cent depending on the assumed income elasticity of demand for imports. From statistics on the share of manufacturing output (see Table 15.3) it would appear that μ was virtually unity up to 1980, with the share of manufacturing output to total output remaining constant over time. This means that the growth of manufacturing output consistent with balance-of-payments equilibrium was exactly the same as the over-all balance-of-payments constrained growth rate. Now productivity growth in manufacturing industry over the period 1950 to 1964 was 2.7 per cent per annum, which is approximately equal to the rate of growth of total output and manufacturing output, and thus is consistent with the economy retaining labour in the manufacturing sector over the period and the economy moving into payments deficit. From the mid-1960s to the early 1970s, however, productivity growth accelerated, but the growth of manufacturing output permitted by the overall balance-of-payments constraint did not rise commensurately and hence manu-

TABLE 15.3

Manufacturing employment and output in the United Kingdom since 1950

	Share of manufacturing employment in total employment (%)	Share of manufacturing output in GDP at constant (1963) prices (%)	Level of manufacturing employment (000)
1950	34.7	29.3	8519
1955	35.9	30.6	9222
1960	35.8	31.0	8850
1965	35.0	31.1	9028
1970	34.7	31.7	8910
1975	30.9	29.1	7488
1980	30.2	29.5	6807
1984	26.1	24.7	5517
1989	22.9	23.5	5167

Sources: Brown and Sheriff in F. Blackaby, *Deindustrialisation* (London: Heinemann, 1979) and *Monthly Digest of Statistics* (various editions).

facturing employment declined. During the rest of the 1970s, productivity growth slowed but output growth slowed even more, and was actually negative in 1980, causing further (sharp) falls in manufacturing employment, as shown in Table 15.3. In the 1980s a further wide discrepancy arose between the rate of productivity growth in manufacturing and the rate of growth of industrial output leading to a further shedding of labour. Such was the state of the economy that the level of manufacturing output effectively showed no increase at all between 1979 and 1987. Clearly, the explanation of the slow growth of manufacturing output over time cannot lie in the lack of factor supplies, but must be attributed to constraints on demand. As we argued in the previous chapter, the problem seems to lie in the characteristics of the goods that the UK produces and sells at home and abroad. The British treat them as 'inferior' goods and so does the rest of the world.

Not only do imports rise in response to domestic income, but they may also rise *autonomously* independent of increases in income or output, through, for example, the liberalisation of trade or changes in taste. Import penetration is often thought of in this latter sense (although clearly an income elasticity of demand for imports greater than unity will also lead to a rise in the ratio of imports to income). An autonomous increase in imports unmatched by an autonomous increase in exports will contract output and employment in the industry concerned. Most sectors of industry in the UK have experienced substantial import penetration over the last 20 years at least (see Chapter 10). The import penetration has largely come from Europe, particularly Germany, and Japan. The trade balance with the EC and Japan worsened to a significant degree over the decades of the 1970s and 1980s compared with other country groupings. Since the EC and Japan grew faster than the UK there was clearly substantial import penetration of the UK market compared with the UK penetration of the EC and Japanese markets. Winters (1987) has shown that prior to 1973 (when the UK joined the EC), EC countries were gradually increasing their share of the UK market, but after 1973 their shares rose considerably, while shares of non-EC countries continued to decline at faster rates. By 1979, over one-half of UK imports from the original six EC members could be attributed to UK accession. An estimated £8–12 billion of additional manufactured imports were generated, almost all displacing domestic sales. By contrast, UK exports to the EC increased by about £4.5 billion while those to other countries decreased by £1.5 billion *vis-à-vis* what otherwise would have been the case. There is evidence of a positive relation across industries between the extent of import penetration and the decline of industrial employment (Thirlwall, 1982b).

A TRADE STRATEGY FOR THE UNITED KINGDOM

To halt the process of deindustrialisation in the UK, a foreign trade strategy is urgently required. In this section we discuss some possibilities, notwithstanding the fact that most of the suggestions would contravene the Articles of Agreement of the EC. The prevailing mood of free trade, *laissez-faire – laissez-passer* should not be allowed to stifle discussion of alternative economic policies for weak countries in danger of becoming weaker as the competitive process takes its toll. Unequal partners, in any union, need to be treated unequally, if equality is the desired objective.

   Three broad strategies are possible to simultaneously improve the balance of payments and reinvigorate the industrial base, some more promising than others: exchange rate depreciation, import controls, and export promotion. Some economists still put their faith in currency depreciation to arrest Britain's industrial decline, but we have questioned whether exchange rate depreciation can permanently improve a country's balance of payments consistent with a higher growth rate. It would seem that the currency depreciation would have to be continuous to put a country on a higher growth path consistent with balance-of-payments equilibrium, but in any case it is highly inflationary and the evidence would suggest that it cannot be relied upon to rectify balance-of-payments disequilibrium.

A second possibility is import controls. There are legitimate economic arguments for various forms of protection, one of which is the famous infant industry argument; another is if the social cost of labour is less than the private cost of labour because of unemployment. Some of the arguments for protection are arguments for tariffs; others arguments for subsidies. Protection to control imports alone, however, would be a very inward-looking strategy, and there are many weaknesses and disadvantages of such a strategy. First, if import controls take the form of tariffs, a once-for-all tariff may reduce the *level* of imports, but it is unlikely to reduce the *rate of growth* of imports permanently which is what is required if the country is to move to a higher growth path without balance-of-payments difficulties arising. To reduce the rate of growth of imports permanently would require an ever-increasing tariff level in the same way that it is recognised that a *continual* depreciation of the currency would be necessary to achieve the same objective if that were a feasible policy. Secondly, if price uncompetitiveness is part of the problem, tariffs are a policy of adjusting the internal price structure to the internal cost structure, while what is required is an adjustment of the internal cost structure to the external price structure. The danger is then that once the limits of import substitution have been reached there is no basis for further improvement in the balance of payments. Faster export growth is jeopardised and virtually precluded because an unfavourable internal cost structure has been protected. Many developing countries have paid dearly for this import substitution strategy at the expense of promoting exports. If demand is at all important for achieving high levels of output and productivity, and for reaping economies of scale, it is much more sensible to orientate domestic industry to the virtually unlimited world market, as Japan learnt to do a long time ago, and which countries like Korea, Singapore and Taiwan have also learnt to do. A third disadvantage of tariffs is that by raising the internal price level a loss of welfare is incurred. It is true that the revenue gained from tariffs could be used to reduce indirect taxes on goods but there is no guarantee that this would happen.

An alternative form of import controls would be import quotas. To be effective, however, in reducing permanently the rate of growth of imports, they would have to be comprehensive covering virtually all imports. Otherwise, as demand was expanded there would be a switching from imports with quotas to imports without, and imports would continue to grow. There could also be complex administrative problems in allocating the scarce imports between competing uses.

Whichever form import controls take, however, they are all isolationist and inward-looking. A dynamic growth and development policy cannot be based on pure protectionism. There must be an export strategy as well. The counter-argument to these criticisms has three elements: firstly that import controls work quickly to get an economy back to full employment; secondly, that in the movement back to full employment, investment will rise, technological progress will accelerate and average costs of production will fall, producing dynamic benefits which will raise the rate of growth of exports; thirdly, that if controls discriminate against surplus countries this will help to raise the growth of world income and consequently UK exports too. There is some force in these counter-arguments, but it requires a very much greater act of faith to believe in dynamic benefits stemming from import controls than in the benefits that could accrue from an investment and taxation policy deliberately orientated to raising the rate of growth of exports. The dynamic benefits from import controls are supposed to arise as firms move along downward sloping average cost curves towards full capacity utilisation. There can be little doubt that cost curves are downward sloping at less than full employment, but what happens under this strategy when full employment is reached and there is no more scope for import substitution? The dynamism produced by import restrictions ceases. By contrast an investment policy to encourage exports, which also relieved the balance of payments constraint on demand, would also move firms along the same downward sloping cost curves, but at the same time, by inducing structural change, the policy could put exports and hence the economy on a permanently higher growth path. Import controls and import substitution may be a quicker route to full employment than an industrial strategy to raise exports, but they are inferior as a growth strategy if export growth remains unchanged.

The policy of import restrictions will also no doubt help to raise the growth of world income provided the composition of imports is altered against those countries with balance of payments surpluses. However, if the world income elasticity of demand for UK exports is lower than for other countries, (which it is), a rise in the growth of world income will *worsen* the *relative* performance of the UK economy. In other words, a policy of import restrictions does nothing to raise the propensity of other countries to buy UK goods and thus would simply consolidate the UK position at the bottom of the growth league table. By contrast, if an investment strategy, working through the tax system, could induce structural change in favour of activities producing goods with a high income elasticity of demand in world markets, the growth of world income would be raised in the same way as under import controls (by relieving the economy of the balance of payments constraint on demand) and at the same time the growth rate of UK exports would be higher and hence the overall growth of output.

Those who advocate import controls are understandably preoccupied with the short-run, but there is also a need to stand back and to consider the longer run issue of the UK economy's chronically slow underlying growth rate compared to other developed countries. All the evidence suggests that a necessary condition for a faster long run rate of growth of output and living standards is a faster rate of growth of exports, which import controls do nothing to foster directly. If one examines intercountry differences in export and import propensities, it is not so much the overall UK import propensity which looks so alarming but the abysmally slow growth of exports compared with other countries. This, in turn, seems to have very little to do with relative price differences, but with a very low income elasticity of demand for UK goods in world markets due mainly to the supply characteristics of the goods such as their design, reliability, delivery, marketing, servicing and quality in the widest sense. Regardless of 'quality' we also know that some goods have an intrinsically lower income elasticity of demand because they are 'inferior' goods (goods produced to cater for low income markets as opposed to high income markets). There is no hope of improving this fundamental weakness by import controls (or by currency depreciation for that matter).

No attempt has ever been made in the UK economy to develop a coherent strategy of export-led growth. The primary task of economic policy in the United Kingdom must be to develop a strategy of export-led growth based on a judicious mix of taxes and subsidies to alter the allocation of investment resources and the composition of output in favour of exports. UK export performance is a function of the *types* of goods produced and the *division* of output between domestic and foreign markets. Tax incentives could be used both to alter the structure of production and to raise export performance within the structure. The structural change required is to induce an allocation of resources in favour of technologically progressive industries producing goods with a high income elasticity of demand in world markets. The policy could be integrated with an industrial strategy and linked to a system of investment grants and allowances. Investment incentives could be discriminatory according to various growth criteria. A complementary strategy would be to relate investment grants and allowances to the proportion of output exported which would tend to bias both the structure of output and the composition of output towards exports if manufacturers are at all responsive to differential rates of return. In addition, it would be possible simply to make exporting more profitable by remitting corporation tax on export earnings. A number of other things could be done: exporting firms might be offered cheaper credit for investment; an attempt could be made to raise the status of marketing in firms; encouragement could be given to foreign language training, and finding room for engineers in the board-rooms of firms. An economic environment, supported by government, in which firms can take the long view and be assured of adequate support relative to competitors, would also seem to be important. We reproduce below a letter to the *Financial Times* from the Director-General of the Council of Mechanical and Metal Trade Associations which illustrates that our concerns and proposals suggested above are not simply those of 'ivory tower' economists, but shared by those who work in industry itself.

Those who have been involved in export marketing of capital goods know very well that success only comes from a sustained campaign, and instant results do not arise from a favourable exchange rate. That is one reason why this Association strongly advocates an industrial strategy developed jointly by Government, industry and the City with the objectives of identifying broad future markets, and then setting the right climate in which manufacturing industry can market over the long term. Industry cannot do this if its decisions are heavily influenced by short-term attitudes of City financial interests, and changing political regimes. The Department of Trade and Industry (DTI) should take the lead to set up a strong body drawn from all three parties to determine ways of bringing our UK act together with real consistency, as has been done so successfully in Japan and France. If we had had a strategy on these lines 10 years ago, manufacturing industry would not have suffered so severely in recent years. There is another factor which has as profound influence on export efforts. Success, particularly in overseas project business, is highly dependent on the financial package the supplier can offer. Increasingly over recent years contenders have looked to their governments for help to enable them to offer these packages. The support our industry has had has been quite inadequate compared with that given to overseas competitors. On level terms, we do not fear competition, but we need at least the same degree of backing from our Government as the others get. The £8 billion manufacturing industry represented by this Association is ready and able to take on any competitor overseas; but it needs the stability of a long-term UK strategy, and at least the same degree of government financial assistance as our competitors receive.[2]

An export-led growth strategy of the type described here may violate the spirit of international trading agreements and particularly the Articles of Agreement of the EC. Article 92 of the Treaty of Rome lays down that state aids which distort competition are incompatible with the EC. It does specify, however, two forms of permissible regional aid: (1) aid intended to promote economic development in regions where there is a low standard of living or serious underemployment, and (2) aid intended to facilitate the development of *particular* activities or economic regions, provided that it does not affect trading conditions adversely. In one sense, any subsidy or tax concession to any activity distorts 'free competition'. On the other hand, 'free competition' itself may affect trading conditions adversely if it means that a country languishes economically and under-utilises its resources. In these circumstances, support for activities to achieve a fuller utilisation of resources could enhance the volume of trade for all. It is in this spirit that support for export activities within regional groupings should be assessed. Given the UK's long-term economic dilemma and the massive full employment deficit on the non-oil account of the balance of payments, one might hope that there would be a good deal of international sympathy for the kind of strategy here outlined whether Britain remains a member of GATT and the EC or not. At least the water could be tested, as other EC countries have done from time to time with respect to both import restrictions and export promotion. Just how far a weak country could go would be interesting to see. With the completion of the single European Market in 1992, some mechanism will be required to permit countries to deal with structural balance-of-payments problems and the associated poor economic performance.

THE FUTURE

We are not optimistic about the future for two major reasons. First, North Sea oil revenues are declining and will continue to decline. Nothing can be done about the deflation of this cushion, which up to now has helped to fill the growing gap between manufactured imports and exports, unless a dramatic rise in oil prices leads to further exploration and oil discoveries. Furthermore, it is unlikely that exports of services will grow sufficiently to fill the gap left by oil, let alone to offset the growing balance-of-trade deficit in manufactures. The second worry concerns the implications for British manufacturing industry of the *single European market*. The creation of a single European market, in which all barriers to trade in goods and factors of production are removed, is a major step along the way to complete European integration (and some would hope to a United States of Europe) which was started with the signing of the Treaty of Rome in 1957 and the creation of the European Community. If past experience is anything to go by, however, the prospects for British industry look bleak. As an extract from the *Financial Times* remarked, 'European industry is heading for a drastic and painful restructuring which will lead to the disappearance of many companies and could create higher unemployment in the next few years.'[3]

Britain remained outside the EC until 1973. It then became a member on the pretext that access to a larger market would enable industry to reap economies of large-scale production and therefore enhance its competitiveness. More competition and less protection was to blow the cobwebs off British industry and enable it to compete more effectively in international markets. A government White Paper in 1970 entitled *Britain and the European Communities: An Economic Assessment* (Cmnd 4289) argued that there would be:

dynamic effects resulting from membership of a much larger and faster growing market. This would open up to our industrial producers substantial opportunities for increasing export sales, while at the same time exposing them more fully to the competition of European industries. No way has been found of quantifying these dynamic benefits, but if British industry responded vigorously to the stimuli, they would be considerable and highly advantageous. The acceleration of the rate of growth of industrial exports could then outpace any increase in the rate of growth of imports, with corresponding benefits to the balance of payments. Moreover, with such a response, the growth of industrial productivity would be accelerated as a result of increased competition and the advantages derived from specialization and larger scale production. This faster rate of growth would, in turn, accelerate the rate of growth of national production and real income.

A further White Paper in 1971, *The United Kingdom and the European Communities* (Cmnd 4715), promised much of the same. The miserable economic performance of the British economy was compared with the vastly superior performance of the EC, with the optimism expressed that:

> Her Majesty's Government is convinced that our economy [will be] stronger and our industries and peoples more prosperous if we join the European Communities than if we remain outside them. . . . Improvements in efficiency and competitive power should enable the UK to meet the balance of payments costs of entry over the next decade as they gradually build up. . . . [The] advantages will far outweigh the costs, provided we seize the opportunities of the far wider home market now open to us.

The much-heralded beneficial winds of change turned into a gale of destruction for much of manufacturing industry, as might have been predicted from both economic theory and experience that when weak countries join free-trade areas or customs unions, the strong countries benefit at their expense. There is nothing in the doctrine of free trade that says that the gains from trade will be equally distributed among partners. Indeed, some countries may lose *absolutely* if the gains from specialisation that free trade permits are offset by the unemployment of resources which comes about if import growth exceeds export growth, and the growth of output internally has to be constrained because of balance-of-payments difficulties. The doctrine of free trade ignores the balance-of-payments implications, implicitly assuming that the balance of payments looks after itself and that full employment is maintained.

There is precious little evidence that Britain joining the EC has raised the underlying growth rate of the British economy consistent with balance-of-payments equilibrium. On the contrary, there is evidence that the budgetary costs of entry, the extent of import penetration from Europe, and a growing trade imbalance in manufactures, particularly with Germany, have tightened the balance-of-payments constraint on Britain's growth rate.

With the complete liberalisation of trade, and the removal of all restrictions on the movement of capital and labour, the European Commission is predicting substantial global benefits, including a 4.5 per cent rise in GDP in the Community as a whole, a 6 per cent reduction in prices, and employment gains of 1.8 million (see the Cecchini Report, 1988); but it says nothing about the *distribution* of gains between member countries.

These further moves towards liberalisation will probably strengthen the centrifugal forces already apparent within the Community by which the rich regions and countries get richer and the poor, poorer. The Single European Market does not augur well, therefore, for British industry, or for the British economy which is still chronically weak.

There can be no guarantee that the mobility of factors of production, such as labour and capital, between countries will equalise the rewards to factors of production, as orthodox (neoclassical) theory predicts, and that therefore *per capita* income levels will be equalised between countries. Orthodox theory says that factors of production migrate in response to differences in economic opportunity – and this is true – but the predictions of the theory seem to conflict with the facts. As labour migrates from a depressed to a more prosperous region or country, the supply of labour and unemployment is supposed to fall in the depressed region (with the demand for labour unchanged), so that wages rise, while in the more prosperous regions the increased supply of labour (with demand unchanged) is supposed to depress wages. Capital is supposed to 'migrate' the other way from prosperous regions where the wage rate is higher (and the rate of profit lower) to depressed regions where the wage rate is lower (and the rate of profit higher).

That is the neoclassical story, but it is a very static story which ignores the dynamic interactions between the supply and demand for factors of production as migration takes place. For example, as labour migration takes place it brings with it its own demands – in the form of demand for local goods, the provision of local services, housing and so on – so that the demand for labour increases with the supply of labour in the prosperous region, while in the depressed region from which the migrants come the demand is depressed. The equilibration of wages may not take place.

Likewise, as far as capital is concerned, the location of regional investment is not simply a function of relative wage rates, but also a function of productivity and the expected strength of demand. Therefore new investment is just as likely to flow to prosperous regions to which people are migrating as to depressed regions where the wages may be lower. Investment and employment growth tend to be complementary in the productive process.

All this is to say that initial differences in the level of development between regions and/or countries do not necessarily set up forces which eliminate those differences. On the contrary, forces are set up which may perpetuate and even widen these differences. The operation of these forces has been called by the Swedish economist, Gunnar Myrdal, the 'process of circular and cumulative causation'. These forces are factor mobility and free trade which lead to 'virtuous circles of growth' in strong regions and countries and 'vicious circles of poverty' in weak regions and countries. If the theory of circular and cumulative causation is correct, liberalisation will further widen regional/country disparities in levels of prosperity in Europe.

It must not be forgotten, too, that Britain is not only economically weak and relatively poor compared with many of its partners; it also lies on the geographic periphery of Europe. It is not in the 'centre' of the market for goods and services, but it is the 'centre' of a market that always exerts a strong gravitational pull. It is not an economic accident that the relatively depressed regions of the UK are on the geographic periphery of the UK or that many of the depressed regions of the EC lie on the geographic periphery of Europe.

There is reason to be worried for the future, not only as a result of the effects of the operation of free-market forces pulling investment and skilled labour from Britain to the centre of Europe, but also because the Articles of Agreement of the EC make it increasingly difficult for countries to pursue an independent economic policy, at least as far as the functioning of the real economy is concerned. It cannot offer incentives to industrial development because that means unfair competition; it cannot discriminate in favour of particular activities because that distorts competition; and it cannot restrict trade. Furthermore, if the idea of complete monetary union was adopted, with a European Central Bank and a common currency, countries would lose control over exchange rate policy and monetary policy as well. Britain in Europe would become like Scotland, or Wales, or any other region within the UK, or like the states within the USA; that is, completely at the mercy of market forces as far as economic performance is concerned, devoid of any instruments of economic policy, and with depressed regions dependent on the largesse of a central administration. This must be the worry for British industry, and therefore the British economy, in the 1990s.

Notes

CHAPTER 1

1. This replaced the 'liquidity balance' concept in 1965 on the recommendation of the Bernstein Committee. However, in 1976 an Advisory Committee on the Presentation of Balance of Payments Statistics recommended doing away with all 'balances' for fear that they may mislead.

2. The old measure of total currency flow measured by the *balance for official financing* excluded the allocation of Special Drawing Rights and gold subscriptions to the IMF.

3. A basic balance-of-payments surplus or deficit will not necessarily lead to an accumulation or decumulation of foreign-currency reserves, or to a change in the exchange rate, because the surplus or deficit may be fully offset by private short-term capital movements.

CHAPTER 2

1. Subscriptions to the IMF take two forms: 75 per cent is given in the country's own currency (e. g. £ in the case of the UK) and 25 per cent in gold.

2. Official reserves are part of what used to be called official financing. In Chapter 1, we noted that official financing is no longer itemised separately in the balance of payments. Official reserves, however, form a large part of what used to be called official financing.

3. It is possible to conceive of the change in reserves over a given period being zero yet there has been intervention in the foreign exchange market. If intervention in part of the period were exactly matched by intervention of the same magnitude but in the opposite

direction, then the change in reserves over the whole period would be exactly zero. Thus the size of the change in reserves may not always be an indication of the degree of intervention over the period.

4.   This buffer-stock view of reserves can be contrasted with the view that international reserves comprise an international monetary base, with the volume of international reserves ultimately affecting the level of world inflation. See, for example, Heller (1976) and Chrystal (1989) for expositions of this view and Williamson (1982a) for a critique.

5.   See, for example, Heller and Khan (1978), Frenkel (in von Furstenberg, 1983) and the various comments on Frenkel's paper by Purvis and Masera.

6.   The official price of gold was raised from $35 dollars per ounce to $38 dollars per ounce in December 1971.

7.   See, for example, Corden (1983) and von Furstenberg (chapter 11) for a short analysis of the historical development of the SDR.

8.   IMF quotas refer to the amounts which individual countries have to contribute to the IMF's resources. They are based on a country's importance in international trade and as such the US has remained the country with the largest quota throughout the history of the IMF. Quotas determine access to funds, voting rights with the IMF and the allocation of SDRs.

9.   See von Furstenberg (1983, especially chapters 11 and 12) for an account of the changes in valuation, interest rates and liquidity of the SDR which have sought to make it a more attractive international reserve asset.

10.   See Lessard and Williamson (1987) for the case of Latin America and Gibson and Tsakalotos (1990) for the EC.

11.   US banks were unable to compete for funds with other US financial institutions because of the operation of Regulation Q. Regulation Q limited the interest rate which banks could offer on time deposits. When monetary conditions were tight market interest rates would rise above the Regulation Q ceiling. Other financial institutions were able to raise their interest rates on time deposits. The banks, however, were not and this resulted in a large movement of funds from bank time deposits to deposits with other financial institutions. The banks therefore found themselves short of funds and

went to borrow dollars in the euromarkets to meet the demand for loans in the US.

12. For a detailed account of exchange controls in the UK and how they operated see Parker (1978) and Bank of England (1977).

CHAPTER 3

1. Bullionists believed that the only real money is gold (and/or silver). Many of their views were derived from those of the mercantilists. The system of the Gold Standard can be said to have links with the ideas of bullionism.

2. The literature on PPP is enormous. On the importance of the assumptions of PPP, see, for example, Isard (1978, 1987), Katseli (1979), Krueger (1983) and MacDonald (1988).

3. See, for example, Katseli (1979).

4. Katseli (1979) notes that this was recognised as early as 1928 by Zolotas.

5. See Chapter 5 for the derivation of the Marshall-Lerner conditions.

6. Frankel and Froot (1987) provide a useful outline of the various methods of expectations formation. They also test to determine the method of expectations formation in the foreign exchange markets.

7. See, for example, Dornbusch (1976) and MacDonald (1988) for proof of this.

8. Note that Dornbusch (1976) relaxes this assump r=:: V of the article. We can note that Dornbusch shows that ii we assume departures from full employment, then overshooting is no longer a necessary outcome of the adjustment process.

9. This is derived as follows:

$$0 = \delta \left[\alpha(e + p^* - p) - \sigma i + \gamma y - y \right]$$
$$\Rightarrow \quad 0 = \delta \left[\alpha(e + p^* - p) - \sigma(i^* + \theta(\bar{e} - e)) + \gamma y - y \right]$$
$$\Rightarrow \quad 0 = \delta \left[\alpha e + \alpha(p^* - p) - \sigma i^* - \sigma\theta\bar{e} + \sigma\theta e + \gamma y - y \right]$$
$$\Rightarrow \quad 0 = \delta\alpha e + \delta\sigma\theta e + \delta[\alpha(p^* - p) - \sigma i^* - \sigma\theta\bar{e} + (\gamma - 1)y]$$

$$=> \quad \delta\alpha e + \delta\sigma\theta e = - \delta[\alpha(p^* - p) - \sigma i^* - \sigma\theta\bar{e} + (\gamma - 1)y]$$

$$=> \quad [\delta(\alpha + \sigma\theta)]e = \delta[\sigma i^* + \sigma\theta\bar{e} - \alpha (p^* - p) - (\gamma - 1)y]$$

$$=> \quad e = (1/(\alpha + \sigma\theta))[\sigma(i^* + \theta\bar{e}) - \alpha (p^* - p) - (\gamma - 1)y]$$

10.   Dornbusch's model, in this sense, is similar to the monetary app; 'ach to exchange rate determination. This approach is examined in detail in Chapter 7. In the monetary model, the exchange rate is seen as the relative price of foreign and domestic money and moreover it is determined in the money market alone. For example, an excess supply of domestic money leads to exchange rate depreciation, whereas an excess demand for money leads to exchange rate appreciation. The introduction of the bond market in portfolio theory and the implications of the interaction between the money and the bond market implies that portfolio theory is much broader than the monetary theory.

11.   See, for example, Dornbusch and Fischer (1980).

12.   See, for example, Allen and Kenen (1980), who develop one of the most comprehensive models.

13.   See, for example, MacDonald (1988), Allen and Kenen (1976), and Genberg and Kierzkowski (1979).

14.   This can be derived using equations (3.22) to (3.25). Taking (3.25):

$$
\begin{aligned}
EB^* &= W - M - B \\
&= W [1 - m(i, i^*) - b(i, i^*)] \qquad \text{if we assume money and} \\
&\qquad\qquad\qquad\qquad\qquad\qquad\qquad\quad \text{bond market equilibrium} \\
&= b^* (i, i^*)W \qquad \text{since } m + b + b^* = 1
\end{aligned}
$$

15.   See Frankel (1979) for a discussion of the real interest rate different 'l model of exchange rate determination. This is a modified version .f the monetary theory and it argues that exchange rate changes are a function of differential inflation rates in addition to differential income, wealth, money supplies, and nominal interest rates.

16.   See, for example, Flood and Garber (1982) and Blanchard and Watson (1982) for surveys of some of the early work on rational speculative bubbles.

17.   The gold specie system which preceded the gold bullion

system differed in that the domestic coinage itself consisted of gold. However, the mechanism of international adjustment under the two systems was the same.

18. The convertibility of the domestic currency into gold was abandoned by most countries during the First World War.

19. This part draws on Dennis and Nellis (1984) and Midland Bank Review (1979).

20. It should be noted that the final decision to join the exchange rate mechanism was probably not taken on economic grounds, but rather for political reasons. There was a growing dissatisfaction that the UK seemed to be outside of the main decisions taken by the EC. With moves towards more fixed exchange rates and ultimately monetary union, which we discuss later, it was felt to be important that the UK was not left behind, with little influence over the decisions which were about to be taken.

21. These figures are taken from Davies (1989).

22. This view is taken, for example, by Kaldor (1970) and provides a case for regional policies.

23. Such stabilisation programmes normally involve attempts to reduce inflation, cuts in government spending and conditions which can favour asset holders.

24. All countries with the exception of Greece, Spain, Portugal and Ireland had to remove their controls by July 1990. Greece, Spain, Portugal and Ireland all had the possibility of extending the use of their controls beyond July 1990, of which they have taken advantage.

CHAPTER 4

1. Throughout the chapter and the book, exports and imports are defined in such a way that the national income equals the national output. The difference between income and output is net factor payments abroad.

2. For expositions of the theory, see Cripps and Godley (1976) and Rowan (1976).

3. The traditional approach to the foreign-trade multiplier is introduced first in order to dismiss it later.

4. We assume for simplicity that the import coefficients attached to autonomous and induced consumption are identical.

5. If so, we have $\lambda_a = (\Delta M / \Delta T)_a$ and $m_a = (\Delta M / \Delta Y)_a$, where T is total expenditure. Since $\Delta Y_a = (\Delta T - \Delta M)_a$ $m_a = \lambda_a/(1 - \lambda_a)$, or $\lambda_a = m_a/(1 + m_a)$. Likewise for λ_b. Substituting for λ_a and λ_b in equation (4.39) gives equation (4.40).

6. The real-balance effect derives from the assumption that people desire to hold a constant proportion of their real income in the form of real-money-balance holdings. If the price level goes up, the real value of money holdings goes down, and to restore the real value the demand for nominal money must increase.

CHAPTER 5

1. In terms of domestic currency the Marshall-Lerner condition becomes more stringent starting from deficit, i.e. $E_x (pX/M) + E_m > 1$. This leads to the possibility that while the trade balance may be improved in terms of foreign currency, it may not be improved in terms of domestic currency.

2. Divide the top and bottom of the first half of the expression by S_x and the top and bottom of the second half by S_m.

3. Starting from payments equilibrium the same result can be derived, measuring changes in the balance of payments in domestic currency.

4. Some mitigation is provided by the Export Credits Guarantee which introduced in 1975 a scheme to provide exporters of capital goods costing more than £2 million with a manufacturing period of more than two years with cover against inflation on fixed-price contracts.

5. If the competitive advantage of devaluation is maintained, the *J*-curve will become a square-root sign (Masera, 1974), and if it disappears the curve will come down to the level at which it started, leaving the balance of payments unchanged.

6. The barter terms of trade is the ratio of export prices to import

prices measured in a common currency, and changes in the barter terms of trade give a measure of the change in the real purchasing power of exports over imports.

CHAPTER 6

1. Specifically, this concerns the suggested idea that all balance-of-payments deficits are *caused* by an excess supply of money.

2. Except for the possibility that devaluation might increase productivity if the traded-goods sector has higher productivity than the non-traded-goods sector. (This will be discussed later.)

3. Changes in absorption will also have an effect on income. We incorporate later the interaction between changes in income and absorption.

4. Assuming, of course, people have the extra money income to increase their money expenditure in line with prices. If not, the saving would be 'forced'.

5. This section draws on Thirlwall (1979a).

6. The same formula in a different form has been presented by Johnson (1958), but it is not clear how it is derived.

7. Johnson (1958) is guilty of this, intentionally or not.

8. By Walras's Law, which says that the sum of excess demands and supplies in all markets must sum to zero.

CHAPTER 7

1. An alternative approach suggested by Coppock (1978, and in correspondence) is to distinguish between traded and non-traded goods. Let $X_g = X_n + X_t$, where X_n is the excess demand for non-traded goods and X_t is the excess demand for traded goods ($= -B$). The budget constraint leads to $X_n + X_t + X_m \equiv 0$. Then, if $X_n = 0$, $X_m = -X_t = B$.

2. The growth of reserves (R) can be shown (see Johnson, 1973) to be inversely related to the growth of domestic credit expansion (D) according to the following expression:

$$dR/R = \left(- \frac{1 - r}{r} \right) dD/D$$

where r is the ratio of reserves to the money supply. The growth of reserves is also positively related to the growth of income, through the increased demand for money, implying that the higher a country's growth rate (holding the supply of money constant), the greater its balance-of-payments surplus. But how can a higher growth rate be financed without an increase in the money supply? The evidence does not square with the theory.

3.   Employing the earlier distinction between traded and non-traded goods we would have $X_n + X_t + X_m + X_b \equiv 0$. If $X_n = X_m = 0$, then $X_b = -X_t = B$.

CHAPTER 8

1.   It is possible (see the *IS-LM* curve analysis later) for fiscal policy to improve the balance of payments by raising interest rates to such an extent that higher capital inflows exceed the increase in imports. In this case the *BB* curve would be positively sloped and the problem of assignment would not arise. Mundell's model ignores the interrelation between fiscal policy and interest-rate changes.

2.   In terms of the model outlined above, if Y_1 is external balance, Y_2 is internal balance, X_1 is monetary policy and X_2 is fiscal policy, then monetary policy should be assigned to external balance and fiscal policy to internal balance because $a_{11}/a_{21} > a_{12}/a_{22}$.

3.   There are a number of other factors which may increase the impact of fiscal policy and reduce the impact of monetary policy which are too involved to discuss at this introductory level. For a useful survey, see Currie (1978).

4.   For a derivation of the slopes of the *IS* and *LM* curves in an open economy, see Stern (1973, pp. 312–16).

5.   Assuming that capital movements are not sensitive to income, in which case the schedule may slope downwards.

6.   This is ruled out of Mundell's original model discussed earlier.

CHAPTER 9

1. Unemployment in the middle of 1966 was still at a record low of 1.1 per cent.

2. The estimated annual magnitude of the surcharge effect is of the same order (if not higher) as the estimated annual impact of the 1967 devaluation (see later), which suggests that controls on imports can be at least as effective as devaluation.

3. The figures shown in Table 9.4 are different from those published at the time.

4. But this is also implicit in Worswick's procedure.

5. Probably because of the removal of the import surcharge.

6. See Chapter 6 for an exposition of this concept.

7. A 1 per cent movement in the rate is intended to be equivalent to a 1 per cent change in sterling's rate against all currencies as far as the effect on the UK trade balance is concerned.

8. The deficit first appeared in 1982 on an overseas trade statistics basis, and in 1983 on a balance of payments basis.

9. Abridged from A. P. Thirlwall, 'The Panacea of the Floating Pound', *National Westminster Bank Quarterly Review*, August 1974.

10. For a fascinating catalogue of quotes (and academic somersaults!) see Hutchison (1977).

11. Hence Houthakker and Magee's conclusion that 'Britain can therefore only grow half as fast as the rest of the world in the long run if it wants to maintain its exchange rate'. It does not follow, however, that the appropriate long-run solution is to allow the exchange rate to depreciate.

CHAPTER 10

1. A 'Koyck' distributed lag function could also be used to estimate short- and long-run elasticities if it takes time for imports to adjust to changes in the independent variables; but for a tractable solution it would have to be assumed that the distributed lag-adjustment weights attached to each of the variables were the same.

2.   For the experience since 1967, see Table 11.4 in the appendix to Chapter 11.

3.   The official statistics only go back to 1970, but unpublished data are available from the Treasury for the period 1963 to 1970.

4.   It is important that the rise in the ratio of exports to output should reflect a genuine improvement in exports and not a fall in output induced by the increase in imports via the workings of the Harrod trade multiplier. For a discussion of this topic, see Kennedy and Thirlwall (1979c).

CHAPTER 11

1.   For good discussions of this topic, see Ball (1961) and Cooper, Hartley and Harvey (1970).

2.   Good discussions of the various measures are contained in HM Treasury's *Economic Progress Report*, February 1978, and in Enoch (1978).

3.   The empirical magnitude of these effects will depend on the order in which the summations occur. Here it is *i* first and *j* second.

CHAPTER 12

1.   Exceptions to this statement would be countries able to attract a continual net inflow of long-term or short-term capital despite a growing current-account deficit.

2.   See Chapter 5.

3.   This result would also obtain if the Marshall-Lerner condition was just satisfied. Krugman (1989) has called this formula the 45-degree rule since one country's growth rate relative to all others (y_B/z) will be equiproportional to the ratio of income elasticities (ε/π). See the reply by Thirlwall (1991).

4.   For a more extensive discussion of the Harrod trade multiplier and its empirical application, see Thirlwall (1979b, 1982a, 1986); McCombie (1980, 1989); Williamson (1984); McGregor and Swales (1985, 1986), and Bairam (1988, 1990).

CHAPTER 13

1.   This is not to say, of course, that the capacity growth rate is exogenously determined.

2.   Kaldor, once an advocate of currency depreciation to improve export performance, later turned against it because of its inflationary repercussions domestically.

3.   That is, the relationship between the rate of growth of productivity as the dependent variable and the rate of growth of output as the independent variable, which when tested empirically gives a coefficient of about 0.5. The law is not simply an empirical generalisation, however. In the mathematical appendix of Verdoorn's original article he also develops a predictive model (see Thirlwall and Thirlwall, 1979).

4.   Our simple rule enunciated in equation (12.8) gives a balance-of-payments equilibrium growth rate of 2.6 per cent.

5.   The parameter values and estimates of the variables (rates per annum) used were $\eta = 1.5$, $w_t + \tau_t = 0.26$, $r_a = 0.01$, $p_f = 0.28$, $\varepsilon = 1$, $z_t = 0.03$, $\lambda = 0.5$, and $\pi = 1.51$, and the exchange rate fell by about 4 per cent per annum over the period.

CHAPTER 14

1.   The relation between the two elasticities is as follows. The income elasticity of demand for exports (ε) is x/y. The elasticity of world trade with respect to world income could be expressed as $\lambda = t/y$. Thus the elasticity of exports with respect to world trade is ε/λ. If $\lambda > 1$, which it is, then the elasticity of demand for UK exports with respect to world trade will be less than the income elasticity of demand for UK exports.

2.   High research intensive activities are where R & D is greater than 2.8 per cent of sales; medium research activities – R + D 1.1 per cent – 2.8 per cent of sales; low research activities – R & D less than 1.1 per cent of sales.

CHAPTER 15

1.   This chapter draws heavily on Thirlwall (1982b and 1983) and Bazen and Thirlwall (1989).

2.   9 January 1987.

3.   23 November 1988.

References

Adams, F. G. *et al*. (1969) *An Econometric Analysis of International Trade* (OECD, Paris).

Alexander, S. (1952) 'Effects of a Devaluation on a Trade Balance', *IMF Staff Papers*, April.

Alexander, S. (1959) 'Effects of a Devaluation: A Simplified Synthesis of Elasticities and Absorption Approaches', *American Economic Review*, March.

Allen, P. R. and Kenen, P. B. (1976) Portfolio Adjustment in Open Economies: A Comparison of Alternative Specifications, *Weltwirtschaftliches Archiv* 112 (1.).

Allen, P. R. and Kenen, P. B. (1980) *Asset Markets, Exchange Rates and Economic Integration* (Cambridge, Cambridge University Press).

Anderton, R. and Dunnett, A. (1987) 'Modelling the Behaviour of Export Volumes of Manufactures: An Evaluation of the Performance of Different Measures of International Competitiveness', *National Institute Economic Review*, August.

Anderton, R. and Desai, M. (1988) 'Modelling Manufacturing Imports', *National Institute Economic Review*, February.

Argy, V. and Porter, M. C. (1972) 'The Forward Exchange Market and the Effects of Domestic and External Disturbances under Alternative Exchange Rate Systems', *IMF Staff Papers*, November.

Armington, P. S. (1970) 'Adjustment of Trade Balances: Some Experiments with a Model of Trade Among Many Countries', *IMF Staff Papers*, November.

Artis, M. J. and Taylor, M. P. (1987) 'Exchange Rates, Interest Rates, Capital Controls and the European Monetary System: Assessing the Track Record', in Giavazzi, F. Micossi, S. and Miller, M., *The European Monetary System* (CEPR, Cambridge University Press).

Artus, J. R. (1973) 'The Short Run Effects of Domestic Demand

Pressure on Export Delivery Delays for Machinery', *Journal of International Economics*, February.

Artus, J. R. (1975) 'The 1967 Devaluation of the Pound Sterling', *IMF Staff Papers*, November.

Artus, J. R. and Sosa, S. C. (1978) 'Relative Price Effects on Export Performance: The Case of Nonelectrical Machinery', *IMF Staff Papers*, March.

Atkinson, F. and Hall, S. (1983) *Oil and the British Economy* (London, Croom Helm).

Bacon, R. and Eltis, W. (1976) *Britain's Economic Problem: Too Few Producers* (London, Macmillan).

Bacon, R. and Eltis, W. (1978) 'The Non-market Sector and the Balance of Payments', *National Westminster Bank Quarterly Review*, May.

Bairam, E. (1988) 'Balance of Payments, the Harrod Foreign Trade Multiplier and Economic Growth: the European and North American Experience 1970–85', *Applied Economics*, December.

Bairam, E. (1990) 'The Harrod Foreign Trade Multiplier Revisited', *Applied Economics*, June.

'Balance of Payments: Methods of Presentation' (1964) *Bank of England Quarterly Bulletin*, December.

Balassa, B. (1963) 'Some Observations on Mr Beckerman's "Export-Propelled" Growth Model', *Economic Journal*, December.

Ball, R. J. (1961) 'Credit Restrictions and the Supply of Exports', *Manchester School*, May.

Ball, R. J. (1967) 'The Case Against Devaluation of the Pound', *Bankers' Magazine*, April.

Ball, R. J., Burns, T. and Laury, J. S. (1977) 'The Role of Exchange Rate Changes in Balance of Payments Adjustment: The U.K. Case', *Economic Journal*, March.

Ball, R. J. and Drake, P. S. (1962) 'Export Growth and the Balance of Payments', *Manchester School*, May.

Ball, R. J., Eaton, J. R. and Steuer, M. D. (1966) 'The Relationship Between United Kingdom Export Performance in Manufactures and the Internal Pressure of Demand', *Economic Journal*, September.

Ball, R. J. and Marwah, K. (1962) 'The U.S. Demand for Imports 1948–1958', *Review of Economics and Statistics*, November.

Bank of England (1977) *A Guide to UK Exchange Controls*, London.

Bank of England Quarterly Bulletin (1981a) 'An Inventory of UK External Assets and Liabilities: End-1980', *Bank of England Quarterly Bulletin*, June.

Bank of England Quarterly Bulletin (1981b) 'The Effects of Exchange Control Abolition on Capital Flows', *Bank of England Quarterly Bulletin*, September.

Bank of England Quarterly Bulletin (1982) 'An Inventory of UK External Assets and Liabilities: End-1981', *Bank of England Quarterly Bulletin*, June.

Bank of England Quarterly Bulletin (1983a) 'The External Balance Sheet of the United Kingdom: Developments to End-1982', *Bank of England Quarterly Bulletin*, June.

Bank of England Quarterly Bulletin (1983b) 'UK Banks' External Liabilities and Claims in Sterling: Geographical Analysis', *Bank of England Quarterly Bulletin*, September.

Bank of England Quarterly Bulletin (1984) 'The External Balance Sheet of the United Kingdom: Developments to End-1983', *Bank of England Quarterly Bulletin*, June.

Bank of England Quarterly Bulletin (1985) 'The External Balance Sheet of the United Kingdom: Developments to End-1984', *Bank of England Quarterly Bulletin*, September.

Bank of England Quarterly Bulletin (1986) 'The External Balance Sheet of the United Kingdom: Developments to End-1985', *Bank of England Quarterly Bulletin*, September.

Bank of England Quarterly Bulletin (1987) 'The External Balance Sheet of the United Kingdom: Recent Developments', *Bank of England Quarterly Bulletin*, November.

Bank of England Quarterly Bulletin (1988) 'External Balance Sheet of the United Kingdom: Recent Developments', *Bank of England Quarterly Bulletin*, November.

Barker, T. S. (1968) 'Devaluation and the Rise in U.K. Prices', *Bulletin of the Oxford Institute of Economics and Statistics*, May.

Barker, T. S. (1970a) *The Determinants of Britain's Visible Imports 1949–1966*, Department of Applied Economics, A Programme for Growth No. 10.

Barker, T. S. (1970b) 'Aggregation Error and Estimates of the U.K. Import Demand Function', in *The Econometric Study of the United Kingdom*, Hilton, K. and Heathfield, D. (eds) (London, Macmillan).

Barker, T. S. (1977) International Trade and Economic Growth: An Alternative to the Neoclassical Approach, *Cambridge Journal of Economics*, June.

Barker, T. S. and Lecomber, J. R. C. (1970) ' The Import Content of Final Expenditure for the U.K. ', *Bulletin of the Oxford Institute of*

Economics and Statistics, February.

Barna, T. (1963) 'Fast- and Slow-growing Products in World Trade', *National Institute Economic Review*, August.

Basevi, G. (1973) 'Commodity Trade Equations in Project Link', in Ball, R. J. (ed.), *The International Linkage of Economic Models* (North-Holland, Amsterdam).

Basevi, G. (1988) 'Liberalization of Capital Movements in the EC: A Proposal with Special Reference to the Case of Italy', *European Economy*, May.

Batchelor, R. A. and Bowe, C. (1974) 'Forecasting U.K. International Trade: A General Equilibrium Approach', *Applied Economics*, June.

Bazen, S. and Thirlwall, A. P. (1989) *Deindustrialisation* (London: Heinemann).

Beckerman, W. (1962) 'Projecting Europe's Growth', *Economic Journal*, December.

Beckerman, W. (1963) 'Some Observations on Mr Beckerman's "Export-Propelled" Growth Model: A Reply', *Economic Journal*, December.

Beenstock, M. and Minford, P. (1976) 'A Quarterly Econometric Model of Trade and Prices', in Parkin, M. and Zis, G. (eds), *Inflation in Open Economies* (Manchester, Manchester University Press,).

Bird, G. (1985) *World Finance and Adjustment* (London, Macmillan).

Bird, G. (1987) *International Macroeconomics: Theory, Policy and Applications* (Macmillan, London).

Bisignano, J. and Hoover, K. (1983) 'Some Suggested Improvements to a Simple Portfolio Model of Exchange Rate Determination with Special Reference to the US dollar/Canadian dollar Rate', *Weltwirtschaftliches Archiv*, 119.

Black, I. G., Kidgell, J. E. and Ray, G. F. (1967) 'Forecasting Imports: A Re-examination', *National Institute Economic Review*, November.

Black, J. (1959) 'A Savings and Investment Approach to Devaluation', *Economic Journal*, June.

Black, S. W. (1985) 'The Effect of Alternative Intervention Policies on the Variability of Exchange Rates: The "Harrod" effect"', in Bhandari, J. S. (ed.), *Exchange Rate Management under Uncertainty* (MIT Press, Cambridge MA).

Blackaby, F. (1965) *Britain's Share in World Trade in Manufactures*,

Woolwich Economic Papers No. 8.

Blackaby, F. (ed.) (1979) *Deindustrialisation* (London, Heinemann).

Bliss, C. (1985), 'The Rise and Fall of the Dollar', *Oxford Review of Economic Policy*, Winter.

Blanchard, O. J. and Watson, M. W. (1982) 'Bubbles, Rational Expectations and Financial Markets', in Wachtel, P., *Crisis in the Economic and Financial Structure* (Lexington Books, Lexington, USA).

Bond, S. Davis, E. and Devereux, M. (1987) *Capital Controls: The Implications of Restricting Overseas Portfolio Capital* (Institute of Fiscal Studies, London).

Branson, W. H. (1972) *The Trade Effects of the 1971 Currency Realignment*, Brookings Papers on Economic Activity No. 1.

Branson, W. H. Halttunen, H. and Masson, P. (1979) 'Exchange Rates in the Short Run', *European Economic Review*, October.

Brechling, F. and Wolfe, J. N. (1965) 'The End of Stop-Go', *Lloyds Bank Review*, January.

Brech, M. J. and Stout, D. (1981), 'The Rate of Exchange and Non-Price Competitiveness: A Provisional Study within U.K. Manufactured Exports', *Oxford Economic Papers* (Supplement), July.

British Export Trade Research Organisation (1975) *Export Concentration* (London).

Brooman, F. (1970) *Macroeconomics* (London, Allen & Unwin).

Brown, A. J. (1942) 'Trade Balances and Exchange Stability', *Oxford Economic Papers*, April.

Cairncross, A. and Eichengreen, B. (1983) *Sterling in Decline* (Oxford, Basil Blackwell).

Caves, R. (1970) 'Export-led Growth: The Post-war Industrial Setting', in Eltis, W., Scott, M. and Wolfe, J. N. (eds), *Induction, Trade and Growth*, (London, Oxford University Press).

Cecchini, P. (1988) *The European Challenge 1992* (Wildwood House).

Central Policy Review Staff (1975) *The Future of the British Car Industry* (London, HMSO).

Chrystal, K. A. (1989) 'International Reserves and International Liquidity', Conference on The International Financial Regime, University of Surrey, 12–13 September.

Connell, D. (1979) *The U.K.'s Performance in Export Markets – Some Evidence from International Trade Data*, NEDO Discussion Paper No. 6.

Cooper, R., Hartley, K. and Harvey, C. (1970) *Export Performance and the Pressure of Demand* (London, Allen & Unwin).

Coppock, D. J. (1965) 'The Alleged Case Against Devaluation', *Manchester School*, September.

Coppock, D. J. (1978) 'Some Thoughts on the Monetary Approach to Balance of Payments Theory', *Manchester School*, September.

Coppock, D. J. and Metcalfe, J. S. (1974) 'Foreign Trade and the Balance of Payments', in Prest, A. R. and Coppock, D. (eds), *The U.K. Economy: A Manual of Applied Economics*, 5th edn (London, Weidenfeld & Nicolson).

Corden, W. M. (1983) 'Is There an Important Role for an International Reserve Asset Such as the SDR?', in von Furstenberg, G. M. (ed.), *International Money and Credit: The Policy Roles* (International Monetary Fund, Washington DC).

Cornwall, J. (1977) *Modern Capitalism: Its Growth and Transformation* (London, Martin Robertson).

Cripps, F. and Godley, W. (1976) 'A Formal Analysis of the Cambridge Economic Policy Group Model', *Economica*, November.

Crockett, A. D. and Goldstein, M. (1976) 'Inflation Under Fixed and Flexible Exchange Rates', *IMF Staff Papers*, November.

Crossman, R. (1976) *The Diaries of a Cabinet Minister: vol. 2 Lord President of the Council and Leader of the House of Commons, 1966–68* (London, Hamilton/Cape).

Currie, D. (1978) *Monetary and Fiscal Policy and the Crowding-out Issue*, Discussion Paper No. 53 (London, Queen Mary College).

Cuthbertson, K. (1985) 'The Behaviour of UK Imports of Manufactured Goods', *National Institute Economic Review*, August.

Davies, G. (1989) *Britain and the European Monetary Question*, IPPR. Economic Study, no. 1.

Davies, R. (1976) On the Relation Between Product Differentiation and International Trade Flows, University of Bath Discussion Paper.

Dennis, G. and Nellis, J. (1984) 'The EMS and UK Membership: Five Years On', *Lloyds Bank Review*, October.

Deppler, M. C. (1974) 'Some Evidence on the Effects of Exchange Rate Changes on Trade', *IMF Staff Papers*, November.

Deppler, M. C. and Ripley, D. M. (1978), The World Trade Model: Merchandise Trade, *IMF Staff Papers*, March.

Dixon, R. J. and Thirlwall, A. P. (1975a) 'A Model of Regional Growth Rate Differences on Kaldorian Lines', *Oxford Economic Papers*, July.

Dixon, R. J. and Thirlwall, A. P. (1975b) *Regional Growth and Unemployment in the United Kingdom* (London, Macmillan).

Dornbusch, R. (1976) 'Expectations and Exchange Rate Dynamics', *Journal of Political Economy*, October.

Dornbusch, R. (1981) 'Evidence to the Treasury and Civil Service Committee', *Memoranda on Monetary Policy*, HC770 (London, HMSO).

Dornbusch, R. and Fischer, S. (1980) 'Exchange Rates and the Current Account', *American Economic Review*, December.

Duffy, M. and Renton, A. G. (1970) 'A Model of U.K. Exports of Manufactures to Industrial Countries', *Applied Economics*, vol. 2, no. 3.

Dunning, J. H. and Pearce, R. D. (1985) *The World's Largest Industrial Enterprises 1982–1983* (London, Gower).

Eltis, W. (1967) 'Economic Growth and the British Balance of Payments', *District Bank Review*, December.

Enoch, C. A. (1978) 'Measures of Competitiveness in International Trade', *Bank of England Quarterly Review*, June.

Fagerberg, J. (1988), 'International Competitiveness', *Economic Journal*, June.

Fausten, D. (1975) *The Consistency of British Balance of Payments Policies* (London, Macmillan).

Flanders, M. J. (1963) 'The Effects of Devaluation on Exports: A Case Study, United Kingdom 1949–1954', *Bulletin of the Oxford Institute of Economics and Statistics*, August.

Fleming, J. M. (1962) 'Domestic Financial Policies Under Fixed and Floating Exchange Rates', *IMF Staff Papers*, November.

Fleming, J. M. and Tsiang, S. C. (1956) 'Changes in Competitive Strength and Export Shares of Major Industrial Countries', *IMF Staff Papers*, August.

Flood, R. P. and Garber, P. M. (1982) 'Bubbles, Runs and Gold Monetization', in Wachtel, P., *Crisis in the Economic and Financial Structure* (Lexington Books, Lexington, USA).

Frankel, J. A. (1979) 'On the Mark: a Theory of Floating Exchange Rates Based on Real Interest Differentials', *American Economic Review*, September.

Frankel, J. A. and Froot, K. A. (1987) 'Using Survey Data to Test Standard Propositions Regarding Exchange Rate Expectations', *American Economic Review*, February.

Fraser, P. Taylor, M. P. and Webster, A. (1990) *An Empirical Analysis of Long-run Purchasing Power Parity As A Theory of International*

Arbitrage, Dundee Discussion Papers in Economics, no. 3.

Freeman, C. (1965) 'Research and Development in Electronic Capital Goods, *National Institute Economic Review*', November.

Freeman, C. (1979) 'Technical Innovation and British Trade Performance', in Blackaby, F. (ed.), *Deindustrialisation* (London, Heinemann).

Frenkel, J. A. (1981) 'The Collapse of Purchasing Power Parities During the 1970s', *European Economic Review*, 16.

Frenkel, J. A. (1983) 'International Liquidity and Monetary Control', in von Furstenberg, G. M. (ed.), *International Money and Credit: The Policy Roles* (International Monetary Fund, Washington DC).

Frenkel, J. A. and Johnson, H. G. (eds) (1976) *The Monetary Approach to the Balance of Payments* (London, Allen & Unwin).

Friedman, M. (1953) 'The Case for Flexible Exchange Rates', in *Essays in Positive Economics* (Chicago University Press).

Genberg, H. and Kierzkowski, H. (1979) 'Impact and Long Run Effects of Economic Disturbances in a Dynamic Model of Exchange Rate Determination', *Weltwirtschaftliches Archiv*, CXV.

Gibson, H. D. (1989) *The Eurocurrency Markets, Domestic Financial Policy and International Instability* (London, Macmillan).

Gibson, H. D. and Tsakalotos, E. (1990) 'Capital Flight and Financial Liberalisation: A Study of Five European Countries', Paper presented at the European Economic Association Conference, Lisbon, Portugal, September.

Gilbert, R. S. and Major, R. L. (1961) 'Britain's Falling Share of Sterling Area Imports', *National Institute Economic Review*, March.

Godley, W. and Shepherd, J. (1965) 'Forecasting Imports', *National Institute Economic Review*, August.

Goldstein, M. (1973) 'Downward Price Inflexibility, Ratchet Effects and the Inflationary Impact of Import Price Changes: Some Empirical Evidence', *IMF Staff Papers*, November.

Goldstein, M. (1974) 'The Effect of Exchange Rate Changes on Wages and Prices in the U.K.: An Empirical Study', *IMF Staff Papers*, November.

Goldstein, M. and Khan, M. S. (1976) 'Large versus Small Price Changes and the Demand for Imports', *IMF Staff Papers*, March.

Goldstein, M. and Khan, M. S. (1978) The Supply and Demand for Exports: A Simultaneous Approach, *Review of Economics and Statistics*, May.

Goldstein, M., Khan, M. S. and Officer, L. H. (1980) 'Prices of Tradeable and Non-Tradeable Goods in the Demand for Total Imports', *Review of Economics and Statistics*, May.

Goldstein, M. and Khan, M. S. (1985) 'Income and Price Effects in Foreign Trade', in Jones, R. W. and Kenen, P. B. (eds), *Handbook of International Economics, Vol. II* (Amsterdam, North-Holland).

Greenhalgh, C. (1990) 'Innovation and Trade Performance in the United Kingdom', *Economic Journal*, Supplement.

Gregory, R. G. (1971) 'United States Imports and the Internal Pressure of Demand 1948–1968', *American Economic Review*, March.

Gribbin, J. (1971) *The Profitability of U.K. Exports*, Government Economic Service Occasional Papers No. 1 (London, HMSO).

Grubel, H. G. and Lloyd, P. J. (1971) 'The Empirical Measurement of Intra-Industry Trade', *Economic Record*, December.

Gylfason, T. (1978) 'The Effect of Exchange Rate Changes on the Balance of Trade in Ten Industrial Countries', unpublished (IMF, Washington).

Haberler, G. (1949) 'The Market for Foreign Exchange and the Stability of the Balance of Payments: A Theoretical Analysis', *Kyklos*, fasc. 3.

Hacche, G. and Townend, J. (1981) 'Exchange Rates and Monetary Policy: Modelling Sterling's Effective Exchange Rate, 1972–80', in Eltis, W. A. and Sinclair, P. J. N., *The Money Supply and the Exchange Rate* (Oxford, Oxford University Press).

Hagen, S. (1985) *Languages in British Business: An Analysis of Current Needs* (Newcastle upon Tyne Polytechnic).

Hague, D. C., Oakeshott, E. and Strain, A. (1974) *Devaluation and Pricing Decisions* (London, Allen & Unwin).

Hahn, F. (1977) 'The Monetary Approach to the Balance of Payments', *Journal of International Economics*, August.

Harberger, A. (1950) 'Currency Depreciation, Income and the Balance of Trade', *Journal of Political Economy*, February.

Harberger, A. (1953) 'A Structural Approach to the Problem of Import Demand', *American Economic Review*, Papers and Proceedings, May.

Harberger, A. (1957) 'Some Evidence of the International Price Mechanism', *Journal of Political Economy*, December.

Harrod, R. (1933) *International Economics* (London, Macmillan).

Harrod, R. (1947) *Are These Hardships Necessary?* (London, Hart-Davis).

Harrod, R. (1965) *Reforming the World's Money* (London, Macmillan).

Harrod, R. (1967a) 'Assessing the Trade Returns', *Economic Journal*, September.

Harrod, R. (1967b) *Towards a New Economic Policy* (Manchester, Manchester University Press).

Harrod, R. (1968a) 'The British Economy and Prospects for Sterling', *Bankers' Magazine*, January.

Harrod, R. (1968b) 'Devaluation – The Year After', *Bankers' Magazine*, December.

Hawtrey, R. (1969a) 'The Case for a Floating Pound', *Bankers' Magazine*, June.

Hawtrey, R. (1969b) 'A Stable Floating Pound', *Bankers' Magazine*, December.

Heller, H. R. (1976) 'International Reserves and World-wide Inflation', *IMF Staff Papers*, March.

Heller, H. R. and Khan, M. S. (1978) 'The Demand for International Reserves Under Fixed and Floating Exchange Rates', *IMF Staff Papers*, December.

Hemming, M. F. W. and Ray, G. (1959) 'Imports and Expansion', *National Institute Economic Review*, March.

Henderson, H. D. (1949) 'The Function of Exchange Rates', *Oxford Economic Papers*, January.

Henry, G. (1970) 'Domestic Demand Pressure and Short Run Export Fluctuations', *Yale Economic Essays*, Spring.

Hibberd, J. and Wren-Lewis, S. (1978) *A Study of U.K. Imports of Manufactures*, Government Economic Service Working Paper No. 6 (London, HMSO).

Hickman, B. and Lau, L. (1973) 'Elasticities of Substitution and Export Demand in a World Trade Model', *European Economic Review*, December.

Hicks, J. R. (1966) *After the Boom: Thoughts on the 1966 Economic Crisis* (London, Institute of Economic Affairs).

Hirsch, F. and Higham, D. (1974) 'Floating Rates – Expectation and Experience', *Three Banks Reveiw*, June.

Hirsch, S. (1967) *Location of Industry and International Competitiveness* (Oxford, Clarendon Press).

Holmes, P. M. (1978) *Industrial Pricing Behaviour and Devaluation* (London, Macmillan).

Horne, J. (1979) 'The Effect of Devaluation on the Balance of

Payments and the Labour Market: United Kingdom 1967', *Economica*, February.

House of Lords (1985) *Report of the Select Committee on Overseas Trade* (HMSO).

Houthakker, H. S. and Magee, S. P. (1969) 'Income and Price Elasticities in World Trade', *Review of Economics and Statistics*, May.

Hovell, P. (1968) 'Export Pricing Policies', *District Bank Review*, September.

Hughes, J. J. and Thirlwall, A. P. (1977) 'Trends and Cycles in Import Penetration in the U.K.: A Disaggregated Study', *Bulletin of the Oxford Institute of Economics and Statistics*, November.

Hughes, J. J. and Thirlwall, A. P. (1979) 'Imports and Labour Market Bottlenecks: A Disaggregated Study for the U.K.', *Applied Economics*, March.

Humphrey, D. H. (1976) 'Disaggregated Import Functions for the U.K., West Germany and France', *Bulletin of the Oxford Institute of Economics and Statistics*, November.

Hutchison, T. W. (1977) *Knowledge and Ignorance in Economics* (Oxford, Blackwell).

Hutton, J. B. and Minford, A. P. L. (1975) *A Model of U.K. Manufacturing Exports and Export Prices*, Government Economic Service Occasional Paper No. 11 (London, HMSO).

Imlah, A. H. (1958) *Economic Elements in the Pax Britannica* (Cambridge, Mass., Harvard University Press).

Ingram, J. C. (1978) 'Expectations and Floating Exchange Rates', *Weltwirtschaftliches Archiv*, CXIV.

Isard, P. (1977) 'How Far can we Push the Law of One Price?', *American Economic Review*, December.

Isard, P. (1978) *Exchange Rate Determination: A Survey of Popular Views and Recent Models*, Princeton Studies in International Finance, no. 42.

Isard, P. (1987) 'Lessons from Empirical Models of Exchange Rates', *IMF Staff Papers*, March.

Johnson, H. G. (1958) 'Towards a General Theory of the Balance of Payments', in *International Trade and Economic Growth* (London, Allen & Unwin).

Johnson, H. G. (1970) 'The Case for Flexible Exchange Rates, 1969', *Federal Reserve Bank of St Louis*, 52.

Johnson, H. G. (1972) 'The Monetary Approach to Balance of

Payments Theory', *Journal of Financial and Quantitative Analysis*, March.

Johnson, H. G. (1973) 'The Monetary Approach to Balance of Payments Theory', in *Further Essays in Monetary Economics* (London, Allen & Unwin).

Johnson, H. G. (1977a) 'The Monetary Approach to Balance of Payments Theory and Policy: Explanation and Policy Implications', *Economica*, August.

Johnson, H. G. (1977b) 'The Monetary Approach to the Balance of Payments', *Journal of International Economics*, August.

Johnston, J. and Henderson, M. (1967) 'Assessing the Effects of the Import Surcharge', *Manchester School*, May.

Junz, H. and Rhomberg, R. (1965) 'Prices and Export Performance of Industrial Countries, 1953–63', *IMF Staff Papers*, July.

Junz, H. and Rhomberg, R. (1973) 'Price Competitiveness in Export Trade Among Industrial Countries', *American Economic Review*, Papers and Proceedings, May.

Kaldor, N. (1970) 'The Case for Regional Policies', *Scottish Journal of Political Economy*, November.

Kaldor, N. (1974) 'The Road to Recovery', *New Statesman*, 1 March.

Kaldor, N. (1978) 'The Effect of Devaluations on Trade in Manufactures', in *Further Essays on Applied Economics* (London, Duckworth).

Katseli-Papaefstratiou, L. T. (1979) *The Reemergence of the Purchasing Power Parity Doctrine in the 1970s*, Princeton Special Papers in Economics, no. 13.

Kay, J. and Forsyth, P. (1980) 'The Economic Implications of North Sea Oil Revenues', *Fiscal Studies*, July.

Kenen, P. (1975) *Floats, Glides and Indicators*, International Finance Section (Princeton University Press).

Kennedy, C. and Thirlwall, A. P. (1979a), 'The Foreign Trade Multiplier Revisited', in Currie, D. and Peters, W. (eds) *Proceeding of the A.U.T.E. Conference 1978* (London, Croom Helm).

Kennedy, C. and Thirlwall, A. P. (1979b) 'The Input-Output Formulation of the Foreign Trade Multiplier', *Australian Economic Papers*, June.

Kennedy, C. and Thirlwall, A. P. (1979c) 'Import Penetration, Export Performance and Harrod's Trade Multiplier', *Oxford Economic Papers*, July.

Kern, D. (1978) 'An International Comparison of Major Economic Trends 1953–76', *National Westminster Bank Quarterly Review*, May.

Key Statistics 1900–1966, London and Cambridge Economic Service.

Khan, M. S. and Ross, K. Z. (1975) 'Cyclical and Secular Income Elasticities of the Demand for Imports', *Review of Economics and Statistics*, August.

Kindleberger, C. P. (1969) 'Measuring Equilibrium in the Balance of Payments', *Journal of Political Economy*, November–December.

Klein, T. M. (1964) 'The United Kingdom Balance of Payments Accounts', *Economic Journal*, December.

Kravis, I. (1956) 'Availability and Other Influences on the Commodity Composition of Trade', *Journal of Political Economy*, April.

Kravis, I. and Lipsey, R. E. (1978) 'Price Behaviour in the Light of Balance of Payments Theories', *Journal of International Economics*, May.

Kreinin, M. E. (1967) 'Price Elasticities in International Trade', *Review of Economics and Statistics*, November.

Kreinin, M. E. (1977) 'The Effect of Exchange Rate Changes on the Prices and Volume of Foreign Trade', *IMF Staff Papers*, July.

Krueger, A. (1969) 'Balance of Payments Theory', *Journal of Economic Literature*, March.

Krueger, A. O. (1983) *Exchange Rate Determination* (Cambridge, Cambridge University Press).

Krugman, P. R. (1978) 'Puchasing Power Parity and Exchange Rates: Another Look at the Evidence', *Journal of International Economics*, August.

Krugman, P. (1989) 'Differences in Income Elasticities and Trends in Real Exchange Rates', *European Economic Review*, May.

Lamfalussy, A. (1963) *The United Kingdom and the Six* (London, Macmillan).

Lamfalussy, A. (1976) 'Beyond Bretton Woods: Floating Exchange Rates and Capital Movements', in Thirlwall, A. P. (ed.) *Keynes and International Monetary Relations* (London, Macmillan).

Lancaster, K. (1971), *Consumer Demand: A New Approach* (New York: Columbia University Press).

Landesmann, M. and Snell, A. (1989), 'The Consequences of Mrs Thatcher for UK Manufacturing Exports', *Economic Journal*, March.

Laursen, S. and Metzler, L. (1950) 'Flexible Exchange Rates and the Theory of Employment', *Review of Economics and Statistics*, November.

Leamer, E. and Stern, R. M. (1970) *Quantitative International Economics* (Boston, Allyn & Bacon).

Lessard, D. R. and Williamson, J. (1987) *Capital Flight and Third World Debt* (Institute for International Economics, Washington DC).

London and Cambridge Economic Service (1968) *Key Statistics 1900–1966*.

McCombie, J. (1980) 'Are International Growth Rates Constrained by the Balance of Payments: A Comment on Professor Thirlwall', *Banca Nazionale del Lavoro Quarterly Review*, December.

McCombie, J. (1985) 'Economic Growth, the Harrod Foreign Trade Multiplier and the Hicks Super Multiplier', *Applied Economics*, February.

McCombie, J. (1989) 'Thirlwall's Law and Balance of Payments Constrained Growth – A Comment on the Debate', *Applied Economics*, April.

McCombie, J. and Thirlwall, A. P. (1992) *Economic Growth and the Balance of Payments Constraint* (London, Macmillan).

MacDonald, R. and Torrance, T. S. (1988) 'On Risk, Rationality and Excessive Speculation in the Deutschmark – US Dollar Exchange Market: Some Evidence Using Survey Data', *Oxford Bulletin of Economics and Statistics*, May.

MacDonald, R. (1988) *Floating Exchange Rates: Theories and Evidence* (London, Unwin Hyman).

MacGeehan, J. M. (1968) 'Competitiveness: A Study of the Recent Literature', *Economic Journal*, June.

McGregor, P. G. and Swales, J. K. (1985) 'Professor Thirlwall and Balance of Payments Constrained Growth', *Applied Economics*, February.

McGregor, P. G. and Swales, J. K. (1986) 'Balance of Payments Constrained Growth: A Rejoinder to Professor Thirlwall', *Applied Economics*, December.

McKinnon, R. I. (1969) *Private and Official Money: The Case for the Dollar*, Princeton Essays in International Finance, no. 74.

Machlup, F. (1950) 'Three Concepts of the Balance of Payments and the So-Called Dollar Shortage', *Economic Journal*, March.

Machlup, F. (1955) 'Relative Prices and Aggregate Spending in the

Analysis of Devaluation', *American Economic Review*, June.

Machlup, F. (1956) 'The Terms of Trade Effects of Devaluation upon Real Income and the Balance of Trade', *Kyklos*, fasc. 4.

Machlup, F. (1973) 'Exchange Rate Flexibility', *Banca Nazionale del Lavoro Quarterly Review*, September.

Magee, S. P. (1974) 'Prices, Income and Foreign Trade', in *International Trade and Finance: Frontiers for Research*, ed. Kenen, P. B. (Cambridge University Press).

Major, R. L. (1960) 'World Trade in Manufactures', *National Institute Economic Review*, July.

Major, R. L. (1968) 'Note on Britain's Share of World Trade in Manufactures 1954–1966', *National Institute Economic Review*, May.

Marston, R. (1971) 'Income Effects and Delivery Lags in British Import Demand 1955–1967', *Journal of International Economics*, November.

Masera, R. (1974) 'The J-Curve: UK Experience After the 1967 Devaluation', *Metroeconomica*, December – January.

Mayes, D., Buxton, T. and Murfin, A. (1988) 'R & D, Innovation and trade Performance', NEDO, unpublished.

Meade, J. E. (1951) *The Theory of International Economic Policy: Vol. 1 The Balance of Payments* (Oxford University Press).

Meade, J. E. (1966) 'Exchange Rate Flexibility', *Three Banks Review*, June.

Meese, R. A. and Rogoff, K. (1983) 'Empirical Exchange Rate Models of the Seventies: Do They Fit Out of Sample?', *Journal of International Economics*, No. 14.

Meese, R. A. and Rogoff, K. (1984) 'The Out of Sample Failure of Empirical Exchange Rate Models: Sampling Error or Misspecification?', in Frenkel, J. A. (ed.) *Exchange Rates and International Macroeconomics* (Chicago, NBER).

Michaely, M. (1960) 'Relative Prices and Income-Absorption Approaches to Devaluation: A Partial Reconciliation', *American Economic Review*, March.

Midland Bank Review (1979) 'Britain and the European Monetary System', Winter.

Mitchell, B. R. and Deane, P. (1962) *Abstract of British Historical Statistics* (Cambridge University Press).

Morgan, A. D. (1970) 'Income and Price Elasticities in World Trade: A Comment', *Manchester School*, December.

Morgan, A. D. (1971) 'Imports of Manufactures into the UK and Other Industrial Countries 1955–69', *National Institute Economic Review*, May.

Morgan, A. D. and Martin, A. (1975) 'Tariff Reductions and UK Imports of Manufactures 1955–71', *National Institute Economic Review*, May.

Mundell, R. (1960) 'The Monetary Dynamics of International Adjustment Under Fixed and Flexible Exchange Rates', *Quarterly Journal of Economics*, May.

Mundell, R. (1961) 'Flexible Exchange Rates and Employment Policy', *Canadian Journal of Economics*, November.

Mundell, R. (1962) 'The Appropriate Use of Monetary and Fiscal Policies for Internal and External Stability', *IMF Staff Papers*, March.

Mundell, R. (1963) 'Capital Mobility and Stabilisation Policy Under Fixed and Flexible Exchange Rates', *Canadian Journal of Economics*, November.

Mussa, M. (1974) 'Monetary Approach to Balance of Payments Analysis', *Journal of Money, Credit and Banking*, August.

National Economic Development Council (1963) *Export Trends* (London, HMSO).

National Economic Development Council (1965) *Investment in Machine Tools: A Survey by the Management Consultants' Association* (London, HMSO).

National Economic Development Council (1990) *United Kingdom Trade Performance*, Document NEDC (90)10.

National Economic Development Office (1965) *Imported Manufactures: An Inquiry into Competitiveness* (London HMSO).

National Institute of Economic and Social Research (1972) 'The Effects of the Devaluation of 1967 on the Current Balance of Payments', *Economic Journal*, Supplement, March.

Odling-Smee, J. and Hartley, N. (1978) *Some Effects of Exchange Rate Changes*, Government Economic Service Working Paper No. 2 (London, HMSO).

Officer, L. H. (1976) 'The Purchasing-Power-Parity Theory of Exchange Rates: A review article', *IMF Staff Papers*, March.

Oppenheimer, P. M. (1965) 'Is Britain's Worsening Trade Gap due to Bad Management of the Business Cycle?', *Bulletin of the Oxford Institute of Economics and Statistics*, August.

Orcutt, G. H. (1950) 'Measurement of Price Elasticities in International Trade', *Review of Economics and Statistics*, May.

Orr, D. (1978) 'The Customer Rules O.K.', *Sunday Times*, 9 August.

Page, S. A. B. (1975) 'The Effect of Exchange Rates on Export Market Shares', *National Institute Economic Review*, November.

Pain, N. and Westaway, P. (1990) 'Why the Capital Account Matters', *National Institute Economic Review*, February.

Paish, F. W. (1968) 'How the Economy Works', *Lloyds Bank Review*, April.

Paish, F. W. (1969) *Rise and Fall of Incomes Policies*, Hobart Paper No. 47 (London, Institute of Economic Affairs).

Panić, M. (1968) 'British Imports of Manufactured Goods', *Business Ratios*, Winter.

Panić, M. (1975) 'Why the UK's Propensity to Import is High', *Lloyds Bank Review*, January.

Panić, M. and Rajan, A. H. (1979) *Product Changes in Industrial Countries' Trade*, 2nd edn (London, NEDO).

Panić, M. and Seward, T. (1966) 'The Problem of UK Exports', *Bulletin of the Oxford Institute of Economics and Statistics*, February

Parker, A. (1978) *Exchange Controls*, Jordans, London

Patel, P. and Pavitt, K. (1989) 'A Comparison of Technological Activities in West Germany and the United Kingdom', *National Westminster Bank Review*, May.

Pavitt, K. (ed.) (1980) *Technical Innovation and British Economic Performance* (London, Macmillan).

Pavitt, K. and Soete, L. (1980) 'Innovative Activities and Export Shares: Some Comparisons Between Industries and Countries', in Pavitt, K. (ed.), *Technical Innovation and British Economic Performance* (London, Macmillan).

Pearce, I. F. (1961) 'The Problem of the Balance of Payments', *International Economic Review*, January.

Pittis, N. (1989) *On the Exchange Rate of the Dollar: Market Fundamentals Versus Speculative Bubbles*, Department of Economics, Birkbeck College, October.

Posner, M. (1961) 'International Trade and Technical Change', *Oxford Economic Papers*, October.

Posner, M. and Steer, A. (1979) 'Price Competitiveness and the Performance of Manufacturing Industry', in Blackaby (1979).

Prais, S. J. (1962) 'Econometric Research in International Trade: A Review', *Kyklos*, fasc. 3.

Radcliffe Committee (1959) *Report on the Working of the Monetary System*, Cmnd 827 (London, HMSO).

Ray, G. F. (1966) *The Competitiveness of British Industrial Products: A Round-Up*, Woolwich Economic Paper No. 10.

Rees, R. and Layard, P. (1971) *Determinants of UK Imports*, Government Economic Service Occasional Paper No. 3 (London, HMSO).

Renton, G. A. (1967) 'Forecasting British Exports of Manufactures to Industrial Countries', *National Institute Economic Review*, November.

Robinson, J. (1937) 'The Foreign Exchanges', in *Essays in the Theory of Employment* (Oxford, Blackwell).

Robinson, J. (1966) *Economics: An Awkward Corner* (London, Allen & Unwin).

Rosendale, P. (1973) 'The Short Run Pricing Policies of Some British Engineering Exporters', *National Institute Economic Review*, August.

Rowan, D. C. (1976) 'Godley's Law, Godley's Rule and the "New Cambridge Macro Economics"', *Banca Nazionale del Lavoro Quarterly Review*, June.

Rowthorn, R. E. and Wells, J. R. (1987) *De-Industrialisation and Foreign Trade* (Cambridge, Cambridge University Press).

Samuelson, L. (1973) *A New Model of World Trade*, OECD Occasional Studies (OECD, Paris).

Samuelson, P. A. (1964) 'Theoretical Notes on Trade Problems', *Review of Economics and Statistics*, May.

Scott, M. (1973) *A Study of UK Imports* (Cambridge University Press).

Singh, A. (1977) 'UK Industry and the World Economy: A Case of De-industrialisation?', *Cambridge Journal of Economics*, June.

Smith, M. (1986) 'UK Manufacturing: Output and Trade Performance', *Midland Bank Review*, Autumn.

Smyth, D. J. (1968) 'Stop-Go and United Kingdom Exports of Manufactures', *Bulletin of the Oxford Institute of Economics and Statistics*, February.

Smyth, D. J. (1969) 'The Effect of Internal Demand Pressure on United Kingdom Imports of Manufactures', *Journal of Economic Studies*, November.

Sohmen, E. (1961) *Flexible Exchange Rates: Theory and Controversy* (Chicago University Press).

Steinherr, A. and De Schrevel, G. (1988) 'Liberalization of Financial Transactions in the Community with Particular Reference to Belgium, Denmark and the Netherlands', *European Economy*, May.

Stern, R. M. (1973) *Balance of Payments Theory and Economic Policy* (London, Macmillan).

Stern, R. M., Francis, T. and Schumacher, B. (1976) *Price Elasticities in International Trade – An Annotated Bibliography* (London, Macmillan).

Steuer, M. D., Ball, R. J. and Eaton, J. R. (1966) 'The Effect of Waiting Times on Foreign Orders for Machine Tools', *Economica*, November.

Stewart, M. (1977) *The Jekyll and Hyde Years: Politics and Economic Policy Since 1964* (London, Dent).

Stout, D. (1977) *International Price Competitiveness, Non-Price Factors and Export Performance* (London, NEDO).

Swan, T. (1963) 'Longer Run Problems of the Balance of Payments', in Arndt, H. W. and Corden, M. (eds) *The Australian Economy* (Melbourne, Cheshire).

Taplin, G. R. (1973) 'A Model of World Trade', in *The International Linkage of National Economic Models*, ed. Ball, R. J. (Amsterdam, North-Holland).

Thirlwall, A. P. (1970) 'Another Autopsy on Britain's Balance of Payments: 1958–67', *Banca Nazionale del Lavoro Quarterly Review*, September.

Thirlwall, A. P. (1974) 'The Panacea of the Floating Pound', *National Westminster Bank Quarterly Review*, August.

Thirlwall, A. P. (1978) 'The UK's Economic Problem: A Balance of Payments Constraint', *National Westminster Bank Quarterly Review*, February.

Thirlwall, A. P. (1979a) 'The Interaction Between Changes in Income and Changes in Absorption in the Absorption Approach to the Balance of Payments', *Journal of Macroeconomics, Spring*.

Thirlwall, A. P. (1979b) 'The Balance of Payments Constraint as an Explanation of International Growth Rate Differences, *Banca Nazionale del Lavoro Quarterly Review*, March.

Thirlwall, A. P. (1982a) 'The Harrod Trade Multiplier and the Importance of Export Led Growth', *Pakistan Journal of Applied Economics*, March.

Thirlwall, A. P. (1982b) 'Deindustrialisation in the United Kingdom', *Lloyds Bank Review*, April.

Thirlwall, A. P. (1983a) 'Symposium on Kaldor's Growth Laws', *Journal of Post-Keynesian Economics*, Spring.

Thirlwall, A. P. (1983b) 'A Trade Strategy for the United Kingdom'. *Journal of Common Market Studies*, September.

Thirlwall, A. P. (1986) 'Balance of Payments Constrained Growth: A Reply to McGregor and Swales', *Applied Economics*.

Thirlwall, A. P. (1991) 'Professor Krugman's 45-degree Rule', *Journal of Post Keynesian Economics*.

Thirlwall, A. P. and Hussain, M. (1982) 'The Balance of Payments Constraint, Capital Flows and Growth Rate Differences Between Developing Countries', *Oxford Economic Papers*, November.

Thirlwall, A. P. and Thirlwall, G. (1979) 'Factors Governing the Growth of Labour Productivity [translation of P. J. Verdoorn's article in *L'industria*, 1949], in Ironmonger, D., Perkin, I. and Hoa, T. (eds) *National Income and Economic Progress: Essays in Honour of Colin Clark* (London, Macmillan, 1988).

Thirlwall, A. P. and White, H. (1974) 'US Merchandise Imports and the Dispersion of Market Demand', *Applied Economics*, December.

Tobin, J. (1978) 'A Proposal for International Monetary Reform', *Eastern Economic Journal*.

Triffin, R. (1947) 'National Central Banking and the International Economy', *Review of Economic Studies*, February.

Triffin, R. (1960) *Gold and the Dollar Crisis: The Future of Convertibility* (New Haven, Yale University Press).

Triffin, R. (1978) *Gold and Dollar Crisis: Yesterday and Tomorrow*, Essays in International Finance No. 132, Princeton University, December.

Tsegaye, A. (1981) 'The Specification of the Foreign Trade Multiplier for a Developing Country', *Oxford Bulletin of Economics and Statistics*, August.

Tsiang, S. G. (1961) 'The Role of Money in Trade Balance Stability: Synthesis of the Elasticity and Absorption Approaches', *American Economic Review*, December.

Tsiang, S. G. (1977) 'The Monetary Theoretic Foundation of the Modern Monetary Approach to the Balance of Payments', *Oxford Economic Papers*, November.

Turner, D. (1988) 'Does the UK Face a Balance of Payments Constraint on Growth? – A Quantitative Analysis Using the LBS and NIESR Models', ESRC Macroeconomic Modelling Bureau, University of Warwick, Discussion Paper No. 16, September.

Vernon, R. (1966) 'International Investment and International Trade in the Product Cycle', *Quarterly Journal of Economics*, May.

Viner, J. (1964) *Problems of Monetary Control* (Princeton University Press).

Wells, S. (1964) *British Export Performance: A Comparative Study* (Cambridge University Press).

Whitley, J. D. (1979) 'Imports of Finished Manufactures: The Effects of Prices, Demand and Capacity', *Manchester School*, December.

Whitman, M. (1970) *Policies for Internal and External Balance*, Special Papers in International Economics No. 9 (Princeton University Press).

Whitman, M. (1974) *The Current and Future Role of the Dollar: How Much Symmetry?*, Brookings Papers on Economic Activity, No. 3.

Whitman, M. (1975) *Global Monetarism and the Monetary Approach to the Balance of Payments*, Brookings Papers on Economic Activity No. 3

von Furstenberg, G. M. (ed.) (1983) *International Money and Credit: The Policy Roles* (International Monetary Fund, Washington DC).

Williamson, J. H. (1965) *The Crawling Peg*, International Finance Section, Princeton University.

Williamson, J. H. (1971) 'On the Normative Theory of Balance of Payments Adjustment', in Clayton, G., Gilbert, J. and Sedgwick, R. (eds) *Monetary Theory and Monetary Policy in the 1970's*, (Oxford University Press).

Williamson, J. H. (1982a) 'The Growth of Official Reserves and the Issue of World Monetary Control', in Dreyer, J. S., Harbeler, G. and Willett, T. D. (eds) *The International Monetary System: A Time of Turbulence* (American Enterprise Institute, Washington DC).

Williamson, J. H. (1982b) 'A Survey on the Literature on the Optimal Peg', *Journal of Development Economics*, September.

Williamson, J. H. (1983) *The Exchange Rate System*, Institute for International Economics, Washington.

Williamson, J. H. (1984) 'Is There an External Constraint?', *National Institute Economic Review*, August.

Williamson, J. H. (1984) 'International Liquidity: Are the Supply and Composition Appropriate?', reprinted in Milner, C. (ed.) *Political Economy and International Money* (Harvester Wheatsheaf, 1987)

Williamson, J. H. and Miller, M. H. (1987) *Targets and Indicators: A Blueprint for the International Coordination of Economic Policy*, Institute for International Economics, Policy Analyses in International Economics, No. 22 (Washington DC).

Wilson, H. (1971) *The Labour Government 1964–1970* (London, Weidenfeld & Nicolson).

Wilson, J. F. and Takacs, W. (1979) 'Differential Response to Price and Exchange Rate Influences in the Foreign Trade of Selected Industrial Countries', *Review of Economics and Statistics*, May.

Wilson, T. (1976) 'Effective Devaluation and Inflation', *Oxford Economic Papers*, March.

Winters, L. A. (1974) 'United Kingdom Exports and the Pressure of Demand: A Note', *Economic Journal*, September.

Winters, L. A., (1987) 'Britain in Europe: A Survey of Quantitative Trade Studies', *Journal of Common Market Studies*, June.

Worswick, G. N. D. (1971) 'Trade and Payments', in Cairncross, A. (ed.) *Britain's Economic Prospects Reconsidered* (London, Allen & Unwin).

Wyplosz, C. (1988) 'Capital Flow Liberalization and the EMS: A French Perspective', *European Economy*, May.

Yeager, L. B. (1970) 'Absorption and Elasticity: A Fuller Reconciliation', *Economica*, February.

Index